SPANDAU
The Secret Diaries

ALBERT SPEER

Translated from the German by

RICHARD and CLARA WINSTON

ISHI PRESS
INTERNATIONAL

Spandau
The Secret Diaries

by Albert Speer

First Published in German in 1975 as

Spandauer Tagebücher

by Verlag-Ullstein GmbH in Frankfurt/Main – Berlin

This Printing in February, 2010
by Ishi Press in New York and Tokyo

with a new foreword by Sam Sloan

ISBN 4-87187-879-1
978-4-87187-879-1

Ishi Press International
1664 Davidson Avenue, Suite 1B
Bronx NY 10453-7877
1-917-507-7226

Printed in the United States of America

Foreword by Sam Sloan

Spandau
The Secret Diaries

by Albert Speer

This is one of the most amazing books ever written. After being convicted in the **Nuremberg War Crimes Trials**, the prisoners were not allowed to have writing paper, were not allowed to write their memoirs and were allowed only limited visits from their relatives.

However, they were allowed to have toilet paper.

So, on thousands of squares of toilet paper, **Albert Speer** wrote his diary in tiny letters so small that they could hardly be seen, which he was then able to pass to his relatives when they visited him.

By the time Speer was released on **September 30, 1966**, twenty years later, there were more than twenty thousand pages of secret diaries just waiting to be edited and published, but it took him another ten years before he could bear to look at them.

Albert Speer was a brilliant writer and the world should be forever grateful to him for leaving us this work, that addresses and attempts to answer questions the world will always be asking, including:

1. How was **Adolph Hitler**, an obvious madman, totally insane, able to attain and keep such great power?

2. Why did the German people not recognize what was happening and do something about it long before the destructive end?

3. Most importantly: Can this happen again? Could and will another Hitler arise, perhaps not in Germany again? Perhaps in the United States of America? What assurance do we have that a lunatic madman could not enter the **White House** and do much worse than Hitler ever did?

As to the proof that Hitler really was crazy, Speer provides numerous examples. After the **Battle of the Bulge**, the last great German counter-attack, which ended in the defeat of Germany, it was clear that the war was lost. A sensible leader would have dug in and attempted to negotiate a truce or a surrender under favorable terms. This is much the way that the **First World War** had ended.

Instead of doing that, Hitler ordered the **Sixth SS Tank Division** that had just been defeated in the Battle of the Bulge to start an attack on the **Balkans** to the South East by advancing through **Hungary**. Hitler always wanted to attack. The idea of taking defensive positions was completely foreign to him. This is not to mention the fact that the army that he wanted to launch this attack no longer existed.

As to the question of why the German people did not do something about Hitler, once they realized what was happening, Speer laments about the Kennedy Assassination:

> "I feel that the Kennedy assassination is not just an American tragedy, but a tragedy for the world. And I could not help thinking that here only one confused loner was at work, so it seems; he conceived the plan and the assassination was successful. But the attempts on Hitler's life - how many undertakings there were, planned with the precision of a General Staff operation by circumspect cool-headed people, year after year, and never did they succeed, that is the real tragedy."

Albert Speer was unlike any other defendant, in that whereas the others all said that they were innocent of the charges, he admitted his guilt. As to why he did this, Speer explains:

> "I assumed responsibility for all the orders of Hitler that I had carried out. I took the position that in every government orders must remain orders for the subordinate organs of the government, but the leadership on all levels must examine and weigh the orders it received and is consequently co-responsible for them, even if the orders have been carried out under duress.

Foreword by Sam Sloan

"What mattered more to me was to assert my collective responsibility for all the measures of Hitler, not excluding the crimes, which were undertaken or committed in the period from 1942 on wherever and by whomever."

It is a common and seriously mistaken belief that the Nuremberg War Crimes Trials were concerned with the Holocaust and the exterminations of millions of Jews and others deemed undesirable. This was not the case. None of the defendants at Nuremberg were charged with having to do with the Death Camps. The real criminals, such as **Bormann**, **Himmler** and **Dr. Josef Mengele**, may have escaped to South America and were not present at Nuremberg. The case against Albert Speer was weak. He was charged with planning an attack and using slave labor to run his munitions factories. Neither of these are crimes. See if you can find them in law books.

Speer wrote that he was *"duty-bound to face this tribunal, in view of the fate of the German people"*. He notes that in view of the fact that millions of people died because of decisions made by the leadership, a sentence of twenty years in prison, even though he did not commit any crime, seems "fair enough"!!

What is also remarkable is what Speer tells us about the six other prisoners in with him. It appears that all of them were average men, with wives and children, who simply happened to rise to positions of leadership. With the exception of **Rudolph Hess**, who does sometimes seem crazy, sometimes because he really is crazy, other times because he is simply malingering, these are just average men who, on the one hand, are lucky still to be alive after a war in which so many died, and yet are unlucky in that, due to their positions in the **Nazi German Government**, wound up as defendants in the Nuremberg War Crimes Trials.

Sam Sloan
New York NY
February 17, 2010

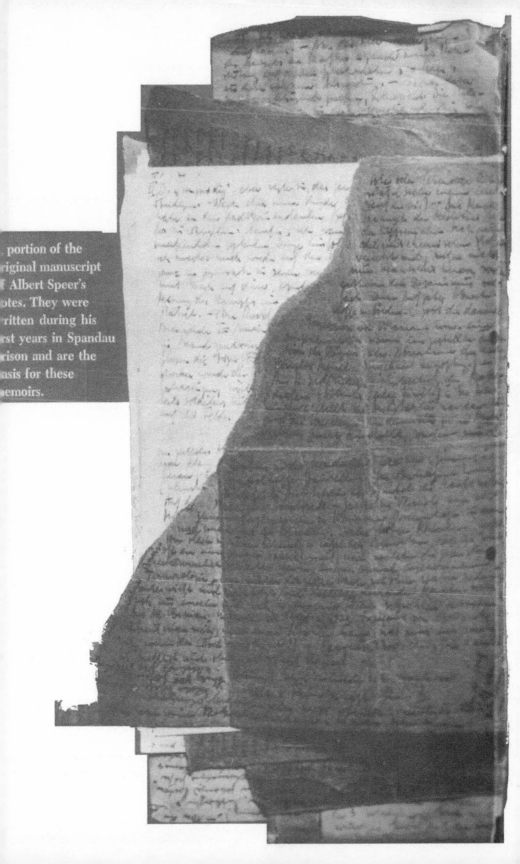

ALBERT SPEER'S SECRET PRISON DIARIES

For twenty years Speer secretly wrote his memoirs in a minuscule scrawl on tobacco wrappings, pages of calendars, and toilet paper. Under constant peril of cell searches, he concealed his notes in the sole lining of a shoe and in the bandage wrapped around his leg to relieve his phlebitis, and managed to persuade sympathetic guards to smuggle them to the outside world.

At the stroke of midnight, October 1, 1966, Speer was led through the prison gates past a barrage of flashbulbs and floodlights into the streets of a Berlin he could scarcely recognize. Waiting for him in the home of relatives were more than 25,000 pages of his notes.

But the prison diaries lay unread for over ten years:

> "... I shied away from looking at that mass of papers which is all that has remained of my life between my fortieth and my sixtieth years. There are various reasons for my presenting this journal now. But ultimately it is an attempt to give form to the time that seemed to be pouring away so meaninglessly, to give substance to years empty of content.
> "Diaries are usually the accompaniment of a lived life. This one stands in place of a life."

> "Speer's new book is - if at all possible - an even more remarkable human document than his Inside the Third Reich. More directed toward inner conflicts, Spandau is a brutally honest, at times full of sarcasm and humor, often terribly painful legacy of the Third Reich and of a man who helped build it as well as destroy it."-
>
> Eugene Davidson

ALBERT SPEER was Hitler's personal architect, confidant, and protege; Reich Minister for Armaments and War Production; and second most powerful man in Nazi Germany at the end of World War II. Speer was also the only defendant of the twenty-two top Nazis at the Nuremberg Trials to assume the burden of guilt for the

Reich's war crimes. He was sentenced to twenty years' imprisonment, and served it in Spandau with six other top Nazi officials - Hess, Raeder, Schirach, Funk, Neurath and Donitz.

Spandau: The Secret Diaries is an intensely powerful, moving, personal narrative - A brilliant individual's effort to retain his strength and sanity during twenty years' nearly solitary confinement through extraordinary feats of self-discipline and moral reeducation. As Specs states, "...these thousands of notes are one concentrated effort to survive, an endeavor not only to endure life in a cell physically and intellectually, but also to arrive at some sort of moral reckoning with what lay behind it all."

Speer offers a spellbinding account of the psychological effects of imprisonment on his fellow inmates their pointless arguments about the bureaucratic policy and war strategies of the Reich, their strict adherence to protocol in their dealings with one another, their petty quarrels over work details, their games to outwit the guards, and Hess's pretended loss of memory.

Speer's gift for recalling events and conversations in vivid, factual detail makes his diary one of the most fascinating chronicles to emerge from the rubble of the Third Reich. He demonstrates his ability to bring the past to life in the many new insights he gives us into the complex personality of Hitler. as in this chilling glance of the Führer's maniacal plan for the destruction of New York.

> "I never him so worked up as toward the end of the war when in a kind of delirium he pictured for himself and for us the destruction of New York in a hurricane of fire. He described the skyscrapers being turned into gigantic burning torches, collapsing upon one another, the glow of the exploding city illuminating the dark sky."

> "Albert Speer's book is a deeply moving human document. It is also of extraordinary political and psychological interest. His self-analysis of the reasons why and how he could have been involved with the

Nazi criminal gang and his remarkably frank account of the change within himself during twenty years are truly convincing. His description of the life of the former Nazi leaders in Spandau prison is a revealing record of the psychology of power bearers who have lost their power. The picture he paints of the four-power prison administration and their bureaucratic methods is often hilarious. This book is a must for anyone interested in the psychological motivation of political action and the problem of guilt and repentance. But beyond this it is so fascinatingly written that I could not put it down before I finished it."

-Erich Fromm

TO MY WIFE

Contents

Preface

MORE THAN TWENTY THOUSAND pages lay before me when I opened the trunk in which my family had stored all the writings that I had sent to them from Nuremberg and Spandau in the course of more than twenty years. There were countless pages of diary notes, authorized letters, and smuggled letters, written in the smallest script I could manage, on leaves of calendars, scraps of notepaper, cardboard lids, toilet paper. Some of the journal was continuous for periods of months, with notations for every day; other sections were written fitfully, with constant gropings for fresh starts and with many gaps where I had broken off in resignation or depression.

What confrontation with these pages after so many years gave to me was a chronicle of prison's daily routine—which was never the routine alone. Throughout the everyday life of imprisonment was reflected the past that had brought me there. If I read the whole thing rightly, these thousands of notes are one concentrated effort to survive, an endeavor not only to endure life in a cell physically and intellectually, but also to arrive at some sort of moral reckoning with what lay behind it all.

The printed pages to which I ultimately reduced the manuscript represent a selection guided by principles of order and evaluation. The deletions consisted above all of repetitions, of sheer banalities, and of the countless fumbling efforts to grasp what I was experiencing. Here and there passages have been moved around, related entries brought together, and dispersed material unified by subject and idea. Everything in these pages is authentic; but the final order is the result of some design. What was lost as a consequence was the infinite monotony of those years, the prolonged depressions, only feebly interrupted by miserable, self-deceptive hopes. For the rest, it was found necessary to disguise most of the names and some dates; many of those who helped me to maintain communication with the outside world, often at considerable personal risk, had to be protected.

For many years after midnight on September 30, 1966, when the gates of Spandau opened for me, I shied away from looking at that mass of papers which is all that has remained of my life between my fortieth and my sixtieth years. There are various reasons for my presenting this journal now. But ultimately it is an attempt to give form to the time that seemed to be pouring away so meaninglessly, to give substance to years empty of content.

Diaries are usually the accompaniment of a lived life. This one stands in place of a life.

ALBERT SPEER
August 1975

SPANDAU
The Secret Diaries

The First Year

An American soldier in white helmet and white shoulder straps leads me down the basement corridors to a small elevator. Together, we ride up. A few steps down another corridor, a door opens, and I am standing on a small platform in the Nuremberg courtroom. A guard hands me earphones. In a daze, I hurry to put them on. Then I hear the judge's voice, sounding curiously impersonal and abstract through the mechanical medium: "Albert Speer, to twenty years' imprisonment." I am aware of the eight judges looking down upon me, of the prosecutors, the defense attorneys, the correspondents, and spectators. But all that I really see are the dilated, shocked eyes of my lawyer, Dr. Hans Flächsner. Perhaps my heart stands still for a moment. Barely conscious of what I am doing, I bow silently to the judges. Then I am led through unfamiliar, dimly lit corridors to my cell. All this while the soldier to whom I am handcuffed has not said a word.

Shortly afterwards, an American lieutenant roughly orders me to take my bedding, table, and my few possessions to a new cell in one of the upper tiers. On the narrow, winding iron staircase I meet Hess, who is also lugging his table. "What did you get, Herr Hess?" I ask.

He looks absently at me. "I have no idea. Probably the death penalty. I didn't listen."

Seven men already sentenced are now in the upper tier, separated from the eleven other defendants who have remained on the ground floor. Only a few hours ago, after our last lunch together, we did not know whether after many years of shared rule, shared triumphs, and mutual animosity we were seeing one another for the last time. For an endless span of time we sat together brooding absently and waiting to be marched together into the courtroom to hear the sentences. But we were summoned one by one and led in by a guard in the seating order we had had during the trial. First Göring, then Hess, then Ribbentrop and Keitel. These men did not reappear. And so the cellar of the Nuremberg court emptied. I was next to last; when I left, there remained only Constantin von Neurath, Hitler's foreign minister until 1938. I still have no idea what sentences the others have received. My impression is that only we seven who have been transferred to the upper tier are escaping the death penalty.

The court psychologist, Dr. Gilbert, visits us in our cells and confirms my suspicion: the men still down below have all been condemned to death. Of the seven of us, the minister of economics, Walter Funk, Grand Admiral Erich Raeder, and Hitler's deputy, Rudolf Hess, have been given life imprisonment; Youth Leader Baldur von Schirach and I, twenty years each; Constantin von Neurath, who was shunted from his post as foreign minister to that of governor of Bohemia and Moravia, fifteen; and Grand Admiral Karl Dönitz, ten years. Gilbert, always eager to add to his psychological knowledge, wants to know my reaction to the sentence. "Twenty years. Well, that's fair enough. They couldn't have given me a lighter sentence, considering the facts, and I can't complain."

Our German prison doctor, Dr. Pflücker, comes on his regular round. He helped all of us with his encouragements during the gloomy months of the trial. But he has no medicines for my excruciating cardiac irregularity; all he can do is give me a few aspirin tablets. To distract me, he tells me that the three acquitted men, Schacht, von Papen, and Fritzsche, wanted to leave the prison a few hours ago, but turned back because an enraged crowd was waiting for them at the street gate. There was general confusion until the Americans offered to let them take refuge in the prison. They are now on the third tier, but their cell doors are open.   •

After our last shared lunch in the cellar of the Nuremberg court, the three had bidden goodbye to us and left to pack their bags. Schacht shook hands with none of us, Papen only with the military men, Keitel, Jodl, Raeder, and Dönitz, while Fritzsche emotionally offered each one of us his best wishes.

After they departed, I grumbled at my own fate for a moment. Didn't I deserve a lesser penalty, if Schacht and Papen were going free? But then, I have just told Gilbert the opposite. I envy the three of them! So lies, smokescreens, and dissembling statements have paid off after all.

October 2, 1946 Tonight I have done a bit of arithmetic. I was twenty-six when I first heard Hitler speak—up to then he had not interested me at all. I was thirty when he laid a world at my feet. I did not help him to power, did not finance his rearmament. My dreams always were concerned with buildings; it was not power I wanted, but to become a second Schinkel.* Why did I insist so stubbornly on my guilt? Sometimes I have the suspicion that vanity and boasting may have been involved. Of course I know in my own heart that I was guilty. But should I have bragged about it quite so much to the court?** In this world, adaptability and cunning carry you a lot farther. On the

* Karl Friedrich Schinkel (1781–1841), the great architect who virtually rebuilt Berlin and Potsdam.—*Translators' note.*

** I assumed responsibility for all the orders from Hitler which I had carried out. I took the position that in every government orders must remain orders for the subordinate organs of the government, but that the leadership on all levels must examine and weigh the orders it receives and is consequently co-responsible for them, even if the orders have been carried out under duress.

What mattered more to me was to assert my collective responsibility for all the measures of Hitler, not excluding the crimes, which were undertaken or committed in the period from 1942 on wherever and by whomever. I said to the court:

In political life there is a responsibility for a man's own sector. For that he is of course fully responsible. But beyond that there is a collective responsibility when he has been one of the leaders. Who else is to be held responsible for the course of events, if not the closest associates around the Chief of State? But this collective responsibility can only apply to fundamental matters and not to details. . . . Even in an authoritarian system this collective responsibility of the leaders must exist; there can be no attempting to withdraw from the collective responsibility after the catastrophe. For if the war had been won, the leadership would probably have raised the claim that it was collectively responsible.

On December 15, 1945, I wrote to my wife: "I am duty-bound to face this tribunal. In view of the fate of the German people one may be too solicitous for one's own immediate family." In March 1946: "I cannot put up a cheap defense here. I believe you will understand, for in the end you and the children would feel shame if I forgot that many millions of Germans fell for a false ideal." Letter to my parents, April 25, 1946: "Don't solace yourself with the idea that I am putting up a stiff fight for myself. One must bear one's responsibility here, not hope for favoring winds."

other hand, am I to take Papen's wiliness as a model? If I envy him, I also despise him. But—I was forty when I was arrested. I'll be sixty-one when I am released.

October 3, 1946   A dreary day. I do some more arithmetic: out of seven thousand three hundred days, plus five leap-year days, nine have now passed. If my pretrial imprisonment and the time during the trial are taken into account, there will be four hundred and ninety-four days less. It's as if I am entering an immeasurably long tunnel.

October 4, 1946   Ever since the sentence was pronounced, our cells have been locked. We can no longer talk to one another or go for a refreshing walk in the prison yard. The loneliness is growing unbearable. So far, not one of us has accepted the offer of a daily hour's walk on the ground floor of the cellblock. What an effect it would have on those condemned to death if they saw us strolling there. They are no longer taken for walks. Now and then one of their cell doors is opened, perhaps for the chaplain or the doctor.

October 5, 1946   Days without interest in anything. Have left even the books lying untouched on the table. If I go on in this twilight state, I foresee that my resistance will totally disintegrate.

October 6, 1946   I have asked for a pencil and fresh paper. Took notes. But contact with the outside world remains restricted to a few lines in block letters on printed forms. This afternoon I suddenly realized quite plainly that my capacity for feeling is atrophying as a result of the adjustment to prison life. Yet that alone makes it possible to endure the pressures of the situation. I might put it paradoxically: Loss of the capacity for feeling increases the capacity for suffering.

October 8, 1946   I must force myself to intellectual activity. Since there are no longer any challenges of this sort now that the trial is over, only the narrowest and most banal area remains to me. I concentrate on the table in my cell, on the stool, on the markings in the oak of the door. I try to grasp these things as precisely as possible and to describe them to myself. A first exercise in— Well, in what? Certainly not in literary activity; but a test of my capacity for observation.

October 9, 1946   For more than a year I have been in this prison, of which I have so far seen only the iron entrance gate and the cellblock. The facades with their small windows are soiled by the dirt and soot of decades. In the courtyard there are a few pear trees, showing that even here life can survive for long periods of time. During the first few days I frequently climbed up on my chair and tipped the upper half of the window to look out into the yard. But the small, high window is too deeply embedded in the prison wall for me to see out. The panes have been replaced by gray celluloid to prevent us from slashing our wrists with splinters of glass from the window. The cell seems gloomy even when the sun is shining. The celluloid is netted with scratches; the outlines of things outside can only be distinguished dimly. It is beginning to grow cold; nevertheless, I sometimes tip down the window. The cold draft disturbs the soldier on guard. He immediately orders me to close the window.

October 10, 1946 Day and night I am under continual observation. A square opening has been cut into each of the heavy oak cell doors at eye level. The grating over the opening can be pushed aside when meals have to be handed through. Evenings, the soldier hangs a light at this grating so that I can read. After seven o'clock the light is turned around; the cell remains dimly lit all night long. Ever since Robert Ley, head of the Labor Front, managed to hang himself by tearing the hem from his towel and attaching it to the drainpipe of the toilet, rigorous supervision has been introduced.

My only previous acquaintance with such prison cells has been in American movies. Now I have become almost accustomed to mine. I scarcely notice the dirt on the walls by now. Years ago they must once have been green. At that time there was also an overhead electric light, as well as some built-in articles of furniture. All that is left of these are the spackled holes where the wooden pegs were. A cot with a straw mattress stands against the long wall. I use some of my clothing for a pillow. At night I have four American woolen blankets, but no sheets. The long wall by the cot gleams with greasy dirt from many previous occupants. A washbowl and a cardboard box with a few letters in it stand on a rickety little table. I need no storage room; I have nothing to store. Under the small window run two heating pipes. There I dry my towels.

The penetrating odor of an American disinfectant has pursued me through all the camps it has been my lot to pass through. In the toilet, in my underclothes, in the water with which I wash the floor every morning—everywhere is that sweetish smell, pungent and medicinal.

October 11, 1946   During the weeks of recess in the trial, when the judges were deciding on the verdicts, I wrote down some scraps of memories of the twelve years with Hitler and had the chaplain send them to a friend in Coburg. It amounts to about a hundred pages. "I think," I wrote in the accompanying letter (I am quoting from memory), "that I am more typical of one side of the regime than all these repulsive bourgeois revolutionaries." And in fact it does seem to me as though the Himmlers, Bormanns, Streichers, and their ilk cannot explain Hitler's success with the German people. Hitler was sustained by the idealism and devotion of people like myself. We who actually were least inclined to think selfishly were the ones who made him possible. Criminals and their accomplices are always around; they explain nothing. Throughout the trial, all the talk was only of those misdeeds that are judicially tangible. But at night in my dimly lit cell I often ask myself whether my real guilt did not lie on an entirely different plane.

Under the impact of the uncanny, almost unbearable stillness that surrounds me, with the only measure of time the changing of the guard outside the cell, doubts assail me whether I accurately portrayed Hitler in those hundred pages. In the effort to explain to myself how I could have succumbed to his fascination for so long a time, I too often called to mind all the minor pleasant episodes: the automobile rides together, the picnics and architectural fantasies, his charm, his concern for people's families, and his seeming modesty. But in recollecting all that, I have no doubt repressed the things that the trial unforgettably reminded me of: the monstrous crimes and brutalities. After all, they are what Hitler really was.

October 13, 1946   A guard goes from cell to cell. He asks whether we want to make use of our right to a daily walk on the ground floor. The yard is still barred to us. I have to get out; the cell is beginning to feel unbearably oppressive. So I ask to go. But I shudder at the prospect of seeing the men in death row. The guard holds out the chromed handcuffs. Linked together, we have some difficulty descending the winding staircase. In the silence, every step on the iron stairs sounds like a thunderclap.

On the ground floor I see eleven soldiers staring attentively into eleven cells. The men inside are eleven of the surviving leaders of the Third Reich. Wilhelm Keitel, chief of the High Command of the Armed Forces, was unpopular and despised; during the Nuremberg trial he grew in understanding and dignity. General Alfred Jodl was Keitel's closest associate. He was typical of the intelligent General Staff officers who were so fascinated by Hitler that they largely cast aside the moral traditions of their class. Hermann Göring, the principal in the trial, grandiloquently took all responsibility, only to employ all his cunning and energy to deny that he bore any specific guilt. He had become a debauched parasite; in prison he regained his old self and displayed an alertness, intelligence, and quick-wittedness such as he had not shown since the early days of the Third Reich. Joachim von Ribbentrop, Hitler's foreign minister, is said to have abandoned his arrogance for a faith in Christ that sometimes strikes a grotesque note. Julius Streicher, the Gauleiter of Nuremberg and one of Hitler's oldest companions, was always an outsider in the party because of his sex-obsessed antisemitism and his flagrant corruption. During the trial, all the other defendants avoided him. Then there is Wilhelm Frick, a taciturn man who as minister of the interior turned Hitler's grudges into laws. Alfred Rosenberg, the complicated thinker and party philosopher, was ridiculed by everyone, including Hitler; to the surprise of all of us, Rosenberg's defense during the trial was able to prove that he had considered the ferocious policy of annihilation in the East a fatal error, although he had remained devoted to Hitler. Then there is Fritz Sauckel, a sailor who rose to be one of Hitler's Gauleiters and who was overtaxed, intellectually and morally, by the wartime assignment to provide Germany with slave laborers from the occupied territories. Arthur Seyss-Inquart, Hitler's Reich commissioner for the Netherlands, sat to my right in the dock for nine months: an amiable Austrian who had tested out as having the highest IQ of all of us. During the trial I had come to like him, because he did not seek evasions, among other reasons. And then there is Hans Frank, governor-general of Poland, whose own diary revealed his ruthlessly brutal actions. But in Nuremberg he freely confessed his crimes, abjured them, and became a devout Catholic; his capacity to believe fervently and even fanatically had not deserted him. Gilbert recently told me that Frank is working on his memoirs. Last of all is Ernst Kaltenbrunner, the Gestapo chief, a tall Austrian with sharp features but a curiously mild look in his eyes, who during the trial in all seriousness denied the authenticity of documents he had signed.

As the rules prescribe, most of them are lying on their backs, hands on the blanket, heads turned toward the inside of the cell. A ghostly sight, all of them in their immobility; it looks as though they have already been laid on their biers. Only Frank is up, sitting at his table and writing away. He has wound a damp towel around his neck; he used to tell Dr. Pflücker he did that to keep his mind alert. Seyss-Inquart looks out through the doorway; he smiles at me each time I pass, and each time that smile gives me the chills. I cannot stand it for long. Back in my cell, I decide not to go back down again.

October 14, 1946   An American guard smiles at me, as though he wished to say: "Courage!" He means it in the simplest way, and I am going to need a good deal of courage to survive the twenty years. But will it not be even harder to face my family and my children? Will it not take still more courage to answer their questions when they come to visit me now or later and want to know how I could have participated in a regime that the entire world feared and despised? They will imply that they will always remain the children of a war criminal. And my wife's courage when she sits facing me and does not say that the ten years just past did not belong to her but to Hitler, and the twenty years that lie before us likewise. And finally, the courage to settle with my-self the meaning of the past and my share in it. I notice how hard, in fact how almost impossible, I already find it to describe even simple and unincriminating episodes with Hitler.

For some time a sound in the distance has been intruding on our si-lence: the sound of hammering. For a moment I felt irritation that they should be carrying out repairs at night. Then the thought suddenly flashed through my mind: they are putting up the gallows.[1] Several times I thought I heard a saw; then there came a pause, finally several hammer blows. Curiously, sometimes these sounded louder to me. After about an hour, complete silence returned. Lying on my cot, I could not shake off the thought that the executions were being prepared. Sleep-less.

October 15, 1946   Nervous all day long. The events of the night have shattered my composure. No inclination to make entries.

October 16, 1946   At some hour of the night I woke up. I could hear footsteps and indistinguishable words in the lower hall. Then si-lence, broken by a name being called out: "Ribbentrop!" A cell door is opened; then scraps of phrases, scraping of boots, and reverberating footsteps slowly fading away. Scarcely able to breathe, I sit upright on my cot, hearing my heart beat loudly, at the same time aware that my hands are icy. Soon the footsteps come back, and I hear the next name: "Keitel!" Once more a cell door opens, once more noises and the rever-

[1] I was mistaken. The gallows were not erected until the last few hours before the execution. See Colonel B. C. Andrus, *The Infamous of Nuremberg* (London, 1969).

beration of footsteps. Name after name is called. To some of these men I was linked by common work and mutual respect; others were remote from me and scarcely crossed my path. Those I feared, primarily Bormann, then Himmler, are missing; likewise Goebbels and Göring. Some I despised. More footsteps. "Streicher!" A loud, excited exclamation follows. From our floor comes a shot: "Bravo, Streicher!" To judge by the voice, that is Hess. Below, the calling of names goes on. I cannot estimate the time; it may be taking hours. I sit with clasped hands.

Perhaps the way these men have ended their lives is preferable to my situation; that is the thought that comes to me this morning. When I spoke to Dr. Pflücker a few days ago about the fear felt by the men awaiting death, he told me he had permission to give them all a strong sedative before the execution. Now the thought of that fills me with something akin to envy: It's all over for them. I still have to face twenty years. Will I live through them? Yesterday I tried to imagine myself leaving prison after two decades, an old man.

October 17, 1946 This morning we survivors have moved down to the lower tier. There we had to clean out the cells of the hanged men. The messtins were still standing on the tables, a few remains of the spare last meal, bread crumbs, half-emptied tin bowls. Papers were scattered, the blankets in disorder. Only Jodl's cell had been cleaned, the blanket neatly folded. On one cell wall was Seyss-Inquart's calendar, on which he himself had marked his last day of life, October 16, with a cross.

In the afternoon brooms and mops are handed to Schirach, Hess, and me. We are told to follow a soldier who leads us into an empty gym. This is where the executions took place. But the gallows has already been dismantled, the spot cleaned. Nevertheless, we are supposed to sweep and mop the floor. The lieutenant watches our reactions closely. I try hard to keep my composure. Hess comes to attention in front of a dark spot on the floor that looks like a large bloodstain; he raises his arm in the party salute.

October 18, 1946 Vast silence in the building. But the atmosphere is curiously changed. It feels as though the tension has relaxed, as though this October 16 had been the goal of all those months of effort by all sides. Even the guards seem to be more equable.

October 19, 1946 From some initial signs I conclude I am beginning to adjust. Obviously, my six fellow prisoners are undergoing the same change. Frequently, nowadays, the cells are opened and instructions issued to the prisoners. I feel no emotion when I obey these requests.

Every morning we clean the prison corridor: Hess, Dönitz, Neurath, and Raeder precede with brooms; Schirach and I mop the stone floor with an evil-smelling disinfectant solution. Dönitz wears a blue admiral's coat, Neurath his hunting fur, Schirach an expensive fur coat with a sable collar, and Raeder his black overcoat with a fur collar given him by the Russians when he was housed in a dacha near Moscow waiting for the beginning of the trial. With the broom on his shoulder, Neurath paces restively back and forth. Six guards in white steel helmets watch this scene contemptuously.

The corridor is about sixty meters long. There are sixteen cells on either side, with dark-gray oaken doors in stone frames painted a greenish gray. The last door leads to the prison office, which is identified by a signboard, like a store. Number 23 is reserved for equipment, number 17 serves as a shower room. Cantilevered iron gangways run along the empty cellblocks on the two upper stories. Ninety-four cells for seven prisoners. Wire netting is stretched along the entire width of these upper floors; it was put there after an imprisoned general in another wing of the prison ended his life by leaping from the top gallery.

This afternoon the prison rules were read out. In addressing a guard or an officer we must come to attention. When the commandant, Colonel Andrus, or a prominent visitor approaches, we are expected to stand stiffly and at the same time fold our arms across our chests, as in the Orient. The American lieutenant on duty commented that we need not bother about any of "this nonsense."

October 20, 1946 This morning I read in Goethe's *Elective Affinities*: "Everything seems to be following its usual course because even in terrible moments, in which everything is at stake, people go on living as if nothing were happening." I used to read such sentences without noticing them. Now I associate them with my situation. In general I notice how my reading is becoming a kind of portentous commentary on my past. I haven't read this way since the end of my secondary-school days.

October 21, 1946 Today I again spent a long time thinking about the executed men. It was only during the trial that I really came to think well of Jodl and Seyss-Inquart. They showed stamina, had a good deal of dignity, and even a degree of insight. I tried to recall a few meetings with them in earlier years. When making this effort, I notice that a barrier is building up in me against any preoccupation with the past. Yet, oddly, I find relief in turning my mind to the past.

In the morning I lie awake thinking about my family. Each time I feel tired and drained afterwards. Today I shall probably muse vaguely for the rest of the evening, as I so often do, burying myself in memories of my youth. My wife and the six children are now living in the cow barn attached to the old gardener's house; my parents are in the gardener's apartment above. What can the days be like for them? I make attempts to picture it to myself, but do not succeed.

October 23, 1946   The upper floors of our wing of the prison are filling with defendants in the trials of the doctors, of the members of the Foreign Ministry, and of the SS leadership. We are kept carefully separated from these people.

A few days ago, Dr. Gilbert bade me a very friendly goodbye and gave me a copy of an article he has written for an American newspaper. In his opinion, I am the only one who showed some discernment during the trial and the only one who will stand by his present views in the future. He does not expect the others, such as Fritzsche, Schirach, and Funk, to do so, and speaks of expedient repentance.

After handing over the voluminous indictment, Gilbert asked all the defendants to comment briefly on what they thought of it. I wrote that the trial was necessary in view of the horrible crimes of the Third Reich, that even in a dictatorship there was such a thing as common responsibility. Dönitz, Gilbert has just told me, took the position that the indictment was a bad joke. Hess claimed he had lost his memory. Ribbentrop asserted that the indictment was directed against the wrong people. Funk tearfully protested that never in his life had he consciously done anything that could justify such an indictment. And Keitel maintained that for a soldier, orders were orders. Only Streicher remained faithful to his and Hitler's lifelong obsession; he maintained that the trial was a triumph of world Jewry.

At that time I wanted to state my belief that a man could not be one of the leaders of a powerful historical entity and then slide out of it with cheap excuses. I could not understand my fellow defendants who refused to take responsibility for events that had happened in their own areas. We had gambled, all of us, and lost: lost Germany, our country's good repute, and a considerable measure of our own personal integrity. Here was a chance to demonstrate a little dignity, a little manliness or courage, and to make plain that after all we were charged with, we at least were not also cowards. I must say, incidentally, that Gilbert always stood by me in the often difficult situations in which I began to doubt whether I was right to take this line during the trial. He did so unobtrusively and without the slightest ulterior motive. He helped all of us, including Streicher, although Gilbert is Jewish. After he has left, I feel something akin to gratitude.

Before going, Gilbert told me some of the details about the last minutes of the executed men. All of them kept their composure. Keitel's last words were: *"Alles für Deutschland. Deutschland über Alles."* Ribbentrop, Jodl, and Seyss-Inquart expressed similar sentiments on the scaffold. Gilbert commented, "During the trial I always said that you were devils, but you're brave soldiers." Streicher's last words were: "Heil Hitler! This is the Purim festival of 1946!"

Now another prison psychologist, Mitscherlich, occasionally walks around in the corridor. His face is emaciated, and he wears overwide dark trousers and a baggy sweater. Easy to see that he's a German. Zealously, he has the guards open for him the cells of the defendants slated for the new trials. He avoids us seven. Probably he has been forbidden to have any contact with us.

November 1, 1946 Again in my mind's eye I see a replay of the nightmarish pictures we were shown during the trial. The prosecution's evidence also contained descriptions of mass executions or gassings that I shall never forget. But in between, if I allow the train of images and associations to flow freely, I discover that the lower stratum of my consciousness tries to balance these out by escaping more and more frequently into pleasant or idyllic memories.

At the same time the profoundly criminal aspects of Hitler's face have emerged more and more sharply. I ask myself: How could you have overlooked that, side by side with him for so long? And yet isn't it understandable that even now the image of the enthusiastic Hitler comes to my mind, the man overwhelmed by his mission, by the grandeur of his plans? I think of our projects, of the hours over the drafting table, of our tours up and down Germany.

One of those tours—I guess it was in the summer of 1936—keeps returning persistently to my mind today. I have a clear image of Hitler as we drive in the big open Mercedes, turning halfway toward me and saying, "I feel safest from assassins in the car. Even the police are not told what my destination is when I leave. An assassination has to be planned long in advance; driving time and the route must be known. That is why I'm afraid that some day I will be killed by a sniper while driving up to a meeting hall. There's no way to dodge that sort of thing. The basic protection remains the crowd's enthusiasm. If anyone so much as ventured to raise a weapon, they'd instantly knock him down and trample him to death."

I no longer recall why on this drive Hitler decided on a detour to Banz monastery. The monks were certainly surprised by the unexpected visit. Hitler was not impressed by the baroque splendor; the style was not one he cared for. But he showed unreserved admiration for the monumentality of the architectural complex as a whole. After the sightseeing he disappeared for a long time into one of the rooms of the monastery. We waited. The abbot had invited him in for a talk, we were told. We did not find out what was discussed.

On the way to Bamberg, Hitler had a picnic place selected in a clearing near the highway. Blankets were brought from the car's trunk, and we sprawled in a circle. After a while he began to talk about the impressive personality of the abbot. "There we have it again, another example of the Catholic Church's clever choice of its dignitaries," he remarked. "The only other institution in which a man from the lowest classes has the chance to rise so high is among us, in the Movement. Peasant boys used to become popes; long before the French Revolution the Church had no social prejudices. And how worthwhile that has proved to be! Believe me, there's a reason the Church has been able to survive for two thousand years. We must learn from its methods, its internal freedom, its knowledge of psychology."

Hitler said all this in a quiet, rather didactic tone. He paused and then went on with his monologue. "But we shouldn't copy it or try to find substitutes for it. Rosenberg's fantasies about an Aryan church are ridiculous. Trying to set up the party as a new religion! A Gauleiter is no substitute for a bishop; a local group leader can never serve as a parish priest. The populace would never respond to that sort of thing. If our leadership tried to go in for liturgy and outdo the Catholic Church, it would be completely out of its depth. It lacks the stature. How can a local group leader consecrate a marriage when everyone in town knows he drinks too much or chases women? It isn't an easy thing to build up a tradition. That not only takes a grand idea but authority, willingness to sacrifice, discipline—and all that for hundreds of years."

Hitler had unusually large, eloquent eyes. Up to this point they had conveyed nothing. But now their expression changed, and he added a few words in a threatening tone: "The Church will come round. I know that crew of black crows well enough to see that. What did they do in England? And how about Spain? All we have to do is apply pressure to them. And our great Movement buildings in Berlin and Nuremberg will make the cathedrals look ridiculously small. Just imagine some little peasant coming into our great domed hall in Berlin. That will do more than take his breath away. From then on the man will know where he belongs."

Hitler said all this in his excited tone, with a curiously panting enunciation. Now the architectural plans carried him away. "I tell you, Speer, these buildings are more important than anything else. You must do everything you can to complete them in my lifetime. Only if I have spoken in them and governed from them will they have the consecration they are going to need for my successors." Then he abruptly broke off and rose; the car was packed, and we drove on.

November 8, 1946 Went to the crude shower cell today. It is divided up by flimsy partitions. Inside is a wood-fired stove for heating the water, and two crates for seats complete the furnishings. Because the shower has no pressure, the whole arrangement is called a "trickle bath." Hess and I shower together, with a guard supervising. One of the German prisoners of war feeds wood into the stove and regulates the supply of water. He was an infantryman on the Russian front. In 1942 we should have had a tank like the Russian T-34, he says, as well as a weapon like the Soviet 7.62 centimeter antitank gun. Hess becomes agitated. "That was treason too, nothing but treason. One of these days we'll be surprised to find out all the treason and sabotage there was." I reply that in the final analysis Hitler himself was responsible for our technical inferiority, that although he had the right ideas about a good many things, he negated his own perceptions by constantly changing his rearmament orders. The German helper and the American guard listen to this discussion with something between boredom and interest.

The shower has been set up in our cellblock to keep us isolated from the defendants and witnesses in the forthcoming "little" trial; these men are being held in the other wing of the prison. A few weeks ago the American soldiers, often careless about such regulations, let our group and theirs overlap in the prison bath. One day I found lying beside me, splashing in the warm bath water with as much pleasure as myself, Sepp Dietrich, Hitler's constant companion in the early years. A rather coarse-grained man with a peasant's sound common sense, he became chief of Hitler's bodyguard after 1933. An ordinary corporal in the first war, he made a remarkable career in the second. By the end of 1944 he was commander of the Sixth SS Tank Army, bearing the title of an SS Oberstgruppenführer, which corresponds to the rank of a full general. Hitler would refer to him as "my Blücher."* I had met Sepp Dietrich for the last time during the Ardennes offensive. He seemed then remarkably indifferent to what was going on; he had left the leadership of his SS divisions to his staff and was living in retirement in a remote forest cottage. He had become, I thought, a grumpy eccentric.

Lying in the tub, Sepp Dietrich told me about the implications of various episodes at Hitler's military conferences toward the end of February and the beginning of March 1945 in Berlin; I had witnessed these episodes but not understood them.

After the lost Battle of the Bulge around Bastogne, Hitler's last effort was directed toward the southeast, against the Balkans. The new offensive was to have the code name Waldteufel. (Perhaps Hitler was thinking of the well-known composer of waltzes, Waldteufel.) As Hitler conceived the operation, the Sixth SS Tank Army, though badly battered in the fighting around Bastogne, was going first to reconquer the Sava-Danube triangle and then, as Hitler boldly traced its course at his big map table, to advance through Hungary to the southeast. "There is every likelihood that the population of these areas will rise as one man and with their help we will go roaring through the entire Balkans in a life-and-death battle. For I am still determined, gentlemen, to wage the fight in the East offensively. The defensive strategy of our generals helps only the Bolshevists! But I have never in my life been a man for the defensive. Now we shall go over from the defense to the attack once more."

In fact, Hitler had almost always followed this principle. He took the offensive in his early years in Munich. His foreign policy of the thirties was offensive, with its unending succession of surprise maneuvers. The unleashing of the war itself had been an example of offensive policy, and he had waged the military conflict in an offensive spirit as long as he was able. Even after the turning point of the war, the capitulation of Stalingrad, he had organized the offensive operation at Kursk code-named Citadel. It was as if he had always known that he had only the choice between the offensive and defeat, as if the loss of the initiative in itself was virtually equivalent to his downfall. For that reason Hitler was doubly shaken when this last offensive also failed, simply ground to a halt in the mud. He gave orders to have the bodyguard and the other SS divisions stripped of their honor armbands. Sepp Dietrich now

* Gebhard Leberecht von Blücher (1742–1819), a famous Prussian general noted for his rough exterior. He was cashiered by Frederick the Great, but ultimately became a hero of the Napoleonic Wars.—Translators' note.

told me that afterwards he had thrown his own decorations into the fire in which the armbands were burning. "You know," he concluded, "Hitler was crazy for a long time. He simply let his best soldiers dash into the fire."

As a commander of frontline troops, Sepp Dietrich had very rarely been exposed to the overcharged, literally mad atmosphere of the Führer's Headquarters, and so he had managed to keep some degree of sobriety and perspective. He had almost never been on the receiving end of one of those Hitler tirades that distorted so many men's grasp of reality. Perhaps I should try to reconstruct one of these monologues, in which Hitler, with voice growing steadily more intense, hammered away at this entourage.

"The Russians have almost bled to death by now," he would begin. "After the retreats of the past few months we have the priceless advantage of no longer having to defend those enormous spaces. And we know from our own experience how exhausted the Russians must be after their headlong advance. Remember the Caucasus! This means a turning point is now possible for us, as it was then for the Russians. In fact, it is absolutely probable. Consider! The Russians have had tremendous losses in matériel and men. Their stocks of equipment are exhausted. By our estimates they have lost fifteen million men. That is enormous! They cannot survive the next blow. They will not survive it. Our situation is in no way comparable to that of 1918. Even if our enemies think it is."

As so often, Hitler had talked himself into an autosuggestive euphoria. "Those who are down today can be on top tomorrow. In any case, we shall go on fighting. It is wonderful to see the fanaticism with which the youngest age-groups throw themselves into the fighting. They know that there are only two possibilities left: Either we will solve this problem, or we will all be destroyed. Providence will never abandon a nation that fights bravely." With solemnity, Hitler paraphrased the Bible: "A nation in which there is even one righteous man will not perish." There was no doubt that he regarded himself as this one righteous man. Among his favorite sentences during these last weeks was the assertion: "He who does not give up wins through." Quite often he would add the remark: "But gentlemen, if we are going to lose this war, you will all do well to provide yourselves with a rope." When he spoke in this vein his eyes gleamed with the savage resolve of a man fighting for his life. "All we have to do is show the enemy once more, by a smashing success, that he cannot win the war. Without Stalin's fanatical determination, Russia would have collapsed in the autumn of 1941. Frederick the Great, too, in a hopeless situation fought on with indomitable energy. He deserved the name 'the Great' not because he won in the end, but because he remained intrepid in misfortune. In the same way posterity will see my importance not so much in the triumphs of the early war years, but in the steadfastness I showed after the severe setbacks of the past several months. Gentlemen, the will always wins!" This was his usual technique—to end his "stick-it-out" speeches with some such slogan.

In the course of such outbursts, which he usually delivered hunched over the map table, gesturing wearily to the tall, silent wall of officers, Hitler in a sense gave the impression of being a total stranger. He really came from another world. That was why, whenever he appeared on the scene in the course of the war, he always seemed so bizarre. But I always thought that the alien quality also constituted part of his strength. The military men had all learned to deal with a wide variety of unusual situations. But they were totally unprepared to deal with this visionary.

November 9, 1946   Overcast day. Too dark for reading or writing. Mused. The fine phrase "lost in thought" precisely describes the vague state of consciousness I remained in for hours. It is part of such a state that everything I thought has evaporated. No notations.

At night, by artificial light, I draw a rendering of the Zeppelin Field. The old version with continuous colonnades. It was better than the later design after all. The first idea is usually the right one, if no basic mistakes have been made.

November 10, 1946   Before the war I saw a movie in which a desperate man fights his way through the waters of a man-high Paris sewer to a distant exit. The image of this man often torments me in my dreams.

November 11, 1946   There have been a good many improvements in the past month. We are allowed to take a half-hour walk daily. But separated. We are forbidden to talk with one another. However, when we are working together we sometimes can exchange a few words, if the guard happens to be in good humor.

November 13, 1946   Several days of reverie. Dense fog outside. The guards are unanimous in their belief that Hitler is still alive.

November 14, 1946 For days, from nine until half past eleven, we have been scouring the spots of rust on the iron plates of the galleries with steel wool. Then the iron is oiled. Stooping makes me giddy, a sign of how weak thirteen months of cell existence leave one.

Today, while musing on the cot, I pursued the question of whether making Germany a technologically backward country will be bad for her. Also whether science and art might not thrive better in an untechnological world. If certain plans are carried out and we are reduced to the status of an agricultural country, may we not be happier than the nations for whom the future now stands wide open? Ironically, Himmler and Morgenthau were not so far apart in their views of what would be Germany's ideal condition. If we take both views for the nonsense they are, there still remains the idea of a nation disbarred from any but cultural concerns. How will Germany deal with that restriction after the present catastrophe? I am thinking of Greece's role in the Roman Empire, but also of Prussia's after the collapse of 1806.

November 15, 1946 Did some drawing. Sketches of a small house. The surrounding landscape gives me special pleasure.

November 18, 1946 Schirach and I load a cart with boards and pull it for a few hundred meters. Work that makes us warm in spite of the rain. The lumber must be fresh from the sawmill, for it smells wonderfully of forest.

November 20, 1946 As we were showering today, Hess disclosed that his loss of memory was faked. While I stood under the shower and he sat on the stool, he said out of a clear sky: "The psychiatrists all tried to rattle me. I came close to giving up when my secretary was brought in. I had to pretend not to recognize her, and she burst into tears. It was a great effort for me to remain expressionless. No doubt she now thinks I am heartless." These remarks will certainly stir a lot of talk, because we were being guarded by an American soldier who understands German.

November 21, 1946 A great deal of drawing. Rendering of a two-family house and of the rear of the Zeppelin Field. Labored over the trees: the occupational disease of architects. Ten years should do it! Resolution: learn how to paint. Romantic fantasies about architecture as a surrogate for my collection of paintings, now lost. I give some of the drawings to the soldiers who ask for them.

November 22, 1946 For days the cell has been cold. I read and write with blankets draped over my shoulders. The Propyläen edition of Goethe's works is very useful, in spite of its chronological arrangement, if you have plenty of time, as I do at the moment. It affords an excellent view of the way various experiences and impressions will often be touched on two or three times before they turn up in Goethe's work as the combined result of a number of different impulses. Goethe finds his material rather than creates it. The generative process cannot be seen so clearly in his finished works. Although we had to learn *Hermann und Dorothea* by heart in school, it has remained one of my favorites, along with Kleist's *Prinz von Homburg* and Goethe's *Torquato Tasso*. The affable, peculiarly "middle-class" sound of the hexameters, the domesticity, the modesty, and atmospheric warmth of that world affect me partly because I belong to it—but also because all that represents the extreme opposite of the overcharged, inhumanly colossal world of Hitler, in which I went astray. Or was it really going astray for me?

November 28, 1946 To distract myself, this morning I noted down the recurring background of daily noises. At seven o'clock in the morning, the defendants in our wing are awakened: "Get up, get up! Let's go!" Like a dog in its kennel, I can distinguish the officers by their voices, the guards by their step. Thumping of many shoes down the winding staircase. Soon after, a cautious shuffling back; the defendants have fetched their breakfast and do not want to spill the coffee.

On the ground floor, at short intervals, is heard the voice of Joseph Mayr, an Austrian farmer, one of the prisoners of war who take care of us: "Bread, bread, bread!" Each time, the call is followed by the brief clink of metal. The seventh time he stops in front of my cell, hangs the night light to one side, and hands in four slices of white bread. A few minutes later: "Cups." Joseph pours the unsweetened black coffee from a pot held through the opening into my aluminum cup, which I extend toward him from my cot. Breakfast in bed, so to speak.

From the upper floor: "How do you feel? Well, good." Next cell: "Good morning, everything O.K.?" Or: "Everything all right? O.K." This is repeated some fifty times. The German doctor is visiting the defendants. Far off, someone is hammering metal. An American soldier whistles "Lili Marlene"; another joins in.

Silence.

Nine o'clock. Footsteps in the galleries, then in the corridor. Every morning the twenty-three defendants of the Krupp company form a line in front of my cell. Through the hatch in my door we smile at each other. Though it is against the rules, Alfried Krupp regularly pauses for a few seconds as the group marches off, and we exchange some words. To my surprise, he is the dominant figure in this group of highly individualistic men.

During my visits to the Krupp works in Essen I frequently had dealings with him. He gave the impression of taking almost no interest in the business, and of being extremely shy. I had the feeling I was talking to a man wholly in his father's shadow, one who had only a vague understanding of my efforts to increase armaments production. His experiences in Nuremberg, however, seem to have brought about a change in him. Perhaps this is also due to his having to represent the house of Krupp for the first time, since he must answer the Allies' charges in place of his father, who is gravely ill. It's a procedure that reflects a curious concept of justice: The father is indicted, but as a surrogate the son is haled before the judge's bench and sentenced.

November 30, 1946 Today Colonel Andrus, the American prison commandant, visited us to inform us that our transfers to Berlin will take place December 15. I shall have to hurry if I am to get through at least a few more volumes of the Propyläen Goethe. We mull over whether we will be permitted to have reading matter in Spandau. The Russians are said to have demanded strict solitary confinement under harsh conditions.

After an hour we are locked up again. Now I have time until lunch.

Did a sketch entitled "Hope." Snowstorm in the mountains. A mountaineer lost in a sérac is trying to find a path. He struggles through deep snow, unsuspectingly working his way out on a tongue of the glacier, which drops off into an abyss.

Half past eleven. "Soup, lunch!" Joseph brings semolina, peas, spaghetti, and meat sauce. Half an hour later, seven times from cell to cell, comes the call: "Messtins," which he is collecting.

For two hours thereafter, as every day, there is the silence of a sanatorium, which I utilize to go on writing. Once again I am obsessed by the thought of Hitler's two faces, and that for so long a time I did not see the second behind the first. It was only toward the end, during the last months, that I suddenly became aware of the duality; and, significantly, my insight was connected with an aesthetic observation: I suddenly discovered how ugly, how repellent and ill proportioned, Hitler's face was. How could I have overlooked that for so many years? Mysterious!

Perhaps I saw the man himself too little and was intoxicated by the tremendous assignments, the plans, the cheers, the work. Only today have I recalled that on our tours of the country, when we were met with so much cheering, we again and again drove under streamers repeating the antisemitic slogans of the very man with whom I had sat at an idyllic picnic listening to songs and accordion playing by his household steward, Kannenberg. I would never have believed this man capable of such a cruel rage for extermination. Sometimes I ask myself: Didn't I even notice those slogans, "Jews undesirable here," or "Jews enter this locality at their own risk"? Or did I simply overlook them as I overlooked Hitler's other face, which represented the reality I had banished from my world of illusion?

Even in the light of the strictest self-examination, I must say that I was not an antisemite. Not even incipiently. That whole world of Julius Streicher always struck me as morbid, twisted. Hitler tended to cut down on his antisemitic remarks in my presence, but of course I was aware that he shared the world of Streicher in a dark, obsessive way. Nevertheless, I am fairly certain that I myself in all those years never made a single anti-Jewish remark to him. Even later, when I was a minister of the Reich, in my official speeches I refrained from participating in the campaign against the Jews; I was never tempted into incorporating even a few ritual antisemitic phrases into my talks for opportunistic reasons. Throughout the entire trial, not a single document turned up that incriminated me in this regard.

And yet—I drove with Hitler under those streamers and did not feel the baseness of the slogans being publicly displayed and sanctioned by the government. Once again: I suppose I did not even see the streamers. Did this partial blindness after all have something to do with *Hermann und Dorothea?* Sometimes it even seems to me that my own "purity," my indolence, make me guiltier. Passion, whether springing from hatred or resentment, is still a motivation. Lukewarmness is nothing.

December 1, 1946 We have just returned from our half-hour walk around the yard at intervals of ten meters. Four soldiers with submachine guns stand in the corners. I took careful note of one of the big pear trees, and afterwards, in the dusk of the cell, tried to sketch my impression. If only the pencil were softer and the underlay harder. It consists of a piece of cardboard from a box of Kellogg's Rice Krispies. Rather playfully, I let the pencil take its course. The tree comes out

well; I look at the drawing repeatedly with as much enthusiasm as, in
the past, I would look at my latest acquisition of a Romantic.

Our Austrian cook wants to build a small house. I have promised to
sketch one for him.

December 2, 1946 Brooded for hours. Confused trampling of
many feet on the wooden floor of the corridor that communicates with
the courthouse. The defendants, perhaps in one of the industry trials,
come from their hearings and half an hour later fetch their supper; ours
is brought by Joseph. Two slices of corned beef, bread, hot tea. The
American chaplain has the cell door opened and comes in to tell me
that we will be allowed to receive Christmas packages from home. I ask
him to tell my wife not to send me any food because we are better off
than they.

Five o'clock in the afternoon. Total quiet. The soldier outside my
door is relieved. The new one greets me joyfully like an old acquaintance and tries to cheer me with a few words. At my request he
readily moves the observation light so that its glow is directed down-
ward.

Every day I learn anew how inhuman we really were. Now I do not
mean the barbarism of persecution and extermination. Rather, the absolute dominion of utilitarian ends, such as I pursued as minister of armaments, is nothing but a form of inhumanity. The American soldiers
who guard us are coal miners, oil drillers, farm laborers. Detached from
divisions that took an active part in the fighting, many of them wear
military decorations whose meaning is unknown to me. The rules call
for rigorous standards of guarding, but these men always balance the
rigor by kindness. There is never any sign of sadism. John, a miner
from Pennsylvania, has actually become something close to a friend. It
is striking that the Negro American soldiers were the first to overcome
the barrier of hostility. Partly on the basis of their own experiences,
they seemed to regard us as underdogs who deserve pity. Even more impressive was the behavior of several Jewish doctors. Even Streicher,
who was despised and treated insultingly by almost everyone, including
us, his fellow defendants, received support from them far beyond the
measure imposed by their duty as physicians. For example, Streicher
was constantly playing with a silly puzzle that required large quantities
of matches. Dr. Levy obtained them for him, although the prisoners
were not supposed to have matches.

December 6, 1946 During the morning's work in the corridor,
Raeder's, Dönitz's, and Schirach's dislike of me for my attitude toward

the Nuremberg trial came out in the open. Schirach, who always looks to someone to lean on, is now following the two grand admirals; during the trial he belonged to my faction, together with Funk and Fritzsche. Today he came up to me in a deliberately challenging manner and declared: "You with your total responsibility! The court itself rejected this charge, as you may have noticed. There is not a word about it in the verdict." The other five prisoners nodded approvingly. I had long been observing them whispering together and drawing aside when I approached. "I stick to it," I answered heatedly. "Even in the management of a company, every individual is responsible for the conduct of the business." There was an awkward silence. Then the others turned on their heels without a word and left me standing there.

Back in the cell. It is shaming, but in fact we did not even act like the management of a company. Rather, relieved of all need for thinking, we left everything to the chief executive officer. Like a management that had been reduced to impotence, to put it rather grotesquely.

In the afternoon I sweep up fallen leaves with Schirach.

I am not suffering from this isolation as much as I did in the early weeks.

December 8, 1946   I am beginning to set up a program for myself, to organize my life as a convict. To be sure, I have only the experience of six weeks to go by, with more than one thousand and thirty weeks still before me. But I already know that a life plan is important if I am to keep going.

But it must be more than a matter of organizing sheer survival. This must also become a time of reckoning. If at the end, after these twenty years, I do not have an answer to the questions that preoccupy me now, this imprisonment will have been wasted for me. And yet I fully realize that even at best my conclusions can only be tentative.

December 9, 1946   At the trial I testified that I had no knowledge of the killings of the Jews. Justice Jackson and the Russian prosecutors did not even challenge this statement in cross-examination. Did they think I would lie anyhow?

It would be wrong to imagine that the top men of the regime would have boasted of their crimes on the rare occasions when they met. At the trial we were compared to the heads of a Mafia. I recalled movies in which the bosses of legendary gangs sat around in evening dress chatting about murder and power, weaving intrigues, concocting coups. But this atmosphere of back-room conspiracy was not at all the style of our leadership. In our personal dealings, nothing would ever be said about any sinister activities we might be up to. I sometimes see Karl Brandt among the defendants in the doctors' trial. One of the reasons I flew back into burning Berlin in April 1945 was to save him from Hitler's death sentence. Today he waved sadly to me in passing. I hear there is gravely incriminating evidence of his having engaged in medical experiments on human beings. I frequently sat with Brandt; we talked about Hitler, made fun of Göring, expressed indignation at the sybaritic living in Hitler's entourage, at the many party parasites. But he never gave me any information about his doings, any more than I would have revealed to him that we were working on rockets that were supposed to reduce London to rubble. Even when we spoke of our own dead, we used the term "casualties," and in general we were great at inventing euphemisms.

Asked the doctor for a sleeping pill, the first in months.

December 19, 1946   For days the temperature has been in the teens. Everywhere there is a shortage of coal, a consequence of the prevailing supply problem. In the cells the temperatures hover around the freezing point. Lacking gloves, I put a pair of socks on my hands; I find I can even write that way.   .

The intervals between entries are growing longer. Almost two weeks since my last note. I must force myself not to lapse into apathy. Worried about the Spandau jail. Five days have now passed since the date we were supposed to have been transferred, and we are still here. Pessimistic moods. I am also afraid I will no longer be able to write there. For I have meanwhile realized how important writing is for this confrontation with myself. What has been written down, formulated with some care, takes on a certain stamp of definiteness.

During the past few days I have made notations on a number of Hitler's remarks. They come to me without great effort; ever since the trial my thoughts are noticeably less inhibited. It is truly astonishing, all that I keep fetching up, and even more astonishing that so many of Hitler's remarks passed by me leaving not a trace. Recently I thought I remembered that in my presence Hitler had been rather reticent about expressing his hatred for the Jews. But he said a good deal more than I recalled in my states of repression. It is disturbing to think that however much we want to be honest, our memory may play us false, depending on the situation.

December 20, 1946   Again the central problem. Everything comes down to this: Hitler always hated the Jews; he made no secret of that

at any time. By 1939 at the latest I might have foreseen their fate; after
1942 I ought to have been certain of it. In the months before the outbreak of the Second World War, which surely did not come at a convenient moment for him, his tirades increased. World Jewry was insisting on war, he obstinately repeated; and later he said that the Jews
alone had instigated this war and were to blame for it. "They also saw
to it that my peace offer of the autumn of 1939 was rejected. Their
leader, Weizmann, openly said so at the time." Hitler spoke as plainly
as possible at the Reichstag session of January 30, 1939, when he asserted that if war came, not the Germans but the Jews would be annihilated. And years later, when everything was obviously lost, he used to
remind his listeners of that statement. More and more often, when he
did so, he would simultaneously bewail the killings of innocent German women and children in air raids. Especially after the heavy raids
on Hamburg in the summer of 1943, in the course of which tens of
thousands of civilians were killed, he repeated several times that he
would avenge these lost lives upon the Jews. If I had listened more
closely, observed more carefully, it would surely have dawned on me
then that he was making such remarks in order to justify his own mass
killings. It was as if the indiscriminate bombing of civilians suited his
purposes, supplying him with a belated apology for a crime long since
decided on and stemming from the deepest strata of his personality. Incidentally, it would be wrong to imagine that in his expression of
hatred for the Jews Hitler literally foamed at the mouth. (We prisoners
were constantly asked whether that rumor was true.) He was capable of
tossing off quite calmly, between the soup and the vegetable course, "I
want to annihilate the Jews in Europe. This war is the decisive confrontation between National Socialism and world Jewry. One or the
other will bite the dust, and it certainly won't be us. It's lucky that as
an Austrian I know the Jews so well. If we lose, they will destroy us.
Why should I have pity on them?"

That was how he used to talk, in military conferences and at table.
And the entire circle, not only the lower-ranking persons, but generals,
diplomats, cabinet ministers, and I myself, all of us would sit there
looking grave and gloomy. But there was also, if I recall rightly, something akin to shamefacedness in our attitudes, as if we had caught
someone close to us making an embarrassing self-revelation. No one
ever contributed a comment; at most someone would sedulously put in
a word of agreement. Now, however, it seems to me that it was not
Hitler who embarrassingly revealed himself, but we. Perhaps I thought
he did not mean it literally; certainly that is how I took it. But how

could I imagine that his ideological fanaticism would stop short just where the Jews were concerned? So what I testified in court is true, that I had no knowledge of the killings of Jews; but it is true only in a superficial way. The question and my answer were the most difficult moment of my many hours on the witness stand. What I felt was not fear but shame that I as good as knew and still had not reacted; shame for my spiritless silence at table, shame for my moral apathy, for so many acts of repression.

December 21, 1946 And then this beastly way of talking! How was it I never really felt revolted by it, never flared up when Hitler—as he did almost all the time in the last few years—spoke of "annihilation" or "extermination." Certainly those who would charge me with opportunism or cowardice are being too simplistic. The terrible thing, the thing that disturbs me much more, is that I did not really notice this vocabulary, that it never upset me. Only now, in retrospect, am I horrified. Certainly part of the reason was that we lived in a tightly shut world of delusion isolated from the outside world (and perhaps also from our respectable selves). I wonder whether in Allied headquarters, as in ours, the talk was not of victory over the enemy but of his "extinction" or "annihilation." How, for example, did Air Marshal Harris express himself?

Afternoon. Of course all such talk was also connected with the ideological fever Hitler communicated to all events, but especially to the campaign against bolshevism. He felt himself the protector of Europe against the Red hordes, as he used to phrase it. He believed in the most literal sense that it was a question of to be or not to be. Again and again he came back to that. The litany of the later years ran: "We must win the war or the peoples of Europe will be mercilessly annihilated. Stalin will not stand still. He'll march on to the west; in France the Communists are already calling for him. Once the Russians have Europe, all our cultural monuments will be destroyed. Europe will become a desert, cultureless, emptied of people, nothing but low trash left and chaos everywhere. Don't forget, Stalin is Genghis Khan come back from the abysses of history. Compared to what's going to happen if we should lose, the devastation of our cities is a joke. We with our two hundred divisions weren't able to stop the Russians; then how are a few Allied divisions going to do it? The Anglo-Saxons will abandon Europe without a struggle. I'm sure of that. They'll leave it to the cannibals. After the big encirclements we found human bones, you know. Imagine that, they ate each other up out of hunger. Just so they wouldn't have to surrender. There you have it, they're subhuman."

I heard him make this last remark repeatedly, and even then the contradiction struck me. For he charged the Russians with being *Untermenschen* for conduct—at least as far as their unyielding determination to resist was concerned—that he again and again demanded of his own soldiers. But this contradiction, which today strikes me as infuriating, did not bother me at the time. How was that possible?

Perhaps the contradiction was somehow resolved in the personality of Hitler and could appear obvious only after his death. It is generally admitted that Hitler admired what he hated; it is really more accurate to say that he hated what he admired. His hatred was admiration that he refused to acknowledge. That is true of the Jews, of Stalin, of communism in general.

Then, too, there was this radicalism in his thinking. It was already there shortly before the war broke out. At the end of August 1939, when Hitler had already decided to attack Poland, he stood on the terrace of his house at Obersalzberg and commented that this time Germany would have to plunge into the abyss with him if she did not win the war. This time a great deal of blood would be spilled, he added. How odd that none of us was shocked by this remark, that we felt ourselves somehow exalted by the fatefulness of such words as "war," "doom," "abyss." In any case, I distinctly recall that when Hitler made this remark I did not think of the endless misfortunes it meant, but of the grandeur of the historical hour.

December 22, 1946   The cell is an icehouse, my breath visible. I wrap the blankets tightly around me. I have underwear around my feet, have put on all available articles of clothing, including the winter jacket that was developed, with my assistance, for the army in 1942. It has a hood that I draw well up over my head.

December 23, 1946   Read an article in the magazine *Fähre* of April 1 on "Psychoanalysis and the Writing of History," by Mitscherlich, the court psychologist, who has been visibly recuperating and has gained a good deal of weight. It is interesting; the rest of the issue seems to me distinctly mediocre. It may also be that I do not grasp the changes in public attitudes, coming as I do from that other world. For the first time I am swept by a feeling of alienation.

Or is it more than that? Where do I really stand? I recognize what was, and I condemn it. But the cheap moralizing that has become a kind of fashion repels me. Perhaps Germany will have to sound like Sunday school for a while. Nor is it that I want to minimize my share in what has come about. But I can't go along with that kind of tone, even though it would make things easier.

December 24, 1946   My improvised sleeping bag has kept me warm all night. Only now, in prison, am I coming to appreciate the inadequacies of the army's winter clothing. Our winter jacket does not keep me warm even here in the cell; it absorbs too much moisture and dries poorly. An ordinarily unfriendly guard comes to the "peephole" and greets me very cordially. He is hoping I'll give him a drawing of the Zeppelin Field.

Ah, yes—tonight is Christmas Eve.

As always, the morning was spent in sweeping and mopping the corridor. Talk with my fellow prisoners. Christmas greetings are exchanged. At eleven o'clock steam thumps in the heating pipes, but the radiator in my cell seems to be blocked. Or else there is too little pressure—the cell is at the end of the corridor.

At two o'clock I have a half-hour walk in the prison yard with Dönitz, Schirach, Raeder, and Neurath. Hess and Funk remain inside. Two guards armed with submachine guns keep watch. We are still required to walk apart. It is well below freezing; I am wearing the winter jacket with the hood up. Dönitz calls out to me good-naturedly that I look—he actually says—happy and contented.

When I come back I find Christmas letters from my wife and my parents on my cot. Altogether disconcerted, I read them, with long pauses.

In our chapel on the second tier there is a Christmas tree decorated with candles, a tinsel angel fastened to its tip. The primitive atmosphere in the cleared-out double cell reminds me of the catacombs of the early Christian congregations. Six of us sing Christmas carols; Hess alone does not take part. Chaplain Eggers, the American, reads a sermon written for us by the Nuremberg clergyman, Schieder. Before we are led back to our cells Funk, with a few jokes intended to hide his Christmassy feelings, hands Dönitz a sausage; with more reserve, Schirach gives me a piece of bacon, since Dönitz and I have not received packages of presents. Neurath gives me some Christmas cookies; later the American chaplain brings chocolate, cigars, and a few cigarettes. I give Dönitz a cigar.

In our wing there is silence; each of us is now locked up for the rest of the day. A woman is singing on the radio.

Three hours later. The thought keeps coming back that this will be repeated nineteen times, and again and again I try to repress that idea. I think of Christmas Eve of 1925, when I visited my future wife at her parents' comfortably furnished apartment overlooking the Neckar River. I was twenty years old. With what I managed to save from my student's allowance I had bought her a bedside lamp with a silk shade and a figure in Nymphenburg porcelain for a base. In Berlin in the spring of 1945 I still had with me the photograph of the table on which her gifts were spread out that Christmas. Then it was lost. I was attached to that picture. After celebrating Christmas with her parents, I went up the mountain to my parents' house, situated in the midst of wooded parkland above the Neckar Valley. It is a house of solid middle-class proportions. The Christmas tree used to be set up in the big living room, in front of a fireplace of old Delft tiles. All my life this scene has remained unchanged; every year we drove home over snow-covered roads to celebrate Christmas. Following the unvarying ritual, the servant, Karl, the maid, Käte, and the cook, Bertha, would be invited to the distribution of the presents. Two fire buckets filled with water always stood beside the tree; my father always chanted a Christmas carol in his unsteady voice. His inability to sing and his strong feelings about Christmas always made the singing sound totally disjointed, and after the first or second stanza he faded out.

Then came Christmas dinner in the adjacent dining room, with its neo-Gothic wooden paneling, where the festive dinner celebrating my baptism had once upon a time taken place. My mother fetched out the tableware she inherited from my grandparents, a Mainz mercantile family: the cobalt blue Limoges dinner service with gold decoration, the polished crystal glasses, the flat silver with mother-of-pearl handles, and candelabra of Meissen porcelain. Karl had donned blue-violet livery with specially made buttons showing a family crest that wasn't altogether legitimate; the maid wore a lace cap with her black silk dress. White-gloved, they served the traditional boiled Westphalian ham with potato salad. We drank Dortmund beer with it, because my father had long belonged to the board of the largest local brewery.

At seven o'clock Sergeant Richard Berlinger comes, as he does every evening. As the security regulations require, he requests my glasses and pencil, then turns the outside light to one side.

December 25, 1946 Chilly night. Today I am the water carrier. Swollen fingers. A few days ago the defendants in the impending trial of the SS leadership were housed on the ground floor. I try to cheer them with a few words; the guard does not interfere. These are all candidates for death row.

To distract myself, I do a lot of drawing in spite of the cold. By five o'clock my fingers are swollen again. I wrap myself in my four blankets and with hood pulled over my head read Timmermann's *Bauernpsalmen*. Later in the evening a hot beverage is brought, but I cannot make out whether it is coffee or tea. From his Christmas package Schirach sends me a large piece of excellent cake and a portion of butter.

Monologues with myself about Napoleon, whom Goethe first branded a monster but ten years later hailed as a phenomenon of world-historical importance. I wonder whether the European Napoleon legend and the cult of the great man connected with it helped to produce that attitude of surrender with which the European bourgeoisie (and the working class, too, which deified its Marx, Engels, and Lenin) succumbed to Mussolini and Hitler. We were all fascinated by towering historical personalities; and even if a man was nothing of the sort, only acted the part with a modicum of skill, we threw ourselves on our bellies. It was like that in Hitler's case. I think part of his success rested on the impudence with which he pretended to be a great man.

December 28, 1946   As I was coming from the shower today, my Christmas package from the family was brought to me. It shocks me by its sparseness. How bad things must be outside! I am deeply touched. My eldest boy, twelve-year-old Albert, has sent me two pieces of fretwork; the other children have pasted silver stars on red wrapping paper. Contemplating these things, I lose my self-control for a while.

Because of a short circuit, the light goes out for some time. A blessing for my eyes, because even at night we live in twilight. At half past ten I listen, leaning against the door, to music from the guard's radio.

Meditations far into the night. I must teach myself to regard the difficulties of imprisonment as a kind of athletic performance.

December 30, 1946   Slept well. The signs of frostbite on my hand are fading. It is somewhat warmer in the cell today; my breath is barely visible.

At half past ten I am linked to a guard by chromed handcuffs and taken out to a conference with Attorney Kranzbühler and Professor Kraus. At the trial Kranzbühler defended Dönitz, while Professor Kraus, a specialist in international law, participated in the defense of Schacht. Both have been assigned to the defense in the forthcoming "minor Nuremberg trials." Dr. Charmatz of the American prosecution team was also present. Naturally I enjoyed this diversion; but that is exactly what makes me a typical prisoner.

My wife has sent me a new issue of the architectural magazine *Bauwelt*. This issue contains the plan developed by Scharoun for the rebuilding of Berlin. The sketch is largely featureless; its only design element is the original river valley of the Spree (which does not show). The city will be divided into utilitarian rectangular areas. No conception of an "architectonic" Berlin underlies this plan, no sense of the city's evolution, and no reference to the problem of the railroad station, to which I once gave such long thought. What a plan like this signifies is a capital that has given up its hopes. The extreme in supercolossal dimensions is followed by renunciation; timidity takes over from megalomania. One extreme or another—that is the real German form of expression. This is of course not so. But a historical situation like the present one suddenly makes us believe it, and oddly, "proofs" then crop up in great numbers, until the truth (which is always difficult and complex) seems altogether obscured.

December 31, 1946   Today is the end of the year 1946. "Albert Speer, to twenty years' imprisonment." It's as if that were yesterday.

January 1, 1947   Began the new year dispiritedly. Swept corridor, a walk, and then to church. Dönitz and I sing more loudly than usual because Raeder is sick and Funk is due to go to the hospital. Only the pressure I was under during the trial made me believe that I believed. Since then I again have the feeling of meaningless rituals during the church services. The narrowness of man's perspective. But these are only the most obvious conditions that color our thoughts. How many conditions must every proposition be subject to, conditions we do not even suspect?

January 3, 1947   I estimate I have now traversed some four hundred kilometers in the prison yard. The soles of my shoes are worn through. I submit a request, with a sketch, to the prison office and receive a pair of used but still good American army shoes.

January 6, 1947   The prison management was not satisfied with our daily cleaning job. What we chiefly tried to do was to stretch the working time to an hour or two by introducing all kinds of elaborations. Leaning on our brooms, we used most of the time for conversation. The job has now been taken from us, and our successors, from the SS leadership, do the same assignment in half an hour. Since then I spend the longest part of the day—twenty-three hours, to be exact—in my cell.

January 7, 1947   Eighteen below zero (F.) in Berlin. People are said to be burning up their last pieces of furniture. Our shower rig has frozen.

January 8, 1947   Dr. Charmatz has just brought a fat interrogation record that I have to sign once more. The already signed copies have been stolen by a souvenir hunter! Charmatz informs me that Field Marshal Milch is asking for me to be a witness in his trial. Milch was one of my friends and, as chief of air armaments, my colleague for many years. A small, fat man with a round, oxlike face. It sometimes seemed to me that the long cigar he frequently held in his mouth was an attempt to imitate Winston Churchill. In spite of his sometimes choleric temperament, the two of us managed to fend off various attempts by his superior, Göring, to sow dissension between us. It will be difficult to confront him in the trial. Milch is being charged with the same crimes as I: Until he handed air armaments over to me in the spring of 1944 he requested and employed forced labor and prisoners from concentration camps.

Of course all these trials are judgments by the victors on the defeated. In various ways I keep hearing that German prisoners of war, contrary to law, are also being put to forced labor in armaments and supply bases. Who here is the judge?

And of course we could argue that our trial was carried out too hastily, that the defense was hampered by the huge number of twenty-one defendants being tried at once. But all such objections, as I still unswervingly believe, are invalidated by the fundamental principle that the leadership of a country that begins a war must accept the same risk that it demands, willy-nilly, of every soldier.

This, I grant, is a realization that I came to only in the course of the trial. Even with the end of the war nearing, I still thought the idea absurd that I as the minister of armaments could possibly belong among the defendants in the trials that the Allies had already announced. At that time, during many idle hours, I had my assistants bring me piles of documents: records of conferences with Hitler, letters or decisions of Central Planning, and so on. Usually stretched out on my bed, I leafed through those documents at random to find passages that might seem incriminating. Once again, I suppose, the narrowness of my perspective prevented me from reading the elements of my guilt in those mounds of paper. At most I saw the interests of my country as a nation waging war, and those interests acquitted me—so all tradition would have it. Consequently, I did not have any of the documents destroyed except for the memorandum of an industrialist who had proposed the use of poison gas against the Soviet armies. On the contrary, I was reassured and ordered that my files be preserved in a safe place. A few weeks later, shortly before my capture, I had them handed over to the Americans as study material. In the trial the prosecution used parts of those files to convict me of crimes against humanity.

January 10, 1947 Thanks to the good nature of one of the guards, I smoked a pipe after dark until eleven o'clock.

January 11, 1947 Signs of grippe, damp hands, pains in my ears at night. Must not get sick!

January 13, 1947 Again spent all day in bed. Drew nothing, read nothing, wrote nothing. I admire Funk for putting up with confinement to his bed in the cell for months at a time without losing his mind.

January 15, 1947 Looked into a mirror again for the first time since August. During the trial I used the glass pane of the interpreters' booth. There I could catch my reflection against dark clothing. This time it is a broken piece of mirror, but it suffices. In months, it seems to me, I have aged years.

January 22, 1947 I had never expected to be one of the defendants in the planned war-crimes trial. Then one day in August 1945, at six o'clock in the morning, one of my associates came rushing into the dormitory of the internment camp. Breathlessly, he stood in the doorway scarcely able to find the words to tell me that I was on the list of the principal defendants in the Nuremberg trial, and moreover that I was ranked in the hopeless third place. I was dumbfounded.

In the camp there was a chemist who was said to possess several capsules of poison such as Himmler had used for his suicide. I cautiously hinted to him that I was looking for such a capsule, but he refused me in evasive language. Why had nobody, neither Hitler nor the proper

SS distribution center, thought of allowing me the same privilege of suicide that was extended to Hanna Reitsch and even to Hitler's secretaries? During this period I heard a lecture by a doctor who casually mentioned that the infusion of a crushed cigar would suffice. But by this time the temptation had already passed; even if I ever could have summoned up the strength for suicide, I no longer had the inclination.

January 23, 1947   Talking gaily and unconcernedly, a child, perhaps the chaplain's, passes through the corridor. This stirs me more than outward events.

January 24, 1947   I owe it to my lawyer, Dr. Hans Flächsner, a Berliner small in stature but possessed of remarkable eloquence, that I have survived the trial in one sense, and to Dr. Gilbert that I survived it in another.

Flächsner, who was assigned to me by the court, explained his idea for a defense: "You will be sitting in the dock third from last. That amounts to being classified one way, whereas Göring, Hess, Ribbentrop, and Keitel are classified another way, at the top. If you go ahead and declare yourself responsible for everything that happened during those years, you are making yourself out more important than you are and in addition calling an inappropriate degree of attention to yourself. That will not only make a dreadful impression but may also lead to your receiving a death sentence. Why do you yourself insist on saying that you are lost? Leave that to the court."

On the whole, this is what we did. For of course I did not want a death sentence. On the witness stand I avoided everything that might have incriminated me except for my admission that millions of the deported were brought to Germany against their will and that I felt generally responsible for the crimes that had been committed. But those were decisive concessions. They also brought me many reproaches from my fellow defendants. Göring in particular kept saying that by incriminating myself I was trying to win the sympathy of the court, but that I'd disregarded the fact that all of them would have to suffer for my admissions. I don't know. Still, I suspect that those noted jurists could not have been so easily deceived—neither by my confession nor by the denials of the others. That is proved by the fact that Hans Frank, the governor-general of Poland, and Hitler's commissioner for the Netherlands, Arthur Seyss-Inquart, who likewise showed contrition, did not escape the death sentence.

January 26, 1947   The fact is that in the courtroom I did win a measure of sympathy, or rather respect.[2] But what Göring said—that I won it by incriminating myself in court—was wrong. Only recently, when I met with the American prosecutor, Charmatz, he told me of a remark Justice Jackson made to Flächsner immediately after cross-examining me: "Tell your client that he is the only one who has won my respect." That was probably because of my effort to tell the truth and not to take refuge in cheap alibis. And then again there is the liking I arouse almost everywhere. I recall my teacher Tessenow, who so conspicuously gave me his backing when I was still a student, and then Hitler, and then these judges, and now many of the guards. It is an advantage to be liked, but to think it nothing but an advantage is being very simplistic indeed. Perhaps in a way it is my life's problem. . . . Some day I must try to work this out completely.

January 28, 1947   For the past several days we have had new guards: refugee Lithuanians. I bade the American guards a reluctant goodbye. But the Lithuanians even permit us to visit the witnesses for the new trials in the other wing of the prison: generals, industrialists, ambassadors, state secretaries, party functionaries. I met many old acquaintances. The doors were open; lively conversations were going on everywhere. I am surrounded by former associates, like the member of an expedition who has passed through great perils. We exchange experiences.

Some distance away I also notice Otto Saur, my former department head in the Ministry of Armaments, who in the end by servile flatteries outmaneuvered me in Hitler's favor. Amused, I watch as he sedulously obeys the order of good-natured Sergeant Berlinger to bring up a pail of water. With repeated bowings and scrapings, he begins mopping. And yet he is a man of great energy—the type who owed his entire existence to the regime. Obedience and dynamism—a fearsome combination.

I recall a characteristic episode that took place in May 1943 in the East Prussian headquarters. At the time, Hitler was being shown a full-

[2] On June 30, 1970, Dean Robert G. Storey, who during the trial served as Justice Robert H. Jackson's deputy prosecutor, wrote me: "As you probably know, you were admired by the United States judges and prosecutors as the least culpable of any of the defendants." On August 2, 1971, in a radio interview with Merrill Frazer, Dean Storey declared: "I shall never forget that Judge Parker in effect said that the defendant who made the greatest impression on the court as telling the truth and being fair was Albert Speer. And then, after a little conversation, he said: 'I personally as a judge thought that a maximum of ten years was a fair sentence.' As I understood, the Russians were in favor of the death penalty for all of them."

size wooden model of a 180-ton tank that he himself had insisted on. Nobody in the tank forces displayed any interest in the production of these monsters, for each of them would have tied up the productive capacity needed to build six or seven Tiger tanks and in addition would present insoluble supply and spare-parts problems. The thing would be much too heavy, much too slow (around twelve miles an hour), and moreover could only be built from the autumn of 1944 on. We—that is, Professor Porsche, General Guderian, Chief of Staff Zeitzler, and I—had agreed before the beginning of the inspection to express our skepticism at least by extreme reserve.

In keeping with our arrangement, Porsche, when asked by Hitler what he thought of the vehicle, replied tersely in a noncommittal tone: "Of course, mein Führer, we can build such tanks." The rest of us stood silently in a circle. Otto Saur, observing Hitler's disappointment, began to rant enthusiastically about the chances for the monster and its importance in the development of military technology. Within a few minutes he and Hitler were launched on one of those euphoric raising-the-ante dialogues such as I had occasionally had with Hitler when we discussed future architectural projects. Unconfirmed reports on the building of superheavy Russian tanks whipped them up further, until the two, throwing all technical inhibitions to the wind, arrived at the overpowering battle strength of a tank weighing 1,500 tons, which would be transported in sections on railroad cars and put together just before being committed to battle.[3]

At our request a much-decorated tank colonel had been brought from the front. He finally managed to say that a single hand grenade or an incendiary charge exploded anywhere near the ventilator opening could set fire to the oil vapors of these vehicles. Hitler, irritated by the disturbing remark, replied, "Then we'll equip these tanks with machine guns that can be guided automatically in all directions from inside." Turning to the tank colonel, he added in a lecturing tone, "After all, I can say for myself in all modesty that I am no amateur in this field. It was I who rearmed Germany." Of course Hitler knew that the 1,500-ton tank was a monstrosity, but ultimately he was grateful to Saur for giving him such shots in the arm from time to time. In the tes-

[3] The year before, in fact, at the suggestion of an engineer, Hitler had actually ordered such a tank built. It was to be armed with a short-barreled mortar having the extraordinary caliber of eighty centimeters. In addition there were to be twin turrets, each armed with a fifteen-centimeter long-barreled cannon. The front armor plate was to have a thickness of 250 millimeters. Four U-boat diesel motors, in combination yielding 10,000 horsepower, were to drive this tank.

tament he drew up shortly before his death, he dismissed me as minister of armaments and appointed Saur my successor.

One other incident occurred to me when I observed Otto Saur so dutifully obeying the guard's instructions. In the last weeks of the war he had obtained permission from Hitler to withdraw to Blankenburg with his staff. Always brash and tough with the captains of industry, he himself lacked even a modicum of courage. Consequently I had an invented text placed in his mail: "Report from the British Broadcasting Corporation: We have learned that Saur, the well-known associate of Speer, has fled from our bombs to Blankenburg in the Harz Mountains. Our airmen will find him out there too." Gripped with panic, he promptly set up his headquarters in a nearby cave.

January 29, 1947   Weakened by another cold. Often dizzy. My physical strength is plainly diminishing; my ability to concentrate is also going.

February 3, 1947   Dizzy in the morning. Cardiac irregularity. I stay in bed and cannot read; the lines swim before my eyes. The doctor is solicitous. As always. In a reverie all day long.

February 6, 1947   Dressed in a ski suit, I go to a hearing as Milch's witness. Empty courtroom. Only three persons present: Justice Musmanno, a Mr. Demmey as the prosecutor, and the defense attorney. Milch is not there. It is good to be back in a large room equipped with real furniture. Strangely, it increases my self-confidence. As I mechanically follow the legalistic game of questions and answers between prosecution and defense, I consider how much strength the bourgeoisie derived from the décor of the world. The security that environmental reliability gives one. The bourgeois's home was the fixed base, the last line of retreat from the outside world, so to speak. Hitler was forever seeking something of the sort. The excessiveness of his buildings, right down to his weekend house, and even the monumental quality of his furniture, reflected how acute this need was for him. And what a light that throws on me.

I go through three hours of testimony in the morning and still feel quite fresh; after lunch a greater expenditure of energy is needed. The prosecution abstains from cross-examining; Milch's lawyer is satisfied, for I declare that in Central Planning the decisions were made by me and not by Milch. In this way I take more responsibility for the levying of labor in occupied Europe, which Sauckel was in charge of, than Milch.

February 8, 1947 My first walk in six days. The weakness seems to be gone. Could it have been only fear of appearing as a witness?

In the evening, under the heading MILCH BETRAYED INDUS-TRIAL SECRETS, I read in the newspaper two sentences about my five-hour testimony, both incorrect. Milch often told me about Hitler's order to show General Vuillemin, chief of staff of the French Air Force, the most secret types of planes when Vuillemin made an official tour of Germany in the late summer of 1938. Milch was even ordered to demonstrate the latest types of flight weapons and disclose our training methods. Even our first electronic equipment for locating planes was not concealed from the guest. Probably, by this demonstration of our technical air superiority, Hitler hoped to make the French government submissive in view of the coming Sudeten crisis. But by 1944 Hitler seemed to have completely forgotten his own instructions. He angrily asserted that Milch had betrayed the secret of radar to the French.

As a witness for Milch I declared that these demonstrations had in practice subtracted from the fighting strength of the German Luftwaffe. On the other hand, Milch could justifiably conclude from the orders that Hitler had no bellicose intentions for the near future.

February 10, 1947 The Lithuanian guards still have trouble abiding by the strict regulations. They repeatedly allow me to go into the witnesses' wing with pail and broom. This afternoon I talked there with several generals, one of whom gave me Guderian's regards. The story is that hundreds of high-ranking military men are being held in the so-called generals' camp fairly near Nuremberg. Many of them have been assigned by the Americans to work on problems in military history. From such conversations I get the impression that people are increasingly representing Hitler as a dictator given to raging uncontrollably and biting the rug even on slight pretexts. This seems to me a false and dangerous course. If the human features are going to be missing from the portrait of Hitler, if his persuasiveness, his engaging characteristics, and even the Austrian charm he could trot out are left out of the reckoning, no faithful picture of him will be achieved. Certainly the generals in particular were not overwhelmed by a despotic force for a whole decade; they obeyed a commanding personality who frequently argued on the basis of cogent reasoning.

Some generals are also trying, so I hear, to represent the failure of the Blitzkrieg against Russia as the consequence of Hitler's leadership. The underlying premise in all such theories is that Germany had a material, technical, and operational superiority that Hitler alone squandered. That, too, is false. I freely admit that I deluded myself about it for a long time, but by now there should really no longer be any doubts on that score.

In the Nuremberg witness wing, Hitler's secretaries are also being held, so I hear. But so far I have not been able to talk to any of these ladies.

February 14, 1947   A few days ago, at my request, Chaplain Eggers gave me the judges' opinions on the sentences in the Nuremberg trial. They amount to a whole book! Today I finished it. Painful reading.

February 16, 1947   We do not know what Hess is up to. Every chance he gets he asks us about things that need doing; he recently questioned Funk about the strengths and weaknesses of each one of us. "All his remarks suggest that he is putting together a new government," Funk commented. "What craziness! Just imagine a list of cabinet members being found under his mattress!"[4]

February 18, 1947   Since nothing is happening, I once again am taking an interest in my dreams, which remain in my mind with curious intensity next morning. In the past I could scarcely recall the dreams of the night.

I am going to an official reception. In the anteroom an acquaintance asks me to smuggle him in, since he has forgotten his admission card. I give him a tray of plates, and disguised as a waiter I accompany him through a door into the open air, where huge tables with white tablecloths are set up. The host, flanked by favored guests, has already taken his seat at the place of honor. Unfortunately, my acquaintance trips

[4] Several months later a statement on the formation of a new government was in fact found in Hess's cell in Nuremberg. He intended to issue it to the radio and press after he had "taken over the leadership of the German government in the territory of the Western zones of occupation with the consent of the Western Occupying Powers." Point 2 of this statement read: "Rudolf Hess gives the order to Speer to help the German people in getting all food and kitchen equipment and transportation together. This can only be done by working together with the Allied Forces." See Eugene K. Bird, *Prisoner Number 7: Rudolf Hess* (New York: Viking Press, 1974), p. 59.

over a wire and sprawls in front of the host with his dishes. I myself am assigned a seat at the adjacent table, where the distances between the guests are abnormally large. Everyone is oddly isolated from his neighbors. We eat in silence.

February 19, 1947 Among the officers, I meet a colonel with whom I had a conference in the Hotel Majestic in Paris in 1943 and with whom, against the embittered opposition of Sauckel, I made the arrangement for setting up "protected industries." The French prosecutors noted that matter in my favor; I still remember the number of the document they introduced into evidence, RF 22. Thereafter, my lawyer no longer needed to offer evidence on this point.

Sauckel had tried to exculpate himself by representing me as initiator of the slave-labor program. In reality I had never needed to spur him on, for he had behaved as if obsessed with his assignment. Moreover, in addition to me there were many other users of foreign labor; of the approximately six million who were employed in Germany in the autumn of 1944, only two million were working for the armaments industry. The majority were distributed among some twenty other branches of production, including mining, chemicals—which, curiously enough, Göring was directly in charge of until the end of the war—agriculture, the railroad, and the postal system.

February 20, 1947 Appeared once more as a witness for Milch. The prosecution has supplementary questions. Afterwards, an interesting discussion with Justice Musmanno on the value of international trials. I said it would have encouraged a sense of responsibility on the part of leading political figures if after the First World War the Allies had actually held the trials they had threatened for the Germans involved in the forced-labor program of that era. Perhaps the trials could have been held without carrying out the sentences, by way of indicating that such verdicts by a victor upon the vanquished had a dubious cast. Had there been such historical precedents, we certainly would have known we were transgressing.

In the evening finished sketching the Californian house for the likable young lieutenant. I enjoy discussing the problems of home building with him.

February 22, 1947 A productive period. In order to turn my mind to other thoughts I have designed a summer house in Maine. An oversized flag is intended to represent American patriotism, which I keep encountering in enlisted men and officers; sometimes it takes the most amazing, often excessive forms.

February 24, 1947 Have repeatedly read through the issues of *Baumeister* that I received from home day before yesterday. Studied details. These architectural magazines have stimulated my desire to draw, and I did a sketch of an area of ruins, with oak trees.

In the afternoon read Margarete Boveri's *Amerikafibel* ("Primer on America") with great interest. Developments in the United States are impressive. A gigantic experiment pitched on a generously conceived scale.

Later I clash with one of the Lithuanian guards on my right to look out of the cell into the hall. He hits me. I refrain from reporting this because, as I tell him, he has lost his country and possibly his family also. The Lithuanian leaves, abashed. If this were reported he would probably lose his job and face punishment.

Outside, first twittering of birds. Nice and warm. Sunbathe my face.

March 13, 1947 In the morning was taken to see Charmatz, the pleasant, intelligent American. I told him I did not want to be called as a prosecution witness in the trials of industrialists. As a former minister, I said, it would be my duty to help my associates and not the prosecution. Charmatz replied in an unusually official tone: "If you are called as a witness by the prosecution and the summons is approved by the court, refusal can lead to conviction for contempt of court." Equally stiffly, I retorted that even so I insisted on my position.

Read Schiller's *Don Carlos* through to the end. Thoughts about the corrupting effect of power.

March 14, 1947 Dr. Charmatz informs me that the prosecution has decided not to call me as a witness.

A newspaper reports that the transfer to Spandau has been postponed again because of differences among the Allies. Birds are twittering outside.

March 18, 1947 First green shoots on the lawn of the prison yard. For several days we have been allowed to talk with one another while walking. I usually walk with Dönitz or Funk. Our conversations circle around prison problems.

This morning, while we are griping about the dull razor blades,

Dönitz abruptly and aggressively says to me that the Nuremberg verdict made a mockery of all justice, if only because the judging nations would not have behaved any differently. Suddenly I realize the futility of reminding him of, for example, the photographs, by way of making him see the moral legitimacy of the verdict. Instead, I argue nonpolitically, pointing out that our conviction might lead to the quicker release of the German prisoners of war, for it is hardly possible to condemn us for violation of the Geneva Convention and at the same time hold millions of prisoners of war for forced labor in mines, in military depots, or in agriculture for years after the war. This argument of mine is borne out by the involved explanation that Lord Pakenham, the Parliamentary under-secretary of state in the British War Office, recently delivered in the House of Lords when he declared that the government must find a middle course between the requirements of the Geneva Convention and the demands of the British economy. Accelerated return of the prisoners of war would imperil the harvesting of this year's crops, he said.

That had been Sauckel's argument, Dönitz replies. The fact remains: he is unable to see the magnitude of the horror. It is fortunate that we are together only half an hour; the walk is too brief for us to develop our opposing views.

Back in the cell. I cannot deny that Dönitz is partially right in his rejection of the Nuremberg verdicts. One striking example of the dubious aspects of the trial was the attempt by the Soviet prosecutors to include in the indictment of Göring a detailed discussion of the bombing of enemy cities. Naturally they did that only because the Soviet Union lacked the planes to conduct mass air raids. The American and British representatives obstinately passed over this recommendation, and even in the death sentence for Göring there is not a word about the destruction of Warsaw, Rotterdam, London, or Coventry. The ruins around the courthouse demonstrate all too plainly how cruelly and effectively the Western Allies on their part extended the war to noncombatants.

But there is another side to this: the Allies' desire for destruction was no greater than that of the Germans, but only their capacity for destruction. I am thinking of a day in the late autumn of 1940, when I was in the Chancellery winter garden talking over with Hitler our plans for the grand boulevard in Berlin. After the victory over France these projects had once again engaged his imagination. In his way, so often utterly passionless, he said, "After the war we will build up Berlin as befits a capital that dominates the world. London will be a rubble heap, and three months from now, moreover! I have not the slightest sympathy for the British civilian populace."

Four years later, in the summer of 1944, Field Marshal Keitel, Chief of Staff Zeitzler, armaments manufacturer Röchling, Porsche, and I sat with Hitler to discuss the crisis caused by the knocking out of the German fuel production plants. "Soon we can begin the attacks on London with the V-1 and the V-2," Hitler declared exultantly. "A V-3 and V-4 will follow, until London is one vast heap of ruins. The British will suffer. They'll find out what retaliation is! Terror will be smashed by terror. I learned that principle in the street battles between the SA and the Red Front." No one said anything. There can be no doubt that in both these cases the hatred and determination to destroy the enemy with any and all methods were comparable. And this is what makes a trial by the victors of the vanquished so dubious. But I take care not to admit this to Dönitz.

March 19, 1947   My forty-second birthday. Sitting on the floor, I take a sunbath in the cell. The small window forces me to move with the sun every half-hour. Spring makes life in a cell harder.

I think of my family. Before 1933 my wife and I usually would go on a ski tour in the Tyrolean Alps for my birthday. Later I merely went on working, and not even Hitler took notice of the birthday. If I had wanted him to, I would have had to drop a hint to Kannenberg, the steward of his household, or better still, to Eva Braun.

In the evening reading a remarkably interesting book by Frederic Prokosch: *The Seven Who Fled.* It describes, among other things, the prison life of a group of convicts. Reading it, I became aware for the first time that an arrogance of the humbled exists. How banal and empty seem to me the lives of the people who pass by my peephole and curiously peer in.

March 24, 1947   Now I have reached twelve hours of sleep daily. If I can keep that up I shall be cutting my imprisonment by a full five years—by comparison with my normal sleeping time of six hours.

March 25, 1947   Dönitz has news from his son-in-law, Hässler, who served on his staff during the war. He is being hired by the British to provide information on the U-boat war. Payment is in British pounds. Dönitz considers this to be good news. Astonishingly, he cannot repress a touch of family pride as he tells me about it.

March 26, 1947   In the middle of August 1942 several industrialists accompanied me to Vinnitsa, Hitler's headquarters in the Ukraine. This was the period of the tempestuous German advance toward Baku and Astrakhan. The entire headquarters was in splendid humor.

After one of the conferences, Hitler sat on a bench at a plain deal table, in the shade of the trees surrounding his frame bungalow. It was a peaceful evening; we were alone. In his low voice, hoarse from all the talking, Hitler began. "For a long time I have had everything prepared. As the next step we are going to advance south of the Caucasus and then help the rebels in Iran and Iraq against the English. Another thrust will be directed along the Caspian Sea toward Afghanistan and India. Then the English will run out of oil. In two years we'll be on the borders of India. Twenty to thirty elite German divisions will do. Then the British Empire will collapse. They've already lost Singapore to the Japanese. The English will have to look on impotently as their colonial empire falls to pieces."

That did not sound like overstatement. There actually no longer seemed to be any resistance to Hitler left in Europe. Laconically, he continued, "Napoleon wanted to conquer Russia and the world by way of Egypt. He would have reached his goal if he had not made great mistakes. I shall avoid such mistakes, depend on that!"

The idea of the power and greatness of the British Empire led him to his own imperial plans. He wanted to incorporate all the Germanic peoples into his empire: Dutch, Norwegians, Swedes, Danes, Flemings. But unlike Himmler, he did not want to Germanize them. For him, the idiosyncrasies of the different stocks, Bavarians, Swabians, or Rhinelanders, always seemed beneficial. He did not want to infringe on their individuality, although occasionally he thought the dialects too coarse. Thus, in a hundred years the different Germanic peoples would contribute to the variety and energy of the empire he intended to found; but the German language would be the general means of communication, like English in the Commonwealth.

In 1938, when Hitler was deciding on the measurements for a new Reichstag building, he left the number of voters represented by each deputy unchanged but doubled the number of seats. He was counting on a government representing one hundred and forty million persons. By 1942 his triumphs and expectations of the future no doubt encouraged him to think in terms of still larger figures.

"The vast expanses of Russia literally cry out to be filled. I'm not worried about that. The German families who will live there in our new towns and villages will receive big homes with many rooms, and soon those rooms will be swarming with children," Hitler said, sitting on the bench in Vinnitsa as we gazed out through the trees at a broad plain. He referred to the belief of historians that the East Goths had paused here sixteen hundred years ago, when they settled for two centuries in the southern Ukraine. Above our heads and far out into the distance sailed fantastically beautiful cloud formations. There was utter silence, except for the occasional sound of an automobile far off. In the course of ten years of being together on an almost private basis, we had become so intimate that I almost had to force myself to remember that I was sitting some fifteen hundred kilometers from Germany with the ruler of Europe and talking in a conversational tone about armored spearheads another twelve hundred kilometers to the east that were just on the point of irrupting into Asia. "If in the course of the next year we manage to cover only the same distance," Hitler said—and he repeated this next day to the assembled industrialists—"by the end of 1943 we will pitch our tents in Teheran, in Baghdad, and on the Persian Gulf. Then the oil wells will at last be dry as far as the English are concerned. . . .

"But in contrast to the English, we won't just exploit, we'll settle. We are not a nation of shopkeepers, but a nation of peasants. First we'll practice a systematic population policy. The example of India and China shows how rapidly nations can multiply." He then elaborated on a system of bonuses that would make every family regard children as a source of additional income. In 1932, he said, Germany had had practically no increase in births, but by 1933 the situation had completely changed. Recently he had looked into the figures and learned that compared with the growth rate of 1932, National Socialist population policy had provided the country with almost three million more people.[5] In the light of such figures the few hundred thousand killed in this war didn't count. Two or three peacetime years would balance out the losses. The new East could absorb a hundred million Germans; in fact, he was going to insist on exactly that.

Hitler said all this in a cool, mathematical tone; he spoke almost in a

[5] In the prewar territory of the German Reich (including the Saar) there were 993,126 live births in 1932. In the same area (that is, without Austria) there were 21,000 fewer births in 1933. Thereafter, however, the increase over the 1932 figures was marked: 1934, 205,000; 1935, 270,000; 1936, 285,000; 1937, 285,000; 1938, 455,000; 1939, 420,000; 1940, 409,000; 1941, 315,000 more births than in 1932. In sum, then, 2,674,000 more persons came into the world than would have been the case if the 1932 birth rate had held steady. See *Handwörterbuch der Sozialwissenschaften*, vol. II, p. 174.

monotone. But I had the extraordinarily distinct feeling that he was there and then arriving at what really mattered to him. This and the buildings, it seemed to me at the time, were his real obsessions. Common to both subjects was his thinking in vast dimensions. His megalomania applied to time as well as to space.

"Let's work it out once more, Speer. Germany has eighty million inhabitants. We can already add to that ten million Dutchmen, who are really Germans, and also—write this down—Luxemburg with its three hundred thousand inhabitants, Switzerland with four million. And then the Danes—another four million; the Flemings—five million. Then the Alsace-Lorrainers, although I don't think much of them."

Only now did his voice become excited, and at shorter and shorter intervals he asked whether I had got it all down, figured it out, added it up. If the result did not meet his expectations, he threw in the Germans in Transylvania or Moravia, then those in Hungary, Yugoslavia, Croatia. "They'll all be brought back to us. As we've already done with the Baltic Germans, and then the three hundred thousand South Tyrolese." The Norwegians and Swedes make together eleven million, Hitler went on. Moreover, all around here he could see these blond, blue-eyed Ukrainian children. Himmler had confirmed his impression that these were descended from the Goths. Gauleiter Forster and Gauleiter Greiser had told him that a good 10 percent of the Polish population really had Germanic blood. He kept hearing the same story from the Reich commissioners for northern and central Russia. He couldn't as yet say how many people out of the eastern populace would ultimately be naturalized as Germans. "But write down ten million anyhow. How many do you have now?"

By this time I had reached nearly one hundred and twenty-seven million. Hitler was still not satisfied and did not calm down until he had once again referred to future high birth rates.

As I sit here trying to reconstruct all the details of the scene, typical of so many others, and as I literally see before me such details as the whitish wood of the new table, I cannot determine what impression this numerical intoxication that Hitler had whipped himself up into made upon me at the time. Was I overwhelmed, or did I see the absolute lunacy of these plans?—for that is what strikes me first now, only a few years later. I can no longer make it out. Only one thing is certain: the orgasmic emotion that seized Hitler as he embarked on such visions was even then totally alien to me. But I cannot say whether what held me back were moral scruples or the skepticism of the technician who reduces everything to a problem in organization. At such times did I have the feeling of witnessing the birth of an empire, or did I feel at least a trace of horror in the face of the wantonness with which millions of human beings were being pushed around the face of the globe? Is not the whole answer contained in my inability to remember?

March 28, 1947   Deportation of labor is unquestionably an international crime. I do not reject my sentence, even though other nations are now doing the same thing we did. I am convinced that behind the scenes during the discussions about German prisoners of war someone will point to the laws on forced labor and to their interpretation and prosecution by the Nuremberg Tribunal. Could the discussion of this matter in our press be so open and critical if for months on end forced labor had not been publicly denounced as a crime? . . . The conviction that my sentence is "unjust" because "the others" are making the same mistake would make me more unhappy than the sentence itself. For then there would be no hope for a civilized world. Despite all the mistakes, the Nuremberg trial was a step in the direction of reciviliza-tion. And if my twenty years of imprisonment could help the German prisoners of war to get home only one month earlier, it would be justified.

March 29, 1947   The missing margin of victory in modern wars is often the last 10 percent. In the Caucasus, for example, on both sides unimportant tank units were fighting one another, the remnants of armored divisions. Suppose that in the autumn of 1942 Hitler, with better armaments and larger numbers of troops, had managed to build up a position extending from the Caspian Sea along the Volga to Stalin-grad. It would have been protected on the south by the insurmountable massif of the Caucasus. Had he succeeded, it would have meant a great step forward in his strategic concept of achieving domination of the world step by step.

My ambivalence troubles me. In the interval I have realized the dangerous, criminal nature of the regime and have publicly acknowledged it. Yet here in this wretched cell I am repeatedly plagued by fantasies in which I imagine how I would have been one of the most respected men in Hitler's world government. Maybe it is the coming of spring after a hard winter in this prison that puts such a disturbing notion into my head. But when I consider that under my direction as armaments minister the bureaucratic shackles restricting production up to 1942 were removed, so that in only two years thereafter the number of armored vehicles almost tripled, of guns over 7.5 caliber quadrupled, that we more than doubled the production of aircraft, and so forth—when I consider that, my head reels.

In the middle of 1941 Hitler could easily have had an army equipped twice as powerfully as it was. For the production of those fundamental industries that determine the volume of armaments was scarcely higher in 1941 than in 1944. What would have kept us from attaining the later production figures by the spring of 1942? We could even have mobilized approximately three million men of the younger age-groups before 1942 without losses in production. Nor would we have needed forced labor from the occupied territories, if women could have been brought into the labor force, as they were in England and in the United States. Some five million women would have been available for armaments production; and three million additional soldiers would have added up to many divisions. These, moreover, could have been excellently equipped as a result of the increased production.

Field Marshal Milch, General Fromm [Chief of the Reserve Army], and I were agreed that a military disaster at the beginning of the war, such as the British experienced at Dunkirk in 1940, would have given a spur to our energies also and enabled us to mobilize unused reserves. That was what I meant when I reminded Hitler in my letter of March 29, 1945, that the war had in a sense been lost by the victories of 1940. At that time, I told him, the leadership had cast aside all restraint.

It is strange: here I am sitting in my cell; I believe in the validity of the trial and of the verdict that has brought me here; and yet I cannot resist the temptation of going back over all the squandered opportunities, the chances for victory that slipped away because of incompetence, arrogance, and egotism.

Was victory really lost only by incompetence? That, too, is probably not so. In the final analysis modern wars are decided by superior technological capacity, and we didn't have that.

March 30, 1947 Have read my notes for the preceding days. Today I am sending a large package of manuscript home; the chaplain is taking it. We still have tacit permission to write memoirs. Frank, Rosenberg, and Ribbentrop also left memoirs behind, so I have heard.

Yesterday I read some comments of Goethe on Schiller's *Wallenstein*. He said in 1799: "Wallenstein's was a fantastic and unnatural career. Founded in a moment, it was favored by extraordinary times and sustained by an extraordinary individuality. But since it was of necessity incompatible with the common reality of life and with the integrity of human nature, it miscarried and went down to destruction with everything connected with it." Perhaps when he wrote these lines Goethe was thinking of Napoleon, whose Egyptian expedition had just come to grief. I myself cannot help thinking of Hitler, although I am aware of how incommensurable he is. Also, I vaguely feel that all such historical comparisons are out of place. Why is that? The man's cataclysmic energy, which turned almost exclusively into destructive channels, again and again? Or his vulgarity, which in hindsight strikes me more and more? And what was it about the living Hitler that so long hid it from me? Questions and more questions. Most of them still remain unanswered for me.

March 31, 1947   The bus that took me under heavy guard to Nuremberg a year and a half ago threaded its way laboriously through ruins. I could only guess where streets had once been. Amid piles of rubble I now and then saw burned-out or bomb-blasted houses still standing by themselves. As we moved farther into the center of the city, I grew increasingly confused, for I could no longer get my bearings in this gigantic rubble heap, although I had known Nuremberg well, since the planning of the buildings for the Party Rallies had been assigned to me. There, in the midst of all this destruction, as though spared by a miracle, stood the Nuremberg Palace of Justice. How often I had driven past it in Hitler's car. Trite though the idea may be, I cannot help thinking there was a deeper meaning to the fact that this building remained undamaged. Now it is being used by Allied judicial bodies.

The thought inevitably recurs that of course the other side committed many war crimes too. But we cannot and may not use those as justifications for the crimes on our own side—that I firmly believe. Crimes are not open to that kind of balanced bookkeeping. Moreover, the National Socialist crimes were of a nature that cannot be compared to anything the other side may have done. After Rudolf Höss, the Auschwitz commandant, had given his extensive testimony, even Göring turned irritably to Raeder and Jodl, exclaiming, "If only there weren't this damned Auschwitz! Himmler got us into that mess. If it weren't for Auschwitz we could put up a proper defense. The way it is, all our chances are blocked. Whenever our names are mentioned, everybody thinks of nothing but Auschwitz and Treblinka. It's like a reflex." Once, after such an outburst, he added: "How I envy the Japanese generals." But that has since proved a wrong conclusion; the Japanese generals received as harsh a verdict as we.

April 1, 1947 From the report card my wife sent me today, it looks as though Albert [the author's eldest son] has a talent for drawing. He should learn a craft. Hilde [the author's daughter, at this time ten years old] decorated her last letter with lovely floral motifs. Inlay carving might be a logical vocation for her; at any rate, that is how I imagine it here in my cell. And if she showed aptitude for cabinetmaking she might make valuable pieces of furniture. Since so much has gone up in flames, all sorts of furniture will be needed. In any case Europe will be going through a lot more turmoil. With a solid occupation Albert and Hilde will be well taken care of; assuming favorable economic developments, they could continue their education on the side. In times of crisis and great unrest, intellectual professions are more severely affected than the crafts. If necessary, with such a vocation they could be sure of earning a livelihood even abroad. Besides, being able to practice a craft promotes self-confidence. At the universities, on the other hand, what the students chiefly learn is intellectual arrogance.

Afternoon. In the chilly cell, the blank paper on my knees, woolen blanket around my shoulders, my thoughts return to the verdict. My juridical guilt is comparatively not so grave, because the victors, especially the Soviet Union, are now doing the very thing I was charged with—they are using prisoners of war for forced labor. Moreover, Allied laws require Germans to work whether they want to or not. Conditions in the Soviet camps, and in a good many of the Western camps as well, are said to be bad, and in some places simply barbarous. I also hear that German workers are being deported; and although in our case the legal rights of the matter may not have been entirely clear, now after the Nuremberg verdicts such measures are undoubtedly a violation of international law. Sauckel's lawyer did make an effort to defend forced labor, since that was the only way to save Sauckel's neck. But since the court ruled that forced labor was a crime, the Allies were committed to adhere to this principle. Such infractions do not negate our responsibility; but they do constitute a responsibility on the other side.

So far, however, it seems as though the other side is hardly worrying about that.

April 2, 1947 Chaplain Eggers brings his four-year-old boy to my cell. The child is the same age as my youngest son, Ernst.

I consider it a mistake on the court's part that it did not admit into evidence the statement by Admiral Nimitz, the American commander in the Pacific. Nimitz said he had been forced to ignore international agreements in the same way that the Germans had. In saying this

Nimitz indirectly admitted to responsibility for the deaths of tens of thousands of soldiers, sailors, and passengers. Naturally I felt some satisfaction that this statement disproved the chief point of the charges against Dönitz. But a principle of law cannot be simultaneously established and negated. The indiscriminate air raids on Berlin, Dresden, Nuremberg, Hamburg, and many other cities—raids whose only purpose was to terrorize the population—were also, like our own raids that preceded them, serious violations of the law established in Nuremberg (insofar as such law was "established" at all, and not in existence from time immemorial, which was the premise of the prosecution and the court).

If I am not to be embittered by these ambiguities, I must fight my way through from acknowledgment of my moral culpability, which I recognized clearly from the start, to a more and more decisive acceptance of legal culpability also.

The moral guilt is undeniable. Up to now it has been hard for me to admit to legal guilt. But were not most of the verdicts based on the committing of such conventional crimes as murder and manslaughter, pillaging and coercion? If I recruited foreign laborers, the fact of coercion was implicit in that act. And that is punishable under the law.

Who could survive twenty years of imprisonment without accepting some form of guilt?

April 3, 1947   Today is Good Friday. Chaplain Eggers has the guard open the door. He closes it behind him and stands with his back to it to block the view of the Lithuanian guard. Without a word he hands me a telegram. His brimming eyes send an impulse of keenest alarm through me. "At ten o'clock in the evening on March 31 Father passed away gently in his sleep. Mother." I have been anxious about him for a long time. Now it has all happened so suddenly.

April 4, 1947   I have been in torment, trying to write a letter to my mother that will not add to her grief. If only I could at least help her by my presence. Never has awareness of separation been so intense and so unbearable.

Our parting outside our Heidelberg house almost exactly two years ago: Father had tears in his eyes when he came back to the car once more, after our last handshake, to bid me farewell. At that time my parents were still intact people. I am glad to have this picture of them. Father and I never talked about our feelings. That was his way, and I have inherited it from him. He had been so successful; life at the age of eighty-four could not give much more to him. Still, he was able to be with our six children in his last months. I hope he will be a model for them, with his Westphalian perseverance, his steadfastness, his optimism.

In the evening I attend the elaborate service in the church, together with several hundred defendants in trials to come. We sit in the gallery, separated from them. Hardly anyone dares to look up at us.

The Good Friday service helped me. But I cannot grasp Father's death. My thoughts cling to that last time we were together in our Heidelberg house.

April 16, 1947   Almost two weeks without an entry. Pointless though it may be, I repeatedly force myself to return to this journal. It is the only form of activity I have left.

We are now allowed to have longer walks, often an hour twice a day. The pear trees are leafing out, and our elms are showing a green glint.

Milch, who was hitherto kept in isolation, has been assigned to our wing. Yesterday they sentenced him to life imprisonment. A harsh sentence, when I consider that the Soviet judges, who usually stand for greater severity, did not take part in it. This is the first time I have been able to talk to him. He tells me about the bacon slabs he has been getting from his longtime girl friend—at the moment she has found refuge on a big farm. I used to meet this pretty little woman with pale complexion and reticent manner in Milch's hunting lodge, near Lake Stechlin, made famous by Fontane,* whenever I went there for an undisturbed talk with Milch. We would sit at the fireplace in the rustic living room, its walls hung with bearskins, antlers, and rifles, drinking old vintages of Louis Roederer—Göring had commandeered the stocks of that fine champagne for himself and his high-ranking officers. (Hitler's court, on the other hand, had to make do with Moët et Chandon.)

Milch enjoyed telling me how he had lashed into "Fatty" (that was Göring) for inaction and laziness. Both men were quick-tempered, and when we had meetings to discuss air armaments they would often sit confronting one another, both red in the face. Once Göring bellowed at Milch, in front of many industrialists and high air force officers, that the failure of Germany's air defenses was all his fault. Milch came right back at him: "You, Reich Marshal, personally issued the orders

* Theodor Fontane (1819–98), German novelist; the reference is to the novel *Der Stechlin.—Translators' note.*

that have brought us to this pass. I vehemently protest your attempt to shift responsibility to me." His reputation was everything to Milch; he would have risked his life for it. During the war, whenever I had any dealings with him, Milch struck me as the typical good patriot, filled with traditional and almost old-fashioned notions of Reich, nation, honor, loyalty, devotion. It saddens me to find him interested now only in his personal fate and slabs of bacon. The country's future obviously no longer matters to him.

April 18, 1947 I read in *Stars and Stripes* that Americans, Englishmen, and Frenchmen are coming out for humane treatment of us seven when we get to Spandau. The Russians, on the other hand, are demanding isolation and more stringent conditions in general. As I doze off at night, confused images pass through my head: dark cells, watery soups, ban on reading, beatings with clubs, harassment, sadistic guards—everything that Fritzsche, the acquitted defendant in our trial, had told us about his months in the cellars of the GPU. Repeatedly I start into wakefulness, bathed in sweat.

April 19, 1947 I reflect on yesterday's bout of fear. How deeply rooted is Europe's dread of alien and uncanny Asia! An experience like last night's shows me that I too have it. In one of the Goethe volumes I recently found a passage in which Goethe answers the Napoleonic Age's dread of the French by referring to the Kirghizes, Cossacks, and Bashkirs who will some day overrun Europe.

In Hitler's march to the east, the idea of world conquest was of course predominant. But there was a touch of that primal dread which wasn't just a matter of propaganda; it was there in Hitler's instincts, and intensified by the atrocities of the Bolshevik Revolution. I always had the feeling that he was not pretending when he fulminated against the horrors of Red revolution and his voice took on a different tone, almost a croak. I have almost to force myself to recall that in spite of the crimes revealed in Nuremberg we were not just a gang of world conquerors babbling nonsense about master races and subhumans. Inside many of us the notion of something akin to a European crusade also subsisted: for the first time in a millennium and a half the tide was flowing the other way, with Europe moving toward Asia. In the final phase of the war we heard about Eisenhower's "Crusade" idea. Quite a few of us had had the same idea in all sincerity; it had been submerged by the barbarities of the Einsatzkommandos. The numerous military formations composed of Flemings, Walloons, Scandinavians, Spaniards,

Frenchmen, and others, who had really joined us voluntarily, indicated that some such mood of European awakening, a European élan, actually existed for a while, although it passed very quickly.

Even Hitler occasionally spoke—in connection with certain countries that he intended to bring under his domination—of setting up client states with conditional freedoms. He presented the Vichy regime in France as a model case. In these considerations of how to organize his future dominion, his ally, Italy, seemed to play no part. Japan he alternately considered as his best ally for the final phase of the struggle for world domination, or again, at such times as he was feeling an exalted sense of his own power, as the vanguard of the "yellow peril." At such times he expressed regret that the British had forced him to promote the spread and strengthening of the yellow race.

April 20, 1947   The American lieutenant has just reminded me that today would be Hitler's birthday.

How many birthdays I spent with Hitler in the Berlin Chancellery, with delegations paying homage to him, with grandiose parades! In 1943, in spite of the ominous military situation, he withdrew to Obersalzberg and in the forenoon received congratulations from the intimate entourage. All dressed up, my children and Bormann's went up to him and offered him bunches of flowers and said their little pieces. Hitler, his thoughts somewhere far off, patted the children's heads while we stood by with the embarrassed pride usual to parents in such situations. Then Heinrich Hoffmann took the inevitable pictures, which on such occasions would be published in the papers.

Aside from this brief scene of congratulations, the day passed like any other of Hitler's working days.

Shortly before, in spite of the unfavorable strategic situation, Hitler had ordered an attack toward the south by way of Novorossiysk, in order to open the way to Tiflis. On this particular April 20 a new division had been sent in to penetrate a strong enemy position. It suffered heavy casualties. Air reconnaissance photos were shown to Hitler in order to convince him of how unsuitable the terrain was for such a breakthrough. But Hitler insisted on the operation's being continued. Cutting off all explanations, he turned to me with the command to build a railroad bridge across the Strait of Kerch so that supplies for further operations in the direction of the Near East would be assured. Only a few months later, by the end of August, the bridge project had to be abandoned. The Kuban bridgehead had proved impossible to hold.

After Hitler had issued this order, he had Otto Saur and me come to his private office on the upper floor. Sitting down at the table, he showed us plans he had drawn himself for a six-man bunker equipped with machine guns, antitank guns, and flamethrowers. "We'll build thousands of this model and scatter them along the Atlantic Wall as additional defenses. Later we'll use the same model on our final eastern boundary deep in Russia." We were taken aback at his having bothered to make a drawing of this sort. Any engineering bureau could have executed it in better style. Hitler seemed to become aware of our feelings, for he said suddenly, "You see, I have to do everything myself. Nobody hit on this idea. Bemedaled generals, technicians, armaments experts surround me, but everything rests on my shoulders. From the smallest to the biggest! Here I am, fifty-four years old, and you can see the condition I'm in. But I'll still have to lead the great clash with the USA. If only I have time enough, there would be nothing finer for me than to stand at the head of my people in that decisive struggle as well."

He drifted off into lengthy expatiations on the role of the individual in history. What had counted had always been the will of a single individual: Pericles, Alexander, Caesar, Augustus, and then Prince Eugene, Frederick the Great, Napoleon. He drew all his heroes from two historical periods: antiquity and the eighteenth and nineteenth centuries. The only exception was Charlemagne, whose empire he occasionally called a prelude to his own plans for European power. I cannot recall his ever, in all those years, mentioning with admiration or even respect either the Salian or the great Hohenstaufen emperors. The Renaissance rulers, France's great kings, such as François I, Henri IV, and Louis XIV, simply did not exist for him. It is probably wrong to say that he had no deep feeling for history, for in fact he saw himself and his role only in historical terms. But his relationship to history was sheer romanticism and centered around the concept of the hero. He might well mention Napoleon and Old Shatterhand* in one sentence.

In the course of his monologue, Hitler pressed a signal button and sent for Bormann. As a special treat for this evening, he wanted to hear *The Merry Widow* on Bormann's record player. The secretary asked whether he preferred to hear the recording with Johannes Heesters and other members of the Gärtner-Platz Theater, or the Berlin performance Lehár himself had conducted for him. Hitler launched into a flood of memories and comparisons, finally concluding that the Munich per-

* A character in the Indian novels of Karl May, Hitler's favorite author. May wrote about the American West without ever having been to America.—*Translators' note.*

formance was after all, in his words, "ten percent better." And so this birthday ended in the salon of the Berghof.

April 24, 1947 Talked with Hess. He keeps to his cell while the rest of us go walking. Like Hitler when things started to go badly, he has built up an escapist world. And once again, as we did with Hitler, we respect his conduct, if only because he has a life sentence before him. Sometimes I have the impression that being a prisoner was always his destined role. Ascetic in appearance, his eyes sometimes wild in their deep, dark sockets, as a prisoner he can again be the total eccentric he was when he moved so strangely in the sphere of power. Now at last he can play the martyr and the buffoon, thus fulfilling the two sides of his personality.

May 5, 1947 For some time the restriction on mail has been abolished. We can write and receive as many letters as we please. It is nearly a year since my wife managed to move with the children from Holstein to my parents' home in Heidelberg. She writes that she is everywhere treated with sympathy. This may partly be because her family, too, were respected citizens of the town. Recently Albert's class teacher said, "You all know what has happened with the father of one of you. Therefore I want you to treat him especially well."

Nevertheless, it is clear to us seven that of all the wives, my wife's lot is the hardest. Schirach's family is being supported by their American relatives; the Neuraths have their estate; Dönitz's son-in-law in London is able to help. Only my wife is entirely alone, and in addition has the six children to look after.

May 6, 1947 On some days Hess seems transformed. Then he too will come out into the garden. Today we walked together and with a touch of cunning he told me about his flight to England. "Have I already told you what Hitler's last words to me were, two days before I took off? 'But fly carefully, Hess!' He meant a flight from Munich to Berlin in the Junkers 52." Hess went on to boast about the way he was treated in England. He said he had had two rooms with bath, a garden of his own. Every day they came in a car to take him out for his walk. The commandant had played Mozart and Handel for him. The food had been generous, a great deal of mutton and pudding, with roast goose at Christmas. A special wine cellar had been placed at his disposal. But petroleum and other things were mixed with the food, he added, and there was that restless, crazed look in his eyes again.

Hess still entertains such notions. He recently asked me to use his sugar ration for a while. "A drug that causes diarrhea has been mixed into it." Yesterday he asked about my experience with it. "Oddly enough, Herr Hess, it had the opposite effect on me. Your sugar gave me acute constipation." Irritably, he took the sugar back.

May 10, 1947 Have been reading an article by Douglas M. Kelley, who made psychiatric studies of us during the trial. He says that Göring in fact presented two faces. Speaking to Kelley, he belittled Hitler. It had not been Hitler's speeches or the party program that persuaded him to join the National Socialist Party, Göring said, but solely ambition to play a part. After the lost war he had been convinced, he alleged, that one or another party of the radical right would win power. Among fifty such organizations he had finally settled on Hitler's party, because it was still so small that he could come to prominence within it. He said he had also admired Hitler's gift for organization and his spellbinding qualities, but that he had never loved Hitler. His admiration had been cool and purely functional. Göring also boasted to Kelley that he was the only one who had had innumerable arguments with Hitler.

To us, on the other hand, Göring always defended National Socialism. He wanted to use the Nuremberg trial as the first step in creating a legendary image of the Hitler era, and mustered all his eloquence to that end. Sometimes he went so far as to demand that we all choose a martyr's death for the future glory of Nazism. Once, before the trial had opened, we were standing around in the prison yard and Göring strutted about as though he actually had held the power of second man in the government. "In a hundred years Hitler will again be the symbol of Germany!" he said in effect. "Did Napoleon, Frederick the Great, or Tsar Peter the Great act any differently? History does not regard them as murderers either. Everything depends on our solidarity. We all have to die sometime. But an opportunity to enter history as martyrs isn't offered every day. At the moment the Germans won't admit it, but of course they know that they were never so well off as under Hitler. One thing is certain: *You others* can do what you like; but my bones will be placed in a marble sarcophagus, and if my bones no longer exist, they'll substitute something else, as is done for saints!" Against my will I was impressed, not only because he put it so forcefully, but because things often actually do turn out that way in history. It wasn't until next day, in conversation with Funk, Schirach, and Fritzsche, that I said, "Now he's puffing himself up. But when he saw we were losing the war, that was the time to behave heroically. If only he had once opposed Hitler. He was still the most popular man in Germany and officially the second man in the state. But he was lazy, and no one kowtowed to Hitler as much as he did. Now he's pretending that his life means nothing to him."

A few days later Schirach brought me Göring's reply: "Göring explicitly warns you to leave Hitler out of it. He told me to tell you that he will incriminate you if you drag the Führer in." Rather more brashly than is my wont, or than I was actually feeling at the moment, I answered that I didn't give a damn about Göring's empty threats, and that he could go to the devil.

May 11, 1947 Spent hours in the yard today: we lay down in the grass under the flowering lilacs. I resolve to walk at least ten kilometers a day, to keep in good physical shape.

On the matter of Göring I should add: The solidarity he demanded began to crumble when Schirach said he was going to denounce Hitler for betraying German youth. Fritzsche, Funk, and Seyss-Inquart also disclaimed any loyalty to Hitler; and even Keitel wavered, wondering whether he should make a statement of culpability. He gave up the idea only after Göring and Dönitz pleaded with him. Frank, the governor-general of Poland, at times condemned the entire regime; Papen and Schacht in any case always presented themselves as innocent victims of deception.

The depressed atmosphere in Nuremberg changed abruptly one day. I remember that we were sitting waiting in the dock during a lengthy special conference among the judges when we heard that Churchill had made a speech sharply criticizing the Soviet Union, denouncing its expansionist ambitions as aggressive and Stalin's methods of rule as cruel and inhuman. This was, after all, the very same Soviet Union whose representatives confronted us on the judges' bench. There was tremendous excitement. Hess suddenly stopped acting the amnesiac and reminded us of how often he had predicted a great turning point that would put an end to the trial, rehabilitate all of us, and restore us to our ranks and dignities. Göring, too, was beside himself; he repeatedly slapped his thighs with his palm and boomed: "History will not be deceived! The Führer and I always prophesied it! This coalition had to break up sooner or later." Then he predicted that the trial would soon be cut short.

Within a few days all the excitement and all the illusions were ground to dust by the daily routine. Sometime afterward Schirach read out his impressive statement acknowledging his guilt in having brought up the young people of Germany to have faith in a man who had been a murderer of millions. Göring was furious and shouted across the dock, loud enough for everyone in the courtroom to hear, that Schirach was a fool, a traitor, a degenerate youth leader whom nobody would listen to a few decades hence when all these democrats were done for.

We others, Fritzsche, Funk, and I, congratulated Schirach at lunch. He was pleased with himself. "With that statement I've put an end to any flowering of a Hitler legend." Schirach is inclined to be yielding and easily influenced, so it was significant that he had resisted the pressure from his former friend Göring. I made rather a thing of proposing that we use the familiar pronoun, addressing each other as *Du*. He accepted this offer with considerable emotion. "Göring will have a stroke," I remarked rather maliciously.

May 13, 1947   Have finished reading the verdict on Milch. His intemperate statements, which today are incomprehensible. Ten or twenty more years of National Socialist education, permeating the lower classes of the population also, would have produced even greater disasters. I've copied Goebbels's last diary entry: "If our leap to great power should fail, at least we want to have left our successors a heritage that will destroy them. . . . The misfortunes must be so monstrous that the despair, the lamentations and the cries of distress on the part of the masses will be directed—despite all attempts to point to us as the guilty ones—at those who want to rebuild a new Germany out of this chaos. . . . And that is my final ploy."

May 15, 1947   My dreams are repeatedly haunted by images relating to Spandau and my fear of the Russians. Göring hoped for conflict among the victors. For me that is a nightmare, for then a situation might arise whereby the Russians in Berlin would have us entirely in their hands at last. Here in Nuremberg we are at least under the jurisdiction of the Americans. In the last few weeks particularly we've been permitted unrestricted correspondence. The rule of silence has been lifted, and the food has been first rate. All these are signs on the part of the prison administration that it is interpreting the prison regulations generously.

May 17, 1947   I hear we are soon to be moved to Spandau. For the first time I receive this news with equanimity.

May 29, 1947   Yesterday I tried to draw up a kind of summary of all my thoughts about guilt and responsibility—then abandoned the attempt. Not because it upset and depressed me. But it suddenly strikes me as tasteless and vain to be forever analyzing the degree of my own responsibility in this catastrophe that engulfed an entire hemisphere. It seems to me that in this kind of thinking I am only maneuvering myself into the old position of leadership—wanting to be first even as a penitent. Who cares whether I have a little more or less guilt?

June 2, 1947   For self-preservation I am forcing myself to make daily diary entries. But I have nothing to say. What's the point!

June 14, 1947   Letter from home. Only makes everything worse.

June 28, 1947   Feeling as though there were some ground under my feet again.

For four weeks I let myself go. I did not draw, hardly wrote, read little. Now I've made plans again for tomorrow. I intend to begin "work" once more. In order to avoid such phases of depression in the future, and in general to introduce some kind of rhythm into my existence, I intend to take vacations from now on. After five or six months, in which I mean to write, read, and study, I'll interpose a break. I've set my first "vacation" for the period from September 1 to September 15.

June 30, 1947   We are still here. Dönitz, Hess, and I think it is only a temporary postponement; the others are convinced that the idea of Spandau has been dropped. But many of us were always inclined to mistake wishes for reality.

July 2, 1947   A three-hour visit from my brother Hermann today. No bars. An American soldier who understands no German was the only person supervising. My brother's optimistic predictions about my future make me hopeful for a few seconds. But back in the cell I sober down.

July 3, 1947   Thinking about yesterday's visit, I realized what difficulty I have had lately in following a conversation. My thoughts and my manner of speech seem distinctly hesitant. When I go outside from the darkness of the cell nowadays I sometimes have a veil before both eyes for half an hour, and the feeling of being dazzled. After prolonged reading everything looks hazy. When I draw, all contours gradually blur. Evenings, before I fall asleep, my eyes fill with tears.

July 6, 1947 Raeder tells me I have a fortunate disposition; I am adjusting to imprisonment more easily than all the others. Even now, he says, after two years I still give the impression of being halfway balanced, which is more than can be said for any of the others.

My temperament may have something to do with it. But it may also come from my ability to organize my life on all planes; the moral aspect by accepting my guilt; the psychic aspect by rejecting almost all deceptive hopes of early release; the practical aspect of disciplining the routine of everyday life, that is, by planning even trivialities: from the cleaning of the cell to dividing time into spells of work and of holiday. Writing down these thoughts is also part of it.

July 8, 1947 The wives of Hess, Funk, Schirach, and Göring are being held along with the wives of other prominent officials in a Bavarian prison camp. The wives of Dönitz, Neurath, and Raeder, as well as my own wife, have so far been let alone. To judge by letters, the women seem to get along with one another even worse than we do. Not hard to see why. Whereas we here are still playing a historic part, though one reduced to banality, they are really just prisoners and nothing more. They don't even have any guilt to their credit. Moreover, in the past each of them was socially a focal point, ruler of a circle that was held together by her husband's power. That, too, is over now. So they have nothing left. The bickering we hear about probably concerns place in a by-now-imaginary hierarchy. But then again, it isn't very different among us.

July 9, 1947 Dönitz's and Milch's wives have been receiving packages from Sven Hedin in Sweden.

July 11, 1947 Have just read what Kelley has to say about me. In his opinion I am one of the most servile, but highly intelligent. Also a very talented architect who devoted himself solely to his work with boyish enthusiasm. A racehorse with blinkers. Now in prison I am inhibited, he says, but still candid.

July 16, 1947 Fine weather; hours in the garden. Brisk walking for two hours to exercise my heart. The other two hours I sat in the grass under one of the pear trees and sunned my back.

My wife's visit has been set for July 27. I hope she will come in time. The newspapers report that we will soon be transferred to Spandau. I have seen a photo of the Spandau prison yard. An ancient spreading linden stands in it. If only it has not been chopped down!

July 17, 1947   Hugh Trevor-Roper wants to send me a copy of his book *The Last Days of Hitler.* He asks for my comments. The book is said to be a great success and partially based on my accounts. I recall dimly that he visited me at Kransberg Castle and showed some reticence and respect for my special situation. His questions indicated that he had thoroughly grounded himself in the subject.

July 19, 1947   Yesterday, Friday, July 18, we were awakened at four o'clock in the morning. A platoon of American soldiers stood around in the prison corridor. A young lieutenant entered my cell and indicated, item by item, what I could take with me. Watch in hand, he tried to hurry me; but it took almost no time to assemble my scanty luggage. A last cup of coffee in the prison office. A tendency on the part of all military men to accumulate lavish reserves of time. For an hour we seven stood around doing nothing, surrounded by a group of American soldiers. Suddenly a shot rang out. For a moment there was great excitement, but it turned out that one of the soldiers, fussing with his rifle, had shot himself in the big toe. We said goodbye to the German prisoners of war, who had taken good care of us. I thanked the American commandant, Major Teich, for the pleasant attitude of his staff. But I quickly added: "Within the framework of the existing prison regulations"—because I did not want to cause him any trouble.

Each of us handcuffed to a soldier, we left the prison, entered two ambulances, and drove out through the prison gate, accompanied by a convoy of personnel carriers. I was glad to put this building behind me; the atmosphere of the trial and the executions still clung to it. In my pleasure at leaving, I felt no concern at the moment. The drive through Nuremberg and Fürth once again showed the thorough destruction of buildings and bridges, but also the reconstruction of a road bridge over the Pegnitz, with its brand-new steel girders. This small structure made me feel intensely excited.

I was given a window seat in a fast, comfortable passenger plane, my guard beside me. After my long imprisonment this flight in glorious weather was a stirring experience. Villages and small towns lay peacefully beneath us, seemingly intact. The fields were planted, and the forests, in spite of all the rumors, had not been cut down. Because life had stood still around me during the recent past, I had lost awareness of the fact that it was going on outside. A moving train, a tugboat on the Elbe, a smoking factory chimney gave me little thrills.

We circled for perhaps half an hour over the buildings and ruins of Berlin. While the Dakota flew in great loops, I was able to make out the East-West Axis, which I had completed for Hitler's fiftieth birthday. Then I saw the Olympic stadium, with its obviously well-tended green lawns, and finally the Chancellery I had designed. It was still there, although damaged by several direct hits. The trees of the Tiergarten had all been felled, so that at first I thought it was an airfield. The Grunewald and the Havel lakes were untouched and beautiful as ever.

At half past eight the handcuffs were snapped on with a quiet click. From the descending plane I could see a column of cars and many soldiers start into motion. We entered a bus whose windows were painted black. It moved at high speed, braking and starting, turning and tooting. One last sharp turn and it came to a stop. Still handcuffed to our soldiers, we got out. Behind us, at the same moment, the gate closed in a medieval-looking entrance. A number of Allied military men were posted about. A command rang out in English: "Take off those handcuffs. None of that here." With a certain solemnity, the American guard shook hands with me in parting.

Inside the building we were shown a wooden bench to sit on. We were wearing our own clothing, which had been returned to us for this trip, for the first time since the trial. Now, one by one we filed into a room where we exchanged these clothes for long blue convict's trousers, a tattered convict's jacket, a coarse shirt, and a convict's cap. The shoes are canvas, with a thick wooden sole. We are being given the clothing of convicts from concentration camps; the officials make a point of telling us this. I was fifth in line. Then I went on into a medical room, where an affable Russian doctor gave me a thorough examination. I made a point of having him note that the first entry read "healthy," so that I would be able to show that later illnesses were the consequence of imprisonment.

After that I passed through an iron door that clanged loudly behind me. The order of our entry decided our prison numbers. From now on, therefore, I am "Number Five." In the cellblock I was assigned to one of the many empty cells. One of us began whistling to work off his nervousness. A guard immediately snapped at him.

July 26, 1947 After an absence of two years, I am back in Berlin, the city I love, the city to which I was going to devote my life work. I imagined the return rather differently. By this year, 1947, many of my buildings were scheduled for completion. The Great Hall, its basic structure finished, was to have dominated the silhouette of Berlin, and the long grand boulevard leading to Hitler's palatial complex was to be traced out. For the first time I fully realize that none of that will ever be built. It will remain drawing-board architecture.

July 27, 1947 So far our treatment has been irreproachable, but extremely cold and aloof. Every day we are led out into a narrow prison yard for half an hour. We are not permitted to exchange a word with one another. The guards, with stern expressions, give us only the necessary orders. Hands clasped behind our backs, ten paces apart, we march around the old linden, which is still here.

Today, for the first time, Jean Terray, the French head guard, made a rift in this atmosphere of ostracism. This rather short, stocky man murmured quite audibly under his breath, "How can one treat them this way? It's a shame."

August 2, 1947 The British director has come into the prison yard and offered to let us work in the garden. "Only those of you who want to and as much as is good for you. It will be to your advantage." All of us accepted.

August 4, 1947 Now we spend many hours every day in a garden of between five and six thousand square meters in area. There are many old nut trees and tall lilac bushes. The garden is choked with weeds growing waist high; no one has taken care of the grounds since the war. The weeds will come right back, because the French prison director insists on having them dug in as green manure.

Spandau Prison is situated in the extreme western part of Berlin, on the edge of the woods and lakes. The life here is healthier than in Nuremberg, and the six hours of work are doing me a great deal of good. My eye trouble has vanished. But in Nuremberg we had plenty to eat; in Spandau we receive the German rations precisely to the gram.

August 16, 1947 Already in Spandau for a month.

I often stoop to pick up crumbs of bread that have fallen from the table. For the first time in my life I am discovering what it means not to have enough to eat.

Communication with the family is worse here. A letter only every fourth week, a quarter-hour visit every eighth week. But my wife cannot afford the expense of the trip. A pity that we just missed the chance to see each other in Nuremberg for a few hours.

August 31, 1947 I encourage myself with the thought that sometime in the future I shall be able to start over again from the beginning. More and more I have been considering how I can systematically deal with these years. I must work out a therapy, so to speak, in order to get through these nineteen years.

My point of departure is that I must do the full twenty years. That means I shall leave here a man of sixty. At that age other men are thinking of retirement. Perhaps I shall then have ten years left. Where should I start afresh? Politics never did interest me; building up armament production was merely a challenge to my talent for organizing things. Even at the apex of my power I always emphasized to Hitler that after the war I wanted to go back to working as an architect. Now, too, the prospect of someday running an industrial firm has no attraction for me—even if somebody should think of offering me such a job. I am and shall remain an architect. That flight over Berlin showed me that the great task I believed in has remained nothing but a sketch. If after these twenty years I still want to do something significant, I shall have to start where I left off in 1933, when I met Hitler. I must not let those twelve years be anything more than an interruption. My old teacher Tessenow's idea of simple and human building has acquired a wholly new meaning for me, and for these times. Back then his sermons were a protest against the megalomania of the industrial age. He deliberately opposed his plain houses with their neat craftsmanship to skyscrapers and factories. But now his aims correspond to the poverty of these times and the crying needs of people. I foresee that he and not Gropius, Miës van der Rohe, or Le Corbusier will determine the future. As his former assistant and favorite disciple it is up to me to carry on his work. It's high time I had done with all these fits of melancholia over the grandiose plans, the unbuilt palaces and triumphal arches; high time for me to find my way back to my beginnings. Why shouldn't I be able to do something about housing for miners and applying my mind to the rebuilding of the cities?

It all depends on my managing to keep in touch with my profession.

September 12, 1947 Fortunately there is no prison library here, filled with the usual tattered, dirty, third-rate light novels. Instead, we put in our requests to the Spandau public library. I have read Strindberg's *The Red Room* in German, am now reading Stendhal's *Rouge et noir* in French. But I should turn to this kind of literature only for relaxation, just as I would in normal life. I very much want to read architectural magazines and technical books to keep up with current developments, that is, resume something like a formal study of architecture. I can foresee that by the time of my release many new building materials and principles of construction will be coming into use. Unfortunately there do not seem to be such technical works in the catalogue of the Spandau public library. Perhaps some will come my way later on.

September 18, 1947 The prison regulations are also helping to give some form to this featureless life. They have set up a work program with a precise schedule determined to the minute. From eight to half past eleven in the mornings and from two to half past four in the afternoons we are required to work. For the remaining time, I set myself my own tasks. I am ready to make a fresh start. I am not unhappy.

The Second Year

October 3, 1947 After two months in Spandau our life is flowing smoothly. Things were a bit improvised for a while because they were still working out the administrative patterns.

Every month there is a change of the occupation troops posted in the towers around the prison and at the gate. First the Russians take over, then the Americans, then the British, and finally the French. As far as we are concerned, the only change is the food. With each change of regime, the director of the group in charge assumes the chairmanship in the conferences among the Big Four. But that hardly makes any difference, since the Soviet director, even when he is not chairman, can at any time say *nyet* or personally intervene.

My cell is 3 meters long and 2.7 meters wide. These measurements would be just about doubled if I counted the thickness of the walls. It is also 4 meters high, so that it does not seem so poky. As in Nuremberg, the glass of the window has been replaced by cloudy, brownish celluloid. But when I stand on my plain wooden stool and open the transom of the window, I see the top of an old acacia through the stout iron bars, and at night the stars.

The walls are painted a muddy yellow, the upper part and the ceiling whitewashed. The top of the table in the cell is .48 meters wide by .81 meters long. The dirty brown varnish is flaking off and the grain of the wood is visible: signs of wear by generations of prisoners. My possessions usually lie on the table: tobacco box, pipes, slide rule, photos, hairbrush, folders, pencils, letters, three books, and the Bible. A Soviet guard recently reproved me, saying that the table could show "more *jista*" (cleanliness) and have more "*cultura*." His reprimand had no effect.

As a substitute for a closet, a small open cupboard .43 by .54 meters hangs in the cell. I keep soap and other paraphernalia on its shelves. My jacket, coat, and towels hang from hooks. The bed is a black iron cot 1.90 meters long and only .79 meters wide. But unlike the beds in Nuremberg, it has a headrest, pillow, mattress cover, and sheets. There are five gray woolen blankets stamped in large black letters GBI. This means they have come from a labor camp run by my former office as Generalbauinspektor (inspector general of buildings) for Berlin. They are made of synthetic fibers and so have no warmth; in addition they are heavy. A mattress filled with cotton batting comes from San Antonio, Tex., according to the American army stamp.

By day I change the bed into a couch by spreading a blanket over the mattress. On this couch I breakfast, read, write, and laze. After a few months I have become so accustomed to the small dimensions of my cell that I have decided to make all rooms small in the buildings I shall someday design. The advantages outweigh the disadvantages. Lying on the couch I can, for instance, get something from the table merely by turning on my side and reaching out. The office in the planned Führer's Palace was to be 650 square meters in area.

As in Nuremberg, the iron cell door has a square opening at eye level. The cell is poorly illuminated at night by a light placed outside. Usually the door is double-locked and barred. If someone forgets, I feel oddly uncomfortable.

Every morning at six there is a knock at the door. This is the signal for getting up. I do it quickly, for a few minutes later the door is opened, to the accompaniment of the ever-present rattle of keys. In trousers and straw slippers, I go out to wash up. Then there is half an hour until breakfast. This is supplied by the nation on duty for the month, from military rations. In July we received ersatz coffee from the Russians, and rye bread at last; we had not had any for more than two years. In August the Americans supplied us again; during the earlier British month we received sugared tea with milk and biscuits. Now it is the turn of the French, but hopes of brioches and good French white bread have been dashed. Whatever the month, we keep losing weight. Recently I had to sew new buttonholes in my prison slacks because they had become too loose around the waist; originally they were too tight.

After breakfast my first pipe. No matter which nation is on duty we receive a tin of American Prince Albert as our weekly ration.

October 4, 1947   Today, by pressing on the button installed in every cell, Funk activated the red disk in the corridor. This is the way we summon the guards. Monsieur Terray called through the hatch in his whispering manner: "I don't have a light. No light. No, nothing in my pocket." Funk teased: "But you always do have matches. There must be one in the other pocket." Terray insists: "I don't have any." Then, suddenly: "Oh yes, here!" Funk plays this game every morning and seems to enjoy it. In the adjoining cell Hess has his stomach cramps and begins to moan: "Oh, oh, oh."

Half past seven. Our doors are unlocked. After greetings exchanged between each guard and each prisoner, we clean our cells. Terray tells Hess, "Get up. Clean up. Make your cell clean. Did you hear?" No answer. Meanwhile we sweep the hall, Schirach often murmuring as he works, without any discernible reason, "Yes, yes, yes, yes." Hess's door is open, the light on; he is lying in bed, blanket drawn up to his chin.

At quarter of eight we return to the cells. Terray calls out, "Ready?" He locks up.

October 5, 1947   Sunday, but we still have no church services. Raeder recently protested. Major Brésard, the temperamental, corpulent French director, merely shrugged and left the hall quickly.

This "hall" is 75 meters long and 5 meters wide, really a cell corridor. Before we moved in, a false ceiling of fiberboard was installed concealing the many-storied shaft with its square of iron walkways usual to prisons. On each side of the hall are sixteen cells.

Recently, for a few minutes all three doors leading to the main gate were open. I could tangibly see the goal that still lies so inconceivably many years away.

Afternoons half an hour in the garden, then locked up in the cell, with plenty of time until ten o'clock at night, when the light is turned off. How can I survive this another nineteen years without severe damage?

I am developing a kind of system not so different from that of Coué.

First persuade myself that the bad isn't so bad at all. Once I've done that, what is really unbearable becomes commonplace, and finally I persuade myself that the situation offers many advantages. My life, I tell myself, hardly differs from a normal though basic existence. That is, of course, sheer madness, for it differs in every respect from life in freedom. But I can go a long way with this method.

In the past I would have said that I would rather die than live under certain conditions. Now I not only live under these conditions, but am sometimes happy. The concept of "a life worth living" is surely elastic.

October 11, 1947   Today, Saturday, we had our first Spandau religious service, in a double cell converted into a chapel. Bare walls painted light brown, a prison table for altar, a Bible on it, a simple wooden cross on the wall behind. Six prison chairs, for Hess will still not take part in the services. In the corner the cell toilet, with a wooden cover. A Soviet supervising officer sat down on it. The French chaplain, Casalis, gave a sermon on the subject: "The lepers in Israel were cut off from the community of the people by a host of legal prohibitions; these were as insurmountable as a prison wall." Raeder, Dönitz, and Schirach take offense; they contend that the chaplain called them "lepers." Fierce discussions rage in the yard and the washroom. I keep out of them.

The situation is probably this: they don't want to hear any truths from the chaplain. In spite of all that has happened, to them the Church is merely a part of the scenery of respectability. No more. It's there for baptisms, weddings, deaths, but it isn't supposed to meddle with questions of conscience. One more instance of how little this class of bourgeois leaders appreciates the moral implications of Christian doctrine. No opposition to the atrocities could be expected on that basis, certainly. Thoughts about the connection between Christian decadence and barbarization. When at the end of the war I decided on active opposition, my stand was not that of a Christian, but of a technocrat. Then how am I different from my fellow prisoners? In the final analysis probably only because I see such connections and can accept Casalis's sermon as a challenge.

October 14, 1947   I can hardly believe it. A prison employee has offered to smuggle letters out for me. Anton Vlaer, a young Dutchman, was conscripted for forced labor during the war and worked in a Berlin armaments factory. There he fell ill and was taken to a special hospital I had established for construction workers shortly before the war.

While in one corner of the yard an American and a British guard eagerly discuss a boxing match, in the other corner this Dutchman whispers to me that he was well treated in our hospital. He remained in the hospital until the end of the war, serving as an orderly in the operating room, and Dr. Heinz, the head of the hospital, took him into his family like a son.

Our toilet paper has since acquired unimaginable importance to me and my family. What luck that no one thought of dyeing it black. I keep the sheets I have written on in my shoes; such padding has its points in the present cold snap. As yet no one has noticed that I am somewhat clumsy in walking. Luckily, the personal searches are very sketchy.

My life, or at least my sense of it, has assumed a totally new quality. For the first time in two and a half years I have an uncensored connection with the outside world. Often I cannot sleep, anticipating the next mail; but often, too, I tremble at being found out. Vlaer has made me promise to say nothing to my fellow prisoners. He is afraid of their loose tongues. To keep down the risks, I have been making only rare use of this new opportunity. I want to see how well this thing works for a few months, and not imperil it by too many letters, which after all can contain only trivialities. But I do have one exciting idea.

If this way to reach the outside world actually proves practicable, my whole existence here will have taken on a new dimension. Up to now I have operated on the assumption that in prison all I have to do is to survive; that I will not be able to accomplish anything meaningful until the twenty years are up. Now I am obsessed with the idea of using this time of confinement for writing a book of major importance: a biography of Hitler, a description of my years as armaments minister, or an account of the apocalyptic final phase of the war. That could mean transforming prison cell into scholar's den. During the walk in the yard I have to keep a tight hold on myself, not to talk about it. At night I can scarcely sleep.

October 15, 1947   A few days ago I was interrogated for two consecutive days in the visiting room, as a witness for the trial of Friedrich Flick, the industrialist. The prosecutor, the judge, and Dr. Flächsner came to Spandau, since permission for me to testify in court had been refused.

The American judge conducted the questioning with calm friendliness: "We have come here, Herr Speer, because we hope you will be able to clarify a number of points for us." The question was whether industrialists could be blamed for requesting the assignment of labor forces. I said that the businessman had had to put in a request for the number of workers needed for the production quota imposed on him. Nor was it for him to say whether he would receive forced laborers or prisoners. Actually, he could not even decide working hours or the kind of treatment his workers received. Fritz Sauckel, Hitler's commissioner general, was alone responsible for all such matters, I pointed out. For practical reasons alone the businessmen in general had resisted the employment of forced labor, I said, and had tried to improve living conditions for the workers. Open disobedience would have landed Flick in a concentration camp; that was what happened to the big businessman Fritz Thyssen, for all that he had rendered notable service to the Party. I hope that I have somewhat refuted the prosecution.

It is very gratifying to me to see that in spite of so many months of imposed silence I can still give good answers for hours at a time, react swiftly to interpolations, make an impression. At the end the judge thanked me and I was allowed to talk with Flächsner for fifteen minutes. A lively and friendly talk. However, the guards of all four nations and one of the directors stood by.

My satisfaction shows me to what extent I have been humbled: all day I have been feeling uplifted because I was addressed as "Herr Speer."

October 18, 1947   Before the service Raeder officially protested to Chaplain Casalis, in the name of five of his fellow prisoners, because the chaplain had referred to them as lepers. They were asking him to preach the Gospel and nothing else. I deliberately took the opposite view, saying: "I am not a neurasthenic. I would rather not be treated delicately. Your sermons should upset me." Much ill-feeling.

October 20, 1947   Sunday. I have plenty of time. At the interview in the visiting room the prosecution started from the assumption that in reality big businessmen like Flick had dominated the government and instigated the war.

If only these people could have been present in the Führer's Headquarters sometime! I recall the discussions about armaments in Vinnitsa or at the Wolf's Lair, to which I used to bring these supposedly almighty industrialists. Except for a single time (and that was, oddly enough, when Röchling made a direct attack on Göring), they were given the floor only to speak on special technological problems. No military, let alone political, questions were even discussed in their pres-

THE SECOND YEAR 73

ence. As for the top captains of industry, people like Albert Vögler, Friedrich Flick, Günther Quandt, or Gustav Krupp, they deliberately kept their distance from Hitler during the war. I would not have dreamed of inviting them to armaments conferences at the headquarters. It is an absurd notion that Hitler would have shared power with Flick or one of the others.

It is true that some of them had come to Hitler's aid in the old days. Unusual though it was for him, Hitler felt real gratitude to these people. There was one industrialist to whom he went on paying tribute even after the man's death: Emil Kirdorf. I recall one time in the Hotel Deutscher Hof in Nuremberg where a small group of us were having tea after inspecting some buildings in the city. Hitler began talking about the financial difficulties the Party had been in shortly before the Depression. Creditors had been pressing for payment and were no longer willing to listen to any kind of political argument; apparently they were going to force the National Socialist Party into legal bankruptcy. "At the time I swore that I would not stand for the Party's declaring bankruptcy," Hitler said. "I would sooner have put a bullet through my head. Then, at the last minute, help came from our dear Frau Bruckmann. She arranged for me to meet Emil Kirdorf. We had a four-hour conference in her house." Kirdorf subsequently took care of most of the debts and made the Party solvent again. You could never be sure when Hitler told such stories that things had actually happened the way he said. Still, the story indicated why Hitler kept a special place in his heart for the old man. Later Hitler even overlooked Kirdorf's frank criticism of abuses under the new government.

Time and again Hitler could display generosity in individual cases. For example, there was the question of a replacement for Dr. Kissel, the deceased general manager of Daimler-Benz. The Board of Directors chose Dr. Haspel, although Himmler and Franz Xaver Schwarz [the National Socialist Party treasurer] were trying to get rid of Haspel and two other directors of Daimler-Benz, all of whom had Jewish wives. After ascertaining that Dr. Haspel and his associates were doing a fine job of running the company, Hitler refused to do anything against them; and so it remained until the end of the war.

On the other hand I do remember that even in peacetime Hitler would occasionally declaim against the ownership of securities. This made me uneasy, because a large part of my parents' assets were in securities. "They bring in high earnings without work. One of these days I'll sweep away this outrage and nationalize all corporations. For compensation I'll issue share certificates with a low rate of interest."

It is now a quarter to seven. The medical aide, Toni Vlaer, is going from cell to cell on his evening round. I hear scraps of conversation, laughter, Hess making his usual fuss. Then the clinking of keys, footsteps on the stone floor, the voice of the French guard Corgnol saying to Vlaer: "*Bon, allez!*" Now silence again. I mean to read for the rest of the evening. All this reminiscing is beginning to bore me. For the past few evenings I have been reading Hemingway's *Farewell to Arms*. This American way of writing with its reporterlike precision is something new, strange, and fascinating to me. I know nothing like it. However, up to the time of my arrest I had practically stopped reading fiction.

At twenty minutes to eight I was interrupted. Dönitz had pressed his signal button. The American guard Stokes opened his cell. Dönitz loudly complained about his eyes, saying he could no longer read. Then I heard him ask: "Has anything special happened?" The American said no. Then whispers, with Dönitz's voice occasionally rising to: "What? Really? What?" Evidently the talk was taking a political turn. I thought I could make out Dönitz praising Taft, but the American did not respond with the heartiness he had evidently expected. The man was a staunch Democrat—which Dönitz did not know. I heard the conversation subside into monosyllables; then Dönitz handed over his glasses. Stokes switched off the light. Shortly afterwards, Funk went to sleep too. Then Raeder's voice: "What time is it?" Stokes tells him the time. Raeder too hands over his glasses. Ten minutes later it is Schirach's turn. I need a light for my pipe and use the opportunity to call the guard.

Now it is wonderfully quiet in the building—the best time for reading, since they are all asleep except for Hess and me. I put Hemingway aside and take up a book on the city in the Middle Ages. Yesterday I decided, as I do every evening, my quota for today. In this regard also I am a pedant. Later, to bring the medieval period more vividly to mind, I mean to read a book about the *Nibelungenlied*.

Twenty minutes to ten. Hess's signal; he hands over his glasses without a word. Light out. In five minutes I too will go to sleep.

I recently devised a kind of meditation exercise before falling asleep. Lying in the dark I try to enter into the closest possible contact with my family and my friends by imagining each of them in detail: their walks, their voices, the characteristic movements of their hands, the way they tilt their heads while reading. I am afraid that otherwise they will slip away from me. I also imagine that perhaps I can establish a kind of telepathic connection with them by this means. Moreover, there must be people who think of me with pity or sympathy, though I do not even know them. Night after night, therefore, I concentrate on one of these unknowns, thinking of an individual, trying to say a few words to a particular person. Addressing myself to unknowns invariably ends with my feeling a strong craving for a better world. Then time stretches out immeasurably. Frequently I fall asleep without having come to an end. But almost always I achieve a state of inner harmony that is akin to a trance.

October 26, 1947   Today Casalis based his sermon on the text: "They that be whole need not a physician, but they that are sick; I am not come to call the righteous, but sinners to repentance." This time he took occasion to say that he is the greatest sinner among us; all the churchgoers were gratified.

November 2, 1947   Long, the British guard, came to work today obviously still "under the influence." He boasted to his fellows of the vast amount of beer he had drunk, and hinted at pleasant company. The party had ended only three hours ago, he said. With Corgnol's approval I let him have my bed and promenaded up and down the corridor, so I could warn him if any superior officer approached. When the time came for us to go out to the garden, he was still unsteady on his feet. He kept swinging the bunch of big prison keys. Suddenly he called out in alarm: "Do you hear those keys? The Russian director! Quick, separate!"

The Russian director did in fact turn up, but not until an hour later. I saluted him, as regulations require. At noon, when I was carrying my lunch into the cell, he called out behind me: "Number Five, come back! You did not salute." I reminded him of my salute in the garden. "You have to salute me every time you see me."

November 18, 1947   At night the area near the high wall is flooded with light from searchlights. Tonight I again stood on the bed and for a long time looked across the darkness of the prison yard and over the one-story buildings at this cone of light. It was snowing, huge flakes drifting down quietly and peacefully as in a filmed fairy tale. In the thin mist contours formed where ordinarily there is only blackness. Bored, the Russian soldier on the watchtower aimed his spotlight at our facade. A few seconds later the light struck me; I was dazzled. The light threw me back into reality; I quickly slipped into bed.

For a long time I listened to the whisper of the falling flakes and watched the shadows of branches on the small illuminated square of my cell wall. Dozing, I remembered the many nights in a hut in the mountains, when we were snowed in. How I always used to love the snow; snow and water were my real loves. Thinking about this, I asked myself whether there are temperaments that belong to a specific element. If so, I would unhesitatingly say that fire was Hitler's proper element. Though what he loved about fire was not its Promethean aspect, but its destructive force. That he set the world aflame and brought fire and sword upon the Continent—such statements may be mere imagery. But fire itself, literally and directly, always stirred a profound excitement in him. I recall his ordering showings in the Chancellery of the films of burning London, of the sea of flames over Warsaw, of exploding convoys, and the rapture with which he watched those films. I never saw him so worked up as toward the end of the war, when in a kind of delirium he pictured for himself and for us the destruction of New York in a hurricane of fire. He described the skyscrapers being turned into gigantic burning torches, collapsing upon one another, the glow of the exploding city illuminating the dark sky. Then, as if finding his way back to reality from a frenzy, he declared that Saur must immediately carry out Messerschmitt's scheme for a four-engine long-range jet bomber. With such range we could repay America a thousandfold for the destruction of our cities.

He hated snow. That was not only after the first winter outside Moscow, when snow and ice put an end to the envisioned Blitzkrieg. Even in peacetime he would shake his head in bafflement when Eva Braun, my wife, and I set out on a ski tour. The cold, inanimate element was profoundly alien to his nature. Almost invariably he showed irritation at the sight of snow.

December 5, 1947   Passing my secret messages has gradually become routine. Sometimes I observe with some alarm that carelessness is creeping in. Are my suspicions being deliberately lulled? Are the authorities trying to trace my connections with the outside world and discover the go-betweens? A few weeks ago I put a piece of folded toilet paper under my bed and trickled a little dust on it to see whether it would be found and then replaced in the same spot. But the dust grew thicker and thicker; no one paid any attention to the paper. Such lack of distrust is really almost insulting.

December 7, 1947   At eight o'clock this morning, during the change of shifts, I held my fountain pen visibly in my hand. That is how I tell the Dutch medical aid that I need more thin writing paper or would like to "mail" letters; that is, pass them to him for sending on.

December 10, 1947   A clash with Dönitz that once again reveals the enormous distance between us—an abyss ordinarily concealed by everyday commonplaces. While sweeping the hall we were at first perfectly easygoing. Dönitz made jokes about my broomstick, which is bent—because I use it more as a support than as a tool, he said. A rather silly but friendly conversation developed. But then it took a sudden turn, I no longer remember just how. I made some chance remark, for which Dönitz reproved me: "After all, this man was the legal head of state in the Reich. His orders were necessarily binding upon me. How else could a government be run?" For all his personal integrity and dependability on the human plane, Dönitz has in no way revised his view of Hitler. To this day, Hitler is still his commander in chief. For years my own attitude toward Hitler was already far more skeptical than Dönitz's is today, after the collapse and the revelations at Nuremberg. Such naïve loyalty as he displays I had only at the very beginning. When I entered into closer proximity to Hitler, and soon afterwards began seeing him every day, my relationship to him far more resembled that of an architect toward an admired patron than of a follower toward a political leader. Naturally his obvious liking for me acted as a kind of emotional bribery, and I felt sincerely drawn to him. But the politician more and more receded for me, and I do not remember ever having a substantive political conversation with him. Of course he often talked about his plans, but that was a kind of clearing the throat on the level of world history.

Politically, he never again fascinated me the way he had done when I was twenty-five, on that November day that I heard him for the first time. Students had taken me along to a mass meeting on Berlin's East Side. Under leafless trees young people in cheap clothes poured toward one of the big beer halls in Berlin's Hasenheide. Three hours later I left that same beer garden a changed person. I saw the same posters on the dirty advertising columns, but looked at them with different eyes. A blown-up picture of Adolf Hitler in a martial pose that I had regarded with a touch of amusement on my way there had suddenly lost all its ridiculousness.

Today, after all that has happened, the once so familiar face of Hitler seems horrible to me. And that is my difference from Dönitz. He too has reservations, notes faults; but for him Hitler still remains the representative of the government, the legal and legitimate chief of state of the German Reich. Any sweeping condemnation of Hitler strikes Dönitz as a kind of treason. And it seems to me that in this view he may have a large proportion of the generals and perhaps of the German people behind him. But his concept of authority seems to me empty. Dönitz does not ask what the authority stands for, what orders it issues, what it conceals. People like him will never realize what has actually happened. The Reich is destroyed, the nation plunges from one catastrophe to the next, but they cling to an abstract idea of loyalty and never ask after causes.

Of course as we talked all this was not brought out in the form I give it as I write it down. But as we walked along side by side, irritably plying our brooms, only half framing our ideas, hardly thinking them through to conclusions, this in essence was what we argued. But I do believe I understood him better than he me.

All of that makes for the gulf between the two of us, both of us nonpolitical. What we have in common, or at any rate had in common, was the fascination we felt for the man to whom we succumbed.

December 12, 1947   During the first months the guards seemed to have distinct feelings of hatred toward us. Now most of them are showing the first signs of sympathy and are trying not to make our lives harder. The French were the first to change. For a long time they have been ignoring a good many oppressive rules, such as the rule of silence. They also let us work or rest as we please, although they watch out that no Russian guards are around. During the early months the Americans followed the Russian line, but they have since become more obliging. The British cannot be swayed one way or another; they show restraint, are not unfriendly, but reserved.

A good many of the Russian guards obviously find it hard to repress their spontaneous humanity and follow the prison regulations to the letter. When they know they are unobserved, they are glad to strike up a conversation with us. In spite of their youth they are not loud; they have an air of almost timid anxiety. It is striking how most of the Soviet guards are short, their higher officers, fat.

The prison regulations are strict. We are still forbidden to talk with one another. We are also supposed to discuss only essential official matters with the guards. According to directives, lights are to be switched on in the cells every ten minutes during the night in order to prevent attempts at suicide. But now, with the tacit tolerance of some of the Russians, these regulations are only partially kept. Also there is never any marching or ordering around; everything proceeds in a rather casual way.

In this regard, too, I cannot understand Dönitz, who holds the guards of the four nations personally responsible for his imprisonment. At the Nuremberg trial he based his defense on the soldier's duty to obey. But now, in Spandau, he blames the guards who stand at the lowest notch in the hierarchy for doing what he declared to be the duty of admirals and generals.

December 13, 1947   Every two hours the guard in the watchtower is relieved. Today I again hear, far off, the American sergeant commanding a squad of ten men. The soldiers are kept in pace with a rhythmic "Hup, hup, hup!" An order of right or left is given at each turn in the path, as though grown men, merely because they are wearing uniforms, can no longer tell for themselves which way a path turns. How odd the soldier's world is. The British, too, do things the same rigid way. This rigidity is usually termed, slightingly, Prussian. The French, on the other hand, come along in loose groups, as if on a family outing. The Russians show up in good order, but without any fuss. A word from the sergeant; the relief proceeds. The relieved soldier cracks a joke; the sergeant and the enlisted men laugh softly.

To my surprise I note that the Russian guards greet their superior officer, the very strict director who holds the rank of major, by shaking hands as if he were an equal. The French have a similar unforced relationship with their superiors. The Anglo-Saxon guards, on the other hand, return terse replies to their director. I repeatedly hear that snappy "Yes, sir!"

December 14, 1947   Today Schirach brought up my quarrel with Dönitz. In our uneventful world that minor disagreement seems to have been the subject of extensive discussion. Dönitz has Neurath entirely on his side, and for once Raeder also; Hess is completely indifferent; this time Funk sides with me; Schirach vacillates. He admits that the entire Third Reich was founded more upon Hitler's personal fascination than upon the attractiveness of an idea. That particularly struck him about his fellow Gauleiters. Powerful satraps though they might be in their own provinces, he says, in Hitler's presence they all seemed small and crawling. He reminded me of how they would grovel before Hitler when he came to the capital of their Gaue, how they would concur with his every phrase, even when the context was completely beyond them. That was true for everything from the staging of an opera to the planning of a building or a technological problem.

Surprisingly, Schirach decides on the basis of these facts that in a sense Dönitz was right in his quarrel with me. The identity of Hitler and the State was so complete, he contends, that it would have been impossible to turn against the one for the sake of preserving the other. In conclusion he threw at me, as his strongest argument: "Don't you see, with Hitler's death it wasn't so much the government as the State itself that ceased to exist. The State was indissolubly bound up with Hitler." I replied, "Just tell that to Dönitz. As Hitler's successor and the Reich's last head of state I'm sure he'll be delighted to hear it."

December 18, 1947   Five o'clock. We are locked in. Donaho, the American guard, a lad high-spirited to the point of silliness, and his haughty British colleague, Hawker, are sitting at their table telling each other jokes. Much laughter. The food cart is wheeled into the corridor with loud thumps. Our tin mess kits are placed on the serving table. One by one we are let out. Schirach fetches the meal for the bedridden Funk. "Let's have this for Funk first. Here is his bladder tea. That's all. Yes, all." Schirach returns from serving Funk muttering to himself "Coffee with milk, with milk, milk, milk."

Ten minutes later the cell doors are locked again. Clatter of spoons on the tin trays. We're still not allowed forks and knives. It would seem that prisoners would prefer to take their meals together, and instead of the everlasting talking by pairs—of course only when no Russians are around—to be able to conduct a general conversation. But when this was proposed by the administration, we unanimously turned it down. We don't really want additional opportunities to be together.

Twenty minutes to six. After the regulation half-hour for eating, the doors are unlocked again, the trays placed on the serving cart and wheeled out. The sparse meal seems to have agreed with Schirach. He sings: "It is all passing, it will all pass." He does not know the rest of the words, so he whistles the melody. He repeats it again and again, singing or whistling. "This is the twelfth time," I comment to Funk. "And still nothing passes, nothing at all," he replies.

December 20, 1947   Incidentally, I too voted against the offer to let us have our noon meal together. I told myself that a company at table sets up an illusion of esprit de corps where no real communication exists. But dialogue is pointless; that is becoming increasingly clear to me. There's no one here I can talk to. The recent clashes with Dönitz and Schirach, all the arguments about authority, loyalty, and fascination, have taught me nothing new. They all talk about fascination; they like to hide behind the word, but what does it mean? If I try to find out where this fascination lay, for them, I get nothing but generalizations. Most of the time, when I do raise such questions, they talk about his talent as an orator and his hoarse, oddly spellbinding voice. Of course he had these things. But these were not all. Sometimes he affected others by his sheer presence. That was what happened to me, at our first encounter. It was in the spring of 1931, in conjunction with the so-called Stennes Putsch, which was a kind of revolt by the Berlin SA. After Hitler had deposed Stennes, he ordered all members of the SA and of the affiliated groups to come to the Sportpalast for a roll call. As a member of the NSKK, the Motorists Association of the National Socialist Party, I too reported to the arena. No speeches were made. Hitler had decided on another tack. Silently we stood, hour after hour. Then Hitler arrived with a small retinue. From a great distance I heard the groups of those who had lined up being reported to him. But instead of going to the speaker's platform, as we all expected him to do, Hitler entered the ranks of the uniformed men. A breathless silence ensued. Then he began pacing off the columns. In that vast bowl, only those few footsteps could be heard. It went on for hours. At last he came to my row. His eyes were fixed rigidly upon the squadron; he seemed to want to take a vow from each man by his look. When he came to me, I had the feeling that a pair of staring eyes had taken possession of me for an immeasurable period of time. One element that impressed me was the fact that Hitler had the courage to walk without protection through the ranks of these SA men who had rebelled against him only days before. In vain I try to explain to myself today how Hitler could exert this psychological power for hours on end. Later I told him about this first encounter, which he was surely unconscious of. But he replied, "I know. I remember you exactly."

December 21, 1947 Quarter after eight in the morning. The medical aide comes. "How would you like a spoonful of Aludrox?" The doors remain open, since we are free of Russians from eight o'clock on. It is raining, so we stay inside the building.

December 22, 1947 Great excitement. I came close to being caught. I had just been trying to fathom once more the nature of Hitler's fascination. For tonight I began considering what this famous fascination would have meant if the Republic had been successful economically and politically. I was on the point of stowing my notes away in the sole of my shoe when suddenly, without warning, I heard voices outside my door. Someone rattles his keys at my observation window. Totally shaken I crushed the paper, took a clumsy and undoubtedly suspicious-looking step over to the toilet, and threw all the notes into it. So far I don't know whether I was observed. After a few hours passed I calmed down. I tried to reconstruct what I had written, but soon lost interest. The subject no longer had the least attraction. A secret hope: that this will happen with the entire past. Liberation by writing things down.

December 23, 1947   As a result of yesterday's incident, my supply of paper has run out. For of course I also threw away the blank sheets as well. I am writing this note on the tobacco wrapper. Tomorrow morning, when Vlaer comes, I'll be holding the fountain pen in my hand.

December 25, 1947   The directors have gone to some trouble to give Christmas Day some special quality for us. First Funk played a few improvisations of his own on the new parlor-organ. Then, for the first time after two and a half years, I heard Bach and Beethoven: a cantata, and the "Gloria" from the *Missa Solemnis.* At first it was almost unbearable, but then a perfect calm came over me. Yet I have all along feared that music would throw me into depression. But in fact I feel light-hearted and happy.

All the same, I am certainly not in a Christmassy mood. Today the long separation from my family weighs upon me even more than it ordinarily does. For that reason I am glad there will be no Christmas packages this year.

December 28, 1947   A few days ago I began developing the design of a medium-sized house. The Russian guards are delighted when I explain my sketches and ask them their opinion. Their response is always the same single phrase: *"Ochin khorosho"* (very good). Since I have not done any architectural drawing since 1942, the detailed drawings give me trouble. Although I have had enough of monumental architecture and turn my mind deliberately to utilitarian buildings, it sometimes comes hard for me to bid goodbye to my dreams of having a place in the history of architecture.

How will I feel when I am asked to design a gymnasium, a relay station, or a department store after I planned the biggest domed hall in the world? Hitler once said to my wife: "I am assigning tasks to your husband such as have not been given for four thousand years. He will erect buildings for eternity!" And now gyms!

January 3, 1948   The food has become more substantial, and the heating is also good. As "chief stoker" I keep our two big iron stoves going. On Mondays I also work as washer-up, and a few days ago for the first time I actually sewed on a button successfully. Our convict's clothing has been replaced; we are wearing more or less civilian suits. The uniform depressed me because it was a perpetual reminder of the concentration camp prisoners who had worn it before me.

February 6, 1948   More than a month's gap in writing. No events, no thoughts, no new impressions.

February 7, 1948   Last night a few scraps of music came drifting down the corridor. *Rienzi*. It's damnable, the way the past keeps coming back to me again and again. I've surely heard the overture often enough, but the years with Hitler came to mind before all other memories.

Summer of 1938. We were sitting with Robert Ley, the organization chief of the Party, in the salon of Winifred Wagner's guest house in Bayreuth. Ley was trying to convince Hitler that the music of a contemporary composer should be used for the ceremonial opening of the Party Rallies in Nuremberg. The National Socialist ideology must also be expressed in musical terms, he contended. It seemed that he had gone ahead and commissioned such a piece from several composers. Hitler and Winifred Wagner remained skeptical, but Ley clung to his idea.

Hitler always took the whole *mise-en-scène* of his mass meetings very seriously. On this occasion, too, in spite of his doubts, he was willing to devote time during one of the blank days in the calendar of the Bayreuth Festival to go to Nuremberg. Together with Ley and some other Party functionaries, we sat in the empty Luitpoldhalle while a large symphony orchestra played the new compositions again and again for a full two hours. In vain Ley tried to elicit comment. Hitler remained mute. At last he said amiably, "I'd also like to hear these people play the *Rienzi* overture. I so informed you yesterday."

I must admit that the familiar sublimity of this work, which hitherto had regularly opened the Party Rallies, came across like a revelation.

Amused, Hitler watched Ley's reaction, enjoying his obvious embarrassment. Then he suddenly became very serious and offered in explanation: "You know, Ley, it isn't by chance that I have the Party Rallies open with the overture to *Rienzi*. It's not just a musical question. At the age of twenty-four this man, an innkeeper's son, persuaded the Roman people to drive out the corrupt Senate by reminding them of the magnificent past of the Roman Empire. Listening to this blessed music as a young man in the theater at Linz, I had the vision that I too must someday succeed in uniting the German Empire and making it great once more."

February 8, 1948   Some weeks ago the directors hit on the idea of having us fold and paste envelopes. Raeder conscientiously keeps a record of the daily production. The finished envelopes are heaped in great piles in an empty cell. When there is no paper for starting the stoves, kindly guards permit the use of the envelopes, so that our production is gradually going up in flames. That confuses and torments Raeder. But the authorities are in one sense relieved; they were worried that our handiwork might be sold as souvenirs.

Hess is usually permitted to remain in his cell. Lying on his bed, he moans and groans whenever a guard summons him to work. I too have occasionally been able to evade the paste detail by drawing up a garden plan on orders from the prison authorities. Then I claimed I could paint; after all, it doesn't take much skill to wield a brush. First I painted part of the hall floor; then I set to work on all sorts of furniture. I am doing that now. I have also occupied myself as a mason. In the hall I chip away crumbling stucco and replace it with fresh plaster.

February 12, 1948   To keep us seven prisoners, a staff of thirty-two is required: four highly paid directors, two of them with the rank of lieutenant colonel, two majors. Each of the directors has a chief guard as his assistant. That is not enough for the French director; he has appointed his chief guard deputy director. To any request he usually answers, very solemnly, "Discuss this matter with my deputy."

Aside from the director and the chief guards, each nation provides seven guards who relieve one another in a complicated twelve-day routine so that two guards and the chief guard always belong to three different nations. The system functions; everyone is busy. They keep each other occupied. Reports are drawn up, conferences called, disputes arbitrated. Spandau is the bureaucratic equivalent to the invention of perpetual motion. Our apparatus already runs almost entirely by itself. Will it continue to run when we are no longer in Spandau?[1]

We are spared the typical prisoner neuroses. In a normal prison, among hundreds of fellow prisoners, we would presumably long ago have gone off the rails. Faced with such a mass of prisoners, the guards scarcely have time for any individual. In Spandau, on the other hand, our interest in life is constantly kept awake by guards concerned about us. The different nations, temperaments, languages, and doctrines introduce change and color into the monotony of our existence. Some of the guards also tell us about their personal affairs. We hear about a father's death, a son's graduation, a daughter's first love. Today, when Reynolds told me about the birth of his daughter, the horrible thought shot through me that I might still be around to hear about her marriage. Thus the lives of others take the place of our own. While our families become more and more remote from us, we become involved in the lives of our guards.

February 14, 1948   The idea of the Hitler biography keeps coming back to me. How to go about it? What sort of structure? How to organize the chaotic mass of episodic material that accumulated in almost fifteen years of intimacy? I am the only person who possesses the necessary qualifications. After the suicide or execution of almost all Hitler's intimates of the early years—Goebbels, Himmler, Ley, Göring, Streicher, Rosenberg, Ribbentrop, and all the other members of his immediate entourage—there is scarcely anyone left who was close enough to him. Hess is still alive, but his muddled mind could never summon up the strength and concentration. Schirach might, but after all he was not close enough to Hitler. Nor did Hitler ever really take him seriously; he was always Baldur, the good boy.

So there's me. Closely linked to Hitler on the factual as well as the emotional plane; but nevertheless remote enough from him by origins and upbringing to recognize, although much too late, the alien, uncanny, evil aspects of his nature. On the other hand, I keep wondering whether I have the requisite abilities to write a major historical work—quite aside from the question of whether I can take a sufficiently objective attitude and adopt the necessary coolness. Still, my life is intri-

[1] In fact it did in November and December 1971, when the last prisoner, Rudolf Hess, was in a British military hospital. Twenty guards continued to carry out their duties, and the relief of the squad guarding the prison took place on the first of the month, between the French and the Russians, according to the rigid forms established by protocol.

cately involved with his. Whenever I feel doubtful I think of a book on the model of Caulaincourt's memoirs of his years with Napoleon, which stood on my father's bookshelves. If only I write down my experiences with sufficient exactness and honesty, I'll have made my contribution.

Sometimes, when I seem to be seeing the past as if it were already behind a veil, I wonder whether my memory is still good enough for me to depict faithfully all the details of my experiences. Do I still see the way he would sit in a car, talk to a person, behave at table? I decide that for the next few days I'll take one of my journeys with Hitler and use it to test my capacity for recollection and description. What I have written up to now amounts to nothing but fragments.

February 15, 1948   In the summer of 1936 Brückner transmitted Hitler's request that I come to his Prinzregentenstrasse apartment in Munich next day. The apartment was that of a private individual of medium income, a secondary-school principal, say, or the head of a savings bank branch, or a small businessman. The décor was petty bourgeois: a lot of imposing oak furniture, glass-doored bookcases, cushions embroidered with saccharine sentiments or brash Party slogans. In the corner of one room stood a bust of Richard Wagner; on the walls, in wide gold frames, hung romantic paintings of the Munich school. Nothing suggested that the tenant of this apartment had been chancellor of the German Reich for three years. A smell of cooking oil and leftovers wafted from the kitchen. Hitler was in the habit of exercising every morning in his bedroom before an open window. He had once told me that for a long time he made himself work with an expander every day. When my face revealed astonishment, he actually showed me an ad from the magazine *Jugend* promising that the use of this device would develop the biceps. One reason the expander was important to him, he went on to say, was that during march-pasts of the SA and SS he often had to hold his arm outstretched for hours at a time, without letting it quiver, let alone resting it. Thanks to his years of training, he said, none of his subordinates could match him in such endurance.

Around two o'clock Hitler emerged in uniform. Only his servant, Krause, was with him. I had brought along some new designs, but to my surprise he greeted me with the news that we were going to drive to Augsburg. "I want to take a look at the theater with you." Then he turned to Brückner and asked whether the Gauleiter had been sufficiently alerted to the fact that he wanted a quiet reception—no crowds, and corner tables to be reserved for coffee in the lobby of the

Hotel Drei Mohren. As we descended the stairs he began enthusing about the Augsburg theater, which had been built by the two most famous theater architects of the nineteenth century. At the entrance we got into the open seven-liter Mercedes. Two passers-by paused and raised their hands shyly in salute. From a side street the escort squad's car joined us.

In Augsburg the Gauleiter, the mayor, the town architect, and the manager of the theater were waiting outside the theater. But to Hitler's surprise a considerable crowd had also assembled. Shouts of "Heil," noise, cheerful confusion—but Hitler strode ill-humoredly into the building. SS guards pressed the crowd back; the gate closed behind us, and we were alone. "Isn't it possible to avoid these crowds?" Hitler snapped. The Gauleiter whom he had addressed, a good-natured, thickheaded, and blindly devoted follower for many years, stammered, "You know, mein Führer . . . when you . . . when you come to Augsburg for once——"

Hitler interrupted irritably: "Now the whole town knows, of course. I explicitly gave orders that I didn't want that. Enough. Now let's see your theater." Hitler turned and preceded us through the foyer to the stairwell. "It's all rather run down," he said, turning to the mayor. "Why hasn't the city taken better care of this jewel? Do you even know who the architects were? Hellmer and Fellner of Vienna, the most famous theater builders in Austria. They created more than a dozen opera houses and theaters all over the world, one more beautiful than the next."

In the auditorium Hitler went into raptures over the rich neobaroque architecture of the galleries and boxes. For almost half an hour he hurried us down the rows of seats, up corridors, into stairwells, backstage, to show us every perspective, every detail, every ornament. Obviously he was enjoying showing off their own theater to the Augsburgers. Suddenly he stood still. The genial, excited enthusiast turned into the statesman. "Gauleiter Wahl," he said, taking a formal tone, "I have decided to have this theater thoroughly renovated and rebuilt. I shall provide for the costs out of my personal funds." The Gauleiter and the mayor both stood at attention. "No question about the need for a new stage and stage machinery. I have considered making Professor Baumgarten, my opera architect, available to you. Everything must be put into first-class shape. The theater is the standard by which the culture of a city or a civilization is measured." With this epigrammatic sentence, Hitler turned on his heel and strode toward the exit. Outside, meanwhile, thousands of persons had gathered, a seething mob that hailed Hitler enthusiastically. The SA, which had been called in, had difficulty opening a lane so that we could drive at a snail's pace to the hotel.

Some time later we sat in the old-fashioned hotel lobby, under palms, over coffee and cake. As always, Hitler finished off many pieces of cake and strudel, urging us all the while with paternalistic concern to take more. He talked excitedly about the diversified backdrop of the medieval cityscape; he had particularly liked Maximilianstrasse. Even then it occurred to me that he had never gone on this way about Vienna, let alone Berlin. And today it seems to me that he always remained a small-town man, feeling strange and insecure in large metropolises. Whereas in political matters he compulsively thought and planned on a gigantic scale, the easily grasped conditions of a town like Linz, where he had gone to school, were really his social habitat.

This provincial mentality was also reflected in Hitler's intention to make the Gaue, the traditional ancient districts based on former tribal occupation, the basis of the political divisions in the Reich. He fostered and cultivated the special qualities of different localities and did not want to have the individuality of the various German racial stocks violated. Holsteiners, Saxons, Rhinelanders, Swabians, or Bavarians were to keep the characteristics they had developed over the centuries. Whenever he came round to this subject he furiously denounced "Jewish leveling," which he said took the soul out of everything.

Six months later I once again rode to Augsburg with Hitler. In the meantime the foundation had been dug out for the new stage. For a long time we stood staring without a word into the pit. Then Hitler inquired about the foundations, the strength of walls, and details of the construction. The Party functionaries and municipal officials discreetly took a few steps backward so that they would not be embarrassed by his questions. Whenever he received an unsatisfactory reply, Hitler displayed his expertise in long technical explanations. I myself could not see why the chief of state of an important country should devote so much time to inspecting building sites. No doubt Hitler enjoyed showing off his knowledge. But probably he was even more pleased at being the motive force of so much earnest activity.

But this time the journey had a more far-reaching purpose. When we were again sitting over coffee and strudel in the Drei Mohren, this time to the accompaniment of light music, he came out with it. "I have been looking at the map of the city," he began. "If we tear down the tumble-down houses in the Old Town, we will have room enough for a grand boulevard. Fifty meters wide and more than a kilometer long.

Then we will also have a connection with the railroad station and relieve the traffic on medieval Maximilianstrasse. And at the end there'll be a new Party Headquarters. That will then form the core of the new Augsburg forum. There'll have to be a tower also, to crown the whole. How high is the tallest tower in Augsburg now, Wahl?" The Gauleiter threw a look of embarrassment at the mayor, who turned for help to the city architect, who finally, after some cogitation, gave a figure. Hitler added twenty meters, saying that in any case the new tower must be higher than the tallest church steeple in the city. The bells in the forum tower were also to be bigger and louder than all the others. Large commercial towns like Ghent or Bruges, and Augsburg too, had thought in this way hundreds of years ago, he said. That was the reason they had put up such buildings as Elias Holl's six-story baroque town hall, the most beautiful in Germany. And that was also the reason that the Perlach Tower close by had been built to a height of seventy meters. Just as, in the Middle Ages, the cathedrals had towered over the homes and warehouses of the burghers, so the Party buildings must surpass modern office buildings. "That is why in general I am against high-rises and skyscrapers. Our cities should not be dominated by plutocratic utilitarian buildings. We are the ones who will shape the new State; our State belongs to the Party and not to the banks."

With practiced, sure strokes, his pencil moving as fast as if he were writing, Hitler sketched his conception on the map of Augsburg. He corrected himself several times until at last he had found the specific form for the dimly conceived idea: "The Gau Headquarters will go here! The tower here! Perhaps we'll put the big new hotel here, and Augsburg must also have a new grand opera. The present theater will be used only for plays." He would make Augsburg a city that did not have to feel put in the shade by the proximity of Munich. Munich had been condescending to Augsburg for years and years; yet at the time of the Renaissance the two cities had been equal in rank. If he carried out his plans for Munich, there would otherwise be a danger that Augsburg would be crushed. "Just consider that I intend to give Munich the biggest opera house in the world, with five thousand seats!" Then he referred to the example of Paris, which had impoverished all the provincial towns; Linz had suffered the same fate because of the closeness of Vienna, he said.

February 21, 1948   This is how far I came during the past few days. But this morning, reading over what I have written, I am no longer quite sure that Hitler really formulated that idea about Party buildings outranking commercial buildings on this occasion in Augsburg. He might have been prompted to say it at another time, in Weimar or in Nuremberg. Moreover, the day before yesterday I tried in vain to conjure up a picture of him during this second visit to Augsburg. What mood was he in? After all, I can clearly remember his variable moods during the first visit. And who was with us? Was Brückner there again? Was Hitler wearing a uniform or civilian dress? All that has slipped away from me, whereas other things, isolated phrases, an angry clearing of the throat, a glance, a change of voice, have been impressed ineradicably upon my memory. That also seems to me the weakness in my description of the second visit to Augsburg: the details are missing, the vivid items that bring out the atmosphere. All my efforts are in vain; I cannot succeed in bringing them back.

Of course that is partly due to the fact that in twelve years spent together, various strata of memory displace one another, especially in the case of a man like Hitler, who was inclined to repeat arguments, phrases, images again and again. What I discover, therefore, is that I have the pebbles of a mosaic which I must put together into a picture. It is all fragmentary. If I am really to set about writing the book, my problem will be to assemble the fragments of remembered material into a coherent, seamless picture. Will I be able to do that?

As far as the second visit in Augsburg is concerned, all I really remember is that at some point Hitler turned to another of his favorite themes: his already almost maniacal passion for building opera houses. He had decided that every sizable town ought to have at least two theatrical buildings. All existing structures were built before the [first] World War, he used to say, although the population of the bigger towns had meanwhile tripled. "We will build opera houses almost exclusively. Opera is for the people; therefore they must be big and have room for the masses at low prices. The youth in particular must be brought into the opera houses. Not starting with the age of eighteen, but much sooner. That way they'll remain loyal devotees of the opera until old age. In Berlin I want to build at least five new opera houses in the various sections of the city."

As was his wont, Hitler bolstered this remark by walling it around with the protection of a general principle based on his own experience and delivered in the tone of a lecture. Any practical objection would then sound like an attack on his experience. Thus he justified his grandiloquent plans for building opera houses by remarking, "So then people come along with figures and tell me that there are only four thousand opera lovers in Augsburg. But I have this to say to them: 'It isn't inventory that creates demand, but demand is created by changed circumstances.' Four years ago, when Dr. Todt and I laid down the route of the Autobahn from Munich to Rosenheim, somebody told me that there's no traffic there. I told that petty-minded person: 'Do you think there'll be no traffic once we have the Autobahn completed?' That is how it will be with the opera houses." And besides, Hitler continued, there would be the further advantage that at last the shortage of Wagnerian tenors would be relieved; as we all knew, things at present were absolutely disastrous. There were plenty of talented voices in Germany; they could try out in the small houses, and in this as in all things the finest voice would emerge the victor from the competition.

February 26, 1948 I really don't know what Bormann—who at that time was still Hess's deputy, but was already very close to Hitler—had against Gauleiter Wahl and the mayor of Augsburg. In any case he used the matter of the theater for a characteristic intrigue. Some two months after Hitler's second visit to Augsburg, while we were standing around on the terrace of the Berghof chatting about this and that, Bormann reported with seeming casualness that he had received a letter from Wahl stating that the first cost estimates for the building project amounted to several hundred million marks. The mayor was requesting, through Wahl, a written statement dispensing him from the financial responsibility. With pretended innocence, Bormann went on: "Should I have Herr Lammers draw up the necessary papers?" That was the cue. Hitler changed color. For a moment he seemed dismayed. Then he burst out, "I always thought Wahl was an idiot! Now he lets that fool of a mayor—what the devil was the man's name?—that fellow Mayr push him into taking such a line with me. Isn't it enough if I guarantee something? Does that bureaucrat have to have it in writing? Nobody gave me anything in writing when I started in 1933." Hitler's voice now became so loud that all those standing around on the terrace could not help hearing, although they pretended to go on with their own conversations. "So he wants something in writing. All right, let him have it. This minute. His dismissal! Here the Augsburgers are being offered something that will distinguish them from all other cities, for after Weimar they'll be the second city to have a Gau forum. Here I am initiating a renaissance for Augsburg, and these asses ask about costs. That time I was in Augsburg I noticed how blank Wahl and that other fellow looked when I outlined my plan. They aren't worthy of it. Tell them that!"

Today, as I reflect on all these plans for the Augsburg Forum which occupied him throughout 1936, it seems to me that this obvious show of preference for Augsburg was connected with something more than Hitler's sincere love for the medieval look and the brilliant history of the onetime city of the Fuggers. For him a distinction conferred on someone was frequently a method for rebuking someone else. Just as he later wanted to use the reconstruction of Linz to humiliate Vienna for the wrongs of his youth, so these projects for Augsburg were affected by the desire to offend Munich, which he accused of trying to make Augsburg into a suburb.

I should tell what came of Bormann's intrigue. Wahl succeeded in getting through to Hitler in Berlin and at a favorable moment changing his mind. Mayor Mayr was permitted to stay in office, but of course he did not receive the requested document. Moreover, he and Wahl were no longer consulted about the preliminary planning. Hitler found in Hermann Giessler an architect who could do just what he wanted. However, the first design for the forum too strongly resembled the Weimar project, which Giessler had also designed. When Hitler found fault with it on that score, Giessler crowned the tower with baroque ornamentation, and Hitler was enthralled. Together they then hit on the idea of covering the blank wall surfaces with colored frescoes. This delighted Hitler even more, because his forum was reviving an old tradition of Swabian architects. Incidentally, money was found for the project by putting a moratorium on all housing. Wahl justified this course in a long article in which he argued that, after all, housing could always be built, but that monuments of such historic grandeur could only be constructed during the lifetime of the greatest German of the ages.

March 12, 1948   Have not written for several days. I feel insecure and spent. For that reason I'm very glad that the garden work has begun again today. The grass is greening, horse manure and fertilizer have been brought in, the sparrows are noisy. I plunged right into the work as soon as we were taken out to the garden this morning.

On the other side Neurath and Dönitz laid out the first beds, Raeder strewed fertilizer, Schirach spread it with the rake. As always a nonparticipant, Hess sat on his bench. Funk had stayed in bed because of his illness. I began raking leaves out of the flower beds. Everywhere the first weeds were sprouting from the soil. I carried the leaves over to a burning place. Long, Hawker, and Dackerman were meanwhile busy with grass fires. Raeder, using a watering can as a pail, carried fertilizer up from the cellar; Schirach dumped it into the wheelbarrow and wheeled it out to the big field.

After an hour Dönitz stopped working. He then sat on the bench with his back against the walnut tree and engaged in long conversations with Dackerman. I too tired quickly and simply strolled around. In the course of this I paid a visit to Hess at his bench. He was in pain. "Don't feel like talking today?" Hess shook his head mutely.

March 16, 1948 A vivid dream last night. A lark is climbing into a blue evening sky. After a while it comes flying to me. With strange confidence it perches near me. Only as I wake up does it occur to me that it was as big as an owl. It also talked to me, pleasantly, of course. But I have forgotten what it said. A feeling that it was an important message.

In the past I often had anxiety dreams in which I plunged down hundreds of meters along unending facades of buildings. Here in Spandau I am spared that sort of thing. My dreams are predominantly pleasant, if only because the setting for most of them is freedom. Evidently the dream life creates a counterpoise to reality. It has a compensatory nature. Here, consequently, I frequently dream of simple walks in an imaginary countryside, often to the accompaniment of colorful sunsets.

In general, impressions of nature displace those of art. I have never returned in dreams to the Palazzo Ducale in Urbino, which made so overwhelming an impression upon me, both in the disposition of the whole and the refinement of the details, so that it always seemed to me the incarnation of everything I myself ever hoped to achieve. But the landscapes of my youth, the Neckar Valley, the Alpine glaciers, the somber Havel lakes, are almost tangibly present in my dreams.

March 26, 1948 For days I have been shrinking from rereading my account of Augsburg. Yet it makes me uneasy that I have had to carry it around with me concealed for such a long time. But low spirits, self-doubt, weariness—I actually feel wretched. I have also been losing weight steadily. Today reached my lowest weight, 146 pounds. That is more than forty-four pounds below my normal weight. I don't dare to lose much more. I consider whether I can go on giving Dönitz, who is eternally hungry, some of my bread. From the irritable mood of the others I can see how severely hunger stretches the nerves.

March 29, 1948 I live in seberal spheres at once. By now I have formed the habit of banishing the Spandau environment from my emotional life. It is unimportant. The sphere of my daydreams is far more important; in them I am with my family, visit the period and the places of my youth, and wander through regions thick with temples, palaces, fountains, and sculptures. Contrast with my nighttime dreams.

But by now what has become most important to me is the world of books. Machiavelli in exile, shunned by friends, literally invited his books to be his guests. He dressed ceremonially for his evening inter-course with them, lit candles. I cannot do that, obviously. But when the bolt at the cell door is slid shut at six o'clock in the evening, I am con-tent. I know that for four hours I can remain alone with my books.

April 2, 1948   At last read the Augsburg chapter straight through. From being kept in my shoe or underwear the paper has almost dis-solved. Deciphering it is laborious. Intensified uncertainty. It seems to me I have given an accurate account of the course of events, but have missed the essence. The first and most superficial objection is simple: if I spend so many pages on every experience with Hitler, I will need sev-eral thousand pages. A more serious difficulty is that I have naïvely let myself get caught up in disparate episodes. In the anecdotal material the typical elements shine through only occasionally, without yet re-vealing their full meaning. Moreover, on those trips to Augsburg Hitler surely discussed political problems; but none of this has stuck in my memory. If I am to be a witness of those years, I must not lose myself in that architect's world and portray Hitler as a great builder who just by the bye happened to be a politician. Probably I must work out a pre-liminary plan that will organize the material. Before I begin I should settle what points are to be emphasized, and how much space I mean to give to specific events and aspects. That should be possible for me to do; my strength always lay in organizing things. Do I have the literary ability? That doesn't really worry me. One of my aims should be to develop spontaneity and not tell the story too abstractly. For example, I'm not sure whether the conversations in the hotel lobby are under-standable and vivid to the reader.

The reassuring element in all these thoughts is that I presumably have nearly two decades at my disposal for this book—a reassurance that at the same time paralyzes me. But at any rate I shall put it off a bit, to gain sufficient distance. The events are still too close and too painful.

April 3, 1948   Today I gave Vlaer the sign. Many pages. But all went well.

April 10, 1948   These years are not useless. What in general would be useless? There is no such thing as lost time. In the course of my daily reading I observe how meager is the basic knowledge of a person trained in technology. How little he really knows and perceives. I look forward with longing to the day I shall find out whether after these years my capacity for experience has intensified.

Hitherto my reading was mostly confined to late-nineteenth-century authors: Zola, Strindberg, Dostoevsky, Tolstoy. Now I have turned to the Italian Renaissance. I am reading books on art and cultural history, but also contemporary sources, chronicles, poems, and philosophical treatises. There are forty thousand books in the Spandau town library. And like a student, I have set up a long-term schedule: for the next year or two I intend to stay with the Renaissance, then classical antiquity, the early Christian period; and perhaps finally I'll study the baroque era. A ten-year program. To conclude it I rather think I should like to write an essay on Giotto's architecture as he represented it in his frescos. There, a century before Brunelleschi, whom the art historians generally consider the first Renaissance architect, the essential elements of Renaissance architecture are prefigured. In general the theme of "the architectonic element in painting" has always attracted me. For what was never built is also a part of the history of architecture. And probably the spirit of an era, its special architectural aims, can be better analyzed from such unrealized designs than from the structures that were actually built. For the latter were often distorted by scarcity of funds, obstinate or inflexible patrons, or prejudices. Hitler's period is also rich in unbuilt architecture. What a different image of it will emerge if someday I produce from my desk drawers all the plans and photos of models that were made during those years. From the books I am reading I extract some ten closely written pages of notes every week for later essays.

April 25, 1948   Every Sunday for three months I have worked an hour or two on a sizable drawing. Finished today. Two pillars of a collapsed temple that is Greek in spirit; in front of it a woman, bowed in mourning. The sun has just risen and already illuminates the capitals. Soon its light will strike the ruins; the woman will straighten up after being crouched over all the night. The drawing is for my mother's birthday.

April 27, 1948   Under the direction of our chief gardener, Neurath, we are planting vegetables. We have already harvested chicory and radishes. Laid down two beds of manure for a hotbed covered by glass frames. Now I am building part of a greenhouse. I work alternatively as mason, carpenter, glazier, and director of operations. As a result of this work in the open air I feel healthy. My torso is tanned. I sleep soundly, awake refreshed in the mornings. No more of those long sleeping spells I used to have during the inactive life in Nuremberg.

For the first time in my life I have been doing physical work for much of the day. And after only a few days of it I see the temptation of going at it whole hog, and probably overdoing it. Evenings my back often aches. Knocked out but content.

April 29, 1948   Still working strenuously and to the point of exhaustion in the garden. I wonder at my own intensity. Yet that has long been my way of working. It was different only at the start, in school and at the university and as a young architect. But soon after Hitler took possession of me, so to speak, I was gripped by that passion for work, which I soon needed like a drug. Even during brief vacation trips, I tried, by driving for long hours from city to city, by looking at more and more cathedrals, museums, temples, or towers, to attain that desired state of evening exhaustion. My relationship to work is a problem of addiction.

Of course my job as minister of armaments used all my reserves of strength. I had to throw myself into the job with an excess of personal involvement in order to make up for my lack of overview, my inadequate knowledge. From morning to night, even during hasty meals, I held important talks, dictated, conferred, made decisions. From conference to conference the subjects jumped around from one problem to the next; I frequently had to find temporary solutions, make decisions of vast import. I suppose I stood the pace only because I would take a trip every two weeks, spending a few days visiting bomb-damaged factories, headquarters on the military fronts, or building sites, in order to gather fresh impressions, to come into contact with practical activities. These tours represented more work, of course, but they also gave me fresh energy. I loved to spend myself to the very limits of my strength. In this I was basically different from Hitler, who regarded the constant activity imposed on him by the war as a terrible burden; he was forever longing to return to the easygoing pace of earlier years.

May 5, 1948   In Spandau only the birds can visit us without a pass. The pitch-black Russian rooks have flown off to the east; a dozen German hooded crows have taken their places. They wage bitter battles for dominance with a pair of kestrels that has recently settled down to nest in a niche on the roof. A pair of wood pigeons that was here last summer has returned exhausted from its winter in Morocco. There are a few tits, two magpies, and recently two partridges actually took a stroll in the garden. A neighbor somewhere in Spandau must keep pigeons. From time to time they settle down on the six-meter-high redbrick wall and watch our activities. To complete the rustic idyll, in the distance several watchdogs can be heard barking.

"Come over here all of you; I have something important to say," Funk calls to us. "The world is evil. Everything is fraud. Even here!" Expectantly, we approach. "There are supposed to be two hundred sheets. But who ever counted them? I have! I went to the trouble. And there are only one hundred and ninety-three." Into our perplexed faces he tosses the words: "The toilet paper, of course." The Russian director, a small energetic man whose name we do not know, appears. We separate. "Why speaking? You know that is *verboten*." He departs, but shortly afterward puts in a surprise appearance in the garden. This time Funk and Schirach are caught talking and warned. Schirach comments scornfully, "That is the dictatorship of the proletariat."

May 11, 1948   For all the closeness that living together enforces, we have hitherto not exposed our private lives. As a general principle, we do not talk about matters relating to our families. An attempt to keep a measure of privacy.

Today for the first time Schirach infringed upon this unwritten rule. While we were preparing a hotbed together, he talked about his parental home in Weimar and his childhood. His father was manager of the theater there; Hitler's passion for the theater led to acquaintance with his father. Before long, Hitler called at the Schirach home whenever he visited Weimar. And as an adolescent Schirach sometimes accompanied the visitor to the theater. Watering can in hand, Schirach recalled Hitler's amazing knowledge of stagecraft, his interest in the diameter of revolving stages, lift mechanisms, and especially different lighting techniques. He was familiar with all sorts of lighting systems and could discourse in detail on the proper illumination for certain scenes. I too had witnessed this. More than once I was present when he discussed the scenery for Wagnerian music-dramas with Benno von Arent, whom he had appointed "Reich Stage Designer" and assigned the job of supervising the décor of operas and operettas. Hitler would gladly have replaced Emil Preetorius, who had long done the sets for the Bayreuth Festival, with the histrionic Arent. But in this case Winifred Wagner remained obstinate; she pretended not to know what Hitler was driving at. In compensation Arent was given other assignments elsewhere that Hitler paid for out of his privy purse. At the Chancellery Hitler once sent up to his bedroom for neatly executed stage designs, colored with crayons, for all the acts of *Tristan und Isolde;* these were to be given to Arent to serve as inspiration. Another time he gave Arent a series of sketches for all the scenes of *Der Ring des Nibelungen.* At lunch he told us with great satisfaction that for three weeks he had sat up over these, night after night. This surprised me the more because at this particular time Hitler's daily schedule was unusually heavy with visitors, speeches, sightseeing and other public activities. Another time, when Arent was commissioned to stage *Meistersinger* as the opening performance for the Party Rally, Hitler again took a close interest in every detail, considering what sort of lighting would best do for the moonlight scenes at the end of the second act. He went into ecstasies over the brilliant colors he wanted for the final scene on the mastersingers' meadow, and over the romantic look of the little gabled houses opposite Hans Sachs's cobbler's shop. "We must bring the masses illusions," he once said in 1938, after he had given directions to SA delegates concerning the deployment of the Storm Troopers in the Luitpold Arena. "They need illusions not only in the movies and the theater. They have enough of life's grim realities. Just because life is grimly real, people have to be exalted above the routines of every day."

Hitler's ideas about staging were unquestionably not the most modern, but they certainly accorded with Richard Wagner's directions. Ruthless though Hitler could be in sweeping aside troublesome traditions, in the interpretation of Wagner's operas he was conservative, so that he regarded almost imperceptible modernizations as dangerous innovations needing careful weighing. One of the reasons he intervened in the appointments to all important theatrical posts was just this desire to preserve tradition and to keep overbold innovators out of positions of power. In August 1942, for example, he told me that he had just decided in favor of Karl Elmendorff as director of the Dresden City Opera. Even in so minor a matter as Furtwängler's declaration in April 1936 that he would not conduct for a year (except in Bayreuth), Hitler insisted on approving the text of the statement.

Schirach's and my conversation, although conducted in a murmur because of the guards, had become quite lively. Kneeling side by side in the hotbed, we thought of more and more anecdotes illustrating Hitler's mania for the theater, which we had once taken as proof of his universal genius, but which now strikes us as peculiar and immature.

Schirach contributed an item about Hitler vociferating about the vanity of conductors, that he regarded Knappertsbusch as no better than a military-band leader, that he mistrusted Karajan because he conducted without a score and so could not catch blunders on the part of the singers. That was extremely inconsiderate of the public as well as the singers. Schirach also thought Hitler would probably have interfered if Karajan had not been a protégé of Göring's, just as Knappertsbusch enjoyed the protection of Eva Braun, who had a girlish partiality for the conductor because of his manly good looks. Among the hardships Hitler thought the war had imposed on him was his having to forsake this whole world of the performing arts. Whenever Goebbels visited the Führer's Headquarters, Hitler would ask him first of all how his favorite singers were. He would do the same with Schaub when the adjutant returned from trips to Berlin. He was eager for gossip, and the bombing of an opera house pained him more than the destruction of whole residential quarters. He once told Schirach that he loved Bayreuth so much that he liked to imagine spending the last years of his life in that culturally pre-eminent little town so impregnated with the spirit of Richard Wagner.

May 13, 1948 Today—again in the hotbed—Schirach asked me where Hitler got those extraordinary sums for his private purse. Could the income from *Mein Kampf* have covered the multitude of expenditures? he wanted to know. After all, Hitler had not only financed productions and new theaters, but had also supported young artists, built up a large collection of paintings, and finally paid for luxurious Berghof with the teahouse and the Eagle's Nest on the top of the mountain. Together, we reckoned up his income and arrived at a sum that came nowhere near covering such expenditures. Then I remembered the story of the stamp. One day his photographer, Hoffmann, had called Hitler's attention to the fact that he could demand a royalty for the use of his portrait on every stamp, and Hitler had unhesitatingly taken up the suggestion. A third source of income was the Adolf Hitler Endowment Fund of German Industry, which Bormann invented. This put additional millions at his disposal. Once a year Hitler invited those businessmen who had shown themselves unusually generous to an evening party in the Chancellery. After an impressive banquet the best singers from the Berlin opera houses offered a gala program. In 1939 I was present when several leading industrialists presented Hitler, for his fiftieth birthday, with a coffer containing some of Richard Wagner's original scores. It included the bound four-volume

Rienzi manuscript and the scores of *Das Rheingold* and *Die Walküre*. Hitler was particularly excited by the orchestral sketch for *Die Götterdämmerung;* he showed sheet after sheet to the assembled guests, making knowledgeable comments.[2] Bormann did not miss the chance to point out to Hitler that the collection had cost nearly a million marks.

Schirach ended our conversation with a poke at Göring. At any rate, he said, Hitler had spent all his money on artistic purposes. Göring, on the other hand, had practiced the same kind of blackmail of industry, but had amassed huge funds solely to satisfy his lust for luxury. In personal matters, Schirach said, Hitler had had a rather ascetic bent right to the end, but Göring had been a good-for-nothing spendthrift.

We agreed on that.

May 15, 1948   My wife is to make her first visit. An hour's visit has been approved, the sum of the four quarter-hours accumulated in the course of the year at Spandau. To judge by Flächsner's visit, no privacy is allowed. It is merely a question of seeing each other again. No sooner has permission come through than terrors beset me that she might be arrested while traveling through the East Zone. I ask Pastor Casalis to inform my wife that she absolutely should not come.

May 16, 1948   Last night in bed I thought about my conversation with Schirach. It is extremely liberating to have at last had a talk with a fellow prisoner about matters of substance aside from the everyday routine of prison. Moreover, it was the first conversation in several months about Hitler and the past that was not marred by irritability.

Yet it seems to me that we concentrated too exclusively on Hitler's fondness for Wagner, for he loved operetta just as much as he did Wagner's grand operas. In all seriousness he regarded Franz Lehár as

[2] On September 17, 1973, Frau Winifred Wagner informed me that toward the end of the war she tried to persuade Hitler to transfer these valuable manuscripts to Bayreuth. Hitler, however, held that he had placed them in a far safer place than she ever could. The following manuscripts were involved:
1. Original score of *Die Feen.*
2. Original score of *Das Liebesverbot.*
3. Original score of *Rienzi* (four volumes).
4. Original clean copy of the score of *Das Rheingold.*
5. Original clean copy of the score of *Die Walküre.*
6. Original duplicate of the orchestral sketch of *Siegfried,* Act III.
7. Copy of the orchestral sketch of *Die Götterdämmerung* prepared by Hans Richter and several copyists.
8. Orchestral sketch of *Der Fliegende Holländer.*
Perhaps this listing will enable some reader to provide a clue to the whereabouts of these lost documents.

one of the greatest composers in the history of music. Hitler ranked *Die Lustige Witwe* [The Merry Widow] as the equal of the finest operas. Similarly, he felt that *Die Fledermaus, Der Vogelhändler,* and *Der Zigeunerbaron* were sacred portions of the German cultural heritage. After one performance of *The Merry Widow* conducted by Lehár himself, then in his seventies, the composer was introduced to him. For days afterward Hitler expressed his pleasure at this significant meeting. He loved ballet as much as he did operetta, but expressed his repugnance at the way the dancers displayed themselves in their close-fitting leotards. "I always have to look away," he commented in disgust. On the other hand he bluntly termed modern interpretive dance, of the kind created by Mary Wigman or Palucca, a cultural disgrace. Goebbels once coaxed him into going to such a performance, he told me; he'd never do that again. The Höppners of the Berlin Municipal Opera, on the other hand, were a different matter entirely, the very essence of beauty. He frequently invited them to tea in his private rooms. With the two sisters sitting to either side of him on the sofa, he would even in my presence hold each by the hand, like a worshipful teenager. For a while Hitler was crazy about an American dancer who performed almost unclothed in Munich. Through the intercession of Adolf Wagner, the Gauleiter of Munich, he invited her to tea; aside from Unity Mitford, she was the only foreigner who was ever admitted to his circle. Hitler made it quite plain that he would lay siege to her if it were not for his accursed official position.

May 25, 1948   Last night's dream: our dachshund comes out of the woods. One of his sides is torn open, the bones protruding. The dog licks my hand. I cry.

August 8, 1948   Have sat for a month over an extremely detailed drawing that tries to say: The destroyed life work must not be allowed to become the end of all hopes. A wooden barracks symbolizes my new standards. The columns of the portico of the Great Hall were thirty meters high. I show them as ruins. My wife and I in the foreground. Heads covered with a shroud.

Unfortunately the governors have turned down my request to have the drawing sent home. Only letters are allowed, they inform me.

August 24, 1948   For three months I have produced no notes. Alarming sign. Is my vitality giving out? Constant hunger. Weakness. Have again lost weight. The meals are still meted out according to the

German rations. Unfortunately, for some time now there has been a
ban on using any of the vegetables we planted in the meals for prisoners. They now go only to the mess for the staff. I help myself out by
eating raw vegetables. I take the youngest and tenderest leaves of red
cabbage, lettuce, and green cabbage. Cauliflower and new potatoes taste
good even uncooked. Of course that is against the rules, but the guards
pretend not to see—even some of the Russians. Recently Taradankin,
who is especially rigid, caught me stealing cauliflower for the third
time. The governors imposed a week of solitary. I was not allowed to
read or write. The punishment came to an end today.

Robert Dackerman, a Jewish American guard who is particularly decent, is trying on his own initiative to improve our nutrition. A few
days ago he made a fire in the garden and baked some early potatoes.
With scallions and lettuce hearts they tasted as good as the best delica-
tessen at Horcher's. After a while Taradankin came into the garden,
carefully inspected the embers of our fire, and ill-naturedly removed the
last of the potatoes.

August 25, 1948   Today Dackerman brought us the dried mak-
ings for a big pot of pea soup. All afternoon we were happy and lazy.
Pushing gluttony to the limit, with the support of the British guard
Pease we built a fire again and baked more new potatoes.

August 26, 1948   Since our tête-à-tête in the hotbed a few months
ago, my relationship with Schirach has become more and more relaxed.
Today he told me about a remarkable affront Hitler delivered to the
Hitler Youth in the early summer of 1938. After a visit in Dessau for
the dedication of the new opera house, Hitler had watched a parade.
Shortly before, for reasons of foreign policy, he had ordered that the
Hitler Youth were no longer to take part in public parades. Allegations
had been repeatedly published abroad that the Hitler Youth was a
paramilitary organization. Now, after the march-past of other organizations, Hitler saw units of the youth group approaching. In the
presence of all the dignitaries, Schirach said, he shouted at his adjutant,
Julius Schaub. Then he ordered Gauleiter Jordan to have the Hitler
Youth turn back at once. Barely a hundred meters from Hitler's car
thousands of young people who had come great distances from the
countryside and small towns and had waited for hours were stopped
and sent back. The scandal, the offense to the Gauleiter, the disappointment of the boys—all that left Hitler completely cold. Schirach
saw the act as evidence of Hitler's intemperateness, but I disagreed. It

rather seems to me that once more Hitler was putting on a calculated outburst. His purpose was to drive home a lesson; from now on his orders were to be obeyed meticulously. For he could well assume that word of the incident would spread like wildfire through the leadership of the Party. Compared to the salutary results, what did a few disappointments and a scandal in a small town in Saxony amount to!

August 29, 1948   Book distribution today at a quarter after five. The library, an empty cell, is unlocked. On one side shelves with our personal books, which we brought with us from Nuremberg. The lion's share has been provided by Hess, who in England was able to buy an impressive number of books, even some rare editions, because during his imprisonment he received a captain's pay (in keeping with international agreements, since he had landed in a captain's uniform). Raeder sits down at the table; Hess goes to him and reports: "Number Seven. I am returning: Zinner, *Sternglaube und Sternforschung* [Astrology and Astronomy]." He mentions his number because Raeder has several times used it in addressing him. Then Hess looks over the book list. Meanwhile Schirach returns Bernauer's *Theater meines Lebens*. Raeder notes down the choice. Since Hess has still not made up his mind, Raeder grows impatient. "Have you finished yet?" he asks. Hess decides on a book entitled *The School of Danger*. When Raeder objects that it is about mountaineering, he replies angrily, "No matter."

Outside in the corridor Dönitz says to me that if he were a guard he would inspect the pockets of my trousers; my behavior has been highly suspect. As best I can, I pretend amazement. But maybe I have really become too careless and am incurring suspicion. For in my right pocket, wrapped in my handkerchief, I was carrying the notes of the past several days.

August 30, 1948   Frequently I hear the whistles of the tugboats on the Havel very close by, a sound that makes me melancholy. At the same time it arouses a rather odd thought; I begin wondering whether one of our sons should not become a sailor. I imagine the free and untrammeled life of a captain on board his own tugboat.

Just twenty years ago yesterday, about a kilometer away from this cell on the Spandau shipping canal, Margarete and I set up the two collapsible boats and began our honeymoon trip on the Havel, paddling to the Müritzsee in Mecklenburg. That sort of thing expressed our sensibility; it was typical of our generation's hostility to civilization. In those days we were always dreaming of solitude, of drives through quiet river valleys, of hiking to some high mountain pasture, camping in some remote meadow studded with fruit trees. We never felt drawn to Paris, London, or Vienna, and even the classical heritage of Rome did not lure us. We always preferred—until 1933—the cliffs of Sweden to Roman temples.

During the last days of the war a curious coincidence prompted me to retrace our honeymoon trip. On the night of April 24, 1945, I bade goodbye to Hitler in his Berlin bunker and toward morning took off from near the Brandenburg Gate in a Storch. During the second third of the flight Soviet fighter planes appeared. The pilot flew the light reconnaissance plane just a few meters above the surface of the Mecklenburg lakes and the canals that connect them. Close to the edge of the woods I saw beneath me one part of my life sweeping past. Far, far.

September 24, 1948   In another week I shall have made it through two years. One tenth. There remains a curious feeling of emptiness, as though these years had not existed.

Today, after a thorough examination, the British doctor found me in perfect health. In fact I do feel in many respects better than in the past, during times of great strain. A good many of the nervous symptoms that once troubled me have vanished. Moreover, in the three and a half years of imprisonment I have not once been seriously ill.

Since Nuremberg I have not looked in a mirror. Now, in the water of the fountain, I discover that my hair is turning white. My features have also sharpened. But after all, everyone grows older.

September 26, 1948   I have heard from Frau Kempf, my former secretary, that Otto Saur made a surprise appearance as chief witness for the prosecution on the last day of testimony at the trial of Krupp. In the past Saur was the strongest advocate of coercive measures for increasing production, a ruthless slave driver on the industrial front. In the final phase his blatant opportunism caused me serious difficulties. Now he is serving the prosecution; he has remained the same man. I would not wish it for anyone, but if any of my close associates has ever deserved to be tried, Saur is the man.

September 28, 1948   Nut harvest. For probably the first time in a quarter of a century I have been climbing around in nut trees. The wind blows. The falling nuts are gathered by the guards. But I too appropriate twenty or thirty a day. When our Grand Admiral Dönitz eats nuts against the rules, he usually seeks cover under a low-hanging branch. His head and torso are then concealed by the leaves. But his hands remain plainly in sight, busily cracking the shells—like a child who covers his eyes to make himself invisible. The Russians find this slip so amusing that they do not interfere.

The Third Year

October 20, 1948 Right at the beginning of the third year one of those rumors that have kept cropping up since the beginning of our imprisonment reached us. It began with a message to my wife from Frau von Mackensen, Neurath's daughter. My wife sent me the letter in question, dated October 10, via our clandestine route: "Perhaps I am telling you what you already know when I inform you that our prisoners are no longer in Spandau but have apparently been, for the past month or so, in a house on a side street off the Kurfürstendamm, a villa with barred windows guarded by English soldiers. I have now received this news from four different sources, and today it was confirmed as authentic by a gentleman from Nuremberg. The other report, that they were taken away by plane yesterday, appears for the present to be incorrect."

This rumor has touched off all kinds of speculations among us.

October 24, 1948 The medical aide brings a basketful of thirty new books from the Spandau Municipal Library. Raeder with his assistant librarian, Schirach, has been busy for an hour entering the books in a register that he keeps with such care that one might think he is administering thirty battleships instead of that many books.

Selecting books from the Spandau catalogue is one of the few autonomous acts we are permitted. Funk usually orders philosophical works, Schirach literature and literary criticism, Hess history (which often does not come through), and I works on art and architecture.

For the past twelve months I have been reading four to five hours daily. I still find it hard to grasp the difference, beyond generalities, between classical antiquity, the Renaissance, European classicism, and my own efforts. At best I might say that Paestum or the Greek temples on Sicily have a more powerful and more emotional effect upon me than all the works of the Italian Renaissance. The same is true for Prussian classicism, most of all the work of Gilly and Schinkel. Hitler was affected altogether differently. When he returned from his visit to Italy in 1938 he spent whole evenings talking about the tremendous impression the Florentine Renaissance had made upon him, especially its imperial fortifications style. Of course he was sentimental about classical antiquity; at least once in his life, he said at the time, he wanted to see the Acropolis. But how often we drove over Schinkel's Schloss Bridge, past the museum island so shaped by his work, and I cannot recall that Hitler even once remarked on the admirable portico. And once, during the war, I gave Hitler a book on that brilliantly gifted architect Gilly (who unfortunately died too soon); I had always regarded him as a genius of architecture and the example I strove to follow. But Hitler never afterwards so much as mentioned the book.

It was curious that even in architecture he simply could not relate to Prussia. The current opinion seems to be that he was the epitome and end product of the Prussian spirit. Nothing could be more wrong. For in fact he was Habsburgian, basically anti-Prussian. Strictly speaking, the element he loved in classicism was the opportunity for monumentality. He was obsessed with giantism. Troost, it seems to me, temporarily led him in the direction of austerity in the early thirties, so that contrary to his true inclinations Hitler called the Haus der Deutschen Kunst [House of German Art] in Munich a miracle of modern architecture. But his real preferences were for arched passageways, domes, curving lines, ostentation, always with an element of elegance—in short, the baroque. That extended to his feeling about the Ringstrasse in Vienna. He went wild over its architectural richness; he reached for pencil and pad to express his enthusiasm. His sketches tended to dwell on certain motifs: heavy cornices or stone window casings, enormous piers, and occasionally gigantic recessed arches in unorganized structures. There was, when I recall them to memory, a curious sameness about everything he drew. His columns, for example, were always stark, but he praised me for the gilded capitals of the New Chancellery. I observed that he did not know how to convey in his sketches the ornateness he extolled in words. I also realized that he was so pleased with my New Chancellery because of its relative wealth of ornamentation. Accordingly, when I designed the grand boulevard that was to be the center of Berlin, the world capital, I tried to put into it all the variety of a cityscape that had evolved in the course of centuries. It was a congeries of styles. The Führer's Palace as I conceived it was a play upon Pompeian motifs: two-story colonnades with Empire-style ornamentation of gold and bronze. For Göring I designed an Office of the Reich Marshal whose model, in the back of my mind, was the Palazzo Pitti in Florence, with sweeping baroque stairways in the interior. The Vault of the Field Marshals was a kind of Nibelungen architecture, and the projected Town Hall with its granite towers stirred memories of late-medieval cityscapes. But when I consider it today, I believe my design was essentially a failure. In spite of some good details, what primarily came through was not variety but monotony and emptiness. The Berlin Hitler and I would have built had nothing in common with Prussian classicism, austere and sparsely ornamented, which drew its strength entirely from its proportions.

I see in retrospect how far astray he led me from my beginnings and ideas.

November 3, 1948   We are shut off from the outside world. No newspapers or magazines. Even with historical books, we are only allowed those dealing with the period before the First World War. The guards are strictly forbidden to tell us anything about political events. It is against the rules for them to talk to us about our pasts or to refer to our sentences. Nevertheless, we know more or less what is going on. I have just found out, by a little trick, that Truman won the election in the United States yesterday. I said casually to Thomas Letham, the Scottish chief guard with the pink baby face: "So Truman was reelected after all!" He looked up in astonishment: "How do you know that? Who let it out?" So I knew.

For Christmas presents I have asked the family for two bright peasant print handkerchiefs and a sketchbook.

November 21, 1948   Now there is garden work in winter too. Depending on the weather, I turn the soil or paint our corridor. I lay a board between two rickety ladders and balance on it two meters above the ground while the whitewash runs over my head and hands. It soon stops being fun, but I tell myself that this is a kind of balancing exercise for future hikes in the mountains. Every day I climb up and down the ladders perhaps a hundred times. A hundred times two meters makes an altitude of two hundred meters. Prisoner jokes.

A few days ago, when I was moving the ladders, a heavy hammer I had placed on top of one fell on my head. Four stitches needed to close the wound.

December 7, 1948   A week ago an American medical commission examined us and then increased the rations. Now we are getting creamed soups to accustom our organisms to richer food.

For infraction of the rules I have again been penalized: a ban on reading for a week. A happy result is that I experienced the world of *Don Quixote* with greater keenness. But I shall have to be on my guard against attacking windmills in prison. On the whole the tone of my notes seems to me more disciplined and tranquil now. The questions of guilt, responsibility, and punishment, all those self-justifications and self-accusations, no longer dominate as they did previously. The part of the sentence already served increasingly settles the score. During my weeks of preoccupation with the Renaissance, I did not once think about the war, armaments, and criminality. Along with all this the feeling grows that Spandau is a kind of home. That too is worrisome.

December 28, 1948   Have written nothing for three weeks. But today something new has totally upset me. My wife sent me the copy of a letter from Mrs. Alfred A. Knopf dated October 28. The wife of the well-known American publisher who has published the works of Thomas Mann in the United States would like to bring out my memoirs.[1]

In my isolation I had completely lost the feeling that the outside world could still be interested in me. Everything has been going along so smoothly—and now this incredible interruption. It bothers me, but at the same time excites me. After weeks of reverie I want to return to my past after all. By bringing it to consciousness and writing it down I'll make sure I have the material I will need for the major book on Hitler

---

[1] "I realize," she wrote, "that there is very little to be expected from Albert Speer at this time and the possibilities of what we discussed earlier are dimmer than ever before. I am still interested but if we will have to wait too long, perhaps the material will not have the same importance that it had months back."

that I think of more and more frequently. At present I can still recall almost every detail, and can effortlessly reconstruct a good many conversations almost word for word. I am still close enough to the events, and my preoccupation with those years has sharpened my memory. In Nuremberg I was able to write a first draft on Hitler; it has already been revised and corrected. Here in Spandau I must send my notes off by my clandestine route, rough though they be. An enormous file of notes will accumulate at home; later I can organize them and use them as the basis for the book.

January 3, 1949   From hints we know that the alliance between West and East has broken down. The conflict has led to disputes over access routes into Berlin. Now Berlin is said to be blockaded. And in fact day and night transport planes roar over our building. In the garden we puzzle over the consequences of all this for us. We gradually come round to the idea that if there should be a final break between West and East, prisoners would be returned to the nations that captured them. Consequently I would go to the British. A reassuring prospect.

Today, with Funk, I washed our laundry in the bathroom. The room fills with steam; moisture runs down the walls. We keep moving around vigorously to warm ourselves, our wooden clogs clacking on the stone floor. Long, the British guard, withdraws to the anteroom. For some time Funk's favorite subject has been corruption in the Third Reich. He tells me about several freight cars of women's stockings and undergarments that Göring had shipped in military trains from Italy in the summer of 1942, to be sold in the Reich on the black market. Accompanying the goods was a regular price list, so it was quite clear what huge profits could be expected. I dimly recall the affair. One day Milch angrily informed me that Air Force General Lörzer had been entrusted with the task of organizing these wholesale black market activities. Lörzer was a close friend of Göring's from the First World War, and like Göring had received the Pour le Mérite medal as a fighter pilot. Pilly Körner, Göring's assistant secretary and deputy in the Four Year Plan, had also taken part in these deals. The absurd part of it was that the traffic involved mostly goods that Germany was obliged under export agreements to ship to her Italian ally, items that were turned around and sent back right after crossing the Brenner. As he went over these matters, Funk's indignation mounted. He stood still, exclaiming, "What a dirty business!" Working away at the laundry, I retorted that as minister of economics he should have intervened and reported the racket to Hitler. "What do you mean?" he replied. "After all, I had no idea where it stopped, and besides, Himmler undoubtedly had dossiers against me in his files."

In a speech to the Gauleiters in the autumn of 1943 I myself had warned that in the future we were going to check up on certain obscure import and export affairs. This earned me a great deal of ill feeling and did not discourage the black marketeering in the least. Today I sometimes think that Hitler consciously tolerated or even deliberately promoted the corruption. It tied the corrupt men to him—doesn't every potentate attempt to consolidate his rule by gestures of favoritism? Besides, corruption corresponded to his notion of the right of those wielding power to take possession of material goods. Authority, he thought, also needed outward show; the common man was impressed only by display. He liked his satraps to live in castles and palaces; he definitely wanted them to be ostentatious. My own resistance to such conduct basically testified to my naïveté. How little Funk and I had ever grasped the cunning that underlay Hitler's tactics in the exercise of power.

January 10, 1949 During the past two months of British and American administration I've gained fifteen pounds. The German proverb "Behind bars even honey tastes bitter" does not apply to me. Fortunately, the Russian month always brings an ascetic phase. I don't mean that only in the sense of the provisions; the sparser food also changes one's whole sense of life. Surprisingly, my feeling is that the period under the Russians is better for me intellectually. The monastic orders certainly knew the connection between deprivation and stimulation of the mind.

January 28, 1949 Subjects wear out. Since we hear nothing, or only bits of chance information, about the outside world, and since no future is visible, we repeatedly entangle ourselves in the same snarls of the same subjects. One might assume that we convicted war criminals would have no moral relationship to the past, that we would try to regard what has happened primarily as a historical process, independent of ethical categories. But actually all of us here moralize incessantly: on that profligate Göring, that fornicator Goebbels, that drunkard Ley, that vain fool Ribbentrop. Funk takes the lead in this. Today he began on Streicher—who, it must be granted, everyone avoided, and who even under the Third Reich was considered disgusting. We reminded Hess today that it was he, supported by my friend Willy Liebel, the mayor of Nuremberg, who brought about Streicher's fall from grace. Hess reacted with a mixture of annoyance and absent-mindedness.

Hess had been a bitter opponent of Streicher all along. When Hitler was in Nuremberg at the end of 1938 Hess had his first chance to take up cudgels against Streicher, but he got nowhere with Hitler. Yet there was plenty of evidence of corruption in the way Streicher and his Nuremberg cronies had enriched themselves out of confiscated Jewish property. After prolonged urging, Hess, with the support of Mayor Liebel, finally succeeded in having Streicher's conduct brought before the highest Party tribunal. When the court decided against Streicher, Hitler showed extreme displeasure at the verdict. He rebuked the chairman, Reichsleiter Buch, a major in the regular army. Buch was an obstinate old officer, he said, who had often arrived at wrong verdicts out of political stupidity. At times, Hitler said, he actually considered removing Buch. But Bormann, who had married Buch's daughter, was always protecting his father-in-law. That, incidentally, was a first sign of how much influence Bormann had by then acquired. In the end, the condemnation of Streicher was allowed to stand. Until the end of the war he lived in a kind of exile on his estate, Pleikertshof, some distance from Nuremberg. He was actually forbidden to enter the city. Living with him was his thirty-five-year-old secretary, a strikingly pretty woman whom he married shortly before the end of the war, and who was also the only person who had the courage to appear as a witness for Streicher. The contrast between the two was amazing, absolutely incomprehensible.

During the war years Hitler was often sorry that he had yielded and agreed to the banishment of Streicher. In nocturnal conversations at Headquarters he remembered that after all it had been Streicher who, by bringing his Nuremberg followers over in a body into the National Socialist Party in 1922, had taken a decisive step toward the consolidation of the Party. Nor did he forget that during the confusion on the morning of November 9, 1923, when the Putsch had already failed, Streicher had been one of the few to keep calm, and had delivered a fanatical speech in the Marienplatz, trying at the last moment to change the course of events. It is indicative of Hitler's contradictory nature that he bemoaned a matter that he could have changed simply by issuing an order. A word to Bormann would have sufficed to restore Streicher to his post as Gauleiter.

Streicher was aware of Liebel's antagonism; in 1938 he sent his personal adjutant to present Liebel with a large bouquet of thistles for his birthday. In the dock at Nuremberg Streicher one day turned to me with an expression of hatred and gratification that I shall not forget for the rest of my life and snarled: "I had your friend Liebel, that swine, shot a few hours before the Americans arrived!" During the last weeks of the war Streicher, asking no leave, had left his place of banishment and taken over the leadership of the Nuremberg Gau again. Liebel, who during the past several years had been chief of the Central Office in my Ministry, had ignored my advice in March 1945 and had returned to Nuremberg, to serve there as mayor during these last days of the war. The chaos of this period gave Streicher the opportunity for his revenge.

January 31, 1949 At last we have finished painting the corridor. It took us three months. Now we are beginning on renovation of our cells. My fellow prisoners, who at first made fun of my work program, are by now participating as helpers or apprentices. The dull muddy yellow of the cell walls is giving way to a soft green hue that is separated from the whitewashed upper half of the wall by a dark green stripe. I am making the door a stronger tone of the wall color; the furniture is being painted a red-brown, the window frame with white enamel. Goethe says somewhere that soft green has a reassuring and calming effect. I can now test this on myself.

Formerly I gave as much thought to the colors of the marble that was to sheathe the Palace of the Führer and the regime's other sacred structures as I now give to the colors of our cells. Hitler always accepted my choices. Which reminds me of an episode: once at dinner Hitler told his listeners that he had personally selected all the varieties of marble in order to coordinate colors. Hadn't he noticed that I was sitting at an adjoining table? What so took me aback was and is the fact that he was still clutching at glory in such ridiculously trivial questions, when he had long since been astounding the world.

In military conferences, too, Hitler quite often presented as the fruit of his own reflections technical details that my experts, Professor Porsche or Stieler von Heydekampf, had instructed him on just a short while before. He also liked to claim that "last night"—although a conference might not have ended until nearly morning—he had "studied" a scientific or historical work of hundreds of pages. We all knew that he firmly believed in reading only the end of a book, because everything important was to be found there. At worst, it might be necessary to leaf through a few more pages, perhaps even letting yourself be caught up in a passage here and there, and soon you would appropriate everything a book had to offer. How intense and uncontrollable this man's desire to show off must have been!

February 3, 1949 Our Frenchman from Champagne, François Roulet, a clumsy but straightforward fellow, greets grumpy Dönitz at breakfast time with: *"Mon général, comment ça va?"* Then they have a long talk, although a few days ago Dönitz solemnly declared that for a whole year he would not speak to a guard. Each of us has developed his own pattern of behavior toward the guards and directors. Hess is unfriendly, regards them as his personal enemies, and receives all reprimands with unruffled, contemptuous calm. Neurath and Raeder are reserved, polite, and somewhat forbearing. Dönitz vacillates, now huffily acting the high-ranking naval officer and keeping his distance from everybody, now genially seeking contact. Schirach and I are basically on good terms with all those who are on good terms with us. A tacit agreement has gradually taken shape, however, that Schirach's closer friends are not mine and mine not his. The older men criticize the two of us because we do not show more restraint toward the staff. Funk, who occasionally hits on pithy phrases, admonished us today: "Even humane guards are still guards."

With the passage of time the seven of us are becoming increasingly cranky and headstrong. Contacts among us have frozen into their early patterns; new friendships have not formed. Funk and Schirach were always close; today they are an inseparable pair, constantly quarreling and making up. Their interests lie chiefly in literature and music. Systematically, they inform each other about their reading, pick out quotations, exchange opinions. Raeder and Funk, making their rounds of the garden as if it were the daily promenade at a fashionable spa, love to talk about their mutual ailments. Hess and I have been classed as solitaries. Schirach, Raeder, and Dönitz are distinctly cool toward me, although they occasionally find a few words to say to me. They disapprove of my consistent and basic rejection of the Third Reich. Hess, on the other hand, is so eccentric that no one can get close to him. But I have a degree of sympathy for his oddities and even some liking for him; his response is prickly. Neurath remains even in this environment a nobleman of the old school, always amiable, helpful, modest. He never complains. That gives him a certain dignity and an authority which, however, he never exploits.

February 4, 1949 Recently Funk has started a friendly talk with me every few days, but my own ineptness at small talk hampers things.

Another obstacle is Funk's tendency to wallow in self-pity. But sometimes he gives even his laments an ironic twist. He also likes to mourn
the loss of his onetime corpulence and recollect vanished sybaritic pleasures. Raeder is sometimes ready for a brief chat on insignificant matters. Dönitz, with whom I was once quite friendly in the line of our
official duties, seldom talks with me, and when he does, usually makes
covert nasty remarks. Since he is not very witty, I suspect that he plans
his quips during sleepless night hours.

Raeder and Dönitz have their difficulties with each other. Raeder,
who in the spring of 1943 was replaced by Dönitz as commander of the
navy, is now seventy-two years old, and still vigorous. He still regards
Dönitz, fifteen years his junior and his former subordinate as chief of
the submarine forces, as an overambitious officer. Dönitz, for his part,
blames his predecessor for his policy of bloated surface vessels. Thanks
to Raeder, he says, the German navy entered the war with only some
fifty U-boats, of which only ten could be permanently operating in the
Atlantic. Today, talking at length with Neurath in the garden, he excitedly argued that England would have been forced to her knees as early
as 1941 if Germany had had three hundred U-boats, as he had
demanded, at the outbreak of the war. It had been Raeder's fault, he
said, that until the middle of 1940 only two U-boats a month slid down
the ways. The navy command had not built even half the 24,000 tons
of submarines permitted under the 1935 Naval Treaty with England,
he pointed out. Spade in hand, I watched Neurath listening with polite
interest to the grand admiral's tirade. Whenever the two passed by me
on their round, I could hear only Dönitz's agitated voice.

Raeder treats Dönitz with the condescension of a superior officer,
which particularly irritates him. As for Dönitz's allegations, Raeder ig-
nores them. The two usually avoid each other. The disagreement will
not be settled, but I have the distinct feeling that Dönitz is only waiting
for the chance to denounce what he considers to be omissions in the
German preparations for war. He wants to point an accusing finger at
Raeder.

Among us are passive types who pass the time by endless talking.
Among these are Funk, Schirach, and—a taciturn and absurd variant of
the type—Hess. The active types who go to pieces without occupation
are Raeder, Neurath, Dönitz, and I. We have at any rate got rid of
titles. Raeder is no longer the grand admiral and Neurath no longer
foreign minister. But from fear of going downhill, we are careful to
maintain a certain degree of formal manners among ourselves. In any
case, we look so bedraggled with these clumsy shoes, shapeless pants,

big numbers painted on backs and knees, and hair cropped by crude military barbering, that we become aware more keenly than ever of the importance of forms. In this world without privacy we set up barriers against too much intimacy. Such barriers have protective value. We still address each other as "Herr," continue to respect precedence, and politely wish each other good morning and good night.

At two o'clock Charles Roques of the French staff unlocks all the cells and calls out, "Gloves and socks are on the table." We have been without these articles for several weeks; they have just come back from a women's prison, mended. All the others rummage through the pile. The Frenchman turns reprovingly to me because I am still sitting on my cot: "See to your things. Otherwise they'll all be gone." In response to a question from Long, the Englishman, Schirach explains for perhaps the hundredth time, "I've really explained it to you often enough. Hess and Speer don't mark their socks. They simply refuse to. Of course we others all do. I even darn my number in."

After they have all returned to their cells I go to the table. There are no socks left. Evidently Hess has again stocked up. Last month twenty pairs were found in his cell.

February 5, 1949   The days pass swiftly and leave little memorable behind. Today ten wild geese flew across my small segment of sky. First signs of spring. The buds are fat on our lilac bush.

A few weeks ago Casalis gave me Karl Barth's *Epistle to the Romans*. Barth phrases everything with great firmness. That appeals to me. As I understand him, the Christian commandments represent virtually infinite values, which even a saint can only approximate. It is given to no one to remain without fault. Every human being inevitably sins. But I must confess that for pages at a time I could scarcely grasp Barth's thought. After the services today I said to Casalis that faith seems to me like a tremendous mountain range. Tempting from a distance, when you try to climb it you run into ravines, perpendicular walls, and stretches of glacier. Most climbers are forced to turn back; some plunge to destruction; but almost nobody reaches the peak. Yet the world from on top must offer a wonderfully novel and clear view.

February 14, 1949   With the directors' approval Neurath today divided up the garden and assigned each of us an area. The size of the parcels is adjusted to our taste for work. This solution has its advantages, for previously the hard-working had to fill in for the lazy.

A visit from my wife is not possible because of the blockade.

Through Casalis's mediation my cousin Hildebrecht Hommel, who teaches in the Berlin Theological Seminary, came today. I was worried about this first personal visit in Spandau. Behind me sat an American, an English, a French, and a Russian guard. An additional representative of the Allies was sitting in a corner taking notes on our conversation. Still another sergeant, French, escorted Hildebrecht. Two close-meshed wire gratings only ten centimeters apart separated me from the visitor, so that we could scarcely see each other's faces. My cousin, whom I had previously never met, made a pleasant impression. My constraint disappeared. What would our common ancestor, old Count Pappenheim, hereditary marshal of the Holy Roman Empire of the German Nation, have thought if he could have seen his descendants in this situation?

February 15, 1949 An odd fit of high spirits. When Schirach asked me the purpose of all those pots of white paint, I replied, "Don't you know? The directors have ordered the coal bunker to be whitewashed so that they can better check on whether the briquets are kept clean. Isn't that crazy?" "Is such a thing possible?" Schirach asked incredulously. Outraged, he rushed off to Pease and Dackerman to give them the news.

While I was spreading fertilizer in the garden today, I calculated that with my trips back and forth I am daily covering between nine and ten kilometers. Training for future hikes. The wheelbarrow takes the place of the rucksack.

February 18, 1949 I dreamed of a long tramp in the woods on the northern banks of the Havel lakes, although there are no woods there. Large deciduous trees reminded me that before the war, on my initiative, a beginning was made in the reforesting of Grunewald, which had been planted with evergreens after being cleared during the time of Frederick the Great. I was recently told that in the intervening years the tens of thousands of saplings have grown into forests, one of the few remaining traces of my activities. If in a hundred years Grunewald should really be green, that will be my work.

Tired of walking, in the dream I wish for a bicycle and immediately have one. I now ride along side-paths, using low gear on the uphill stretches. At last I come out onto one of the broad promenades I planned for Grunewald: some day it was to be a vaster Bois de Boulogne, with restaurants, riding stables, playgrounds, and sculpture gardens. At once I leave the promenade and take a path that leads high up along the slope and affords an unreal view of the Havel lakes, with their tree-covered islands. In the dream, romantic landscapes like those in certain paintings in my collection slide in front of this view: I see stone pines and cypresses; white temples gleam on islands; and in a semicircle to one side stand bleached sculptures.

Evening. Since six o'clock, when the door was locked behind me, I have been sketching what I can remember of my plans for parts of Grunewald. It was to be converted into a carefully shaped park for the common people's enjoyment. A visit in 1937 to the Paris World's Fair, for which I had designed the German pavilion, gave me the inspiration for this concept. At the time French friends had taken me to the Bois de Boulogne, and the alternation of forested areas, well-designed land-scapes, greenswards, and artificial lakes, all joined by pleasantly curving gravel paths, had remained fixed in my memory as far superior to our sparse Grunewald with its sandy paths. This partiality for consciously created landscape was confirmed by my visit to Italy with my wife and Magda Goebbels that same year. In Rome, for example, we became acquainted with the gardens of the Pincio and of the Villa d'Este. Hitler, who in any case had no taste for the rather tart appeal of Prussian landscapes, was instantly won over. Goebbels, on the other hand, as Gauleiter of Berlin, opposed the plan—the whole idea seemed to him to sound too feudal a note for a proletarian city like Berlin. He pointed out that from time immemorial Berliners had been accustomed to going out on Sundays with their whole families "into the country" and not into some belatedly laid-out aristocratic park. But as always, it was Hitler who decided things. Only a year later we began cutting down groves here and there and, instead of pines, establishing nursery plant-ings of deciduous trees. Goebbels, incidentally, was quite wrong. We had not the slightest intention of transforming this vast area of woods, several square kilometers in extent, into a formal park. The intention was only to intersperse here and there small oases of horticulture. The impressions of Rome and Paris, but also of the gardens of Sans Souci, Schönbrunn, and many German provincial capitals, had made me con-scious of the special beauty of sculptures against the backdrop of na-ture. This feeling coincided with Hitler's repeated insistence that sculp-ture must be freed from the dungeon of bare museum halls. He was the first in a long time, he said, to restore sculpture to its proper place in the whole aspect of cities, in the squares, on the boulevards, and in the new forums for the people. Next to architecture, he loved sculpture most. The area around the Chancellery was adorned with classical and contemporary sculptures. And he enjoyed visiting sculptors' studios to convince himself of the progress in creativity being made in *his* epoch.

My friend Arno Breker was his favorite sculptor. After the conquest of France, Breker introduced me to his old teacher Maillol, who in the early decades of this century led French sculpture to a new flowering. Things were bad for him; bronze was no longer available, and in those desolate times collectors had become rare. Breker therefore made the surprising suggestion that we enlist his old friend in the project for the redesigning of Grunewald. Maillol spontaneously agreed when at a dinner in the Coq Hardi I proposed that he create sculptures for Berlin's great new park. Maillol was touched; at the age of eighty, he said, this was his first government commission. Over all the years the French government had never commissioned anything from him. Early in 1945 I heard that the original model of what is perhaps his most beautiful and most important figure, the *Méditerrané*, created at the beginning of the century, had been smashed to pieces by members of the Resistance because it had been mistaken for a work done on my commission. Another story was that it had been destroyed on the assumption that it was a work by Arno Breker.

February 25, 1949   It is raining today. When eleven o'clock comes, time for the daily walk, Hess begins to groan. When we others go out, he remains lying on his cot. Stokes orders him: "Number Seven! Go for a walk!" Curious, we linger in the corridor and listen to a protracted discussion. "Seven, you'll be put in the punishment cell. You must go out!" Shrugging, Hess gets up and without demurring goes into the punishment cell, which is furnished only with a chair and table.

March 3, 1949   Today I asked myself whether the man I served, whom I certainly revered for long years, was even capable of such sincere emotions as friendship, gratitude, loyalty. I sometimes have my doubts about his real feelings toward Eva Braun; his old associates said that he probably did really love Geli Raubal. In the world of men he seemed genuinely fond of me, of his chauffeur, Schreck—of whom he actually had a portrait in his study, beside a picture of his mother—and the only other person I can think of is Mussolini. I believe that something like a feeling of friendship existed between the two, and probably was even stronger on Hitler's side. One counterargument is that in the final phase of the war Hitler wanted to take the northern provinces away from Mussolini. But that had more to do with disappointment at his ally's inadequate military performance, and with a surge of hatred, vengefulness, and sense of betrayal directed against Italians in the Badoglio camp who had gone over to the enemy.

In all the years before the end, however, the friendship was evidently close; and if I had been asked to name a person toward whom Hitler showed genuine attachment, I would always have mentioned Mussolini. But recently I recalled the day that this friendship was founded. In September 1937 Mussolini had come to Berlin. Together, he and Hitler had driven down the East-West Axis, which Benno von Arent had transformed into a triumphal avenue by the use of several hundred white cardboard pylons. Hitler was so taken with these that he decided to have them executed in stone someday. Side by side at the Maifeld, Hitler and Mussolini addressed a crowd of hundreds of thousands. In the evening, as soon as Mussolini departed after the grand banquet in the Chancellery, Hitler showed extreme gratification. The Duce, he said, was now so impressed by him that Italy was forever bound to Germany. Subsequently, we spent a few more hours together in a more intimate circle. Hitler was once more going on about Mussolini's Caesarean look when Goebbels interposed. He was surely speaking in the name of all present, he said, if he called attention to the enormous difference between the Duce and the Führer. After all, the Führer was quite another kind of personality. In Italy Mussolini might be something special, a Roman among plain ordinary Italians, as the Führer had sometimes remarked; but here in Berlin he was, after all, just an Italian among Germans. At any rate he, Goebbels, at times had felt that the Duce had come walking out of an operetta.

Hitler's initial response to this seemed to be one of contradictory emotions. His new friend was being denigrated, but at the same time he felt flattered and stimulated. When Goebbels followed this up with two or three skillful remarks, Hitler began imitating a few of Mussolini's poses that had struck him as outré: the outstretched chin, the right hand braced against the hip, the straddle-legged stance. While the onlookers laughed obediently, he flung out a number of Italian or Italian-sounding words like *patria, Victoria, macaroni, bellezza, bel canto, telegrafico,* and *basta.* His performance was very funny.

Turning serious again, Hitler proudly related how he had won Mussolini over, during the latter's stay in Munich, to the new German architecture. He boasted of having given him a lecture on modern architecture, and said that the Duce was now convinced that the designs of his official architect, Piacentini, amounted to nothing. At the 1940

World's Fair in Rome, Mussolini had said, he would show what he had learned in Munich and Berlin.

March 12, 1949   Now the renovation of the cells is complete. We have even received new beds with steel springs. For the first few days their resilience was so strange that I could not sleep. On the long wall I have pasted up photos of my parents, my wife, and our children. Alongside these hang reproductions of a bronze head by Polyclitus, Schinkel's sketch of a palace on the Acropolis, an Ionian capital, and a classical frieze. The first thing I see from bed every morning is the Erechtheum on the Acropolis.

Today Pease told me in a whisper of rumored changes in the prison setup. Because of the political conflicts, the joint enterprise with the Russians is to be dissolved. An hour has been approved for my wife's visit. But I would like to postpone it until June. Perhaps by then everything will be very different here.

March 13, 1949   I forgot to finish that story about Mussolini's buildings.

A few months later Hitler saw the first sketches for the World's Fair in Rome. The idea was that the buildings would later serve as a kind of government center. "He didn't understand us!" Hitler exclaimed. "A meaningless copy without any impact. But maybe it's better so; we will keep the lead." At the same time he instructed Hermann Giessler—who was already busy with building the Gau forums in Augsburg and Weimar, with the reconstruction of Munich, and with the comprehensive rebuilding of Linz—to design an impressive German pavilion for the Rome World's Fair.

It's strange, but I myself never came into any contact with Mussolini. During his stay in Munich I was once introduced to him and we exchanged a few words. Later, during those hapless days at Lake Garda, SS Obergruppenführer Wolff wanted to obtain an invitation from Mussolini for me, but I thought it tasteless to visit him under these humiliating circumstances, as if he were some object for sightseers. Today I regret having missed this opportunity.

March 14, 1949   All morning I glazed windows for the hotbeds, sowed peas and carrots in the first bed, planted pansies, violets, lilies of the valley, and asters in others. Neurath, Dönitz, and the rest prefer to raise vegetables. The flower seeds supplied by the prison authorities remain for Schirach and me. In addition I have established a tree nursery with fifty walnut seedlings. They are supposed to need ten or fifteen years to reach bearing age. I hope that some successors here will harvest the first nuts.

Because of bad weather this afternoon, after the noon break we had to sweep thick layers of dust in the upper stories. These assignments at least give me a chance to look out over the high walls. Only now do I have a more accurate idea of where the prison is located. Very close by I can see the highway to Nauen, along which I drove with my family on many a weekend to visit friends on Sigrön Estate, near Wilsnack. Spandau Prison must also have been visible from that road, but I surely did not notice it.

March 16, 1949 Compared to my Nuremberg buildings, which in their blocklike severity introduced an early Oriental motif into architecture, reminiscences of Assyria or Egypt, in the simultaneous Berlin buildings I employed livelier articulation and richer details. I ventured excursions into taboo ornamentation and produced lusher outlines, for by then the sort of thing I had already built had become fashionable. I tried to differentiate myself from a growing band of imitators by developing a new style.

There had never been an ideology of National Socialist architecture, although I constantly read assertions to that effect. The one thing necessary was superdimensionality. Hitler wanted to impress, and also to intimidate, the people by vast proportions. In this way he expected to provide psychological buttresses for his own rule and that of his successors. To this extent, the program was ideological. But this did not affect the style. That is my point.

March 18, 1949 To my surprise the Soviet director has just come into my cell. He looked around to see whether everything was in order, said in an aloof but not unfriendly tone, *"Kak dee la?"* (How goes it?), and vanished without waiting for the reply. I had just been busy writing. Lucky that the door is locked and bolted twice, so that there is always a certain amount of noise when it is opened. I lie on the bed, face toward the door, legs drawn up, with a large book on architecture resting on them as a lap desk.

I recently introduced a new system. When there is an alarm I no longer thrust my papers into my jacket pocket. I keep the top button of my trousers unbuttoned; one swift movement, covered by the book, and the letter vanishes into my underdrawers. That is where I also keep my reserve stock of paper and my letters to be answered: my underwear is my writing desk! Using bandages that I need for my sometimes swollen leg, I have closed the bottom of the underdrawers, so that notes or letters cannot fall out when I walk. My preferred cache for writing material is in the bend of the knee, since the paper then does not show by stretching my trousers as I work.

March 26, 1949   It is painful that I cannot be present at my son Albert's confirmation. We had a good relationship, but when I returned from my long working days, usually very late, to our house in Berlin-Schlachtensee, only my wife would be waiting up for me. The children would have gone to bed long since. Often I did not see them for an entire week. As armaments minister during the war I was so busy that they grew up almost without a father. I was just a man who occasionally looked in and brought the sweets. The letter I am trying to write for Albert's confirmation makes me realize that it is becoming harder and harder for me to speak to him as a father. I no longer have the right tone toward him. Also, there is a lack of new impressions; we have no new experiences together. Undoubtedly it is becoming harder and harder for the children to retain any conception of what I am like.

May 3, 1949   Five-week interruption, but not out of lethargy. I reached for the T square and angles, and for the first time in years have completed a design that is fully worked out. Happy about this activity, and also about a new version of my upper-middle-class house. I was so carried away by the work that I again started to make detail drawings of facades to scale. This design seems to have turned out particularly well, with a severe street front and an informal south side.

May 13, 1949   Beautiful spring weather. John Hawker, who is normally rather aloof, tells me that preparations are going forward in Berlin for a foreign ministers' conference which is expected to bring relaxation of the tensions over Berlin. Probably Hawker intends to dispel obstinate rumors to the effect that we will be transferred to the vicinity of Hamburg because of the political differences among the Allies. Another guard, the cheerful American Donaho, confirms the report. It is reliable, then; Hawker might only invent news in order to rob us of hopes.

The sky today looks as though it had been washed in blueing; it seems possible to see through to its very depths. Ordinarily this effect can be had only in the mountains. At least I have only noticed it there, on climbs, while skiing, or at Obersalzberg. Only in the perspective of Spandau do I fully realize how relaxed, how familial the atmosphere there was—more like the summer residence of a prosperous industrialist than the mountain castle of the inaccessible Führer who had so painfully adopted the statesman's pose, and who even in my memory is increasingly assuming the features of a historical abstraction.

On the terrace we would stand around informally while the ladies stretched out on the wicker reclining chairs with cushions covered in red-and-white gingham. The ladies sunned themselves as if they were at some spa, for being tanned was the fashion. Liveried attendants, select SS men from Sepp Dietrich's Bodyguard Regiment, with perfect manners that seemed a shade too intimate, handed around drinks: champagne, vermouth and soda, or fruit juices. Sooner or later Hitler's valet would appear and report that the Führer would join us in ten minutes; that he had retired to the upper floor for a few minutes after a long conference. On one such occasion, already more than an hour past the time set for lunch, I remember short, lively Dr. Otto Dietrich, Hitler's press chief; the surgeon Dr. Karl Brandt, who always had to be on hand in case there should be an accident or an attempted assassination; Colonel Schmundt, the armed forces adjutant with the unforgettably protruding ears; army adjutant Engel, always ready to joke; Wilhelm Brückner; and of course Martin Bormann, whose inept old-style gallantries toward the ladies failed to draw any response, except from one of Hitler's younger secretaries, who would break into shrill giggles. At the news of Hitler's imminent arrival, the buzz of conversation becomes more muted, the bursts of laughter cease. The women drop into murmurs as they continue chatting about clothes and traveling. Eva Braun takes her movie camera from the reclining chair; with her is Negus, a black Scottish terrier named after the emperor of Abyssinia. She prepares to film the entrance.

Hitler appears in civilian dress, in a well-tailored suit that is somewhat too loud. His tie is not well chosen. Weeks ago Eva Braun several times proposed that she pick out suitable ties from his collection, but he ignored the offers. In spite of the good weather he is wearing a velours hat with a wide brim, somewhat wider than the fashion, because he tends to sunburn. Perhaps he also prefers pallor; at any rate, his color is not healthy. His slight paunch gives his whole appearance a portly, comfortable cast.

Hitler greets each of the guests with friendly words, asks about everyone's children, personal plans, and circumstances.

From the moment of his entrance the scene has changed. Everyone is tense, visibly trying to make a good impression. Yet Hitler wants an air of unforced sociability that will not seem servile but will instead put people at their ease and cover over the fact that once back in Berlin these same people will revert to their usual fawning manner. Here Hitler tries to be genial, and by his behavior encourages us to act relaxed.

Another half-hour passes before we are asked to table. Hitler leads the way alone, Bormann following with Eva Braun. We pass by the cloakroom. In high spirits, one of the young adjutants tries on Hitler's hat, which a servant has just laid aside; the hat falls down over both his ears.

Although Hitler's familial interest in us was plainly more a matter of form than genuine concern, he was still less constrained on these occasions than at any other time, and scarcely ever tried to pose. He sometimes claimed that women became hoarse with excitement in his presence, but the ladies at Obersalzberg did not. Rather, they had to hold themselves back from playing their innocent jokes on Hitler also. In this private environment he could not conceal weaknesses, although he tried hard to do so.   .

Sometimes his efforts to live up to his conception of statesmanlike dignity produced rather amusing effects—as when he addressed princes as "Serene Highness," or exaggeratedly played the cavalier with ladies. In 1934 I accompanied him to Weimar, where he paid a respectful call on Nietzsche's sister. In greeting her he performed the most formal of bows and handed her a gigantic bouquet of flowers, which his servant immediately had to take from her again, because it was too huge for the lady to handle and obviously embarrassed her. In her living room Hitler employed ceremonious forms of address that I recall to this day with amazement and amusement. "Most gracious and respected madam," he began, "what a pleasure to have the privilege of finding you in the best of health in your esteemed home. Along with expression of my unchanging reverence for you and your estimable brother, permit me likewise to transmit to you on the occasion of this visit a modest gift in the form of an annex contributed by me to this home so linked with a great tradition." Hardly knowing what to say, Elizabeth Förster-Nietzsche offered us seats.

In 1939, when my mother was taking care of our children at Obersalzberg so that my wife and I could go off for a vacation, Hitler frequently invited her to dine with the intimate circle. As I later heard, he seemed to have taken a liking to her, and he must have expressed his respect in much the same sort of antediluvian phraseology he had used with Nietzsche's sister. My mother, otherwise singularly blind in political matters, changed her opinion of Hitler and his staff after these visits. "How nouveau riche everything is there. Even the way the meals are served is impossible, the table decorations crude. Hitler was terribly nice. But such a parvenu world!"

June 14, 1949 The Berlin blockade stopped over a month ago, which made my wife's visit possible. It was torment, perhaps more for her than for me. Under the eyes of these five or six other persons we were unable to say a single natural word. Nevertheless it was a great event. At least we saw each other for an hour. It made me very happy that she looks so much better. Three years ago, the last time we sat facing each other, shortly before the verdicts were pronounced in Nuremberg, she seemed tired and careworn. This picture of her stayed with me all through these three years, and preyed on my mind.

June 15, 1949 I am smoking the pipe that Margarete brought me as a belated birthday present. It is at the same time a memory of Grandfather. He was a passionate hunter, and when he told his grandsons stories about hunting he used to make a great fuss about thoroughly packing a similar pipe.

Recently I read that Thomas Carlyle's wife disliked pipe smoke as much as my own wife does. Carlyle would sit down on a low hassock in front of his fireplace and blow the smoke up the chimney. Since we have no chimney at home, I will have to have a funnel built with outlet to the outside. But for the present I am still here.

June 17, 1949 It occurs to me that at Obersalzberg we ourselves stayed longer at the Berghof with Hitler than in our old frame house, which had once been a small boardinghouse until Bormann acquired it, as he did all other properties on the mountain, and assigned it to us. How high-spirited my children were whenever I had time to drive them, in our fast BMW sports car, at high speed over the serpentine road that Bormann had blasted out of the rock to Hitler's Eyrie 800 meters higher up the mountain. The children laughed and shouted with pleasure the more the tires squealed on the switchbacks.

June 18, 1949 Yesterday I began reading Aeschylus's *Oresteia*, which was written during the years in which Pericles, with his architect, Ictinus, was building the Parthenon: an expression of Athenian confidence after the Persian Wars.

Sometimes Hitler invited Bormann's children and mine for chocolate and cake. They were washed up, dressed in their best clothes, and instructed to be cordial and friendly. But they would not let us crack the whip; they acted uninhibitedly, and Hitler did not win them over. He did not have the knack of winning children's affection; all his courting of them met with no response. Once he took the trouble of sitting on a bench beside my daughter and letting her show him her first efforts at writing. For a few minutes our eldest son looked on with some interest, but ran off abruptly when Hitler tried to draw him in also. The children tried to go off by themselves as quickly as possible—a normal reaction, but an unusual experience for Hitler.

I recall something else in this connection. On certain days the SS opened the gates of the Obersalzberg property. A column five yards wide, consisting of thousands upon thousands of admirers, filed past Hitler, who stood in a raised place, visible to all. People waved; women shed tears of exaltation. Hitler would point out one child or another to his chauffeur, Kempka, and an SS man would then lift the child above the crowd. Then the inevitable group picture would be taken; Hitler seemed to be avid for such pictures. The children themselves often looked rather unhappy.

I nearly made myself sick to my stomach breaking in my pipe.

June 20, 1949   After making sure that nobody is watching, Pease whispers to me that the Western zones of occupation have again become an independent state and have taken the name "Federal Republic." The East Zone has proclaimed itself the Democratic Republic. Whatever the details, four years after the downfall of the Reich there are, instead of the occupying powers, political entities governed by Germans.

The exacerbated political conflict is matched by the guerrilla war between West and East over our garden work. The Russian director is insisting that several small flower beds that are in full bloom be removed at once. Flowers are inappropriate in a prison garden, he says; besides, there is no provision for them in the rules. The Western Powers are constantly violating the stringent agreements, he complains. After protracted negotiations a compromise is reached: no new flowers may be planted, but those already growing in the garden will be allowed to remain.

July 24, 1949   Russian month. Fasting time. In the morning there is a third of a liter of thick barley soup, chicory coffee, a few slices of bread; in the afternoon a sour-tasting watery soup and the same quantity of bread; in the evening mashed potatoes, unpalatable meat, a small dab of butter, and again bread. This goes on day after day without the slightest variation. When I gripe at the monotony of the food, the guard tells me, "In Moscow the supplies for an expedition to the far north were assembled. On the approved list was a phonograph and fifty records. When the explorers in their tent wanted to hear music, they discovered that fifty copies of exactly the same record had been sent."

July 26, 1949   Today in the yard, overhearing a snatch of conversation between Dönitz and Schirach about Hitler, I was suddenly startled by the realization of how coldly I think and write about him. After all, I was constantly around him for more than ten years, owed my rise and fame to him. What is more, I also felt comfortable in his company—at least in the peacetime years. Was I consciously or unconsciously dissembling when I did not notice his clumsy exaggerations, his ill-chosen ties, his excessive bouquets—or am I now deceiving myself and others when I incessantly belittle him, even to myself? If I remember rightly, during the past few months I have not mentioned a single engaging trait of his; and in fact I no longer feel a trace of loyalty to him. Is that betrayal?

July 27, 1949   Have continued to reflect on my relationship to Hitler. The theme of faithlessness.

July 28, 1949   I cannot talk myself out of it; I am faithless. And that is not only because Hitler has forfeited all claim on my loyalty; loyalty to a monster cannot be. But I sometimes ask myself whether there is not some inexplicable instinct within me that always, whether I want it or not, makes me succumb to the spirit of the times; as though the prevailing current always carried me along. My feeling of guilt at Nuremberg was certainly completely sincere, but I wish I could have felt it in 1942. I would also have more confidence in my own judgment if today, at least from time to time, I were in opposition to the *Zeitgeist*, which now totally condemns Hitler. But I too can now hardly discover any good side in him; at any rate, none that offsets his monstrous crimes. In the light of those crimes, what can faithlessness possibly mean?

August 1, 1949   A rainy summer of cold winds, thunderstorms, and frequent showers. Nevertheless, I am tanned. The Russians marched off at twelve o'clock. Now American soldiers are back on the watchtowers. Whereas the Russians' submachine guns were mostly pointed toward our side, the garden, the Americans stand with their weapons pointed toward the outside.

For lunch there was mutton, baked potatoes, and so many other good things to eat that I shall probably lie awake until midnight. In the afternoon we were weighed by the American doctor. Each of the prisoners has lost about six pounds in the past month.

Hess, too, has benefited by the change in diet. A few minutes after the inspection we sat together on a bench in the sun. I tried to strike up a conversation with him. Since political subjects are delicate and lead nowhere, and since on the other hand he comes to life only when the talk centers around the old days, I brought up Eva Braun. I told him about an episode that indicates Hitler's extreme coldness. One day in the spring of 1939 a distraught Eva Braun, who sometimes poured out her heart to me, told me that Hitler had offered her her freedom to leave him and find another man—that he could no longer be all she wished to her. He had made this proposal bluntly, but perhaps it showed that momentarily he had an inkling of how many sacrifices a girl had to make to be his mistress. Hess, who at first had listened attentively, soon waved aside what I was saying with a bored air, and I went to work.

September 11, 1949 Another six weeks have passed. One month after another. Somewhere I have read that boredom is the one torment of hell that Dante forgot.

September 30, 1949 The end of the third year. The sensational events of our summer were: Hundreds of sparrows stole the sunflower seeds. We had a miserable vegetable harvest. But my flowers are doing well; among them there now are lupines from English seeds, of a beautiful pink. I have again read dozens of books wearily, with no conviction. Pointlessly, I go on studying English and French. Soon I shall take up T square and angles and again begin designing a house. Pointless.

The Fourth Year

October 18, 1949   Funk underwent an operation a few days ago. The
Western doctors wanted to perform it in the American hospital, but the
Russian director refused to allow it. An army-type mobile operating
unit was brought to Spandau. The difficult operation was carried out
by a French surgeon. Three guards had to be present, because the rules
require it. One fainted. There was a coffin ready at hand in the cellar.

Funk is being cared for by a French nurse. We do not see her, since
as soon as she appears we are locked up. I am just as glad, for after so
many years of not being in the company of women, I am afraid of
being gauche and clumsy.

October 22, 1949   Funk is out of danger. He is mad about Made-
moiselle Antissier, but to his grief she does not reciprocate his feelings.
However, she allows him his illusions.

October 24, 1949   Adenauer, the former mayor of Cologne, is said
to have become head of the new West German government. I recall
Hitler's calling him a capable man; that must have been in 1936, at tea

in Nuremberg's Deutscher Hof. Liebel had brought the conversation around to the importance of mayors, in order to puff up his own work in Nuremberg. Adenauer, Hitler commented at the time, had had the foresight and determination to create the Cologne green belt with its system of peripheral highways; he had also attracted important builders to Cologne and built a unique fairground on the right bank of the Rhine. To this day, Hitler said, he was impressed by the vision Adenauer had shown in plunging the city into debt. What did a few ridiculous millions mean as against a bold city plan, an architectonic conception? It was a pity that Adenauer's unreasonable political stance prevented Hitler from making use of the man.

Hitler praised Adenauer for his stubbornness: in fact he would have clashed with that difficult man as soon as he encountered him. He once tried to make an arrangement with one of these autocratic mayors, and although the man was not unsympathetic toward the "national revolution," in no time at all the two were at odds. "The obstacles this man Goerdeler in Leipzig is putting in my way!" Hitler would say, repeating a complaint I had often heard from him before. "He's well aware how much I want to have the new national monument for Richard Wagner built. I told him myself that I approved of Hipp's design. But he's constantly devising new maneuvers to prevent the demolition of the shabby old statue that an incompetent sculptor put there." Hitler's voice took on a sharper tone. "Goerdeler knows very well—I've even discussed details with him—that I particularly like those glorious giant reliefs, that the whole is to be done in the best Untersberg marble. I had to fire Goerdeler from his post as Reich commissioner because he worked too bureaucratically. If he doesn't show some sense soon, he can no longer remain as mayor. Remind me of that in six months, Bormann."

And in fact in 1937 Goerdeler lost all his official positions. None of us at the time could have imagined that seven years later the erstwhile mayor of Leipzig would be picked by the conspirators to be Hitler's successor.

October 26, 1949   In line with my measures for self-preservation I have begun an exercise program intended to strengthen heart and muscles. I shall fill a pit approximately one hundred and fifty cubic meters in volume with sand, by removing a mound from another part of the garden. In addition I have measured off distances of one and two hundred meters, and occasionally run these lengths. The doctor has prescribed gym shoes for me. After having done no running for years I find my performance discouraging.

November 2, 1949   After a few days of running exercises my knee is swollen. The doctor has prescribed bed rest. I am swallowing a vast number of pills and taking a vitamin cure.

Family photos accompany every letter from Heidelberg. I hold them in my hand again and again, comparing them with older pictures—at least in this way I can follow the children's development. I have been puzzling over one of the photos that came today: the forehead is obviously Fritz's, and the haircut also suggests one of the boys, but the chin looks like Hilde's and the eyes are altogether Margret's. Could it be Margret, after all, with her hair cut short? I hope it doesn't turn out to be Ernst. Only recently I mistook Ernst for Arnold.

More than four years have gone by since the last time I saw them. Ernst, the youngest, was one and a half then; today he is over five. Arnold is entering his teens, and Albert is already fifteen! In another five years three of my children will be adults. In the past I looked forward with pleasure to this period in the lives of my children. Now I feel more and more intensely that I have lost the children forever, not just for the duration of my imprisonment. How are the natural feelings going to begin again after twenty years? Sometimes I fear that if I were to reappear prematurely, it could only disturb the process of growing up. In the course of such brooding I sometimes wonder whether it might not be better if I never went home again. What are they going to do with a sixty-year-old stranger?

November 4, 1949   Still in bed. Again read for five hours today. Brooding. Homesickness. Longing for the family. Pains in chest and around the heart.

Tormented myself for several hours today with the thought that my family has forgotten me and my wife is leaving me. Fantasies? Or in such wild notions is my unconscious responding to fears of facing the family, fears of homecoming?

November 5, 1949   Depression. The will to persevere very feeble.

November 7, 1949   Dream in the afternoon: My wife and I are quarreling. Angrily, she walks some distance away from me in the garden. I follow her. Suddenly only her eyes are there. They are full of tears. Then I hear her voice saying she loves me. I look steadily into her eyes; then I embrace her firmly. I wake up and realize that I have wept for the first time since my father's death.

November 8, 1949 After awakening yesterday, a muted mood that lasted all day long. At the same time a feeling of being freed from the almost unbearable pressure of the last few days. My obsession that I have lost my family has evaporated.

November 18, 1949 For the past few days, during each of the noonday rests, Jack Donaho has brought me a book just published outside. The author is Günter Weisenborn, a playwright who wrote a play on U-boats that I saw in Berlin during my student days. Under Hitler he was sentenced to the penitentiary, and this book, entitled *Memorial*, is a diary of those years. In one passage Weisenborn recalls seeing Hitler, before the outbreak of the war, sitting with his intimates in the Munich Künstlerhaus:

The person whom they called the Führer was this evening playing the good fellow with a look of kindly wonderment in his eyes. When this person spoke a few words, all the paladins sitting around him leaned forward obsequiously, all toward the same point: the despot's mouth with the smudge of a mustache above it. It was as though a warm wind of humility had silently bent those proud stalks, so that I could no longer see anything but the folds of blubber at the napes of the necks of our country's leaders. . . .

Fat-faced Hitler received this wave of servility. He in turn leaned discreetly toward Speer, who sat to his right and occasionally spoke a few politely bored words. The homage that billowed toward Hitler he transmitted to Speer; it was like a relay race of devotion. Speer seemed to be somehow admired, beloved; and it was he who raked in the tributes as if they were so much small change.

Strange to read such observations in this cell. They remind me of the remark my associate Karl Maria Hettlage made after Hitler had paid an evening visit to my studio, that I was Hitler's unrequited love.

It was not pride. Nor was it the effort to keep my distance from Hitler. When I think of it from my present vantage point, it may have been that all my human relationships were marked by aloofness, and that aloofness was perhaps only a variant of shyness. On the other hand, there I was, a young man of thirty being told by everyone that he was building for the millennia—and I felt crushed by the enormous responsibility. I saw myself historically. Probably I would have liked to show Hitler my total veneration; but I was never able to express feelings freely. I could not even in this case, although quite often it seemed to me that he stood high above all the people I knew, probably even above my father, whom I truly revered.

November 20, 1949 Have continued to reflect on the deeper reasons for my reserved attitude toward people. Of course the twelve years in the aura of Hitler's power must have taken from me that spontaneity I surely had at times in my youth. I had better not tell myself that it was only the effect of the great personality and the historic tasks that weighed me down. It was also bondage in the commonest sense of the term, not only in the sublimated, psychological sense. After all, I was entirely dependent on Hitler's whim for achieving my ambitions. Hitler might have called me an architect of genius yesterday, but who could guarantee that he would not be saying tomorrow, "I like Giessler better than Speer"? From 1943 on he probably did actually prefer my Munich rival to me.

Soon after I had received my first major architectural assignments from Hitler, I started occasionally experiencing feelings of anxiety in long tunnels, in planes, or in close rooms. My heart would begin pounding, I would struggle for breath, my diaphragm would feel heavy, and I had the feeling that my blood pressure was rising precipitously. After a few hours such attacks subsided. Anxieties while I enjoyed full freedom and power! Now in my cell I am free of such symptoms.

At the time, I underwent a thorough medical checkup lasting several days. It was undertaken by Professor von Bergmann, the famous Berlin specialist in internal medicine. He could find no organic defects. The complaints vanished without medical treatment after the beginning of the war, when Hitler's interest turned to other matters and I was no longer the focus of his attention, or of his affection either.

Recently I read in Oscar Wilde: "To influence a person is to give him one's own soul. He does not think his natural thoughts or burn with his natural passions. His virtues are not real to him. His sins, if there are such things as sins, are borrowed."

But while reading *The Picture of Dorian Gray* the thought flashed through me: the dandy preserved his good looks by the portrait's taking over all the ugly features. Suppose I am now transferring all my moral ugliness to my autobiographical likeness? Would that be a way to escape alive?

November 22, 1949 I have been on my feet again for the past two weeks. On instructions of the Russian doctor I am supposed to walk for a few minutes every day at intervals of half an hour.

The church towers in the vicinity are just striking 11:00 P.M. The cell light was switched off long ago. But a glow falls on my small drawing board through the large peephole. As I write, all my senses are keyed up to catch the slightest alarm. That is more difficult now, since some of the guards are wearing rubber-soled shoes. The intention is obviously not to disturb our night's rest, but it complicates those four or five hours we have really to ourselves every day. Now, however, the Russian Mushin with his tough leather-soled boots has taken up his post in the corridor. For tonight I can work undisturbed.

To return to *Dorian Gray*, or the borrowed personality: as a result of my meeting with Hitler, something alien to me, something hitherto remote from me, certainly came into my life. I, who was basically a modest fledgling architect without any marked character of his own, suddenly began thinking in surprising terms. I dreamed Hitler's architectural dreams. I thought in nationalistic categories, in imperial dimensions—all things that did not belong to my world. At any rate, since Nuremberg I have convinced myself of this concept of Hitler as the great seducer. But was he really that? Did he lead me away from myself? Yet whatever I may say or write, the complicated feeling of being bound to him persists to the present day. In view of that, might it be more accurate to say that he actually led me to myself? Suppose I take a new look at my conceptions of architecture. I arrive at the following:

The things I wanted to build in the thirties basically came precisely from that refusal to accept modernity that had guided me when I was Tessenow's assistant. It was no accident that neither Gropius nor Miës van der Rohe attracted me as a young architect, but Tessenow, with his feeling for solidarity, simplicity, craftsmanship. Hitler did not lead me away from myself in that respect. My distaste for big cities, for the type of person they produced, and even my incomprehension of the amusements of my fellow students, together with my passion for rowing, hiking, and mountain climbing—all this was part and parcel of the romantic protest against civilization. I regarded Hitler above all as the preserver of the world of the nineteenth century against that disturbing metropolitan world which I feared lay in the future of all of us. Viewed in that light, I might actually have been waiting for Hitler. Moreover— and this justifies him even more—he communicated to me a strength that raised me far above the limits of my potentialities. If this is so, then I cannot say he led me away from myself: on the contrary, through him I first found a heightened identity. I might even pursue the question further to the point of asking whether Hitler—what a curious idea!—is not the reason for my now, in prison, finding still another new identity. Without the experiences and insights I acquired as a result of those years with him, would I ever have learned that all historical grandeur means less than a modest gesture of humaneness; that all the national honor of which we dreamed is insignificant compared to simple readiness to help others? How strangely I find my viewpoints shifting.

November 23, 1949   Today I received a letter from my mother, in which she reminds me that Anneliese Henkell was engaged during the First World War to my uncle Hermann Hommel. If my uncle had married the energetic Anneliese, my mother asks, would her future husband, Joachim von Ribbentrop, ever have become ambassador to London and ultimately foreign minister?

I saw Ribbentrop once when I was seventeen and my parents had taken me along with them to Wiesbaden. He impressed me because he carried an umbrella in spite of the cloudless sky, and held a bowler in his hand. This tall, fair-haired man, who always held his head very high, struck me as arrogant and inaccessible. Up to that time I had seen such almost absurd models of the English gentleman only in humor magazines.

Ribbentrop's undersecretary, Martin Luther, one day told me about a remark made by the foreign secretary's mother-in-law, the wealthy co-owner of the Henkell champagne firm: "Odd that my dumbest son-in-law should have gone the farthest." A few months later Ribbentrop sent Luther to a concentration camp because Luther, doubting his chief's intellectual abilities, had cooked up an intrigue with Himmler to overthrow him. Himmler protected his former cohort and saw that he was given the safe post of librarian in the concentration camp. Such mutually antagonistic Party men as Göring, Rosenberg, Goebbels, and even Bormann would for once agree whenever the talk turned to Ribbentrop. All regarded him as haughty, stupid, a fool who wanted to do everything himself. The foreign minister's much-discussed vanity also became evident to me after I visited his official residence, the former presidential palace, which was rebuilt during the war at great expense. In almost all the public rooms were photographs of Hitler in wide silver frames with long, flattering dedications to Ribbentrop. They stood everywhere: on chests, desks, and buffets. When you examined them more closely, you saw that Ribbentrop had simply had many prints made of the same one.

November 24, 1949   In the corridor today I happened to overhear Dönitz saying that Ribbentrop was the person really responsible for the war, because of his arrogance and his misjudgment of British reactions. As I heard Raeder agree, I recalled a scene that must have taken place in the summer of 1939. On the terrace of the Berghof Hitler was pacing back and forth with one of his military adjutants. The other guests respectfully withdrew to the glassed-in veranda. But in the midst of an animated lecture he was giving to the adjutant, Hitler called to us to join him on the terrace. "They should have listened to Moltke and struck at once," he said, resuming the thread of his thought, "as soon as France recovered her strength after the defeat in 1871. Or else in 1898 and 1899. America was at war with Spain, the French were fighting the English at Fashoda and were at odds with them over the Sudan, and England was having her problems with the Boers in South Africa, so that she would soon have to send her army in there. And what a constellation there was in 1905 also, when Russia was beaten by Japan. The rear in the East no threat, France and England on good terms, it is true, but without Russia no match for the Reich militarily. It's an old principle: 'He who seizes the initiative in war has won more than a battle.' And after all, there was a war on!" Seeing our stunned expressions, Hitler threw in almost irritably, "There is always a war on. The Kaiser hesitated too long."

Such epigrams usually transported Ribbentrop into a state of high excitement. At these moments it was easy to see that he alone among us thought he was tracking down, along with Hitler, the innermost secrets of political action. This time, too, he expressed his agreement with Hitler with that characteristic compound of subservience and the hauteur of an experienced traveler whose knowledge of foreign ways still made an impression on Hitler. Ribbentrop's guilt, that is, did not consist in his having made a policy of war on his own. Rather, he was to blame for using his authority as a supposed cosmopolite to corroborate Hitler's provincial ideas. The war itself was first and last Hitler's idea and work.

"That is exactly what neither the Kaiser nor the Kaiser's politicians ever really understood," Ribbentrop was loudly explaining to everyone. "There's always a war on. The difference is only whether the guns are firing or not. There's war in peacetime too. Anyone who has not realized that cannot make foreign policy."

Hitler threw his foreign minister a look of something close to gratitude. "Yes, Ribbentrop," he said, "yes!" He was visibly moved by having someone in this group who really understood him. "When the time comes that I am no longer here, people must keep that in mind. Absolutely." And then, as though carried away by his insight into the nature of the historical process, he went on: "Whoever succeeds me must be sure to have an opening for a new war. We never want a static situation where that sort of thing hangs in doubt. In future peace treaties we must therefore always leave open a few questions that will provide a pretext. Think of Rome and Carthage, for instance. A new war was always built right into every peace treaty. That's Rome for you! That's statesmanship." Pleased with himself, Hitler twisted from side to side, looking challengingly around the attentive, respectful circle. He was obviously enjoying the vision of himself beside the statesmen of ancient Rome. When he occasionally compared Ribbentrop with Bismarck—a comparison I myself sometimes heard him make—he was implying that he himself soared high above the level of bourgeois nationalistic policy. He saw himself in the dimensions of world history. And so did we.

We went to the veranda. Abruptly, as was his way, he began talking about something altogether banal. For months Zoshchenko's book, *Sleep Faster, Comrade,* had been a topic of conversation at the Berghof. Hitler repeatedly related episodes from it until he became choked with laughter. Bormann was ordered to send a chauffeur to Munich to buy a copy of the book for each one of us. I never found out which he appreciated more, Zoshchenko's humor or his criticism of the Soviet Union. At the time I probably didn't give the matter much thought.

This evening I've had my first cognac in more than four years. Given me by Jack Donaho. Just a small glass. But the consequences were devastating. Unsteady legs, giddiness. I lay down on the bed. At the same time I had some difficulty repressing the impulse to sing or whistle. After an hour I got up again. In the flush of having mastered my unsteadiness, I went over to Hess. He only said, "What's the matter with you?"

November 25, 1949   To go on with yesterday's entry: When the war began a few months later, the war that had loomed behind these conversations all through the summer and autumn months of 1939, the pressure on me was relieved, and not just in a psychological sense. I became steadily freer physically also. Now adjutants and generals formed Hitler's entourage, and I was able to lead a private life again for the first time in years. Without Hitler, I drove to Obersalzberg with the family in my BMW, painted wartime gray. Meanwhile my office improved and refined building plans and perfected the wooden models.

It seemed to all of us that with every passing month we were almost effortlessly drawing nearer to the reason for the arches of triumph and the avenues of glory. The Great Hall and the Berlin Palace of the Führer suddenly acquired a real background: the victories in Poland and Norway, the conquest of France. In the crypt of the Soldiers' Hall innumerable places were reserved for the sarcophagi of the commanders of these campaigns.

How merrily we headed for catastrophe! Hans Stephan, one of my closest associates, drew a series of caricatures. One of them shows, in the midst of gigantic temples, a small weekend cottage that has been left over, a last vestige of an idyllic past. Mounds of rubble, vast excavations, and pile drivers show what awaits the people of Berlin when the work begins. A hapless group of pedestrians is led by police across the new grand avenue, down which the traffic roars forty cars abreast. A gigantic crane intended to pick up a huge drum for a column in the portico of the Great Hall picks up the Reichstag building by mistake. The eagle on the globe of the world crowning the dome twists its excessively long neck to look three hundred meters down to the ground. It calls on a kestrel flying by to find out what those renewed shouts of *"Heil"* below the cloud cover are all about. Heavy howitzers are firing in order to raze the apartment houses that stand in the path of the grand boulevard. Two years later that job was done for us by Allied bombers.

November 28, 1949   Gloomy November weather; Spandau is thickly veiled in mist. Depression. For hours I have been trying to force myself to write, but apathy paralyzes me.

December 3, 1949   Today I learned from Pease that more than a year ago Frau Schirach broke with her husband and has entered on a new relationship. But after all, theirs was a marriage in which she was partly after his power and he was partly after her money. The children are supposed to have taken their father's side. It's a sign of my isolation from the other prisoners that I first hear about this from a guard.

Pease simultaneously hands me a letter that has come through official prison channels. It informs me that Arno Breker sends his regards. Evidently things have worked out better for him than for me. The last time I saw him was in Paris in 1941, before I was appointed minister of armaments. We used to meet in a famous restaurant in Bougival on the Seine, and were served by Maître François like old friends. We sat in the sunshine, a loose group of Germans and Frenchmen, on the terraces of a garden laid out on the side of a hill: German officers and French artists, industrialists, aristocrats. A few eccentric Americans were included. Here there was nothing to recall war, enmity, the Resistance.

After these dinners we sometimes went up to the small top-floor apartment of Alfred Cortot and sat on rolled-up rugs because there were not enough chairs. Cortot played Chopin or Debussy. I shall never forget his playing of *La Cathédrale engloutie*.

How different were the official functions for Breker and me which were arranged by Otto Abetz, the German ambassador to Paris, and his French wife. There the French artists gave the impression of being tight-lipped and constrained. Perhaps this was because these were parties given by the victor. At any rate, in small groups and when they felt they were not under surveillance, they were cordial and open. At the embassy functions they were awkward. Cocteau showed none of his charm and wit; fragile Despiau sat glumly in a corner of a sofa under a huge tapestry; Vlaminck, a sensitive giant of a man, stood around scarcely opening his mouth; Derain talked with French colleagues; Maillol seemed embarrassed; and Cortot, too, was visibly constrained. Even the city planner Greber, who in 1937 had given me friendly assistance in building the pavilion for the Paris World's Fair, did not say a word in response to my offer to help him.

December 25, 1949   Pleasure at gifts from home: warm ski socks and a calendar have passed the censorship. Our Christmas dinner was prepared with care. Each of us received a new good dark-brown corduroy suit. To match the Van Dyck brown, I shall order two flannel shirts, a scarf, and warm slippers from home.

December 26, 1949   "We want to be able to nip every uprising in the bud," Hitler commented in 1940 when he looked over the defensibility of his planned Berlin palace. Resolutely he repeated his favorite idea, which in the course of the years had become a kind of obsession: "There will never be another November 1918!" He added, "Those who take to the streets in times of unrest will be smashed. Enemies from the days of the Weimar Republic, whether they are in concentration camps or in their homes, will be shot at once. I'll also settle scores with the Catholics. Within a few days hundreds of thousands will breathe their last. I'd like to show how tough, prompt action can take care of a revolution right at the beginning. All those who are waiting for it will have a surprise." It may be that Ribbentrop was thinking of such remarks when, years later at the Nuremberg trial, he declared that if Hitler had been in power in 1914–18 the war would not have been lost.

December 27, 1949   Today Hess surprised us by declaring that he has once again lost his memory. After all these years he is again asking Schirach, Funk, and me grotesque questions. He maintains that he has never seen our British director, who makes his rounds almost every day. In despair he asks what this stranger is doing here. In the garden he asks me who the Rosenberg is whom Schirach has just been talking about. In order not to offend him, I dutifully tell him. Half an hour later Funk comes over. "Imagine, Hess just asked me who Rosenberg was." I wonder what is prompting Hess to come out with all these old crazy tricks again.

In the evening I have a chance to pay Hess back for his little games. In the library he picks up the memoirs of Schweninger, Bismarck's personal physician. "Who is Bismarck?" he asks with amazing calm. "Don't you know that, Herr Hess? The inventor of the Bismarck herring, of course." Everybody laughs. Hess, insulted, leaves the library cell. Later I go to his cell and apologize.

January 6, 1950   Today in the hall a conversation took place that is characteristic of the general idiocy of prison. The participants were the British guard Long, this time half sober, the medical aide Mees, and I. Off to one side, silent and watching the scene with a studied lack of interest, was the subject of the conversation, Rudolf Hess. Reproachfully, Long holds out to me a tattered shirt and asks, "What is this?"

"A shirt," I inform him.

Slightly irritated, Long replies, "I don't mean that. What kind of shirt?"

I continue to take his questions literally. "A torn shirt."

Long shows signs of uncertainty. "But how did it get into the pail?"

I point out that according to the instructions we received some time back, worn-out clothing is to be thrown into the regular garbage pail.

"But I don't understand that," Long comments. "The pails go down to the cellar and the civilian employees have access to the cellar."

I show my surprise. "But what harm can a torn shirt do among the employees?"

"You don't understand," the guard replies. "It's one of Number Seven's shirts!"

I still don't understand, and look over at Hess. "So what? What is so special about Hess's shirts?"

Long is stunned. "You don't see? Haven't you heard of the things the German generals sold for souvenirs after the war? Not only their medals, their pistol belts, riding boots, epaulettes, even their pocket knives and family photos."

I shake my head. "But a torn shirt—of Hess's." Once again I look across the hall at Hess, who is leaning on a broomstick gazing mutely at us with a certain degree of contempt.

"But of course, no question about it," Long says. "What do you know about souvenirs? Or how crazy people are? Even today a shirt like that is easily worth ten marks, maybe even twelve. And think of what it will be worth in a hundred years!"

I pretend to be convinced. "You're right about that. Then it would certainly bring in a hundred and fifty marks. And there are seven prisoners, three of them with life sentences. Why, that certainly makes—well, say, four hundred shirts. How much will they come to in a hundred years? Just figure it out."

Long begins to beam. Triumphantly, he turns to the medical aide. "Sixty thousand marks! Those shirts are worth sixty thousand marks. And you let them go down to the cellar where the employees can get at them!"

I intervene. "But a medical aide is not responsible for security."

Long is annoyed. "If you empty the pail," he says, continuing to address Mees, "you must also check it. Just think of all the stuff that might be taken out of the prison along with the pails."

Mees shakes his head. "You're right. But I still refuse to check the pails before they go out. Am I supposed to stick my hands in and rummage through them? That's your job if it's anybody's."

Long pondered for a moment. Then he decided: "We'll have to change the routine. All torn and used-up prisoners' clothing will have to be listed. It was a mistake to list only the new clothing. The old stuff is much more important. We'll have to keep books. Every discard must be written down. That's how we'll handle it. I'll take care of whatever's necessary."

Vigorously, Long strides off. But I know that nothing will be done. Long, like the other guards, has become sluggish from years of doing nothing. The operation of a prison almost inevitably demoralizes the guards as well as the guarded.

January 7, 1950   Last year an American eye doctor examined us. Today Donaho showed me an article from the *Saturday Evening Post* in which the doctor reports on his visit in Spandau and comments, "Speer was very different from his fellow-prisoners. He is certainly the most vital of them, but perhaps also the most dangerous." What in the world must go on in the head of a visitor, and a doctor at that, for him to think a prisoner incarcerated for almost five years and tormented by states of depression is "vital" and "dangerous"?

February 14, 1950   Another visit from my wife, for the first time in eight months. One hour! I feel revived and almost happy.

In spite of all the letters, including the smuggled uncensored ones, imagination is always pallid and misleading. An hour sufficed to show that I have been interpreting her letters in far too gloomy, far too anguished a spirit. Probably some of my own bitterness has consistently entered into these letters. For she herself seemed so tranquil and serene that in the future I must keep this impression before me when I write to her. At the beginning of a letter, as before every movement in music, there really ought to be an indication of its character. Something like: "Cheerfully serene, but with grave background," "Somber, but not despairing," "*con moto.*"

A few hours before her visit I asked for needle and thread so that I could sew on a few buttons. After I had threaded the needle and then fetched my coat, I could not find the threaded needle. I searched the surface of the bed, then, a sign that I was beginning to lose my head, foolishly removed the pillow, then the blanket. I took the bed apart, took off my jacket and trousers, examined my underclothes, practically carried out a physical search of my own person. My eyes filled with tears. Exhausted and despairing, I sat down on the bed and saw the needle and thread lying on the floor at my feet.

February 15, 1950   Perhaps I'll postpone my wife's next trip until August; then we'll be able to have three-quarters of an hour. Or to October; then there would even be an hour. With short half-hour visits we are all worked up during the first quarter hour at seeing each other again, and during the second at having to say goodbye.

February 20, 1950   The last four evenings I have had to take Theominal, because my heart is taking leaps. They are extrasystoles which, as a medical paper reports, can be attributed to the monotony of modern life and isolation within mass society. The symptom is common.

My wife brought with her two handsome flannel shirts. How a fine article of clothing intensifies one's sense of self. Formerly I used to take the wheel of my five-liter sports car with the same feeling. Now a shirt does it.

April 1, 1950 This morning I played an April Fool joke on Funk. I told him that the American doctor who just examined us had prescribed half a bottle of champagne every night for me, to combat my poor circulation. I even produced the cork of a champagne bottle, which Funk pensively and nostalgically turned in his hand. "My circulation is much worse than yours!" he exclaimed, and I could hardly keep him from calling for the doctor immediately.

April 6, 1950 Ambassador François-Poncet has requested Director Brésard to ask Neurath and me whether there was anything we wished. "Of course, to be free," was the message I sent back.

April 7, 1950 Today Schirach suddenly exclaimed during the garden work, "Clouds are moving in from the west. We shall probably have rain." His mode of expression struck me—under normal circumstances he presumably would have said, "It's clouding over. Going to rain," or something like that. We all talk a kind of stylized book language. For example, Funk always refers to the sandy soil of Brandenburg as "the good earth." Schirach "dines" when he eats his prison fare. Neurath says that he wants "to linger a moment longer in the spring sunlight." Perhaps this has something to do with the rule of silence, which is still officially imposed. After nearly five years we say only a few sentences a day when Russians are present. For four or five hours books are our intellectual companions.

By now I have read nearly all the books on the Italian Renaissance in the Spandau library. The designs of Delorme and the *noblesse* of, say, the palace of Ancy le Franc make me realize for the first time that something can be great without being massive, and that the impact of precisely this kind of classicism lies in its avoidance of effects. Fundamentally, this restraint of the French early Renaissance makes the fortresslike Florentine palaces seem vulgar. The latter were my ideal during the years in which I designed the Führer's Palace. The development of German art in that era is disappointing. Someone like Wendel Dietterlin, for example, simply does not stand up in comparison with Delorme. In Dietterlin a few elements of classical antiquity are imposed upon a mannered late Gothic. Everything seems picturesque rather than clear; there is no inner freedom. Now, too, I realize where the overornate Renaissance facades of the Heidelberg Schloss, which stands only a few hundred meters from my parents' house, had their origin.

Fundamentally, the Renaissance skirted Germany when it spread from Italy to France and England. Perhaps one of the roots of Hitler's successes may be traced to this failure on Germany's part to participate in humanistic culture.

April 9, 1950   For several weeks Hess has been refusing to get up in the mornings, to wash, to go for his breakfast. He says he is in such pain that he cannot stand it. Several times there have been noisy scenes with the guards in his cell. In response to the shouts of "Get up! Out of bed, out!" Hess could be heard whimpering: "Pain! I can't. I can't go on. Don't you see how I'm suffering? It's terrible!" Now the American doctor has given orders that Hess must get up for an hour in the morning, wash and clean his cell, but that he may then lie down again. I am no longer allowed to bring him his food. Obviously the doctor thinks Hess is malingering. An X ray has shown nothing significant.

April 13, 1950   My birthday package: a pair of pajamas and several cakes of soap. It was delivered to me today after a four-week delay.

April 14, 1950   An American psychiatrist has paid a call. Hess did his best to show that his mind was failing. We others tried to escape as quickly as possible from the obtrusive questions. The doctor spent a half-hour on me. I would be interested in reading his report.

April 17, 1950   Chief guard Terray informs us that the directors have agreed on a change of regulations; from now on all wall decorations are forbidden in the cells. A few family photographs are still permissible.

Depressed, I took down the reproductions of classical art, memories of my real world. I am pained more by this senseless harassment after long imprisonment than by the actual loss.

April 20, 1950   "Herr Speer, I have my memory back!" Hess exclaims as he comes toward me. "Want me to prove it?" Unasked, he bursts out with detailed information on literature and history, referring mostly to matters I know nothing about. Can the psychiatrist have produced this cure?

April 27, 1950 After four weeks of work, have completed the designs for a large country house. I like my second solution best. I am now better at trees; I practiced them in the cell in Nuremberg.

May 26, 1950 To divert myself, during the past few days I have designed a modest home in ranch style for Jack Donaho. A small bungalow corresponding to his modest income. He wants to build somewhere in the southern part of the United States. As relaxation from this small scale, which is really not in my line, I immediately begin sketching a larger house, the kind I would build if someday I should have money again.

By orders of the directors, our British chief guard, Letham, has been made responsible for the garden. He has returned from his vacation back home in Scotland with flowering plants and seeds; his brother runs a nursery there. But we are worried about these improvements. We are afraid the flower beds may prompt the Soviet director to clamp down. He recently declared that all this business of working in the garden was bad for discipline and made guarding us more difficult. He would rather see us again walking round after round every day, ten paces from each other, hands behind our backs, as we did three years ago.

June 1, 1950 Chaplain Casalis, who has cared for us for three years, is going to Strassburg. His sermons have taught me the meaning of faith. He tolerates no halfway measures and is effective because of his total commitment. Perhaps in the future, too, his influence will help me through these Spandau years.

In order to keep from losing my composure during his last sermon, I tried translating his words into French. Afterward we were able to sit down together for half an hour because no Russian was present. Deeply moved, in bidding him goodbye I said with full conviction, "May God preserve your strength."

June 7, 1950 Renewal of the strict ban on eating fruit while we are in the garden. Since I happen to be working in the strawberry beds, the governor sends Mushin to watch me. But at regular intervals the good fellow ostentatiously does a military about-face and shows me his back. I can rely on his remaining in this position until I have eaten my fill of strawberries.

June 18, 1950 My flowers are doing magnificently. I have arranged with Letham that next year, if I am still in Spandau, I shall give a large area over to a flower garden. Letham says he will see to it.

Evening. In a clandestine letter my wife informs me that Heliopolis Verlag in Tübingen, which also publishes Ernst Jünger, got in touch with her on May 25. The house would like to publish my memoirs later on. Along with the letter from Mrs. Knopf, that is the second inquiry! I would not have thought that anyone is still interested in me. I tell my wife to put them off in a pleasant way, without closing the door on future possibilities. Even though I have begun making notes here, I would need three or four years after my release to work them up into book form.

June 22, 1950 A late spring is approaching its end. During these weeks in 1950 the first building phase of the new world capital, "Germania," was to have been completed. When I promised Hitler this deadline in 1939, he spoke enthusiastically about a great world's fair that would be held in the still empty buildings in 1950. In 1939 we had begun on the principal structure, the Great Hall; the clearing of the building site was already going on, and the granite was on order. Several shipyards had received contracts to build special ships to transport the granite blocks from Scandinavia. Today I wonder whether all this was only intended for show, since of course word of this deadline got around among diplomats and intelligence people; and it seemed obvious that even the briefest war would necessarily cross up all our plans. How remote all that is. Another world! When I recall it, I am gripped neither by melancholy nor anger. It is merely alien to me.

June 23, 1950 For me personally, the great change did not take place until February 8, 1942. As Hitler's architect, nothing would have happened to me after a lost war; I would not even have been called up before the German denazification authorities. Probably I would have been just another Breker, a better-known Giessler. No one would have brought an architect to trial. My associates who worked with me on the plans for Berlin are back at work today, so my wife writes; they are doing well as city planners and architects and are even able to help out my family.

July 3, 1950 A large water beetle is moving in the direction of Wannsee. Neurath, Dönitz, Raeder, and I stand around the insect and several times try to make it change direction. After two or three circles it always sets out again on the same course. Talk about animal instinct. We have become animal lovers. I have even forbidden the others to chase mice in my part of the garden.

July 8, 1950   In some of my recent notes, I wrote something to the effect that the world of the grandiose buildings I planned for Hitler had become very remote. But tonight, as I lay sleepless, my thoughts kept turning to those buildings repeatedly. Perhaps bidding goodbye to this whole dream world is harder for me than I am willing to admit. After I awoke I sketched from memory several of the Berlin and Nuremberg buildings. The last things I actually built for Hitler were barracks and shelters—an extensive bungalow project in a small pine forest in Vinnitsa, for example. Several winding walkways suggested a parklike, gardened area. It was all in strange contrast to the miserable villages and the dirty town of Vinnitsa.

One day Hitler had been making fun of the primitiveness of the country's inhabitants, as was his wont. Göring fell in with jokes about using beads in trade with the natives, as if they were African savages. Next morning, an unusually hot and dry day, I set out with a few companions to drive around the countryside and see something of these conditions. But when I entered one of the mud huts, I was offered bread and salt in welcome. In the corner of each of these small houses was an icon decorated with flowers. On that day I was able to drive around the country without an armed escort. Only six months later Hitler's brutality had transformed this world; partisan groups had formed everywhere and were putting up a bitter struggle against us.

July 10, 1950   This morning the tension with Schirach came to an open break. His hostility was kindled over a broom, of all things. Suddenly he snarled at me: "How dare you take my broom! An outrage!" I said I would not stand for his insolent tone. "I'm insolent?" He almost exploded. "Your general arrogance is getting on everyone's nerves here. Don't you notice that?" Now we have stopped greeting each other.

As a matter of fact, a few days ago Funk warned me about his friend Schirach, saying that he was speaking against me to the guards and our fellow prisoners, questioning my ability to keep a secret, and warning everyone against talking with me. And in fact, since then the others have hardly been talking with me. I have drifted from my occasional resolves to maintain strict silence. I don't seem made for that sort of thing, and seize every chance to have a talk with the guards. I find relief even in chatter about trivial matters.

But presumably the quarrel with Schirach will not last long. Spandau is not a place for bearing grudges. Anyhow, we have already enacted quarrel and reconciliation several times. The first occasion was shortly after my appointment as armaments minister, when I flew from Silesia to Vienna to settle some questions in regard to armaments. At that time I sent word to Schirach, then Gauleiter of Vienna, asking him to come to the airport so that during the long ride into the city we could discuss production. But he did not come; he gave my adjutant the message that only heads of state were entitled to be met by a Gauleiter. He would be prepared to see me at any time at his headquarters. For my part I sent word back to him that he could call on me at the Hotel Imperial if he wished.

This bickering over protocol, which was just as childish as our latest dispute, prevented all contact between Schirach and me until the end of 1944. Whenever I came to Vienna on inspection tours, Schirach was allegedly traveling. He sent his deputy to the conferences, and each time I informed him that I would be delighted to receive him in the Hotel Imperial.

At the beginning of the war Schirach was still in Hitler's favor. In the summer of 1942 Hitler is said to have remarked to a small group of intimates that he was expecting great things from Schirach. Possibly Schirach saw in me a rival for power; that would explain his conduct in Vienna.

July 21, 1950   In spite of Schirach's open disapproval, Funk sat down beside me on the garden bench today. We are both listless from the monotonous food of the Russian month. Five steps away from us is a bed of cucumbers. Suddenly Funk says after a pause, "I would like to eat a cucumber. How about you?" I say no. Long pause. Funk sits still until I comment: "This is psychologically interesting. Probably you lack the energy to stand up alone." Funk shakes his head apathetically. "No, that isn't it. But if you would do it, I would ask you to bring me one."

If only to annoy Schirach, who is busying himself nearby, rake in hand, making nervous movements of his arms, I use the occasion to have a good talk with Funk. We go from one thing to another and finally arrive at Hitler's plans for the settlement and development of the conquered eastern territories. We reflect on how that would have kept us occupied for the rest of our lives. It would have been my task to plan and supervise the layout of towns, military bases, highways, and so on. Funk would have had to direct the economic development of the areas. He tells me about Hitler's idea of devising a system of economic exploitation by using differentials in the value of currencies. "I doubt whether the enormous war debts could really have been worked off in this way. Hitler's extensive building programs in the East would have led to tremendous new indebtedness."

Along with the new towns, gigantic cemeteries were to be established, looking like the tumuli of the ancient world, but rising to heights of a hundred meters and more. Wilhelm Kreis, who was also to build the heroes' crypt on my grand avenue in Berlin, had already designed various versions of these so-called "citadels for the dead," and Hitler had approved them. In addition to Himmler's fortress villages, many new towns were to spring up in the vicinity of the existing Russian towns. As models, Hitler would mention Regensburg, Augsburg, Weimar, or Heidelberg. These towns were to be as different as possible from each other. It was perfectly all right for us to copy familiar buildings, so that even in Russia a feeling for the homeland could develop. In antiquity, Hitler would say, no attempt was made to develop new forms of temples for, say, the colonial cities in Sicily. He also wanted to use a great deal of color. He recalled the "Theresian yellow" to be found in any territory where the influence of the Hapsburg monarchy extended, even deep into the wilds of Montenegro. Our own buildings in the Ukraine, in White Russia, and as far as the Urals must always be identifiable as products of German culture.

One day, toward four o'clock in the morning, when all of us were completely worn out and scarcely listening, Hitler came out with the surprising thesis that these towns ought to reproduce the tight, crooked patterns of medieval German cities. It was a grotesque idea, to place huddled Rothenburgs or Dinkelsbühls in the broad Russian plains with their enormous available space. But Hitler could summon up reasons. After all, the towns would be liable to attacks from bandits. The tighter the circumference of the city walls, the better the inhabitants could defend themselves. The density of medieval cities was a direct result of the insecurity and the feuds of those times, he argued, not cultural backwardness.

In the immediate vicinity of these German-style cities Hitler wanted to establish industries. All the raw materials and coal you wanted were available in ample quantities, he pointed out. Armament works also had to be planned for, so that our armies posted on the borders of Asia would have no supply problems.

"Well, Funk," I said, getting up, "all that is only seven years ago. And now I'll get you your cucumber."

Late in the afternoon, in the cell, I recall other items in Hitler's plans for the East. Above all, I realize how concrete and tangible it all must have been for Hitler. He often showed us sketches in which he had, for example, calculated how long it would take a German farmer living on an entailed estate in the southern Ukraine to drive to Berlin. Significantly, Hitler used a Volkswagen as the basis for his calculations; he wanted to build a million of these cars a year after the war. Porsche, at their last conference on tanks, had again assured him that the car would be able to keep up a steady speed of sixty miles an hour, he told me. That meant a farmer from Kiev or Odessa would need about thirty hours to reach Berlin. In every sizable village, Hitler commented on another occasion, there must be a stop that would always have the same name, Gasthof zur Post, as in Bavaria. This proposal was another example of his obsession that the German farmer lost in the expanses of Russia must find way stations where he could feel secure and in a homelike environment.

Illustrating his points with his own sketches, Hitler would sometimes talk to the minister of transportation, Dorpmüller, about a modern railroad system that was to have a track width of no less than four meters. In this way, he said, the trains would have a useful width of six meters; this would allow for really handsome sleeping compartments, virtual bedrooms, on both sides of a central aisle. He decided that the height of the cars would be from four and a half to five meters, so that two-story cars with compartments of two to two and a half meters in height would be possible. These are house measurements; and evidently that is how Hitler conceived the new railroad system for the East. It must be spacious, because whole families would have to live on the trains for days on end. "But we'll make the dining car one story. Then, with six meters in width and thirty meters in length, we'll have a height of five meters. Even in a palace that would make a handsome banquet hall, as Minister Speer here will corroborate." Hitler wanted separate lines for passenger cars and for freight cars; sometimes he wanted to make the lines four-tracked. There were to be two east-west lines across all of Europe, one beginning north at the Urals, the southern line beginning at the Caspian Sea. "That's where we'll be in luck with our colonial empire. The maritime empires needed a fleet; building and maintaining a fleet costs thousands of millions." Even while we were sitting together, Hitler ordered Dorpmüller to start working on the plans and figures at once. He had made a rough estimate, he said, that a freight car of such proportions could move a hundred tons or more. A whole train, therefore, would be able to transport as much cargo as a middle-sized ship, say about three thousand tons. These would be his convoy trains, and no submarines could sink them.

The gray-haired minister of transportation nodded uncertainly. He seemed confused by the assignment.

July 23, 1950 At night I sometimes hear the Russian soldiers loudly calling a few words to one another from tower to tower. They have telephones, but they prefer to shout. Or else they sing melancholy songs, sometimes with one taking the lead.

July 24, 1950 Beaming with pleasure, Pease today told me that a certain Herr Siebenhaar, chairman of the Wittenau Reichsbanner,* had gathered the addresses of twenty-five foreign workers whom I am said to have freed from concentration camp.[1] Forty Berlin workers want to testify to that under oath, and some of the foreigners are also prepared to confirm my having helped them. In the meanwhile old Siebenhaar has died, but his son is going on with these efforts. It is touching; they want to address a petition for my release to the military government.

July 26, 1950 For some time we have been hearing rumors of a disturbing development in Korea. We didn't believe them. But today Jack Donaho brought a newspaper with him. It is much worse than I imagined: open war. Eastern forces rapidly advancing to the south, American troops in flight. Will this spread to Europe?

Our familiar Russian guards were recently changed, perhaps to avoid their being influenced by their Western colleagues, who have found a sort of lifetime job here. The new Russians are unusually friendly. One of them, the Tatar Begmu, gives the impression of being particularly

---

* Social Democratic paramilitary organization of the Weimar period.—*Translators' note.*

[1] According to the record of my conference with Hitler from June 3 to 5, 1944, Point 21 (Ba R 3, 1509), I reported to Hitler concerning an allegation by my office manager, Schieber, dated May 7, 1944 (Ba R 3, 1631) that the SS was proceeding more and more recklessly in removing large numbers of foreign workers from our factories by using trivial infractions as pretexts for arresting them and sending them as delinquents to the SS's own camps. Between thirty and forty thousand workers a month were involved. I demanded that Hitler order these workers returned forthwith to their original factories. Hitler promised to talk with Himmler, but Himmler denied the charge. It is possible that my associates obtained lists of names from some plant and succeeded in getting some of these workers back.

good-natured. *"Kamerad,* what you doing?" was his invariable phrase during the first few days. Perhaps he was assigned to a post in the German Democratic Republic and landed here by some bureaucratic error. But his friendliness persists, even after being told he should not call us "comrade."

Today Corgnol took out his dentures in Begmu's presence. The Tatar shook his head incredulously and looked into Corgnol's mouth to see whether there were any teeth in it. He obviously thinks the whole thing is a joke.

July 28, 1950   When the Russian soldiers in the watchtowers are relieved three days from now, we will breathe a good deal easier, at least for the next three months. Whichever side provides the guard in Spandau possesses the power in the crunch; it can occupy the building overnight. We hear that an English general remarked recently, "Even if the Spandau prisoners were hanged by the Russians, we couldn't do anything. We are not going to start a war on their account."

At any rate they would not be hanging Dönitz and me. He still has a certain interest for them because of his experience in submarine warfare; and in my case, the interest would lie in my experiences with bombing, despite the conditions of the atomic age. Or am I overestimating my value? At any rate, it increases my sense of my own worth to think that a world power could suddenly take an interest in "Number Five."

August 3, 1950   Today I advised my wife to flee if the Russians should start overrunning West Germany. I have asked the American director to give me the means to commit suicide if the Russians should occupy Berlin. Five years ago I made a similar appeal to Justice Jackson when rumor had it that the Nuremberg defendants would be turned over to the Russians. At that time I received no reply.

Just now the noise of children playing gaily is borne in on the wind. Fortunately the wind does not often come from this direction.

September 21, 1950   No entry for six weeks. Disturbed and depressed. What is the use, I keep asking myself, since everything is lost anyhow? This morning a new political sensation: Pease whispered to me that day before yesterday the Western foreign ministers had decided on energetic defense of the Free World. The most exciting part of the news for me: Germany is to be rearmed! Five years after Nuremberg. The moral impulse that resulted from defeating Hitler's empire has almost entirely dissipated.

In the course of the day I was told of this great turning point in policy toward Germany twice more, each guard naturally speaking under seal of silence as far as his fellow guards are concerned!

September 22, 1950 Brooding tonight. I keep asking myself whether my imprisonment will not become much more difficult for me in the future. In a certain sense it has by now lost its moral significance. Will I continue to be incarcerated for fifteen more years for having done things that now, because of Korea, are going to be done again?

September 24, 1950 Tonight I dreamed I was a soldier in a small unit. Suddenly an officer rushed into the room. "Alarm! It's starting tomorrow. War. We're going into action first thing in the morning." Dazed with sleep, I ask the time of the attack. "Five forty-five in the morning." I am reassured; so I can sleep a while yet. Confusingly, my present existence as a prisoner mingles with my dream prison life. In Spandau we are allowed to stay in bed until six o'clock.

September 28, 1950 I ruminate in prisoner fashion—every day brings me closer to death, but there is a pull that opposes this push. And so I have been living for years, or at any rate can imagine it so, in a temporal state of suspension. My future is blocked off from me, but it alone gives meaning to this present life.

Time is flying faster again. The months hasten by. Yesterday, in the garden, it suddenly occurred to me that the fourth year is already approaching its end.

The Fifth Year

October 6, 1950   The Directorate approved a visit of only three-quarters of an hour for my wife, although according to regulations I am entitled to one hour. The Russian director can use his veto right to refuse the accumulation of visiting times.

I have become modest in my hopes: I was happy enough to see my wife even for this briefer time through the double screening. Most of the time we sat facing each other, overwrought and depressed; the minutes passed painfully. Neither of us could pretend to be "natural"; we are not actors.

Pease, ever cheerful, silently beckons me to come to a small observation hole in our iron door. I am able to watch my wife until she disappears through the outer gate. She is in a hurry to get away, and I can share her feeling. But when she said goodbye this time she gave the impression of being somehow more relaxed.

October 7, 1950   The night after the visit restless sleep full of anxieties. Contrary to my advice, my wife insisted on driving through the Russian zone instead of flying. I am afraid something might have happened to her; in one of my half-waking dreams she has even been arrested. But in the morning Terray stands smiling at my door and whispers reassuringly, "A telegram for you." Because telegraphic communication was not provided for in the regulations, I shall never receive it.

October 9, 1950 At night I frequently hear our cock, a sign that I am sleeping poorly. He crows between two and three o'clock in the morning, during the period of greatest silence. Pause. Then, barely audible, I hear another cock answering from far away. For about half an hour they converse at a distance of perhaps one or two kilometers. What links these two cocks? Did they grow up together? There are many others here in the vicinity, but ours obviously is interested only in this other one, which is comparatively remote.

October 14, 1950 Have begun a fourteen-day sleep cure.

I intend to take the next vacation of this type in March and thus give a rhythm to the monotonous course of the year. This, too, is part of my effort to organize my prison life. Schirach and Funk long ago succumbed to the temptation of taking a sleeping pill every night, year in, year out. That seems to be physically dangerous, and psychologically at least short-sighted.

October 22, 1950 In the middle of the sleep cure I already feel intensified vitality. Accumulated nervousness and many other difficulties seem to have evaporated. I feel more enterprising, actually exuberant. Even my dream world has lost its grayness: last night I visited a large Romanesque Norman cathedral, although I had the distinct feeling of being still imprisoned. I meet the archbishop, dressed in his most splendid vestments. We stroll together through glorious rooms. Occasionally we encounter groups of visitors, who greet him deferentially. I am conscious of how this man's authority flatters me. We go up several flights of stairs. Unexpectedly, on the top floor of the tower, I find myself standing on the outer wall on the crumbling ledge of a window. When I become dizzy, I manage to crawl on all fours back inside. We chat amiably about various matters. Finally the archbishop asks me to deliver the festival sermon for Easter. I point out that I am a layman, and a Protestant to boot, but he is not dissuaded. I bring up additional arguments: If I deliver the sermon the Soviet Union will draw highly undesirable conclusions and oppose my premature release. The archbishop is finally swayed by this argument.

October 30, 1950 Monday, washday. Dönitz and Schirach wash our socks in a large cast-iron cauldron. Hess and I do underclothes and bedding in the bathroom, thirty meters distant. The guards, who keep an eye on each other, are divided; one of them must watch the five other prisoners who have remained in the cellblock while one goes with the two of us into the bathroom. This increases opportunities for conversations. The bathroom is the principal depot for news.

Stokes, who is ordinarily taciturn and inaccessible, tells me that the North Koreans are by now in full flight from the American troops. The pursuers, supported by other UN forces, are close to the Yalu, the river that marks the boundary between Korea and China. An amazing turnaround; nothing seems impossible. As I throw our dirty laundry into a vat, absently pour in three times the necessary quantity of soap powder, start the coal fire, and bring the water to a boil, Hess indulges in speculations on the continuance of the offensive, which might be carried on deep into China, he says.

Dönitz asks me to help him carry the iron cauldron back to the bathroom. Halfway there we put the burden down, exhausted. "What do you do with the dirty water when you get there?" I ask Dönitz.

"You're right. Pour it out! Why don't we do it right away in the cellblock?"

November 1, 1950 After three years of vainly searching the cells every day, this afternoon the Russians found something in Schirach's bed: a ball of horse manure, carefully wrapped in paper, presumably from the manure we use in the garden. The guards do not know who permitted himself this joke, but it has stirred up incredible excitement. On orders from chief guard Letham the corpus delicti was placed on the table in an empty cell, the adjacent room double-locked. A small spotlight is directed at the table. In response to Letham's report the British director came hurrying to the scene; the cell was unlocked and the spotlight switched on. Without a word the group contemplated the article; then the director turned to go, and all the rest, confused and indignant, trotted after him. No sooner had the cell door been carefully bolted again than the Russian director appeared, asked a few questions, had the door unlocked again, and wordlessly inspected the offending object on the table. This procedure was repeated twice more, since now the American and French directors have also looked into the matter, if only to satisfy the requirements of protocol. Some time later a decision came down from the Directorate: the horse manure is to be brought to the prison secretariat. Its final resting place remains to be decided. Undoubtedly there will be negotiations on this question at the next meeting of the four directors.

November 2, 1950   A grotesque association. Today, as I was describing the inspection scene in front of the spotlighted ball of horse manure, I inappropriately recalled how Hitler, while inspecting the models for new Berlin, ordered a globe of the world to be placed on the great dome as a support for the gigantic eagle. "It ought to hold the globe in its claws," Hitler said. I feel rather ashamed of this extremely prosaic association. Perhaps it was evoked by the spotlighting, which was used in both cases. Who can say?

November 3, 1950   Recently I copied a passage out of Hermann Hesse's *Steppenwolf* to the effect that every human being, no matter how inconspicuous his social role, ought to make an effort not to increase the tensions that exist among people.

But Spandau! Western guards make stupid remarks after the successes of their side in Korea: "All Russians ought to be killed." Some of my fellow prisoners readily agree. Occasionally I point out to one or the other that they were well on the way to forgetting once more the difference between combating a doctrine and combating a whole people. Now some of them are saying—I heard it repeated once more today—that I am pro-Communist. The views I arrived at during the Nuremberg trial, under the immediate impact of having followed a mistaken course for so long, are beginning to be unfashionable.

November 8, 1950   Funk just came into the cell to tell me that Schirach's wife has obtained a divorce. He was not allowed to see a lawyer, although this is a nonpolitical, civilian-court proceeding. I should think it would have been the business of the prison authorities to provide the proper legal representation for him. Schirach gives the impression of not being overly disturbed. But that can also be self-control. I feel sorry for him.

December 11, 1950   Today I learned for the first time, in a clandestine letter from my former secretary, that the military situation in Korea swung completely around weeks ago. An army of two hundred thousand Chinese has succeeded in totally demoralizing the UN troops under the leadership of the Americans. There has been a rout, and evidently the question of using the atom bomb has come up in this desperate situation. The guards of the Western Powers, who always kept

me informed about the successes of their side, have not told me anything about this.

Lucky that we receive no newspapers. Reading them would upset us
terribly; that was what happened during the trial in Nuremberg. If
only this doesn't lead to war!

December 12, 1950   An Advent wreath is hanging in the chapel.
The third candle has been lit. Last Christmas, through the offices of
Chaplain Casalis, the parishioners of the Church of Saint Nicholas in
Spandau presented us with a richly decorated Christmas tree. Unfortunately, Casalis made the mistake of thanking the people in our name.
The Berlin press took up the incident, garnished it with all kinds of
sentimental foolishness, and in the end the Russian director was so irritated that this year he refused our request for a Christmas tree. But he
finally approved an Advent wreath.

December 20, 1950   For days there has been ugly bickering cen-
tering around Hess. He continually complains about pain that keeps
him from getting up. Recently the guards, allegedly on orders from the
directors, lifted the mattress off the bed—Hess is so emaciated that it
was easy—and simply tipped him wailing onto the floor. There they let
him lie. When I protested to one of the guards against this roughness,
he replied, "We're not allowed to lay hands on the prisoners, are we?"
And he grinned.

December 23, 1950   This morning Hess did not eat his breakfast
in the half-hour provided for it. He claims he has stomach cramps. The
Russian on duty, the inflexible Guryev, orders me to take the food
away. When I refuse, he repeats more sharply, "Take it away." I refuse
again, and so it goes six or seven times back and forth: order and refusal, threat of report and punishment. At last Hess notices and asks
what the fuss is all about. When I explain, he says soothingly, "Oh, go
ahead, take it with you." The conflict is over. Guryev asks with real interest: "Why not take away?" I explain that I do not want to act as the
arm of authority against a comrade. When he hears that, he pauses
thoughtfully for a moment, looks closely at me, and then nods in
agreement.

December 25, 1950   Christmas morning starts off with an argument in Hess's cell. The new, strict chief guard, Kovpak, calls on Hess
to wash. Hess replies in a loud voice that he did so last night. Stokes in-

terjects that a normal person washes three times a day. Hess replies, "I'm normal and I wash only once." The quarrel grows more heated after that, and in between Hess shouts, groans, and begs for sympathy. Finally he lets himself be led to the washroom, but then refuses to fetch his breakfast, saying that Speer will bring it. When he is told that that is against the rules, Hess declares with the hauteur of old times that if that is the case he won't have breakfast.

December 26, 1950   Last night Neurath had a mild attack of angina pectoris. He mentions it in the morning, shrugging. According to the medical aide, the doctors are worried that Neurath may die within hours, that his blood pressure is much too high. But "the old gentleman," as everybody calls him, shows no sign; he remains amiable and calm.

No Christmas spirit, and I prefer it that way. At our Christmas concert on records, by now almost traditional, Wilhelm Kempff plays the great Beethoven Fifth Piano Concerto in E-flat major. I was so moved that I was almost grateful to Long for accompanying the beat of the music with his bunch of keys.

I stood for a long time looking out through the window bars. The Russian rooks, their intense black plumage glistening, were doing artistic aerial maneuvers under a low sky, only a few yards away from my window, then cawing and settling down with a peculiar hopping motion. I could not help thinking of the legendary ravens of ill fortune on Kyffhäuser Mountain.

I have collected leftover bread from our meals. As soon as I appear in the doorway, the leader of the rooks comes up, plumage ruffled in excitement. An old rook with a broken bill follows me from branch to branch; only by remaining close to me will it have a chance to snatch a piece of bread. Hess, with his rather meager sense of humor, calls me a raven maniac.

Gloomily, I brood about the last three Christmases of the war. At the time I thought it my duty to spend the day with the Todt Organization crews; in 1942 on the Biscay coast, where bunkers were being built, in 1943 by the Arctic Ocean in northern Lapland; and the last time on the German-Belgian border. The Ardennes offensive was still going on, and the Todt Organization was assigned to restoring shattered bridges. There were speeches calling for perseverance; there was a Christmas dinner; songs were sung by performers and by the men; but not one of these Christmas carols that we six sang today, on the verge of tears.

How could I, all through those years, never have realized that the workers might be missing carols?

When we celebrated Christmas of 1942 in the vicinity of Bordeaux, I heard from the head of the construction unit during the dinner that a group of former so-called Spanish Reds who were interned in a nearby camp had invited me to their Christmas party. Without an SS escort squad—right up to the end of the war this distinction was accorded only to Dönitz, Bormann, Keitel, Ribbentrop, Funk, and Goebbels, in addition to Hitler and Himmler—I drove over to the camp with a small following. The party had already begun. A Spaniard made a short speech to introduce me; the throng responded with faint applause. Folk dances and other popular offerings followed, each time to stormy applause. The rather stiff attitude toward me relaxed only after I had a sizable supply of cigarettes and wine distributed. These Spaniards, who had fought on the side of the Republic, had fled across the Pyrenees to France at the end of the civil war. By now they had been held behind barbed wire for almost three years. They were people with likable, courageous faces; we sat together until late at night, and there was a note of cordiality in our goodbyes.

Two weeks later I told Hitler about the incident and asked him to authorize preferential treatment for these Spaniards. They hated Franco, who had defeated them, I said, and likewise the French brand of democracy that was keeping them imprisoned. "That's highly interesting," Hitler interrupted eagerly. "Did you hear that, Keitel? You know my opinion of Franco. Two years ago, when we were about to meet, I still thought he was a true leader, but I met a fat little sergeant who couldn't at all grasp my far-reaching plans. We ought to keep these Red Spaniards on the back burner—there are many thousands of them, after all. They're lost to democracy, and to that reactionary crew around Franco too—we have real chances there. I believe you to the letter, Speer, that they were impressive people. I must say, in general, that during the civil war the idealism was not on Franco's side; it was to be found among the Reds. Certainly they pillaged and desecrated, but so did Franco's men, without having any good reason for it—the Reds were working off centuries of hatred for the Catholic Church, which always oppressed the Spanish people. When I think of that I understand a good many things. Franco knows perfectly well why he objected only half a year ago to our employing these Spanish Reds. But one of these days"—Hitler stabbed the air with his finger—"one of these days we'll be able to make use of them. When we call it quits with Franco. Then we'll let them go home. And you'll see what happens

then! The whole thing will start all over again. But with us on the opposite side. I don't give a damn about that. Let him find out what I can
be like!"

Hitler had never been able to bear opposition, and he could not forgive the Spanish dictator for having refused to go along with his plans,
in particular for the occupation of Gibraltar. Personal rancor of this sort
invariably counted for much more with Hitler than ideological agreement. That same day he issued orders to treat the "Spanish Reds" well.

December 31, 1950 In a good mood, Corgnol awakens us at six
o'clock singing, "Martha, Martha, you have vanished," and opens the
door. "*Le dernier jour de l'année!*"

January 1, 1951 At the changing of the guards at eight o'clock
Long appears already drunk for the holiday. When I say I would like
to bring a book over to Hess, he opens my cell door, then locks it
behind me, and refuses to admit that an empty cell need not be locked.
A protracted dispute on that question. Then Long strides to my neighbor's door, the key held out in front of him like a spear. Propping himself against the wall with one hand, he aims at the keyhole several
times. After I have handed the book to Hess, we return to my cell in
the same elaborate fashion, but when we get there he refuses to unlock
the door. Nothing I say can make him change his mind. At last he con-
sents to a compromise: he will allow me to enter Funk's cell. With an
inviting gesture he opens Funk's cell door.

Funk is deeply depressed over the turn of the year, for as a lifer, the
year just past has brought him no closer to freedom. To distract him I
tell him a few episodes from my days as armaments minister—trivial but
entertaining stories such as the time an overly nervous lieutenant
arrested me in the vicinity of Calais. Finally, lured by our gaiety, Hess
drops by: Long forgot to lock his cell door. Eyes glittering, Hess un-
folds an idea for illuminating highways. He has read that highway
lighting has been introduced in America, he says. But of course it is
much too wasteful, like everything in America. In Germany, he thinks,
the expenses can be paid for in a much simpler manner, for all cars
would then not use their headlights. This would save current, he maintains, and the erection and maintenance of the floodlights could easily
be financed out of the money thus saved. I object that the cars' genera-
tors would be running anyhow, to supply current to the spark plugs.
He dismisses that; the generator could shut off automatically as soon as
the battery was charged. Thus energy would be stored, fuel saved, and

this saving could be spent on financing the illumination of highways. Reckoned out for all the cars people would soon have in Germany, that would easily amount to more than the highway lights could cost.

We listen speechless, until at last Funk says ambiguously, "At any rate, Herr Hess, I am glad that you have recovered your health." Hess ponders for a moment, then looks sternly at me and orders me to work out the idea in detail. Whereupon he returns to his cell, pleased with himself.

January 6, 1951   After the noon interval, Long went to Hess's cell and called out in a tone of command, "To the garden!" Hess did not stir. "Come on, come on!" Groaning, Hess said he had just had an attack. "Nothing attack, better garden," Long said unrelentingly, in what he regards as German. Again a long, noisy dispute. Finally chief guard Terray appeared and murmured, "It's lovely in the garden." To the surprise of all of us, Hess went along without further protest.

January 12, 1951   Have I the right to laugh at Hess's fantastic idea? What is funny about it is not only the absurdity of the conception hatched out by his poor cracked brain, but also his firm belief in its practicability, the serious way he instructed me to pursue the matter. And in that, I think, there lies a genuine relic of the past: the conviction that everything is feasible, that reality can be ascribed to even the most crackpot of notions. I still remember vividly the way a swarm of reformers and inventors of projects came crawling out of the woodwork after 1933 and crowded all the anterooms of government. All of them had something to offer on which salvation depended, or at any rate progress. And every so often one of them would manage to win backing from an influential functionary, thus obtaining funds and authorization for his project. Dilettantism flourished, and harmless though many of these crackpots were, a few of them proved to be deadly—those, for instance, who conceived the skull measurement theories, the scientifically worthless experiments on human beings, and a host of other experiments. Himmler was one of the matadors in this arena. But sometimes I wonder whether the building projects for Berlin and other such things don't belong in the same category.

January 13, 1951   Perhaps. Perhaps. But why do my thoughts keep returning to that period? Am I closer to Hess than I think? Or is it only the desire for some pastime that makes me constantly fetch up incidents and scraps of memories from the past and try to set them down in words here? Does any such thing as a simple pastime really exist?

One Sunday, at the beginning of April 1943, we accompanied Hitler into his special train at the Berchtesgaden railroad station. For reasons of safety that train was drawn by two heavy locomotives and had a special armored car with light antiaircraft guns following behind the locomotives. Soldiers all muffled up stood on this car throughout the journey, prepared to use the guns. Then came Hitler's car, the central portion of which formed a large salon. The walls were paneled in rosewood. The concealed illumination, a ring running all around the entire ceiling, threw a bluish light that gave a corpselike look to faces; for that reason the women did not like staying in this room. Of course there was a kitchen, and compartments for Hitler's personal needs: a bedroom, a lavishly equipped bath, wardrobe, anteroom, and servants' room. Attached directly to this car was the "command car," which was provided with multiple means of communication to the outside world. In addition it contained a military map room, and thus could serve as a moving Führer's Headquarters. Immediately after that came the car with Hitler's permanent escort, consisting of more than twenty men. Then came the guest cars, in which this time a compartment was assigned to me; then two first-class sleeping cars, a press car, and a baggage car. A second special car with antiaircraft guns brought up the rear of the train.

When we sat around the big table at breakfast at about six o'clock in the morning, Hitler talked again and again about the new Nivelungen Bridge; it was, he remarked, the realization of a dream of his youth. He wanted to pass judgment on two statues at the southern end of the bridge, done by a sculptor named Count Plettenberg, unknown to me. They showed Siegfried and Kriemhild seated on powerful chargers. Even at some distance Hitler began to rave about the figures: "What a beautiful pose! That musculature—masterful! And the straight, sincere look, the resolute way his hand clasps the sword!" Under the horse's body a dragon writhed. "Wonderful!" Hitler exclaimed. "German art. Look at the details of the horse's head. Plettenberg is an artist of glorious talent." He was a different Hitler. The anxieties about tank production, which he had discussed with me the previous evening, seemed to be swept away. "But consider Kriemhild!" he went on. "Look, what a beautiful body. The count's wife must have modeled for that. The pose, masterful." This half-naked Kriemhild with her five-foot-long pigtails, supposed to suggest modesty, actually had a certain lewd quality.

I whispered to someone standing alongside me that the enormous projecting bosom would prove an ideal nesting place for pigeons. "What was that you said?" Hitler asked with some sharpness. Then he went on. "At the other end of the bridge, over there, Gunther and Brunhild will stand. Plettenberg has already provided ideal sketches for them. Once that is all in place, the cornerstone for Linz as a city of art will have been laid. Do you see how neglected the bank of the Danube looks? I want to see Giessler put a row of buildings over there, one more beautiful than the next. Above all, Linz must have a new museum and a new opera house. With the mountains in the background, its situation is far more beautiful than that of Budapest or Vienna. Over there on the slope of the hill we'll put a stadium; from there everything can be seen at a glance. A first-class orchestra is already available for the opera, St. Florian's; Jochum will make it one of the best orchestras in the world." Although Hitler expatiated on his plans with a grave, indeed rather solemn expression, I did not really have the feeling that this was an adult speaking. For a brief second it seemed to me that all this was nothing but a grandiose game with building blocks. But I quickly repressed that thought. It was after all true that the landscape here was more beautiful than in Vienna or Budapest, further downriver. It was true that Linz gave the impression of being rather sleepy and down-at-heels. And what, after all, was so wrong about the project of transforming his own hometown into a cultural metropolis?

January 14, 1951   The Soviet guards, too, have now been issued rubber-soled shoes. Taradankin, who had iron clamps put on his soles and marched noisily up and down at night, has been replaced. Theoretically, the new shoes have been ordered out of consideration for the prisoners, who until recently were wakened every time the guards made a supervisory round at night. But this supposed solicitude creates difficulties for me, since now I scarcely hear the guards approaching.

January 15, 1951   Added comment on Linz (since I had to send yesterday's away). In addition to the large meeting hall Hitler wanted to build, he thought of constructing a gigantic tower, 160 meters high. He would leave only Ulm Cathedral continuing to enjoy its "record height" of 172 meters. But St. Stefan's in Vienna would at last be surpassed, he commented, and by a considerable amount. I remember Hitler saying, "In this way I will right a wrong that was done to Bishop Rudigier of Linz when he planned a tower for the church of Linz that was to be higher than the steeple of St. Stefan's. At that, an order was sent out from Vienna that the Linz steeple would have to be two meters lower than Vienna's." I think it was on that afternoon that Hitler, under the impact of his own enthusiasm, declared for the first time that someday his sarcophagus would be placed in Linz's new landmark, the highest tower in Austria.

The deep impression that the Capuchin vault of the Austrian emperors in Vienna, the Prussian royal tombs in Potsdam's Garrison Church, and recently the sarcophagus of Napoleon I in the Invalides of Paris had made on Hitler caused his mind to turn repeatedly to his own funeral monument. Initially he had wanted to be buried with the victims of the Putsch of November 9, 1923, in the same kind of iron sarcophagus in the Königsplatz in Munich. It would be a grand gesture, Hitler thought, to rejoin the Party friends of those early days at the end. He was also taken with the idea of being entombed under the open sky. In a fit of romanticism he would say that sunshine, rain, and snow made these coffins one with the eternal forces of nature; or he would mention how moved he always was when he looked out of his study on the Königsplatz and saw the spring sun melting the mantle of snow that covered those sarcophagi. Occasionally Hitler had also spoken of burial in the crypt of the Linz tower. On that day in Linz he evidently contemplated as his last resting place the topmost room in the tower, high above the city. But later he occasionally spoke of a funeral plot of his own in Munich, for which he intended to make sketches.

Amazingly, Hitler never even considered being buried in the capital of the empire he had amassed by conquest; at least, I never heard him voice any such intention during the twelve years. He frequently spoke of his tomb as exerting a political influence upon the nation that must not be underestimated. And in fact, when I listened to him discoursing on this subject, I often had the feeling that his desire for an imposing mausoleum for himself sprang less from the usual appetite for glory than from the same didactic political impulse that made him say he wished to rule the Reich for at least a year from the planned Palace of the Führer in Berlin, in order to give the building its sacramental consecration. At the time it seemed to me that he was thinking selflessly; today I realize that such remarks were the utmost form of self-inflation and historical vanity.

Our destination that day was the Linz Steel Works, where the biggest assembly plant in Germany for our superheavy tanks was located. Since we still had some time left, Hitler drove us through the Linz of his youth. He showed us a hotel near the Danube where Karl May, Hitler still remembered, had lived for almost a year in 1901. After that we drove past the former palace of Baron von Thun, where Mozart had composed the *Linz* Symphony in 1783. At the Landestheater, we got out of the car and entered the large auditorium, which probably dated back to the beginning of the eighteenth century. The place was neglected; the plush upholstery of the seats was torn and tattered, the curtain dust-covered. But Hitler seemed untroubled. With visible emotion he showed us the cheap seat in the top gallery from which he had first seen *Lohengrin, Rienzi,* and other operas, and then indicated by a slight gesture that he wanted to be alone. For some time he gazed dreamily into space, his eyes absent, his features slack. Meanwhile we stood around somewhat embarrassed; nobody dared to move, and it must have been more than five minutes before Hitler returned to reality. "To the courtyard, please," he said, his tone an odd mixture of host and museum guide.

We passed through an arched gateway and stood in the famous Renaissance courtyard of the *Landhaus* with its three-story-high stone arcades. "Here you see what burgher pride and patrician self-assurance could produce four hundred years ago. If you compare little Linz of that period with its three thousand inhabitants with the present-day city and consider its future development, you will admit that my plans for this city are no more lavish than theirs."

We drove a few hundred meters farther on to the so-called National Museum (Landesmuseum). "Built by Bruno Schmitz just fifty years ago," Hitler instructed us. "An important architect, as you know. How often in my youth I made a pilgrimage here to admire this splendor. Just look at this richly ornamented gate. And then this sculptured panel above the main floor. It is more than a hundred meters long. And some people would have us believe that that was a decadent era! That it was really an art of decay. Not at all. I myself had some such effect in mind when I drew the frieze for my arch of triumph after the prison years in Landsberg. Breker's designs for that are excellent, but no better than these here. True, later on I let my taste be changed under the influence of Troost. But now that I see this building again I must say it is still one of the peak achievements of German architecture."

Half an hour later we arrived at the Steel Works, which had been established here only after the annexation of Austria. Guderian, the inspector-general of the tank force, and Gauleiter Eigruber were already waiting for us.

January 16, 1951   Interrupted my account of Linz last night. A few times I thought I heard the sound of rubber soles, and finally became so nervous that I put away the writing materials. In the darkness

I recalled the vehement discussions stirred up by Hitler's plan, conceived as early as 1938, for a gigantic industrial plant near Linz. Göring hailed it in the name of the Four Year Plan, but Todt and especially the city planners were against it. Hitler personally had picked out the building site near the city. He brushed aside all objections about the potential problem of industrial fumes, which would be intensified by the prevailing east winds in the Danube Valley. Dr. Todt pleaded that beautiful old Linz would be transformed into a sooty industrial and proletarian city like Essen, but Hitler ignored the argument. He likewise set aside my objection that the huge plant would block expansion of the city along the Danube, its most valuable terrain from the viewpoint of a city plan. His own arguments were by no means romantic; they were quite sober and mathematical. In the long run, he said, his far-reaching plans for Linz would prove feasible only if the city itself could bear the costs of maintaining the new buildings. With the revenue from taxes on the Hermann Göring Works, the future of Linz would be assured for all time to come.

Partly walking, partly driving in the car, we went through the sprawling plant. Covering some 2500 acres, it was about three times the size of the Krupp Works in Essen. We began with inspection of the rolling mill, then the steel foundry, the steel-forging mill, and other workshops. Hitler watched the finishing work on bodies and turrets for heavy tanks. Pleasantly, he responded to the welcomes of engineers and workers, occasionally exchanging a few words with them or shaking a hand.

When we left the big steel plant, Hitler expressed appreciation of modern steel and glass architecture. "Do you see this facade more than three hundred meters long? How fine the proportions are. What you have here are different requirements from those governing a Party forum. There our Doric style is the expression of the New Order; here, the technical solution is the appropriate thing. But if one of these so-called modern architects comes along and wants to build housing projects or town halls in the factory style, then I say: He doesn't understand a thing. That isn't modern, it's tasteless, and violates the eternal laws of architecture besides. Light, air, and efficiency belong to a place of work; in a town hall I require dignity, and in a residence a sense of shelter that arms me for the harshness of life's struggle. Just imagine, Speer, a Christmas tree in front of a wall of glass. Impossible! Here, as elsewhere, we must consider the variety of life."

From the Steel Works we drove a few kilometers eastward to the

Nibelungen Works, the largest tank manufacturer in our armaments program, to inquire about progress in the building of the seventy-ton Porsche Tiger, with which Hitler intended to initiate the offensive near Kursk a few months later. So convinced was he of the superiority of these tanks that he counted on a few dozen of them to turn the tide in the summer campaign of 1943, and thus win this greatest of all wars. Half an hour later all that was far from his mind, and with the same intensity he discussed with Glassmeier, manager of the Bruckner Orchestra then being founded, the idea of an annual Bruckner Festival after the pattern of Bayreuth. When we returned to the special train after these architectural fantasies, musical dreams, and battlefield visions, he was brought harshly back to reality. An adjutant reported the heaviest air raid so far on Paris. It had been carried out in broad daylight with strong fighter protection; the German air defenses had been largely ineffective.

January 23, 1951   During recent weeks I have read a great deal, pretty much of a hodgepodge: Maupassant, D. H. Lawrence, Gerhart Hauptmann, Theodore Dreiser, Schnitzler, Swift.

But the real profit from this reading is a new idea. I no longer read plays; instead, I go to the theater once a week. I buy tickets, leave my coat in the wardrobe, assemble casts, and enter the lobby with an imaginary program in my hand. When the curtain parts, I enjoy the cool draft from the stage with its fragrance of glue, dust, and papier-mâché. Recently I saw Zuckmayer's *Schinderhannes*; I've put Nestroy's *Einen Jux will er sich machen* on my program for tomorrow.

The fantasy world I set up for myself for a few hours is so perfect that at the end of Zuckmayer's play I very nearly applauded.

March 30, 1951   Dreary conversations about the food, as in every Russian month. A slight change in the menu and we are at once at the mercy of banality. I just made Dönitz angry by relating, in the garden, how at the end of 1939 Hitler used to send his four-motored plane to Posen to bring back Christmas geese. Hitler's pilot, Baur, justified this on the grounds that the almost unused plane occasionally had to make a test flight. The geese were intended for packages Hitler ordered sent to his intimates. A curious mixture of middle-class solicitude and a potentate's lavishness, but Dönitz sees it solely as an impropriety. He became quite agitated, but finally found the way out by refusing to believe my story.

April 2, 1951   Am in the last days of my semiannual vacation, with a sleeping pill every night. But today was full of excitement as a result of a letter from my secretary, Frau Kempf. Paul H. Nitze, who interrogated me intensively about armaments and aerial bombing while I was in Flensburg, and who now holds the important post of Director, Policy Planning Staff, in the State Department, wrote expressing sympathy for my situation in Spandau.

April 4, 1951   This sign of concern is momentous to me, although the letter as a whole only expresses regret that Nitze has no way of being useful to me. What is it about the letter that has so stirred me up for days? Probably the fact that, in the midst of this world of underlings, of guards and directors, a man of my own background and position is speaking to me; a former enemy, moreover, who in this way testifies to his respect. Friendly as many of the guards are, I really enjoy not being "Number Five" for once.

April 5, 1951   As an architect accustomed to reckoning the "cubage" of buildings, I have just roughly estimated that the prison occupied by the seven of us has approximately thirty-eight thousand cubic meters. At present-day prices, the costs of construction would run between seven and eight million marks. My one-seventh therefore corresponds to a small palace whose construction would cost more than a million marks.* Never in my life have I lived so lavishly.

We have three kitchens: one for us, one for the guards, and one for the directors. Waitresses serve the guards and directors their meals; not us, of course, although the newspapers have reported that each of us has three waitresses to serve him. There are secretaries, electricians, furnace men, cleaning women, and laundresses. We ourselves keep our part of the prison clean; we wash our own laundry and fetch our own food. Still and all, two cooks and two medical aides work for us.

Two years ago the Berlin authorities were permitted to trim expenses from an annual 400,000 marks to approximately half that. The number of employees was then reduced from fifty to about thirty. Nevertheless, I estimate that the costs still amount to some 300,000 marks. The expenses for the twenty-four men of the Western guards staff probably come to another 400,000. Then there are repairs on the building, as well as expenses for improvements, for maintenance. Fifteen years hence, when my release will be impending, Spandau will have consumed easily 15 million marks.

* In April 1951 the mark was worth approximately $0.25.—*Translators' note.*

The annual budget for Spandau corresponds approximately to what it used to cost to maintain the Berghof.

April 8, 1951 Afternoons when there is such fine Sunday weather I sit in the garden with Funk. Sometimes Neurath will linger nearby, for Funk is a good storyteller and the Russian director has not turned up in the garden for weeks. Today Funk entertainingly relates the story of Hitler's household steward, Kannenberg. In the winter of 1939 Hitler, along with us, thought up the joke of having this butterball of a man sent a draft order to report to the "Fog Troops." Kannenberg was panic-stricken and began anxiously hanging about Hitler—who repeatedly called our attention to this behavior with surreptitious grins. After some days of this, Kannenberg at last gathered up his courage and approached Hitler with the question: Wasn't there anything that could be done about the order? But Hitler pushed the joke somewhat further. No, he said, he could not make an exception; in this government there was no such thing as favoritism, no privileges; this was National Socialism, no longer the corrupt Republic. Kannenberg's eyes came close to overflowing, but Hitler gloated over the man's despair. Finally Kannenberg offered the argument that his dedication to the Führer's well-being might possibly be more important than one man more or less to operate a smoke-generator at the front. Then Hitler began to laugh, and before his relieved and amazed steward's eyes he tore up the official draft notice.

Neurath, for ten years the German ambassador in Rome and London and foreign minister from 1932 to 1937, is speechless. He can understand neither the joke then nor our amusement today. An aristocrat of the old school, he is shocked. "So that's what was going on? Those were the jokes of the chief of state? If only someone had told me that then! So that's the style in which the Reich was governed and gambled away." Shrugging, he turns away. "Toward me Hitler always showed his proper, statesmanlike side." Grinning, though slightly troubled, we watch him walk off. His now thin, old man's figure departs like the era it embodies.

April 20, 1951 Still at work on this house, which puts me in a wholly euphoric mood. Many months of work. With T square and angles again; drew in details; have completed some twelve sheets on the drawing board. Because of the light I did this work during the noon hours when the weather was fine outside.

April 25, 1951   My wife's visit has once again thrown everything into turmoil. Her presence makes me realize that it was not only I who was sentenced in Nuremberg, but she also. It is hard to say which of us suffers more. For days after such a visit I am in no condition to talk with anyone; I go about alone with myself and my thoughts.

Neurath, too, has had a visit. His aged wife and his daughter came together this time. He comes back totally changed. With difficulty he repressed signs of a heart seizure so that his wife would not have that to worry about also. But he says she noticed everything and was pale as death when she said goodbye. Ordinarily composed, Neurath seems distraught today. He says several times that he has finally given up all hope. Wearily he adds that his wife means to visit again in August. "But by then it will probably be all up with me." He is the first among us to give up. Neurath is seventy-eight years old.

To distract myself, I decided to go to a performance of Kleist's *Amphitryon* this evening. The "script" has been lying on my table for some time. For the duration of the first act the illusion persists. But then it begins to crumble. Everything falls apart. Gretel in the visiting room. I realize that I am no longer turning the pages. Parts of our conversation come back to me. In between, Zeus with Alcmene again. There's no point. I stop. I wonder whether this means that my experiment of escaping to the theater is over.

I ask for a sleeping pill for the night. Without thinking, I swallow it immediately. After half an hour it begins to take effect.

April 28, 1951   The lawn has turned green, the chestnut buds are breaking, yellow and blue pansies I set out only day before yesterday are already in flower. After the fresh air in the garden I sleep well again for the first time in days. The garden work has also done Neurath good. Dönitz helps him. But during the nights he has more and more spells of asthma and anxiety.

Pease comes by with the news that the British would like to remove us from Spandau to the West; there we could be held as internees. But I would prefer short imprisonment under the harsh conditions to a longer one under improved conditions. For the rest, it doesn't matter what he thinks or what I think. Nothing changes.

June 4, 1951   I can now do whatever I please in my part of the garden. In the spring I dug out the ground to a depth of about half a meter, and created a sunken rock garden; using thousands of bricks, I made a series of retaining walls twenty to forty centimeters in height. I brought all the bricks from an unused part of the prison area by wheel-barrow, for the sake of exercise. "What are you going to do with those bricks?" Neurath asked. "This is the first time I've ever seen anyone carting bricks into a garden."

Now when I lie on the grass in the rock garden, as I did this morn-ing, these brick retaining walls look like a small city. Flowers surround me. At the moment several pink and a few blue lupines are blooming. Forty to fifty irises will follow them in a few days. In one corner the ferns have unfurled in fresh greenness. Saxifrage, moss pink, delicate harebells, and montbretias droop over the wall or flank the stone bor-der. Sometimes a flower stalk of the saxifrage thrusts upward, looking like a miniature pine tree sown with tiny white blossoms.

My determination to do something, to make something of my time, has now found a new object. I am sick of always merely observing and writing down and then getting rid of what I have written as fast as pos-sible. Nothing tangible remains; before every beginning there is again the same vacancy. This garden, this ridiculous architecture in bricks, has the priceless advantage of being concretely tangible and still there every single morning.

June 14, 1951   As though he has vinegar on his tongue, Hess stands looking at my rock garden with a sour face. "I can't take any pleasure in it. Flowers remind me of outside!" My fellow gardeners are all for useful plants; radishes, peas, onions, strawberries, and tomatoes grow in their beds. Dönitz has become a specialist on tomatoes. He has tomato vines with forty to fifty fruits hanging from them. He is delighted if one counts them in his presence.

June 18, 1951   Yesterday Pease obtained a lipstick for me so that I could color several green strawberries red. Every morning a new American guard has been eating, with obvious pleasure and before our very eyes, the strawberries that have ripened overnight. Now he stands there spitting and cursing; but when he sees everybody, including his own fellow guards, laughing, he finally joins in.

June 25, 1951   A month ago I planted peas, in groups of three, at depths of seven, fifteen, twenty-five, and forty centimeters, and watered them plentifully. Today I undertake a cautious excavation. Even when the eye was down, the shoot turned in a sharp arc and grew vertically upward. None of the many shoots left the vertical by so much as a few degrees, not even those that germinated at a depth of forty centimeters.

Only one pea at a depth of twenty-five centimeters lost its sense of direction and grew into a confused snarl of thick threads.

In greenhouses, heating cables often keep the temperatures under the roots higher than on the surface. So it cannot be the sun's warmth. A pine tree twenty meters tall growing by a shady cliff in the Black Forest does not grow toward the light, but vertically upward. Gravity, then? It is particularly important for technology, which tries to achieve reactions similar to that of the pea, to investigate such guidance mechanisms.

New experiment. I have dug a pit forty centimeters in depth. At the bottom of it I lay out a row of alternating beans and peas. I close off the side toward the south with a pane of glass. Then I fill in the pit with topsoil. The arrangement is such that the surface of the soil is just as far from the seeds as the pane of glass. Consequently warmth and light operate with equal intensity on both sides. If growth is determined by one of these influences, the peas would have to grow toward the glass. But I am still assuming that the plants have a tendency to oppose the pull of gravity.

August 22, 1951   Once again the peas have grown upward with amazing directional impulse, without reacting to the sunlight offered from the side. Out of thirty peas, eleven have found the long way, forty centimeters, to the surface. Two peas gave up after they had grown twenty centimeters, and several others became impatient with this long distance for growing. About eight centimeters under the surface of the soil they sent out side shoots with formed leaves. But these peas, too, were disciplined enough to abandon these energy-consuming shoots after half a centimeter. What vital energy is displayed in these physical achievements, elaborating from a tiny round pea a tube one to one and a half millimeters in thickness and forty centimeters in length. As I suspected, no such strong biological "instinct" can be ascribed to the beans. Out of six beans, only a single one tried to make its way to the surface, and it too gave up several centimeters before it reached its goal, while the others, obviously confused, sent shoots out in various directions from the seed. What brings about such different behavior in such closely related plants?

September 25, 1951   For weeks I have been so tired in the evenings from garden work that I scarcely have any impulse to write. The garden work is gradually becoming, as Hess disapprovingly observes, an obsession. At first I felt it as a liberation. But now I am sometimes fearful of the trivializing effect of such mechanical activity. If I go in persistently for gardening, I may well become a gardener intellectually and spiritually. Survival in prison is a problem in balance.

My lawyer, Dr. Hans Flächsner, a Berliner small in stature but possessed of remarkable eloquence, explained his idea for a defense as follows: "If you go ahead and declare yourself responsible for everything that happened during those years, you are making yourself out more important than you are and in addition calling an inappropriate degree of attention to yourself. That may mean a death sentence. Why do you yourself insist on saying that you are lost? Leave that to the court."

My discussions with Flächsner in the Nuremberg courthouse took place with the two of us separated by a fine-meshed wire grating and watched constantly by an American soldier. At the bottom left of the wooden frame was a slot through which the lawyer could exchange documents with his client; but all papers had to be received by the soldier first.

I did a great deal of drawing while in my Nuremberg cell. I often drew romantic castles to send to my children.

My only previous acquaintance with such prison cells has been in American movies. Now I have become almost accustomed to mine. I scarcely notice the dirt on the walls by now. Years ago they must once have been green. At that time there was also an overhead electric light, as well as some built-in articles of furniture. All that is left of these are the spackled holes where the wooden pegs were. A cot with a straw mattress stands against the long wall. I use some of my clothing for a pillow. At night I have four American woolen blankets, but no sheets. The long wall by the

cot gleams with greasy dirt from many previous occupants. A washbowl and a cardboard box with a few letters in it stand on a rickety little table. I need no storage room; I have nothing to store. Under the small window run two heating pipes. There I dry my towels. The penetrating odor of an American disinfectant has pursued me through all the camps it has been my lot to pass through. In the toilet, in my underclothes, in the water with which I wash the floor every morning—everywhere is that sweetish smell, pungent and medicinal.

Our life in Spandau is flowing smoothly. Things were a bit improvised for a while because they were still working out the administrative patterns. Every month there is a change of the occupation troops posted in the towers around the prison and at the gate. First the Russians take over, then the Americans, then the British, and

finally the French. As far as we are concerned, the only change is the food. With each change of regime, the director of the group in charge assumes the chairmanship in the conferences among the Big Four. But that hardly makes any difference, since the Soviet director, even when he is not chairman, can at any time say *nyet* or personally intervene.

The soldiers are kept in pace with a rhythmic "Hup, hup, hup!" An order of right or left is given at each turn in the path, as though grown men, merely because they are wearing uniforms, can no longer tell for themselves which way a path turns. How odd the soldier's world is. The British, too, do things the same rigid way. This rigidity is usually termed, slightingly, Prussian. The French, on the other hand, come along in loose groups, as if on a family outing. The Russians show up in good order, but without any fuss.

A word from the sergeant; the relief proceeds. The relieved soldier cracks a joke; the sergeant and the enlisted men laugh softly. To my surprise I note that the Russian guards greet their superior officer, the very strict director, who holds the rank of major, by shaking hands as if he were an equal. The French have a similar unforced relationship with their superiors. The Anglo-Saxon guards, on the other hand, return terse replies to their director. I repeatedly hear that snappy "Yes, sir!"

As an architect accustomed to reckoning the "cubage" of buildings, I have just roughly estimated that the prison occupied by the seven of us has approximately thirty-eight thousand cubic meters. My one-seventh therefore corresponds to a small palace whose construction would cost more than a million marks. Never in my life have I lived so lavishly.

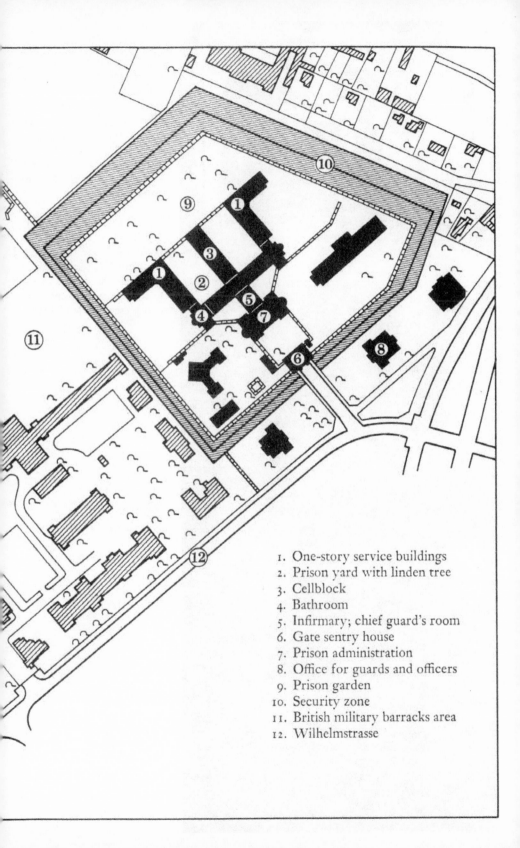

1. One-story service buildings
2. Prison yard with linden tree
3. Cellblock
4. Bathroom
5. Infirmary; chief guard's room
6. Gate sentry house
7. Prison administration
8. Office for guards and officers
9. Prison garden
10. Security zone
11. British military barracks area
12. Wilhelmstrasse

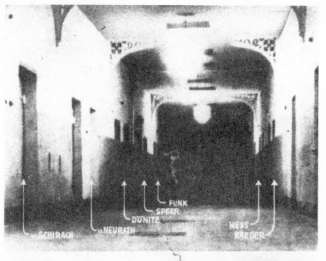

SCHIRACH   v.NEURATH   DÖNITZ   SPEER   FUNK   HESS   RAEDER

The "hall" is 75 meters long and 5 meters wide, really a cell corridor. Before we moved in, a false ceiling of fiberboard was installed, concealing the many-storied shaft with its square of iron walkways usual to prisons. On each side of the hall are sixteen cells.

Every morning at six there is a knock at the door. This is the signal for getting up. I do it quickly, for a few minutes later the door is opened, to the accompaniment of the ever-present rattle of keys.

By pressing on the button installed in every cell, we can activate the red disk in the corridor. This is the way we summon the guards.

My cell is 3 meters long and 2.7 meters wide. These measurements would be just about doubled if I counted the thickness of the walls. It is also 4 meters high, so that it does not seem so poky. As in Nuremberg, the glass of the window has been replaced by cloudy, brownish celluloid. But when I stand on

my plain wooden stool and open the transom of the window, I see the top of an old acacia through the stout iron bars, and at night the stars.

As in Nuremberg, the iron cell door has a square opening at eye level. The cell is poorly illuminated at night by a light placed outside. Usually the door is double-locked and barred. If someone forgets, I feel oddly uncomfortable.

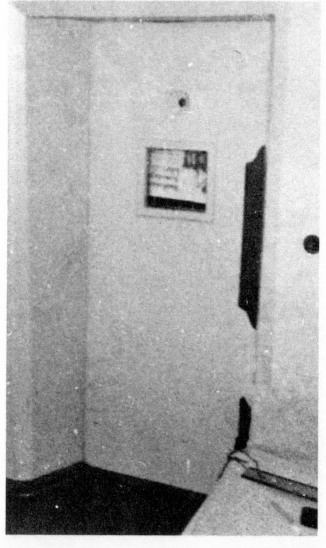

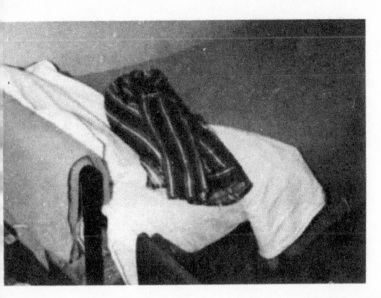

The bed is a black iron cot 1.90 meters long and only .79 meters wide.

By day I change the bed into a couch by spreading a blanket over the mattress.

I draw myself with the blankets wrapped tightly around me, all available underwear around my feet. The cell is an icehouse.

Unlike the beds in Nuremberg, the bed has a headrest, pillow, mattress cover, and sheets.

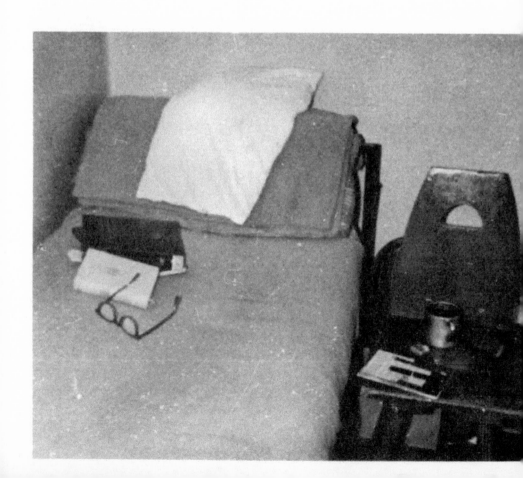

As a substitute for a closet, a small open cupboard .43 by .54 meters hangs in the cell. I keep soap and other paraphernalia on its shelves. My jacket, coat, and towels hang from hooks.

My reading: *Frederick II*, by Kantorowicz, and Cocteau's *Les Parents terribles*.

The top of the table in the cell is .48 meters wide by .81 meters long. The dirty brown varnish is flaking off and the grain of the wood is visible: signs of wear by generations of prisoners.

I cannot pretend to myself: I have been deformed. Granted, my judges sentenced me to only twenty years' imprisonment to make it plain that I did not deserve a life sentence. But in reality they have physically and mentally destroyed me. I'll be an eccentric, fixed on peculiar ideas, pursuing old dreams.

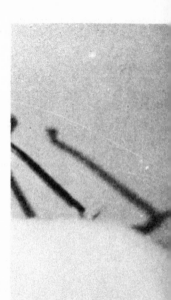

My possessions usually lie on the table: photos, books, and letters.

I have already worked on the memoirs for days. Every morning after dusting the cell I put on a sweater, pull a woolen nightcap over my head, heat up my mind with a big pipe, and open the window vent to provide a

supply of oxygen. At my noon writing session, I have the big manual of construction resting on my drawn-up knees. In this way what I am doing is shielded from inquisitive observers.

29 August 1957

AP/M(57)35.

MINUTES

of the 583rd Meeting of the Allied Prison Directors, held on
29 August 1957.

	Major	SPEIRS	USA	—	Chairman
	Lt.Col.	VICKERS	UK		
	Admin.	FARION	FR		
	Lt.Col.	MAKARITSHEV	USSR		

1. CONFIRMATION AND SIGNATURE OF THE MINUTES OF THE 582ND DIRECTORS'
   MEETING OF 22 AUGUST 1957.

   All the Directors approved and signed the minutes of the 582nd
   meeting.

2. RECAPITULATION OF EXPENDITURES OF THE MONTH OF AUGUST 1957.

   The Directors approved the statement of prison expenditures as
   submitted by the French Director.

3. OTHER BUSINESS.

   (A) EXERCISE HOURS FOR THE PRISONERS.

   The Directors decided that effective 30 August 1957,
   because of the shorter daylight hours, that the prisoners
   would work in the garden from 16.20 hours to 16.50 hours and
   exercise outdoors from 17.45 hours to 19.00 hours.

   (B) DISCHARGE OF WAITRESS.

   The Directors decided to terminate the employment of
   Frau ECKARDT, effective 7 September 1957.

4. DATE OF NEXT MEETING.

   The next meeting will be held at Thursday, 5 September 1957,
   at 11.30 hours.

USA	UK	FR	USSR
Major Speirs	Lt.Col.Vickers	Admin.Farion	Lt.Col.Makaritshev

The Spandau directors ordinarily held a meeting once a week. Detailed minutes of these meetings were prepared.

In spite of all the sedatives I have been receiving for days, today I lost my self-control during the British doctor's visit. I said he was violating

The prisoner was in a highly emotional state this morning. He complained bitterly that he had been moved back from his sickroom to the cell too soon and that, as a sick man, he ~~had bi~~ was being unjustly punished. His emotional state was such that he was beyond reason.

Later in the day he had quieted down considerably, apologising for his outburst in the morning and complaining merely of lack of sleep, of worry and of palpitations.

The impression gained was that he has an acute depressive anxiety state and that more than usual care be taken to see that he can in no way injure himself.

Rather quieter this morning.

To have 1) Tablet Clearanne T b.d.
2) ~~Herabutala~~
Medenal gr X nocte for 3 nights.

The prisoner must not be left to take these tablets himself. They must be given to him and he must be seen to swallow them. If he were able to collect them and take a great many together it would be a simple way of ~~committing~~ suicide.

To have porridge at night.

Make copy for Chief Warder ook

Tablets must be given to a warder or in his presence

his obligations as a physician; he had sent a sick man back to the cell. My psychic state seemed to alarm him more than my physical condition.

At any rate, henceforth I am allowed to take the tablets he prescribed for the next few days only under supervision.

As if turned to stone, Dönitz often stares into space for long intervals.

Now we spend many hours every day in a garden of between five and six thousand square meters in area. There are many old nut trees and tall lilac bushes.

With the passage of time the seven of us are becoming increasingly cranky and headstrong. Contacts among us have frozen into their early patterns; new friendships have not formed. Funk and Schirach were always close; today they are an inseparable pair, constantly quarreling and making up. Their interests lie chiefly in literature and music. Systematically, they inform each other about their reading, pick out quotations, exchange

opinions. Raeder and Funk love to talk about their mutual ailments. Hess and I have been classed as solitaries. Schirach, Raeder, and Dönitz are distinctly cool toward me, although they occasionally find a few words to say to me. They disapprove of my consistent and basic rejection of the Third Reich. Hess, on the other hand, is so eccentric that no one can get close to him. But I have a degree of sympathy for his oddities and even some liking for him; his response is prickly. Neurath remains even in this environment a nobleman of the old school, always amiable, helpful, modest. He never complains. That gives him a certain dignity and an authority which, however, he never exploits.

Among us are passive types who pass the time by endless talking. Among these are Funk, Schirach, and—a taciturn and ab-

surd variant of the type—Hess. The active types who go to pieces without occupation are Raeder, Neurath, Dönitz, and I. We have at any rate got rid of titles. Raeder is no longer the grand admiral and Neurath no longer foreign minister. But from fear of going downhill, we are careful to maintain a certain degree of formal manners among ourselves.

The garden is choked with weeds growing waist high; no one has taken care of the grounds since the war. The weeds will come right back, because the French prison director insists on having them dug in as green ma- nure. Spandau Prison is situated in the extreme western part of Berlin, on the edge of the woods and lakes. The life here is healthier than in Nuremberg, and the six hours of work are doing me a great deal of good.

We are assigned a schedule. Monday is washday. Dönitz and Schirach in the cell-block wash our socks in a large cast-iron cauldron. Hess and I do underclothes and bedding in the bathroom, thirty meters distant. Then the washing is hung out in the garden.

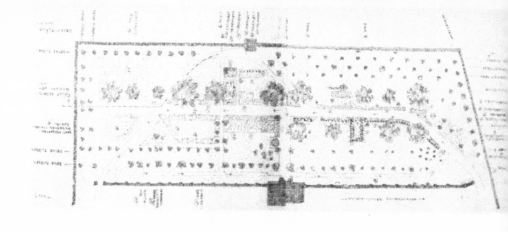

About two years ago, in response to Cuthill's invitation, I systematically set about landscaping our garden, making a park of it. I graded uneven ground into interesting terraces, sowed lawns, planted forsythia, lavender, hydrangea bushes, and roses. In addition I set out twenty-five lilacs of my own raising. Along the paths I have laid out beds of iris two and a half meters wide and fifty meters long. Today seedling pines, birches, and lindens were delivered. With such a wealth of plant materials I can begin to lay out a landscape garden.

In beautiful sunshine and with a fresh breeze from the Wannsee, I took a Sunday walk of several hours. I calculated that I had covered the last kilometers to Vienna and was looking down on the city lying before me from the top of the Kahlenberg.

By steadily increasing the distance I do each day, I have made up for those weeks of confinement to my bed during the winter. My record for one day so far is 24.7 kilometers, my best pace 5.8 kilometers per hour.

For three months I worked
on a drawing. Two pillars
of a collapsed temple that
is Greek in spirit; in front
of it a woman, bowed in
mourning. The sun has just
risen and already illuminates
the capitals. Soon its light
will strike the ruins; the
woman will straighten up
after being crouched over
all night. The drawing
was intended for my
mother's birthday.

Have sat for a month over
an extremely detailed drawing that tries to say: The
destroyed life work must
not be allowed to become
the end of all hopes. A
wooden barracks symbolizes
my new standards. The
columns of the portico of
the Great Hall were
thirty meters high. I show
them as ruins.

I fetched out again the
drawing in which I ex-
pressed my anxiety and
loneliness during my sec-
ond year in Spandau: the
man lost on the icy peak
of a three-thousand-meter
mountain, surrounded by
absolute silence.

The Sixth Year

November 23, 1951   A two-month writing gap, including four weeks of "vacation." Meanwhile the Western Powers have declared that the state of war with Germany is ended. Soon there will be German soldiers again.

November 25, 1951   In my official prison letter today I asked my daughters to knit me a pair of wristlets and a Balaclava helmet for Christmas. The cap should be a cylinder thirty-five centimeters long and sixty centimeters around, with an opening for the face. I've worn something similar on my ski tours.

December 4, 1951   A family letter was withheld from me because I failed to obey a work order from the French director. Nobody but Major Brésard takes this punishment seriously. I am only annoyed because I find it hard to act as if I were indifferent. It costs too much in nervous energy.

December 5, 1951   Saw an article in the *Revue* but was so hurried that I could read only part of it. It was two and a half months old, for even the guards kept this article a secret from us—which also saved us from bothersome questions. An account of our life in Spandau is given, with many distortions. Neurath and I agreed that such polemical articles are bound to deter the Western Powers from urging our early release. The Schirach, Funk, and Dönitz group, on the other hand, seem very pleased. From small signs I conclude that the material for the article was supplied by Funk. Probably he too has a channel to the outside at his disposal; in general it may be assumed that each of the prisoners by now has an illegal means of communication available.

December 6, 1951   Last night in bed I read an issue of the *Revue*. The series is entitled "Behind the Walls of Spandau." The author is Jürgen Thorwald; he claims to have learned that I have not yet been crushed by prison, and continues:

He still believes in himself and in some kind of mission for himself, the nature of which still lies hidden in the future. He still refuses to acknowledge that his life and his undeniable abilities are finished. Alone among the prisoners he fights with all the resources of his lively mind, with his self-control and his wealth of inspiration, to break through the walls of ignorance that surround him. Unshakably, with iron perseverance, he works to preserve his health, running in the yard, working strenuously in his rock garden, alone among the prisoners exposing his body to air and sun at every opportunity during his gardening. Similarly he fights not to lose touch with reality. If he became a half-crazed recluse, he says, he would no longer have a chance.

I read these sentences with mixed feelings.

This article causes the new American guard to decide that I am the most dangerous prisoner. "If we release you, they'll put you right to work rearming Germany. The generals are already all back." But he does not say this maliciously, rather with interest, and basically with respect. It flatters his vanity to be guarding so important a prisoner.

December 9, 1951   This morning I poured a pitcher of warm water into the washbasin and watched absently as it vanished down the drain. This kind of slip has become more frequent of late. A sense of uneasiness.

December 10, 1951   As I have just read in Gaxotte, during the French Revolution the minister of war, Carnot, so swiftly and successfully organized the arming and training of the French army that the young Republic was able to overwhelm the superior Austro-Prussian alliance at Valmy in 1792. Lazare Carnot was, like me, a "licensed engineer"; that is, he too belonged to the guild of technicians and employed chiefly technicians. He demanded and obtained a pledge from the political chiefs of the Revolution that his associates would be protected from harassment by revolutionary zealots. Amazing parallels.

December 11, 1951　Dönitz hopes to be free shortly. A German army cannot be organized, he says, as long as our new allies are holding high-ranking officers in Spandau. He is already discussing with us what he should tell his lawyer about conditions here. Funk, on the other hand, believes in astrological reports that predict that our imprisonment will come to an end next year. Even Western directors and guards give Spandau another two or three years at most. By then Western rearmament will be completed, they say, and then something can also be done about this delicate subject. That is how I see it, too. Actually every day is too much for me, but I must be on my guard against losing my nerve now.

On the other hand the Soviet director, a major, is supposed to have said, so I heard yesterday: "Nobody is getting out of here until he's done time to the last day of his sentence or dies."

December 15, 1951　Perhaps there is a connection between the Russian director's statement and the nasty dream I have had. I am on the tenth floor of a hotel. Splendid view of the sea. Below me a deserted bathing beach. The emerald-green ocean contrasts strongly with intensely yellow sand. A heavy swell. Then my room begins to rock. For a moment the horizon slants. Again a violent rocking motion, but I cannot make out whether it is the horizon or the position of the room that is shifting. After more violent earth tremors, however, the building quite obviously is tilting more and more to the side. The floor slants so steeply that I began to slide. A thunderclap; then everything is dark. The building collapses; I slide faster and faster down a steep track and at last come to a stop on a heap of rubble and dust. Parts of walls and beams thump down alongside me.

In the morning I ask Pease, "Did anything happen last night?" He looks at me in surprise. "Yes, as a matter of fact. Roques fell asleep on his chair, slid off it, and landed on the floor. Did you wake up?"

December 25, 1951　On Christmas Day Wagg and Roulet smuggle in whisky and Chianti—unfortunately at six o'clock in the morning.

We have to drink on empty stomachs, but must not attract attention by being overly cheerful. It gets rather difficult later on when the British prison director, Colonel Le Cornu, pays us a visit. Worried that we may smell of alcohol, we answer all his questions with bowed heads. He concludes that we are especially emotional about Christmas, and in turn becomes very moved himself. He is very diffident about making his requests.

January 1, 1952   A New Year's walk in the afternoon. Always the same: Dönitz walks with Neurath, Schirach with Raeder and Funk. Hess remains for me. I am depressed, and perhaps it is wrong to be drawing up a kind of preliminary balance now. But the temptation to do so is very great on such days. The thought that now the eighth calendar year has began can only be taken with composure if one is in a state of complete apathy. When I consider what I have done in these years, almost a decade of this short life, I realize that all my efforts, all my interest, was directed less to the present than to the past and the future. It has all along been confrontation with the former, preparation for the latter. But preparation for what, really? Whether I learned languages, read books, studied professional journals, exercised—I have always been persuading myself that I must hold out, must not let go. That it was vital to return to real life physically and psychically unimpaired. But isn't this here my real life? Everything points to my staying in Spandau for the remaining fifteen years. Why am I trying to fool myself? I shall leave this prison an old man. What's all this about a new beginning? And then, the children will be out of the house and the family in which I live in my imagination will long since have scattered to the four winds. In my thoughts I go mountain climbing, river boating, undertake strenuous travels. But by the time I come out I'll have gout and a walk of any length will be too much for me. An old man out of days long past turns up again, an embarrassment to neighbors and friends. Anything else is self-deception. I am acting as though a life still lies before me and this is only an interlude. But this cell, that wretched rock garden, my bean experiments and jokes with the guards, are all that is left to me. Beyond that what awaits me is merely a kind of epilogue.

January 3, 1952   Still absorbed in the thoughts of New Year's Day. Trying to understand all their implications. Strictly speaking, my life ended in May 1945. In Nuremberg I pronounced my obituary. That's it.

January 12, 1952 Albert and Hilde went to their first party. They stayed until four o'clock in the morning. Their letter is overflowing with happiness and feelings of anticipation. For them, life still stretches ahead.

February 8, 1952 Since I have no paper I am writing on a page of the calendar that hangs in the cell. In this way the directors unwittingly supply us with writing paper, although otherwise each piece of paper provided us is painstakingly noted.

After washing, Funk talks about a prediction that this year a great statesman will die, whom the Western world will mourn, and another whose death it will joyfully hail. "Two days ago," he concluded, "the king of England's death was mourned." Thereupon Hess says darkly, "Then I will die soon."

February 20, 1952 News has come that Bonn has approved a German contribution of troops for defense. Funk triumphantly declares that now, after seven years, exactly what the Führer prophetically foresaw in the last months of the war has actually happened: that the "unnatural alliance" between West and East would shatter and some day Germans would fight on the side of the Americans and British against the Russians. When I point out to him that the prediction is coming true only in part, since the other half of Germany would probably fight with the Russians against the Western Powers, he is taken aback, gives me an angry look, and stalks off without another word.

February 22, 1952 As though the Russian director means to make it plain that he wants no traffic with the Allies in prison, he has recently taken to appearing in the garden much more often. He forbids talking and demands that we take our walks singly. In addition he insists that the light in the cells not be turned out until ten o'clock at night, even if a prisoner would like to go to sleep earlier. Yesterday there was a violent dispute about that in the presence of the prisoners. The Western Powers, whom Funk has recently taken to calling ironically our "allies," have opposed him with great determination. The British alone maneuver more cautiously.

Kovpak, the Russian chief guard, has made a motion for punishment because Dönitz talked with Neurath.

February 25, 1952 Out of nine hundred applicants, Hilde has been chosen by the American Field Service to go to America as a guest pupil for a year. She will live with a family. Should I have her come for a fifteen-minute visit—the first of the children to visit me here? Schirach sees one of his sons every two months, but after every visit they leave crying. I renounce the idea.

March 9, 1952   With what sort of feelings will Hilde go to America? How will people behave toward her? Will they make it plain to her that she is a convicted war criminal's daughter? Of course she will defend me, with a child's loyalty. What does she really think about me? In general, what do I mean to my children? In their most secret thoughts, which perhaps they do not admit even to themselves?

What will she find harder to take: that I was Hitler's architect who not only built his palaces and halls of fame, but also provided the Party Rally decorations that gave him the backdrop for his acts of mass hypnosis; or that I was his minister of armaments, director of his war machinery and employer of an army of slaves? The architecture I designed for the regime troubles me least; sometimes I match it against the Trocadero in Paris or the Lomonosov University project in Moscow and decide that it was better. But what still troubles me most to this day is my participation in so much overall injustice. I have said that publicly, and I have also said it in letters to the family; and I am really certain that the children feel the same way. For a long time to come it will be their life's problem that their father belonged to the inner circle of despots. Perhaps I ought to write Hilde a few lines on that subject, so that she will be armed to face America. At least I shall be able to help her, out of my own wrestlings, with her problem.

I am very relieved.

March 10, 1952   Drafted note to Hilde. While writing realized that everything is rather more complicated than I thought. How can I best help her?

March 12, 1952   Yesterday I tore everything up. There will be no letter to Hilde. For the more deeply I dug into the problem, scribbling note after note, the more clearly I realized that for the children I am probably the cause less of guilt complexes than of feelings of shame. My involvement in so many wrongs has probably become history to them. For them it must be much more incriminating that I was Hitler's favorite and familiar, who with adjutants and secretaries shared his boring evenings, laughed at his stupid jokes, and listened to his dreary theories of historical philosophy. And heaven knows I cannot write a letter about all that. Not even to myself.

March 14, 1952 Surely my tendency to belittle myself, to accuse myself, does sometimes get carried too far. After all, I was not the only one to succumb to his strange fascination. So did statesmen of importance, men like Hindenburg, Simon, Lloyd George, Mussolini, and many others. For he did not play only on the mass instrument; he was also a master psychologist in the handling of individuals. He perceived the most secret hopes and fears of every interlocutor. Probably he was not so magnificent a statesman as he seemed to us at the time, and certainly, as the second phase of the war demonstrated, he was not a great military commander. But he was and remains a psychologist second to none I have ever met. I can well imagine that historians may someday call him great only to that extent.

Even as a military commander he was inclined to think rather of the psychological than the military potency of a weapon. That was shown early when he devised the siren for Stukas and regarded the demoralizing howl as having a greater effect than the explosive force of the bombs. And his bias assumed strange and militarily unfortunate forms when the submachine gun was ready for production and he delayed its introduction month after month because, he argued, the soldier's use of the rifle forced him to become a good shot and bayonet fighter, and thus called for soldierly virtues. Such psychologizing of all military technology became sheer grotesquery when he begged Rommel and me to develop automatically rotating flamethrowers, which would work in the manner of lawn sprinklers. These, he argued, would be the prime defense against invasion. Judging by experiences in the First World War, nothing was more terrifying to a soldier than a jet of flame aimed at him. The prospect of being burned to death spread panic, whereas death from a bullet always came unexpectedly and was honorable.

By the spring of 1944 more than twenty thousand flamethrowers were produced and available. Some of these were to be placed in the minefields along the Atlantic coast and discharged automatically; in addition, oil storage tanks would have to be set afire by remote control and the landing area converted into a gigantic sea of flames. The objections of military experts meant nothing to him once he began ranting about the devastating psychological effect.

March 27, 1952 Pease told me today that on the Potsdamer Chaussee in Wannsee, right in the middle of the American sector, a

Russian T-34 tank stands as a monument to the victory over Berlin. There are similar monuments everywhere in Europe, Pease says. Basically that is a Hitlerian idea which, I must say, always made me uncomfortable. In the summer of 1941, three days before the attack on the Soviet Union, Hitler, his personal physician, Karl Brandt, and I went for a walk down the broad gravel paths of the Chancellery park. Behind trees to our left lay the long, yellow garden facade of the Chancellery, its large windows framed in gray limestone. The promenade stretched on for some two hundred meters and was flanked at intervals with sculpture; there was a piece by Louis Tuaillon which I had placed there, representing a man taming a bull; there was a nude by Fritz Klimsch; and before Hitler's residential wing, our turning point, a Greek bronze: Poseidon as the Earthshaker angrily striking his trident into the sea. It had been fished out of the ocean near Cape Sounion. But on each circuit we also passed several of those model tanks, Type IV, which reminded Hitler of his great victory boulevard in Berlin. For to the right and left of that grand avenue, stretching on for miles like the avenue of rams at Karnak, captured weapons were to be placed on marble pedestals. I had always had a rather instinctive dislike for this idea; now my feeling was corroborated and intensified by the sight of classical sculptures and technical apparatus side by side. In the form of a query, I indicated my doubts to Hitler, but he seemed not to listen. Instead, he poured out a veritable torrent of words on the impressive, the stunning effect that must necessarily be produced by the display of military triumphs. The fact that his—and my—architecture operated with traditional stylistic elements, with columns, arcades, cornices, pilasters, which were hardly compatible with the caterpillar treads of armored vehicles, or with cannon barrels and gun carriages, seemed to trouble him no more than it does the Russians today. Because he saw only outward effects, he thought in entirely eclectic terms and had no scruples about placing domes beside motors and arcades beside mortars.

I have just been asking myself once more on what my aversion was based. Why do the rams and sphinxes in Egypt, or even so late a sculptural group as Hoetger's Lion Gate near my native city, seem to me aesthetically permissible and even expressive? The answer probably is that the products of industry are not susceptible to monumentalization. In order to achieve real impressiveness and not just the outward effect sought by Hitler (or the Russians), a monument has to have a mythic quality. Technology is always opposed to mythology. Goethe's pen can be exhibited in a museum, but not Zuckmayer's or Hemingway's typewriters. Achilles' sword is not a rifle and Hagen's spear not a flamethrower. Hitler's victory boulevard would have been an embarrassment.

April 1, 1952   Yesterday Neurath had a severe heart attack. Excited coming and going in the corridor, and in between repressed cries. Today we heard that he is close to death. But a slight improvement seems to have come. At any rate, everything is relatively calm today. Recently I have thought relations between us were becoming somewhat warmer, although he always remains aristocratic and aloof. But he is the only fellow prisoner whose absence would be a loss to me.

April 2, 1952   The American director has informed us that he intends to have us taught basketmaking. To our minds that is a discriminatory act and incompatible with the Nuremberg sentences. We were not sentenced to the penitentiary or to forced labor.

After conferring together we all agreed that we must remain unyielding. I am requested to write to my Coburg friend to ask Dönitz's lawyer whether a refusal would justify punishment, let alone reduce the prospects for amnesty.

April 8, 1952   Kranzbühler's reply arrived today. He says that although we should not provoke incidents, penalties will in no way affect a possible amnesty. The lawyer seems to have illusions about our situation, for he simultaneously informs us that it is essential for the Western governors to regard us as gentlemen!

April 11, 1952   This morning when we were summoned to come into the hall for a lesson in basketmaking, we unanimously stated that we would not do this work unless we were explicitly ordered to. None of the guards present was willing to put the summons in the form of an order. Thereupon we returned to our cells without another word, leaving grumpy John Hawker alone with his osier wands. During the past week Hawker had been assigned to, of all places, the Wittenau mental hospital, for instruction in the art of basketmaking. A few hours later the American director informed us that we would not have to weave baskets. But the Russian director, who had originally turned down the whole idea, changed his mind in the face of our opposition. He now began insisting that we be compelled to make baskets.

April 15, 1952   Perplexed. There are always new problems coming along. In all previous arguments over my conduct in the past, arguments with myself and with others, I had to admit that I often confused right and wrong, but I felt that I had never acted disloyally. Loyalty was, so to speak, the last firm ground to which my self-respect could retreat. Today I received clandestinely a letter from an Englishwoman, a Mrs. Anne Fremantle, to my Coburg friend. What she writes at first glance flatters my vanity: that she and her friends, the widows of Freytag von Loringhoven and Adam Trott zu Solz, who were executed as conspirators after July 20, regarded me as the only one of those condemned at Nuremberg for whom they could summon up respect and even a degree of liking. She, Mrs. Fremantle, was considering undertaking something in my behalf, and had recently spoken of her intention to her friends Bertrand Russell and Jacques Maritain. Both of them had said to her that they had no doubts I was the typical loyal man, but that loyalty was a lesser virtue; strictly speaking, in fact, it was really a bad thing, for loyalty always presupposed a certain ethical blindness on the part of the loyal person. If someone really knew what was good and what evil, loyalty would go by the board, they said.

For hours I have been a prey to violent emotions. I can no longer think. I make no progress against this kind of logic. It takes the ground from under my feet. At any rate it is something of a consolation to me that I was loyal not only to Hitler but also to the conspirators. I can still see myself with Stauffenberg after a conference in the Berghof. In addition to the two of us, only Hitler, Himmler, Göring, Keitel, and Fromm participated. Stauffenberg and I stood for a while talking at the foot of the great outside staircase—that was two weeks before the assassination attempt. Stauffenberg was carrying his heavy briefcase, which presumably already contained bombs even then; and on the day after July 20, when the circumstances of the attempt became known, I recalled that during the entire period of the conference he had actually placed this briefcase next to my chair. Now, after the fatiguing session, in the course of which Göring, Himmler, and Keitel had merely nodded assent to Hitler's monologues, Stauffenberg commented that they were all opportunists and psychopaths here; that nobody dared open his mouth. "With you I'm still very glad to talk, but there's no longer any point with these other idiots." He actually said "idiots," and for a moment I was horrified. For although all of us occasionally spoke critically, had a good many things to grumble about, we nevertheless forbade ourselves the use of such words. Nor did I respond to Stauffenberg; the remnants of my loyalty to Hitler kept me from doing so. But at any rate I did not betray him, nor Stieff, nor Fromm and the many others who had confided to me their criticisms of the inadequacies in our leadership. I suppose at least that can be said in my favor.

April 17, 1952 Still on the question of loyalty. It isn't as simple as I thought day before yesterday. Now that I am preoccupied with the matter, it suddenly seems to me that in the Third Reich I heard no word more frequently than "loyalty." It fell from everyone's lips—not only the Keitels and Kesselrings, but the Blombergs, Mansteins, and Kluges all used it to kill their doubts. Not to speak of the Gauleiters, insofar as they were capable of any judgment. Even Göring, debased and addicted as he was toward the end, told me in a long conversation at Karinhall that I would have an easier time breaking with Hitler than he; that he had to be loyal.

But now I ask myself whether loyalty was no more than the rag we used to cover our moral nakedness: our lack of resolution, fear of responsibility, cowardice, all the vapidities that we bombastically called our "duty." The loyalty I practiced to all and sundry, toward Hitler as well as toward Stauffenberg, toward the slave laborers, whom I treated well, and toward Sauckel, who rounded them up for me—what else was that but a form of lukewarmness? Much too late I am beginning to grasp that there is only one valid kind of loyalty: toward morality.

April 18, 1952 I had originally intended to answer Mrs. Fremantle. Now I give up the idea.

April 19, 1952 Hess's attacks are frequently provoked by trivialities that he objects to—a request to go into the garden or to bathe, to clean the cell, or in fact anything that involves physical movement. The threat of basketmaking likewise set him off. Even though the threat is over, Hess goes on complaining and wailing for hours. At night, too. It sounds ghastly in the empty hall. Nobody knows whether he actually is in pain. Even the doctors who believe him doubt that there is any organic cause, for X rays show nothing.

April 20, 1952 Each of us has spells of bad temper and prison psychosis. At the moment Schirach seems to have gone into a tailspin. He has openly broken with me and no longer even responds to my greetings. Why, I don't know. On the other hand, of late my relationship with Dönitz has improved.

The laundry is done. It's raining. Today, incidentally, would be Hitler's birthday.

April 22, 1952 In the garden Neurath, recovered, goes to the entrance of a rabbit hutch. Observing the behavior of wild rabbits is the last thing left to this once passionate hunter. A few weeks ago his family sent him his old hunting vest, a melancholy souvenir. "How often I wore it in my hunting lodge in Balderschwang," he remarks, and launches into a vivid account of the landscape, the woods, and the game. He never says a word about his work as foreign minister and his quarrels with Hitler; he listens expressionlessly to us when we occasionally speak of the past. Sometimes it seems to me that his attitude might equally well spring from forbearance as from indifference. He may have his own ideas. Today Neurath told me how as a young chamberlain he saved Princess Mary, later Queen of England, from a fire in the palace in Stuttgart, and how later on as ambassador to London he regularly provided her with apples from a certain orchard near Kirchheim/Teck in Württemberg. She had greatly enjoyed these apples in her youth.

April 23, 1952 Neurath's silence has something irritating about it; it contains an element of arrogance. What entitles him to such detachment? After all, we are all burdened by the past, almost to the same degree, and we would all of us like to pretend to such detachment. I know I would.

Evening. On our walk in the garden today, I cautiously hinted that to Neurath. Almost abruptly the old man stood still and slowly turned to face me. Quite emotionlessly and in a by no means unfriendly manner, he said, "Oh, for all of you it's just Hitler and the Third Reich that have perished." He said this both wearily and conclusively, so that I did not have the courage to ask what he meant. With an almost kindly nod to me, he continued his round. I loitered behind.

Of course what Neurath said isn't really true. It is in fact unjust. For out of all of us here I am the only one, after all, who made a distinction between Germany and the Third Reich, though very belatedly, and even drew the logical conclusions from that distinction. In Nuremberg there was ample testimony of the way I opposed Hitler's orders for destruction. Does Neurath no longer remember that from November 1944 I insisted on this distinction even when confronting Bormann? I went specially to Karinhall to inform Göring officially, in his capacity of commissioner for the Four Year Plan, that I would no longer obey Hitler's orders to put the needs of producing armaments above the provisioning of the population. Göring sat there in that fantastic jerkin he liked to wear and replied in an almost paternal tone, "My dear Speer, I certainly see your point, but where would we end if the habit of counter-manding orders should prevail? That sort of thing would spread, and soon you too would be left without any authority." Göring thrust aside my objection that we must now think of the nation's survival with a disarming argument: "But surely you cannot pocket your minister's salary and disregard the Führer's orders. Report sick! Or go abroad. I would even be prepared to transfer money for you to Spain, by way of Bernard."

I have drifted from the subject. Will continue tomorrow.

April 24, 1952 Pondering last night. Perhaps Neurath is not so very wrong. At any rate it struck me that here in Spandau everyone is preoccupied with his own province and his own responsibilities. We speak of mistakes we made, of losses we suffered. We think of friends, of family, and if the discussion turns general, Funk and Schirach consider whether the Allies will not quarrel among themselves, as Hitler predicted. But the word that always fell so pompously from our lips, the word "Germany," is never spoken at all. Perhaps the reason is that, except for Neurath, none of us is a real conservative. To various degrees we are technologists, military men, youth movementers, careerists. Only for Neurath do words like "Germany," "nation," or "Reich" and the aura that surrounds them really mean something specifically experienced. The melancholy reticence with which he listens to our discussions, and also the attitude that I felt to be arrogance, perhaps come from a sense that Germany not only lost a war, but both in reality and in the realm of ideas gambled away a historical existence more than a thousand years old. At some time, probably during the first weeks of the war—I no longer remember the context—I heard Hitler speak hypothetically of a *finis Germaniae*. Neurath is the only one of us for whom that has happened. Our bickerings, our charges and countercharges, all our verbose fuming and fussing probably strike him as vulgar. Such behavior helps us. Not him.

April 28, 1952 Sixty books have arrived from the Spandau library, our reading material until the next change, in six weeks. My choice from this shipment: a biography of Jean Paul, the three-volume work by Lord Carter on Tutankhamen, a novel by Schnitzler, Hölderlin's *Hyperion*, his letters, and a biography of him, Dauthendey's letters to his wife, an account of a Polar expedition, the life of Genghis Khan, books on Lucas Cranach, Manet, and Friedrich Preller.

A book on Milan and one on Genoa will have to do as a substitute for traveling.

Now we are also to be getting books from the Berlin central library in Wilmersdorf. To judge by the filing cases left with us, its stocks are inexhaustible.

May 1, 1952   After the conversation with Göring that I mentioned recently he invited me to go for a brief walk in the adjacent wooded park. It was night. For a while we walked in silence side by side. Then he said abruptly that until the fighting ended he must stand by the Führer. But as though to reward my candor, and at the same time to commit himself, he added that what would come after that was another matter. He could count on a degree of friendliness from the Americans, he said: in recent years the press abroad had always treated him more favorably than any of the other political leaders of Germany. Moreover, his many economic ties with such magnates as Deterding and such firms as General Motors would undoubtedly help him. He had witnesses, he said, to prove that he had wanted to prevent the war. I really felt sorry in Nuremberg that I could not come to some kind of agreement with Göring, and after we had finally quarreled in the course of the trial I repeatedly recalled the words he had spoken in parting after our nocturnal walk: "Incidentally, don't worry, Herr Speer. I am not an informer."

May 20, 1952   Letter from my wife. My mother has been paralyzed on one side by a stroke; she lies motionless in bed, has lost the power of speech, and can no longer be communicated with. I must prepare myself for the worst.

May 27, 1952   Depression intensified by my wife's visit. More bad news about my mother. We talked little, and that stammeringly. What is there left to say?

June 10, 1952   The guard Wagg, who ordinarily never transmits any news, has spitefully shown me a press item to the effect that the State Department has refused to grant Hilde an entry visa.

June 13, 1952   Three days ago Raeder complained to the French director about Hess's groaning at night. It's shattering his nerves, he claims. Major Brésard asked Neurath, Dönitz, and me whether Hess disturbed our sleep too, but we said no.

At nine o'clock this morning Major Brésard, who is generally so decent, went into Hess's cell and shouted, *"Allez, allez, 'raus!"* Hess stood up; Brésard ordered the guards to take the blanket and mattress out of the cell until evening. Hess sat on his chair and wailed. At half past eleven Pease had me carry the bedding back in. Half an hour later the Russian director, in an emphatic, friendly tone, gave me the order to take the blanket and mattress out again. In an equally friendly manner I replied that I would not participate in carrying out a measure against a fellow prisoner. But Hess solved the impasse by asking me to do so.

My mother's condition unchanged.

June 14, 1952   When I go to wash at six o'clock in the morning I see Brésard in Hess's cell, gesticulating. The bedding lies in a confused heap on the floor. Pease does not lift a finger to obey the director's order and get Hess out of bed by force. After Brésard has left, Pease says, "In all my years of experience with prisoners nothing like this has ever happened." The Russian director, who shortly afterwards sees the blankets on the floor, also seems to have scruples. "No *kultura*. This not my order; I know not of this measure." But soon afterwards Hess is informed that until further notice the bed and bedding will be removed from his cell from half past six in the morning until half past nine at night.

I suspect Schirach, Funk, and Raeder, Inc., of playing a cunning game. On the one hand they are supporting Hess in his obstinacy, on the other hand inciting the guards against "the malingerer" and disturber of their night's sleep. But when Hess is harshly treated, Funk writes reports to the outside in which he exaggerates Hess's sufferings. This morning when I told him that by adroit questioning I had more or less established that Hess was pretending, Funk replied tersely that it was too late now, that he had already communicated the whole story to his liaison man.

June 15, 1952   Today a notice posted on the cell door stipulated that Prisoner Number Seven may remain in bed every morning until half past nine if he has pain. This is an official acknowledgment that Hess is sick. However, the sickness is not taken seriously, since the medical aide reports that he is injecting only *"aqua destillata"* [distilled water], a trick frequently used with hysterics.

In the medical office this morning Raeder irritably tells the guards Hawker and Wagg that they were wrong to give in, that Hess ought to be handled roughly; he doesn't have any real pain at all. Dönitz is outraged when he hears this. In the washroom he says to Neurath and me, "Raeder would suffer for that in a prisoner-of-war camp. And rightly so, to my mind. That's terribly uncomradely. Hess has a right to malinger if he wants to. We ought to be supporting him. And not to upset him, we shouldn't even tell him that the sedative injection is a trick. You can never tell what he might do then."

June 17, 1952   After four days, Hess has given up. He now rises on the dot, submits punctiliously to the daily routine. Today we lugged our blankets into the garden to hang them up in the sun. Hess carried only one of his blankets over his arm. Behind him chief guard Terray trotted like a kind of butler, carrying the remaining five blankets.

To distract Hess, I sit on the bench with him, chatting. Neurath, accompanied by Dönitz, crosses the garden toward us and asks, "What was the name of that man who was all for a Pan-Europe?"

"Coudenhove-Kalergi," I reply.

After a while Hess asks me, "How come you remember Coudenhove-Kalergi?"

My father was a Pan-European, I tell him.

"Pan-Europe is a good idea," Hess remarks throughtfully. "But unfortunately the only European nation that ever wants it is the one that happens to be at the head at any given time."

I tell Hess that in the autumn of 1943 I wanted to build up a European system of production. But Ribbentrop successfully opposed it on the grounds that as foreign minister he alone should be in charge of all questions of cooperation with other countries. Hess is curious. "What did you intend to do?" I explain that I wanted to combine the various branches of production throughout Europe in "rings," parallel to the system of organization I was using in my ministry. For example, there would be one for coal, another for steel, still others for machinery or electrical engineering. In each case the president would be the outstanding expert in the field, whether he was French, Belgian, Italian, or Norwegian. A German would be the secretary of each ring. Hess, the Führer's former secretary, commented pensively, "You're not so dumb!" For a few minutes we sit in silence. Then Hess says, "After all, the secretary handles everything." By and by Hess raises the question of whether such a European union would have had to strive for autarchy. I say it would not, and point to the Dutch or Danish system. In those countries, in spite of high population density, the import of feeds makes possible the export of eggs, butter, and cheese. But Hess is dead set against any kind of dependence. In that case, he says, during a war Europe would be cut off from feed supplies, and the continent would be done for. I demonstrate my idea by the example of Neurath's estate —the sole source of everything I know about this matter. There, by purchase of feed, they raise a hundred pigs instead of the former ten, and several times the former number of cows. The estate is flourishing. "Well, yes," Hess says slowly, "that's true enough. But Neurath's estate isn't waging any wars."

Five-minute pause. Hess breaks the silence by saying out of context, "I'm annoyed with myself. I no longer have the desire to protest. Now I'm doing what they ask of me. It's a decline, a moral fall, believe me!" I try to bring him round by pointing out all that he gains by making concessions. "It may be so," he replies. "But I'm no longer the man I used to be."

Late that evening Pease comes into my cell. "Here, *Stars and Stripes* reports that your daughter will be allowed to go to America. Congratulations." The newspaper item states that McCloy approached Secretary of State Acheson. In addition, the article says that a prestigious Jewish family has invited Hilde to stay with them. The news stirs me so deeply that I can scarcely restrain my tears. After the door closes behind Pease, I drop on the bed and turn my head to the wall.

June 18, 1952 Have been thinking about yesterday's breakdown. What was it that so shook me about the news that Hilde has received her visa? Is it that the whole incident has forcibly brought to mind my total helplessness as a father? After all, the children must blame me because they cannot even travel abroad without difficulty; and I sit here in this cell and am not even able to give them advice. Or was I overwhelmed by the thought of McCloy's intercession, and perhaps even more, that the offer of a Jewish family whom I do not know also means a partial rehabilitation for me? My daughter, whom I cannot help, helps me to take a first step back into honorable civil life.

June 29, 1952 Today, after the service, the chaplain gently broke the news I have long expected: My mother died four days ago.

We are ordered into the garden. I stoop over the flower beds so that no one can see my face, and absently pull weeds. My fellow prisoners briefly commiserate. They avoid formal expression of condolences, in keeping with our habit of not intruding into one another's emotional lives.

July 4, 1952 Today Raeder rebukes me with unexpected vehemence for an innocently intended remark about Hitler's contempt for other human beings. Schirach joins in the rebuke; Dönitz and, strangely, Funk also look on with obvious satisfaction. Schirach in particular chides me for disloyalty. One cannot condemn Hitler, he says, for never giving up and holding out to the last day. In fact, that is practically the only thing about him that can be admired. Even when he was nothing but a wreck of a human being he tried to turn the course of destiny. In that, Schirach says emphatically, Hitler was certainly not being untrue to himself.

As always, we do not pursue the dispute; each of us returns to his cell. After the key has turned in the lock, I try to establish for myself when what they call my treason began. Was it during the early days after July 20, 1944, when it began to be rumored that my name had figured on the conspirators' list of cabinet ministers? Or was it in September, when I sent a memorandum to Hitler for the first time arguing that a material basis for victory no longer existed? Or, finally, was it in the course of that monologue of Hitler's in the Chancellery at the end of November 1944, when he cynically and with utter contempt for humanity spoke of the destruction of Germany?

I still remember how he began with a crude joke almost as soon as he had invited me to sit down. With a sweeping movement of his arm he indicated the destruction outside the window. "What does all that signify! Speer"—he made a motion as though he meant to grip my arm—"in Berlin alone you would have had to tear down eighty thousand buildings to complete our new building plan. Unfortunately the English haven't carried out this work exactly in accordance with your plans. But at least they have launched the project." He made an effort to laugh when he saw me remaining grave. "We'll rebuild our cities more beautiful than they ever were. I shall see to that. With more monumental buildings than they ever had. But to do that we must win the war!" Even now the old passion for showy buildings could carry him away. He had altogether forgotten the concession he had made to me a year before, that immediately after the war he would let me build nothing but housing for a while. But I could not contradict Hitler as he sat there exhausted in his chair, clutching his trembling arm. In any case, by now it no longer mattered all that much what he had to say about the future.

Hitler went on, "These air raids don't bother me. I only laugh at them. The less the population has to lose, the more fanatically it will fight. We've seen that with the English, you know, and even more with the Russians. One who has lost everything has to win everything. The enemy's advance is actually a help to us. People fight fanatically only when they have the war at their own front doors. That's how people are. Now even the worst idiot realizes that his house will never be rebuilt unless we win. For that reason alone we'll have no revolution this time. The rabble aren't going to have the chance to cover up their cowardice by a so-called revolution. I guarantee that! No city will be left in the enemy's hands until it's a heap of ruins." He let his head droop, then straightened up with a sudden jerk. "I haven't the slightest intention of surrendering. Providence tests men and gives the laurel to the one who remains undaunted. As long as I live we will withstand this testing. It's the man who can be ruthless, not the coward, who wins. Remember this, it isn't technical superiority that proves decisive. We lost that long ago. I know that too. Besides, November has always been my lucky month. And we're in November now." Hitler grew more and more passionate. "I won't tolerate any opposition, Speer. When the war is over, the people can vote on me for all I care. But anybody who disagrees now is going straight to the gallows without question. If the German people are incapable of appreciating me, I'll fight this fight alone. Let them go ahead and leave me! The reward always comes from history alone, you know. Don't expect a thing from the populace. They cheered me yesterday and will wave the white flag today. Gauleiter Florian himself told me one such incident. The people know nothing of history. You cannot imagine how sick I am of it all."

I had often heard Hitler arguing that only the great individuals decide the course of history. And he had repeated until we were tired of hearing it that he with his allegedly iron nerves was indispensable. Even before the war he had used that argument to justify the necessity of beginning the conflict during his lifetime. But I had always thought that his immense energy was to be devoted to the cause of the German people; and he had after all said again and again how much he would prefer to listen to music, build, and sit on his mountaintop. Now all these masks of the aesthete and the man of the people had dropped away. Nothing but iciness and misanthropy came to the fore. And the intimacy with which he drew us into these thoughts had actually become physically repulsive to me. "My dear Speer," he concluded, with an attempt to find his way back to our old closeness, "don't let the destruction confuse you. And you mustn't be bothered by the people's whining."

That had been said in a tête-à-tête, but every one of us had heard him go on this way—including Funk, including Schirach, including

Dönitz. Yet Hitler in this mood, much as they may otherwise criticize him, still impresses them. They take as soldierly virtue what in reality was merely his callousness at the prospect of total destruction. At least in this respect he is still a kind of Frederick the Great to them. To me he is only Attila.

July 10, 1952   Rodin's *The Cathedrals of France*. For pages I have been reading without knowing what I am reading. In my parents' home much of the time. At low ebb.

July 22, 1952   Donaho has just nonchalantly distributed to each of us a bar of chocolate and a bottle of beer. As always Hess refuses, saying that these things are illegal. Hastily, I gulp down my first beer in seven years; but I hide the chocolate in a sock so that I can eat it quietly tonight.

July 24, 1952   Hilde on the Atlantic. At the last moment she and a few other students were shifted from a freighter to the *United States*. Chief guard Felner says that McCloy, who has ended his duties as high commissioner in Germany, is returning on the same ship.

Conversation with Brésard on my wife's accomplishment in raising the children. Deep feeling of gratitude. I consider a symbolic gesture. Perhaps an unobtrusive way of showing my feelings would be to give her, on the day of my release, the same kind of gold watch I gave her once before when I saved up for it out of my student's allowance—the watch went astray during the weeks after the end of the war.

August 30, 1952   Donaho has brought with him *Nuremberg Diary*, by Gilbert, the prison psychologist at Nuremberg. I must admit that he reproduces the atmosphere with amazing objectivity. His judgments are on the whole correct and fair; I would hardly have put it very differently. Nevertheless, it remains a curious experience to see moments of the most extreme anxiety of my life reconstructed so objectively. This is a new experience: reading about oneself as though one were long dead.

At the same time my secretary has sent a book by Donald Robinson: *The Hundred Most Important People in the World Today*. From 1943 to 1945 Robinson was chief historian on Eisenhower's staff, and I am on his list. Naturally I am pleased to see myself as an important man. But I have my doubts about Robinson's prediction that the world will soon be hearing from me again. He thinks I will be released in five years. I would be then fifty-two. A second career?

September 3, 1952   Late at night, Hilde's first report. She has been taken in for a year by a wealthy American Quaker family who live in Hastings-on-Hudson. Her hosts have children her age, with whom she is getting on well. When Hilde arrived in Boston, the family was there with their cabin cruiser, and they went by water to New York. The intimacy of ship life dispelled the awkwardness of the first few days.

September 7, 1952   Returning from garden work, I saw the Russian guard, Guryev, leaving my cell. He had used the daily inspection to pile bedding, clothing, and all my other possessions in a heap. On the table paper and drawing materials lay in a welter. My nerves gave way and I refused to enter the cell, although the cook was already waiting with the food outside the iron door of our cellblock; he is not allowed to enter until all the cell doors are locked. Letham spoke soothingly to me, urging me to be reasonable, while Guryev watched my outburst with interest. After some minutes I gave in and lay down exhausted on the bedstead. I did not go to fetch my meal.

September 10, 1952   Again chaos in my cell. It is even worse than the confusion of three days ago. I wonder what Guryev can possibly have against me. At my request the British director on duty, Le Cornu, comes to see. He obviously disapproves of what has happened. The new guard, Eburne, also shakes his head. Hess, on the other hand, is rude to me, perhaps because I told him about Donald Robinson's book. I try to appease him, but he becomes even nastier and more hostile.

September 19, 1952   Eleven days ago, on September 8, I applied for approval of a visit from my wife in October. In response to my question about why I had received no word as yet, Le Cornu confides that the Russians have made approval dependent on my first being punished. "I don't give a damn. I want the visit in any case." This evening Le Cornu simultaneously informs me of approval of the visit and punishment "for delaying to go into his cell." As he tells it, the Russian director has also filed a report that I disappeared for several hours during an American shift, which isn't true.

An official notice is posted on my door: "On September 19, 1952, the

Directorate has ordered Prisoner No. 5 to be punished as follows: a) For one week he is not permitted to go into the garden. b) For one week, from waking time until 5:30 P.M. he will be locked in a special cell containing only a table and a chair. c) For one week he is not permitted to have books and writing materials between waking and 5:30 P.M. The punishment begins on September 20, 1952 (incl.) and ends on September 26, 1952 (incl.), Signed, Le Cornu, Lt. Col."

September 22, 1952   As the price for my wife's visit, so to speak, I now sit for eleven hours daily in a cell provided only with chair and table. So far the pencil concealed in the radiator has not been discovered, and toilet paper is available in any quantity. So I pass the time. Today is the third of these seven days. But the kindly British doctor has at my request secretly prescribed three tablets of Theominal for me. It simply wipes out the psychic effect of the punishment. To everyone's astonishment I am as fresh as I was on the first day, whereas with the same punishment Hess was writhing on the floor after four days.

Terray unlocks the door, murmuring, "I'll give you a break. Go wash the laundry." Smiling, I ask him to read the notice on the door. I don't want any amendment of an unjust punishment.

September 24, 1952   Fifth day. Neurath and Hess are openly showing their sympathy, and Dönitz cautiously expresses his concern; I am avoided by Funk, Schirach, and Raeder. They have predicted to the guards that my collapse will come today. Evidently my calmness irritates them. Strange, what has happened to us. What animosities thrive under conditions of excessive proximity!

Funk has just come to my cell. "Funk, how are you coming with your prediction?" I ask through the door.

"You're being perverse as usual. I need something dramatic for my reports. You have to shout, groan, collapse. Instead you're laughing and cracking jokes!" At this moment Neurath pays me a visit at the cell door and tells me that from 1935 on, at the order of his doctors, he took two or three Theominal tablets daily because of his heart trouble. He recommends this drug to me because it also has a tranquilizing effect. No doubt Neurath's physical complaints at that time were produced by Hitler's foreign policy, for the foreign minister was one of those who attempted to tame Hitler. But at the same time those tablets brought Neurath to Spandau—they took away his heart trouble, but simultaneously removed his scruples.

September 26, 1952   Last day of the punishment. A small owl has settled down for his daytime sleep on a tree just two arm lengths away from me. In the adjacent washroom Dönitz is being shaved by the medical aide. "Don't press so hard, please. I'm not a rhinoceros." Pause. "No, no, lion hunting isn't all that easy. I also hunted antelope and bushbuck." Pause. "So, what do I owe you?" Dönitz is replaced by Schirach. "Rumors about relaxation of the conditions of imprisonment? I hope they don't increase the number of letters and visits. Because then we'll no longer have any reason to complain. What else is new?" he asks Mees.

Funk sneaks around in the corridor. A French guard is snoring. Far away I hear someone unlocking a door. To Funk: "Quick, wake Monsieur Corgnol up." It is only common decency to alert a sleeping guard when someone is coming. What else is there for them to do but sleep? It was a false alarm. Corgnol unlocks my door. "Would you like to stroll in the corridor? If someone comes go right back in." Pacing back and forth with me, to cheer me up he tells me that Major Brésard frequently tries to catch guards asleep between three and five o'clock in the morning. He runs the last fifty meters—which, given his short size and tubbiness, must look funny. But he always finds the guards awake. As soon as his plump figure appears at the gate, the man on duty there, even if he is a Russian, rings the telephone.

At five o'clock, mess time. In half an hour the punishment period will be over. I am eating in the special cell for the last time.

September 27, 1952   Some time ago the guard Long asked me to work out the route for a tour of the Black Forest. Now he has made his trip and tells me about it. Names full of memories come up: Hundseck, Titisee, Höllental, Konstanz. I ask about the old marketplace in Freudenstadt. "The Frogs—you know, that's what we call the French—burned down all of Freudenstadt when they marched in. But everything has been rebuilt, much finer than it was."

The Seventh Year

October 3, 1952 In the garden I pass out the latest news I have received from Long: Soviet Congress opens. Secret ties revealed between the Russians and the French administration in Berlin. Hess, too, wants to hear the latest; but Guryev appears behind his back without Hess's being aware. I quickly ask, "Herr Hess, could you hold this plank for me?" Dumbfounded by this outrageous request, he moves off without a word and sits down on a bench. Later I say to him, "That was the only way I could warn you." "But that was also a particularly weird request," Hess replies drily.

October 5, 1952 A week ago nine pages of notes were found under Dönitz's mattress. Luckily they were written on official paper. The authorities suspect they were intended for his memoirs. In the trash pail I found fragments of the report of a conference of directors at which the incident was discussed. The new Russian director demanded that Dönitz's reading and writing be banned for two weeks because in the notes he described activities that took place in fascist Germany. But no verdict could be agreed on.

The new Russian director, energetic as they always are at the start, confiscated Schirach's "Watchwords," a calendar with Bible texts for every day. Schirach used it to keep a record of medicines prescribed and family birthdays.

The Russian officer who monitors our religious services and sits on the toilet that still disfigures our chapel heard the phrase "be forearmed" several times during the sermon. Report: the chaplain spoke about armaments. Now he has to submit his sermon in writing before delivering it.

October 6, 1952 Vexations again. This afternoon Major Andreyev was in the garden. I had just transplanted lilies of the valley. He tells his interpreter to warn me: "Those new flowers." I reply that they are transplanted and transplanting is permitted. He shakes his head irritably. "No, transplanting also forbidden. Please! The flowers will be removed at once and destroyed."

The Russian officers move off. Letham, the Scot, says didactically, "You know, orders are orders. My experience is to obey all orders. Don't think, just obey. That's best." I reply a bit skeptically, "I don't understand you and this world anymore. In Nuremberg I was commended for disobeying Hitler's orders, and here I get punished if I don't obey." He doesn't understand that either; it is something beyond his horizon.

October 7, 1952 This afternoon, Donaho climbed into one of the nut trees and started cawing. He has already been given a warning by the directors "because he sat in a tree and gave vent to the noises of a raven," as the official record of the directors' conference puts it. Selinavov, a new and popular Russian who pays little attention to his directors' general directives, laughs at the cawing American and in broken German begins telling about bears, capercaillies, foxes, northern lights that make the night bright as day, and much, much, much snow. Then guards and prisoners together shake down nuts. After a while all our garden implements are hanging up in the branches. Selinavov fetches the garden hose and begins spraying down the nuts one by one. As so often happens, chance put a comment in my way. After a severe illness of three weeks Goethe once wrote to his girl, Kätchen Schönkopf: "A foolish thing with us human beings. When I was in merry sprightly company I was cross. Now I am abandoned by everyone and am jolly."

October 12, 1952   Long clandestine note of Hilde's from Hastings. She is happy and enjoying her courses. John McCloy's parents-in-law live in the same town and have invited her to tea. She met McCloy and his wife there. If I had faced an American court, McCloy said, I would long ago have been freed.

The Russians are said to have accepted a proposal by the Western high commissioners to allow us more letters and more visits, so Pease says. Perhaps a result of the Adenauer démarche. Funk becomes excitable. "I don't want any more letters; I want them to stop switching on the light every half-hour at night." Roulet probes: "How is it you always know the latest news? Who tells you things?" I give my tried-and-true answer: "In this case you yourself, don't you remember?" He too has a touchy conscience over having occasionally furnished us with news.

October 14, 1952   Big quarrel among all of us because of the lighting problem. Everyone wants something different. Dönitz, Neurath, Hess, and I are against Schirach's proposal that a weak blue bulb be screwed into the socket, because in that case we could no longer read. Violent discussion. Funk backs off ten paces and berates first Neurath and then all of us. When he starts using vulgar epithets, I shout back: "You sound like a truck driver!" He clears out. The first scene of this sort in seven years and, worse yet, in the presence of a guard.

October 15, 1952   When we return from the garden work we find that the prison electrician has replaced one of the two-hundred-watt bulbs by a forty-watt bulb. Since the lighting fixture is installed at a height of three meters and for reasons of safety protected by wire-glass, the illumination is considerably reduced. Hess is indignant. "This is inhuman! Am I to ruin my eyes?"

October 22, 1952   Donaho has at last smuggled in the magazine I wanted to see, with the latest types of airplanes. To my great surprise I see that since 1945 nothing fundamentally new has been produced in the field of fighter planes. I recall von Lippisch's "all wing" project which so fascinated the Americans in Kranzberg; it has now been carried out by the British in the form of a four-jet bomber. In January 1945 I discussed the possibilities of a supersonic plane with Messerschmitt. He thought we could not be very far from the technical achievement of such a plane. Now, I read, a speed of twenty-two hundred kilometers per hour has been attained. It is already seven years since that discussion. Strange, to sit here in my cell and encounter these old projects which I tossed around for years and which others are now carrying out. I can still remember—when was that?—talking with the pilot of the Me[sserschmitt] 163 at the Rechlin experimental field; he reported violent shaking of the fuselage as the plane approached the sonic barrier.

Even more exciting for me are the blueprints and reports on the British Comet, with which the age of passenger jet planes is beginning. In the spring of 1945 I had the ambition to take a first passenger flight in a jet plane. An Me 262 was to transport me from Berlin to Essen. But General Galland, the fighter plane commander, countermanded the experiment for reasons of security.

I have never heard of Wankel again. At that time he was working on a kind of rotary motion engine, and I had to provide funds and materials because some technicians thought it extremely promising.

In Nuremberg I spoke of the diabolic aspects of technology and deplored the strange turn my life had taken, transferring me from the ideal world of art to technology. Again and again I longed to return to architecture. But now, as I held this magazine in my hand, the fascination of that phase of my life once again overwhelmed me. To be honest, I must admit to myself that flipping through the new architectural magazines, which are on the whole very monotonous, leaves me far more indifferent.

October 23, 1952   Eburne, the fat and easygoing Englishman, has promised me *Time* for today. In order to be able to read the magazine in peace I agree not to go into the garden, feigning a cold. The French doctor on his daily round proposes a Chinese treatment for it. "I'll stick a gold needle into this vein in your right hand for a few minutes and the cold will be gone."

Night before last I was awakened by Guryev switching the light on and off three or four times in succession every quarter hour. I complained to Terray while Guryev was on duty at the gate, and Terray helpfully wrote up a report to the directors. Today he told me that Guryev had delivered a counterreport stating that the French chief guard had delivered his reprimand dressed in a sweater and wearing slippers. "Orders not official unless given in correct uniform," Guryev argued.

October 24, 1952   After twenty-four hours I announced that my cold was over. The doctor is content with his acupuncture.

There has been a pleasing development in the electric-light war. Yesterday a British eye doctor, a lieutenant colonel, came from Hanover, examined the light by day, and merely said, "That's proof." In the afternoon Terray secretly changed bulbs. "But show no pleasure, not even in front of the other guards. The three Western directors have tacitly agreed to permit it."

October 30, 1952   Kovpak, the sandy-haired Russian, gives me a friendly smile. "Today wife come." But a real cold this time makes me droopy. Our conversation drags more lamely than ever. My wife tells me things about the children, about Hilde's American experiences, and much else of which I have long since heard through the clandestine mail. Brésard, moreover, sat down close beside my wife and stared fixedly at me.

Evening. Petry, the new French guard, is an Alsatian. He gives the impression of being a sympathetic fellow—and also confides his worries to us. Today he was complaining about corns and his troubles in love. The combination amuses me. His visit with me lasts for an hour. The only advice I can give him is: "Be a man. And I mean that in respect to both your complaints."

At nine o'clock I take the last sleeping pill of my autumn vacation and go to bed, but soon am awakened by a loud discussion in the corridor. Major Andreyev wants to wake up all the prisoners who are already sleeping. Petry vainly opposes him. The light is switched on in all cells. Andreyev calls out in a loud voice, "Why sleep? Not yet ten o'clock. Sleeping before ten o'clock forbidden. Regulations. Get up, please!" He departs, a victor. But three minutes later the French guard switches off the light. I go back to sleep.

November 18, 1952   Petry has brought with him an issue of the magazine *Carrefour*. In it Georges Blond reports, in the form of a fictional dialogue, on my last visit to Hitler on April 23, 1945, a few days before his suicide. The article is entitled *"L'extravagant M. Speer."* I show it to Hess, commenting, "One of these days the episode will make a good technicolor movie." Laughing, Hess replies, "But demand a guarantee that the actor who plays your part wear a halo." We suggest to each other dramatic touches for the sentimental reconciliation scene twenty meters underground. Laughing loudly, we make up more and more new movie scenes. Yet at the bottom Hess is the only one of the group who feels sympathy for my melodramatic return to Berlin that day, perhaps because the idea of saying goodbye comes closest to his romantic notions of honorable behavior.

Perhaps I too was activated by romanticism. Also a trace of bygone loyalty and even gratitude. But surely there was also the impulse to put myself in the hands of fate. In those last days of the war so many reports of horrors had reached us, stories of rapes, mass killings, spontaneous lynchings; even such episodes as the death of Gauleiter Mutschmann, who in bitter cold weather was driven naked on a cart through Dresden, then beaten to death. Such tales could not fail to make their impression on us. The prospect of being hanged from the nearest lamppost after the conquest of Berlin seemed to me a better choice than slave labor in Siberian mines. By openly opposing Hitler and confessing to him that I had sabotaged his orders for destruction, I was, as it were, seeking divine justice in an ordeal. All I know with absolute certainty is that I was not acting out of disappointment over all my lost dreams or out of despair over the collapse of Germany. All I wanted was to shuffle off the responsibility for my future life.

Had I known at the time that twenty years in Spandau awaited me, I would surely have taken even a stronger line against Hitler. Sometimes now, when I am at the end of my strength, it seems to me an overwhelming tragedy that Hitler at the time was so weary and in such a forbearing mood that he responded to my confession of open disobedience with emotion instead of with an order to have me shot. That would have been a better rounding off for my life.

November 19, 1952   How well considered was everything I wrote yesterday? It is easy to say that you prefer death to a long imprisonment. But how relieved I was in Nuremberg when my earphones reverberated with those words: "Albert Speer, twenty years." Even if I am kept here the full twenty years, at least it is life.

November 20, 1952   Hitler. Suddenly he has again become present to my mind. I had almost driven him from my thoughts. How long it is since I have written about him. Almost nothing for years, I imagine, aside from anecdotes and an odd remark here and there. I have no way of checking on that. If I look searchingly into myself, I must say that this is scarcely due to my having rid myself of him. Rather, it seems to me that I have been evading him because he still has too strong a hold on me. Whatever turn my life takes in the future, whenever my name is mentioned, people will think of Hitler. I shall never have an independent existence. And sometimes I see myself as a man of seventy, children long since adult and grandchildren growing up, and wherever I go people will not ask about me but about Hitler.

What would I reply? I saw Hitler in moments of triumph and moments of despondency, in his headquarters and stooped over the drawing board, in Montmartre in Paris and deep underground in the bunker. But if I were to describe a single scene in which he was everything at once and his many faces really merged into one, I think of a relatively minor incident, nothing more than a walk in the snow.

It was probably during the second half of November 1942. Matters at Stalingrad were going very badly. In view of the depressing news, Hitler left his East Prussian headquarters and sought refuge at Obersalzberg. Dr. Morell had urged him, as he so often did, to take a few days' rest. Surprisingly, this time Hitler complied. He had his adjutant telephone my office and ask me to come to Berchtesgaden. At the Berghof he liked to gather his old cronies around him. Their familiar faces and innocuous jokes could free him from his gloomy moods. His military entourage, meanwhile, was quartered in the village down below.

When I arrived at the Berghof in the evening, we exchanged only brief greetings. As was his habit these days, Hitler sat in silence in front of the big fireplace, staring for hours into the flames. The following day, too, he was tired and dispirited. Toward noon he asked us to join the daily walk to the Teahouse farther down the mountain.[1] It was one of those dismal Obersalzberg days, with west winds driving low-lying clouds from the plateau of Upper Bavaria down into the valley. These clouds piled up against the surrounding mountain slopes, producing steady falls of snow. In spite of the noon hour, it was dark, but at least the gusts of snow had let up. Hitler came down from the upper floor in his shabby field-gray windbreaker. His valet handed him his worn velours hat and a cane. Pleasantly, with a somewhat remote cordiality and as though he were seeking my tacit understanding, he turned to me. "You come. I'd like to talk a bit." Turning to Bormann, he went on, "Stay behind with the others." We walked down the path, which had been newly cleared of snow. To the right and left were low walls of snow; in the background the Untersberg. The clouds had dissipated; the sun was already low in the sky, casting long shadows, and the Alsatian dashed barking through the snow.

[1] Hitler would walk down to this Teahouse below the Berghof almost every day. On the other hand he very rarely turned his steps toward the higher Eagle's Nest, or Eyrie, often wrongly called the Teahouse.

After we had walked in silence side by side for a few minutes, Hitler suddenly said, "How I hate the East! The snow alone depresses me. Sometimes I think I'll even stop coming to this mountain in winter. I can't stand seeing snow any longer."

I said nothing; what reply could I have made? Subdued, I walked along at his side. He went on talking without inflection about his antipathy to the East, the winter, the war. Lately he had been complaining, to persuade himself and others, of how he was suffering because fate was forever forcing him to do nothing but wage war. Abruptly he stopped, thrust the cane into the ground, and turned to face me. "Speer, you are my architect. You know that I always wanted to be an architect myself." His voice low, sounding as though all strength had been drained from him, he went on: "The World War and the criminal November Revolution prevented that. Otherwise I might today be Germany's foremost architect, as you are now. But the Jews! November ninth was the consequence of their systematic sedition." Hitler grew excited. One could practically see the gears beginning to mesh as he wound himself up into his old rage. His voice gained strength too; it became louder, passing after a while into a hoarse staccato. An old man, a man who was really already defeated, stood there in the snow impotently squeezing out his stored-up bitterness, his toxic resentments. "The Jews were doing it even then. They organized the munitions strike too! In my regiment alone hundreds of soldiers lost their lives. The Jews made me go into politics."

Often before, he had declared that the defeat of the Reich, the humiliation of the nation, and the dishonorable Revolution of 1918 had made him a politician; but he had never put it this way. Yet I distinctly had the feeling that he had started on this walk solely for the sake of a little distraction, so that he could forget the depressing news from the battlefronts. When we set out he had probably not even thought of the Jews. But the snow evidently brought the wintry plains of the East to his mind, and to escape these odious images he had taken refuge in thoughts of that old adversary who from the outset had stood behind all the failures and threats of his life. Never before had I felt so clearly how absolutely essential the figure of the Jew was for Hitler—as an object of hatred and at the same time an escape. For now he had found what the landscape of his beloved mountain and this winter walk could not give him. The tightening noose around the armies at Stalingrad, the intensifying air war, Montgomery's breakthrough at El Alamein—obviously he had forgotten all that, and his dawning recognition that the war was already lost.

As though the outburst had exhausted him, he went on talking without excitement, in the same weary manner as before, drained of energy. "You know, Speer, I have never really lived like other people. In the last thirty years I have sacrificed my health. Before the First World War I often did not know what I was going to live on next day. In the war I was an ordinary frontline soldier. Then came the Revolution and my mission, and with that the difficulties began, for ten long years. Anyone else would have given up. But fate wanted it so; Providence helped me."

We began walking somewhat faster. "Then when I was called to head the nation, I wanted to create Germany anew—with you, Speer— erecting buildings and more buildings. Germany was going to become the most beautiful country in the world. Just think of what we would have made of Berlin! Paris would have been nothing by comparison. But they've spoiled everything for me. They always read my offers as signs of weakness. They thought I was easily frightened. They thought that of *me!* What does that crew know about the Führer of National Socialist Germany! But we'll get hold of them! And then we'll settle accounts. They'll find out who I am! This time not one will escape. I've always been too lenient. But no more. Now we'll settle accounts." He called Blondi, the Alsatian, who had run on ahead.

At the time I often wondered whether Hitler still believed in victory. It is indicative of the atmosphere in the top leadership that I never candidly discussed this question with the few higher-ranking military men with whom I had a personal friendship that went beyond official relations, such as General Guderian and Grand Admiral Dönitz, or with whom I even used the pronoun of intimacy, the *Du*, like Field Marshal Milch. At most I tried to sound them out with a few anxious hints. Today it seems to me that in spite of all his invocations of Providence, even Hitler was uncertain. This walk, with its continual shifts of mood from depression to aggression, from self-pity to delusory projects for the future, was typical of Hitler's unstable state not only on this day, but in general. During the war such shifts could be observed almost daily.

As though to bolster his confidence, he began citing examples from history. "Now I know," he said, "why Frederick the Great decided he had at last had enough after the Third Silesian War. I've had enough for a lifetime too. This war is robbing me of the best years of my life. I wanted to make history not with won battles but with the buildings you and I designed together. Those barbarians almost conquered the empire once before; they were at the gates of Vienna. But there, too, a

great man opposed them and drove the Asiatics back. How our old empire flourished then, after Prince Eugene's victory. Remember that beautiful baroque Vienna sprang up immediately after the hour of gravest
danger. It will be like that for us, too, after we have won. In the same
way we will build palaces and glorious buildings. They will be the
monuments of our victory over the Bolshevists."

Have I reproduced that more or less accurately? Has the character
been made plausible? I must remember that, after all, I am always listening to his voice, hearing him clear his throat, seeing his slightly
stooped figure before my eyes. After my release I must listen to records
and look at films to see whether he has shifted in my memory, and
whether the sinister or repulsive features have been thrust too much
into the foreground. For if that were the whole Hitler, how is it possible that he captivated me so, and for more than a decade?

November 26, 1952   Yesterday I had to write many letters, and
comically today my left wrist is so swollen that the bone has disappeared. In the medical office Dönitz comments, "It's high time a blood
sample was taken." Funk, always more pessimistic, says, "The hand is
blue and red. Very bad. Looks like a severe nervous disease." The Russian doctor bandages the hand and prescribes Salizyl four times a day.
In addition I am not permitted to go into the garden.

I had to write so much because I now have two routes to reach the
outside. A new American, who shall be called Frederik, thinks that in
view of my large family the official number of letters is far from
sufficient. Through him I can now write as many as I want. I would
not have thought him capable of so much active sympathy; he has a
rather insensitive face, and is scared to boot; he breaks into a sweat
when he merely considers the risks he is taking.

For that reason I would have been glad to decline his offer, because
my opportunities are already sufficient. But Frederik might suspect
that I already had a liaison with outside. That must not be. But I don't
know what is going to happen if a third and a fourth offer their assistance. I would have to write letter upon letter every night, until my
right hand as well becomes totally numb.

November 29, 1952   The first Sunday in Advent. The Advent
wreath is hung up in the chapel. In the evening Major Andreyev in
person removes it from the cellblock. Shortly thereafter the British director turns up and comments, "This fool of a chaplain didn't ask per-

mission." But Colonel Le Cornu takes the action of his Russian colleague calmly.

As he has been doing every evening, Hess makes my bed, because I am still not permitted to move my heavily bandaged hand. I use the opportunity to inform him that his wife has published his letters as a book. Hess becomes feverishly excited at this news. When he hints that he considers it quite natural for him to be ahead of the rest of us as an author, I put a bit of a damper on. "You should be grateful to the censor for always scissoring out your crazy ideas about politics. This way you are published purified, virtually a model democrat." Hess laughs and pretends to be shocked. All the same, my wife liked the published letters to Hess's son. Since she dealt with many other matters concerning Hess in her last clandestine letter, I read passages to him while he is making my bed. "Did your wife know about those things you undertook against Hitler toward the end?" he asks. "No," I reply, "I didn't want to involve her. . . . Thanks very much for the bed." Hess replies generously, "The letter was thanks enough for many beds. Please give your wife my warmest regards." What I like about Hess is that he does not take my views, which must be a horror to him, as a basis for being hostile to me, as Dönitz does.

December 2, 1952 Today Dönitz had a half-hour talk with his wife. After he came back he commented ironically: "It was very pleasant, almost intimate. Only the Russian interpreter, the French *sous-chef*, a guard, and one or the other of the directors, alternately, were present."

December 4, 1952 In the garden Hess tells me that in his last letter he enjoined his son always to carry out the duties of chivalry and honor. "Aha," I say, "you already have your eye on posterity." Hess laughs, but grows thoughtful when I ask him whether under Hitler the wives of Severing or Thälmann would have been allowed to publish their husbands' letters in book form. "Of course not," he answers emphatically. I pursue my questioning: what would he say if the Federal Republic forbade the publication of his letters? "That wouldn't do at all," Hess replies, shaking his head. "They have democracy now. If they did that, they'd no longer have it."

December 5, 1952 Dönitz has illegally read an extract from the official history of the British Admiralty. He is wildly pleased because the British share his viewpoint: that neglect to build hundreds of

U-boats before the beginning of the war, or at least during the first few years, was the crucial strategic error. Again and again he stresses that he will bring up all these points against Raeder in the full light of publicity once he and Raeder are free. He grows very excited when he talks about this.[2]

December 6, 1952 Kranzbühler has talked with important personages of the Western countries, so he writes in a clandestine note to Dönitz. It would be best, he says, if we were to count on serving our full time. We discuss this information with peculiar calm. The idea that we might someday be free again has by now vanished into the realm of unreality.

December 11, 1952 Le Cornu, who has been our British director these many years, comes to bid goodbye. He has just seen Neurath and Dönitz; there are tears in his eyes and his voice trembles. "This is your new director," he says, indicating the officer standing behind him. Then he gives me his best wishes for the future, and a forbidden handshake. I thank him "for all you did, but more for what you wanted to do." Even Hess confirms that the departing director acted "like a gentleman," but on principle does not shake hands with him.

December 15, 1952 The guards are forbidden to bring books with them into the cellblock. Tonight the indefatigable Major Andreyev opened the top button of an American guard's jacket and took out a book. This is a kind of border incident, since a Russian officer is not permitted to touch an American soldier.

December 16, 1952 Mr. John Egerton, the new British director, formerly a judge, is going from cell to cell. In a notebook he writes down our wishes. In these five years in Spandau we have not heretofore experienced such conscientiousness and concern. When supper is handed out, he orders that all the doors be opened simultaneously. For the first time we stand together at the serving table. There is no apparent reason why we should still be let out and locked up again singly, since we spend many hours together in the garden.

But in comes his colleague Andreyev and snaps at us, "All return to the cells immediately. But only one after the other." We trudge back;

---

[2] In his *Memoirs: Ten Years and Twenty Days* (trans. by R. H. Stevens, Cleveland, World Publishing Co., 1959), Dönitz represses this sharp criticism of Raeder.

what else are we to do? I hear fragments of a heated argument between the two directors. The Englishman: "But then the food gets cold."

The Russian is unmoved. "No matter. What's forbidden is forbidden."

The Englishman replies coldly, "We shall see each other at the conference."

From the official letter to Dönitz it appears that his wife was received by the pope, who was friendly and sympathetic. This news has given Dönitz an enormous lift. Years ago Neurath's daughter saw the pope, and Frau Funk, the archbishop of Cologne. A veritable pilgrimage has begun, although we are all Protestants. I am glad that my wife will not visit the pope.

December 22, 1952 Kovpak was too vigilant today. Twice I could not hand over my material. I must keep all that I have written with me overnight. And it has been quite a lot recently. Loquacious Christmas season!

December 23, 1952 This time it worked. Sent off my notes in the morning.

In the afternoon unfriendly Guryev inspects Neurath's pockets. Triumphantly he removes two small pieces of chocolate. Since the ball of horse manure was found, months ago, this is the first time the shakedowns have yielded anything. I promptly get rid of ballast; several sheets of paper are dumped into the toilet. But we are not searched.

Immediately thereafter the Soviet director, Andreyev, comes with his interpreter to question Neurath while the prisoner is presumably still shaken. But Neurath declares calmly, "Chocolate? I found it on my table when I came in from the garden. I thought it was probably from my Christmas package."

The new English director seems out of sorts when he comes into the corridor. He snaps at the complacent Guryev so loudly that all of us can hear it, "Don't stand around with your hands in your pockets. And take that cigarette out of your mouth in the presence of an officer. What kind of behavior is this! Did you understand me? Besides, I want to talk to the prisoners alone. Go away."

Dönitz comments, "How modest we have become. We are pleased when an officer behaves like an officer."

January 1, 1953 At midnight I was awake, thinking of my wife, children, friends. I knew that in the same minute they were thinking of me. Through the open window came sounds of shots, shouting, and bells ringing. So the old year ended.

In the morning, friendly greetings in the washroom. Schirach and Raeder shake hands with me for the first time in a long time and give me their best wishes. "What do you expect of the new year?" Schirach asks.

"I have made a firm resolution never to be irritable," I reply.

Astonished, Hess says, "Really? I already am." He looks discouraged.

The French chief guard comes and in spite of his speech defect manages to say solemnly, "I wish that the walls of the prison may be shattered this year." Other Western guards also express amazingly friendly wishes for a rapid end to our imprisonment.

January 7, 1953 During the last few days Major Brésard has tried in vain to find out who gave the chocolate to Neurath. He is said even to have had the garbage pails examined in his presence, in hopes of finding the remnants of the chocolate wrappers. Today the four directors met for a special session on this question. Ten witnesses, so we are told, were summoned for questioning and had to wait in the anteroom for from two to six hours, among them the Russian who had made the find. Sitting alone in a corner, he was cut by his comrades; partly because they were losing an afternoon off on his account, partly because they feel that Neurath, who is almost eighty, is welcome to the chocolate. In the evening the British director informs the delinquent of the verdict: "The conference has decided that you are not to be punished because you took the chocolate. But you are given a warning because you did not promptly hand it over to the nearest guard as soon as you found it."

January 20, 1953 The "chocolate affair" scared many of the guards; sources of information dried up for a few days. But now they are beginning to flow again.

And promptly there is great excitement. Funk tells us in the garden: "A plot has been uncovered. Skorzeny, the man who liberated Mussolini, is said to have wanted to kidnap us, using two helicopters and a hundred men. Along with this there was to be a Putsch. All of us were going to serve as a new government, headed by Dönitz as Hitler's successor. The British Secret Service has arrested Naumann, Goebbels's undersecretary, the former press chief, Sündermann, and Gauleiter Scheel. The newspapers are headlining the whole thing."

Apparently Dönitz wanted to keep this news from me. "But I

couldn't help hearing you talking with the American a while ago," I say. "According to what I've heard, you're Number One in the new government of the Reich——"

Excited, he interrupts me: "What nonsense. They ought to let me out of here so that I can issue a statement that I have nothing to do with it. I condemn Hitler's system, and I never had anything to do with SS men like Skorzeny." There was a short pause. "But I am still and will remain the legal chief of state. Until I die!"

I pretend astonishment. "But there has been a new chief of state for the longest time. Heuss was elected, after all."

"I beg your pardon," Dönitz insists. "He was installed under pressure from the occupying powers. Until all political parties, including the National Socialists, are permitted to function and until they elect someone else, my legitimacy remains. Nothing can change that one iota. Even if I wanted it changed."

I try persuasion. "If I were in your position I would renounce my rights."

Dönitz shakes his head in despair at such incomprehension. "You simply refuse to understand. Even if I renounced the office I would remain chief of state, because I cannot renounce it until I have appointed a successor."

At this point I too became obstinate. "But even emperors and kings abdicate after a revolution."

Dönitz sets me straight: "They always appointed a successor. Otherwise their abdication had no validity."

I play my trump card. "But then you're in luck that the crown prince is dead. Otherwise there would be three of you." Then it occurs to me that Prince Louis Ferdinand is alive, and I ask, "Tell me, what arrangement did you make in 1945 with the head of the House of Hohenzollern?"

Neurath, shrugging, puts in, "This idea has become an obsession with him."

January 24, 1953   Reassuring news that McCloy in America has called the plot a soap bubble, that Adenauer has denounced the alleged revelations. In fact it has come out that the whole Skorzeny "affair" is more or less a journalistic fiction.

January 26, 1953   A book on building construction has arrived. It is written in a dense style and with as small print as an encyclopedia. With the cooperation of the British director, my wife gave the book to the Wilmersdorf central library, and it was then delivered to me from the stock of that library. For the first time I am obtaining a systematic survey of the progress of the last five years. At the moment I am working through the section on wood joints. My head is a whirl of pegs, dowels, tongue-and-grooves, tenons, dovetails.

February 3, 1953 We have been given orders to paint the hall, which by now has become gray and dull. When was the last time? I no longer remember; the years merge in my mind. We immediately set to work, beginning with whitewashing the ceiling. How strong is the impulse in man to make himself useful. The directors obtain a paint sprayer. Dönitz and Schirach pump while I direct the apparatus at the ceiling. The Russian director looks on with interest. But no paint comes out. As I screw off the clogged jet, a stream of white lime solution strikes me in the face. For the first time I see the Russian director laughing loudly. Angry, but as if wholly by accident, I turn the stream from the spray gun into the hall, whereupon everybody flees, including the director. Immediately afterwards the jet becomes clogged again. From the ladder I call down to Dönitz: "Make the mixture thinner. More water in the pot." Then it becomes fun to spray. In a few hours the hall is finished. Years ago it took me several weeks with the brush.

But when I look at the dried ceiling a few hours later, it is merely coated with a pale gray mist. Dönitz put too much water into the lime soup.

February 5, 1953 Meanwhile the oil paint has arrived. It is gray, or as Letham proudly declares, "battleship gray." For my taste it is too somber. Using the coloring powder that is intended for the upper parts of the wall (ochre, yellow, and umber), I mix up a livelier, more imaginative color, which is approved by Dönitz and Schirach. Using the same proportions, I then mix in the entire supply of coloring materials.

February 6, 1953 We begin work at nine o'clock as usual. Letham looks at the color sample. "Oh, what sort of color is that? That's not gray, is it?"

I admit it is not.

Uneasy, he says, "Oh, but don't change the color! You know, the American director decided on battleship gray. Don't do that." He speaks in a rather tearful voice, as if to a child who must be treated kindly and urged to mend its ways.

"Yes, I understand," I reply. "But I've already mixed all the paint to that color."

Metham is thrown into despair. "Oh, oh, what have you done? Really?" Troubled, he walks away. We set to work.

February 12, 1953   One of the four Berlin city commandants frequently inspects the prison. Today the new French commandant of Berlin arrived, accompanied by a train of directors, adjutants, and guards. In front of my door I heard someone say, "This is Speer." He had himself introduced: "May I present the new commandant of the French Sector, General Demiau." He gave a proper military salute; such are the trivialities that attract one's notice. Then he wanted to see my sketchbook, found a few appreciative words to say, and left with a compliment on my French.

February 17, 1953   During the noon rest Frederik slips me the first installment of a series on Dönitz's government, which is being published under the title "The Twenty-Three-Day Fourth Reich." Dönitz must already have read it, for he looks distinctly complacent when he talks with Frederik. For my part, I read the whole thing with rather irritable feelings, for a large part of it is viewed wrongly; most of the individuals are seen in a heroic light, and almost everything is distorted. The tenor of the article is plain from the statement by Dönitz that is used as an epigraph for this first installment: "I have nothing to apologize for and would do everything all over again just as I did then." All this makes me want to record many details of that period that come back to me now.

When I went into the garden after reading the article, Dönitz came up to me and stood beside me. The two of us looked across the snowy field at the red prison wall, eight meters high. Of course he assumed that I had read the *Illustrierte Post.* But he asked with pretended indifference, "Anything new?"

I wouldn't gratify him, and merely said tersely, "No." After a pause of several minutes, during which we regarded the wintry garden with a seemingly bored air, I asked, "What about you—anything new on your mind?" Lengthy pause as the admiral ponders. "No."

Amused, I remark, "I suppose this is rather the way conversations go among old salts."

February 26, 1953   A notice on Neurath's door: "For health reasons Number Three has been issued an armchair." "I don't need one at all," Neurath grumbles. But apparently his occasional bouts of asthma are taken more seriously than he likes. This afternoon his chair was delivered. I could scarcely believe my eyes: it comes from the Chancellery and was designed by me in 1938.

The damask upholstery is tattered, the sheen faded, the veneer scratched, but I still like the proportions, especially the curve of the rear legs. What an encounter! Wagg says the chair came from a furniture warehouse belonging to the city of Berlin.

Evening. I am really grateful for the chance that brought me face to face with a part of my own past. It is, moreover, a past still entirely unburdened by war, persecution, foreign laborers, guilt complexes. Nor is there anything about the piece of furniture itself that I find embarrassing, nothing exaggerated, nothing pompous. It is a plain chair, good craftsmanship. Could I still design something like that? Perhaps later I might like to design furniture instead of buildings.

Only on reflection do I gradually realize that this simple chair in Neurath's cell may be the only thing I shall ever see of all my work during those years. The Chancellery has already been eliminated; the Nuremberg Rally site is to be demolished. Nothing else is left of all the grandiose plans that were supposed to transform the architectural aspect of Germany. How often Hitler said to me that our buildings would testify to the greatness of our epoch after thousands of years—and now this chair. Oh yes, and a small cottage that I built for my wife's parents in Heidelberg, when I was still a student. Nothing else.

Will those plans survive at least as an idea? How many never-built schemes and projects have become a part of the history of architecture? In an account of building in our time will there at least be one plate showing work by me? Granted, it was late architecture, still another attempt—how many have there been?—to build in the classical mode. But that was always evident to me, without bothering me.

Yet sometimes it seems to me that I am a terminus, a kind of last classicist. I don't particularly mean this in terms of form or style. I have never believed the innovators who maintain that pillars and portals are no longer permissible. Such elements have persisted for four thousand years; and who has the right to rule that they are no longer possible today?

Something else is bringing this style, and presumably all traditional styles, to an end: the fact that the craft traditions on which the forms of the past were founded are now dying out. There are no longer masons who can hew a cornice out of stone. Soon there will be no more carpenters who can fit a stairway, no plasterers who can make a ceiling.

And if a Palladio, a Schlüter, a Schinkel were to come along a hundred years from now, he would have to work with steel, concrete, and glass. Our era, no matter how well or ill it may have built, was truly the farewell to a long and venerable tradition. It may not be mere chance that nothing has remained of all our plans. Nothing but a chair.

March 4, 1953   Today I passed by Dönitz's cell to fetch clean sheets. His door was open; he eagerly beckoned me to come in. His face had suddenly become several years younger. He pointed out the caption for a news photo of him: "The man who saved the lives of hundreds of thousands."

March 8, 1953   A few days ago, stimulated by the series perhaps, I began writing down my "memoirs." I have been hesitating for so long, making false starts, rejecting samples, finally beginning to doubt my ability altogether. Now I began writing as if it were the most natural thing in the world. So far it has given me little trouble. I am full of eagerness to write and happy to have a task that will last me for years. However, I have made it easy for myself. I did not begin with Hitler, but with my home and childhood.

I am setting myself a daily stint: an average of one closely written page a day. In four years that will yield approximately fourteen hundred pages—a good-sized book.

March 9, 1953   It was suspiciously quiet today during the noon pause. Since I wanted to go on with the opening passages of my memoirs, I made certain nobody was spying by stuffing my pipe and flipping the signal that I needed a light for it. When it was brought to me, I caught a glimpse of Selinavov painting the edging. Reassured, I went to work.

In the evening came the news of Stalin's death. Has been dead for several days. Now the second man who cast a pall over this century is gone. It means nothing to me.

March 17, 1953   Have already worked on the memoirs for ten days. Every morning after dusting the cell I put on a sweater, pull a woolen nightcap over my head, heat up my mind with a big pipe, and open the window vent to provide a supply of oxygen. At my noon writing session, I have the big manual of construction resting on my drawn-up knees. In this way what I am doing is shielded from inquisitive observers.

I find it something of an advantage that aside from a few smuggled books I have not been allowed to read anything on contemporary history. I am writing blind, so to speak.

March 18, 1953   As I recently read in Stefan Zweig, Casanova would never have written his autobiography had he not spent his last years in a wretched little town in Bohemia. For me, Spandau is that small town. Here I find the solitude I need to draw up a balance sheet. While the others spend hours in the garden trading shared opinions about the past, I am considering what really happened.

March 19, 1953   All this evening of my birthday I have kept going at the memoirs to distract myself. Of Cellini someone said, "An artist of whom virtually nothing but an autobiography is left!"

Interruption. Funk at my peephole. "Come over to my cell. I have to show you something interesting." Irritated by the disturbance, which violates our usual social forms, I do not react. After fifteen minutes Funk is back. "Do come, it's really interesting." I have my cell unlocked. "Put out the light!" Funk says. "Do you see the moon with the stars in front of it? That is the Turkish sign for good luck." Long is bored, because Funk showed him the same thing a few minutes ago, and disappears. In the darkness Funk thrusts a cup toward me and whispers, "Quick, drink! To your forty-eighth birthday! What you dream tonight will be fulfilled." Where in the world can he have got this excellent cognac?

March 21, 1953   Today as we were planting a chestnut sapling Funk said, "We'll be here to sit in the shadow of this tree."

News that Malenkov will be Stalin's successor. The example of Bormann showed how advantageously situated a secretary is to become a dictator's successor. After Lenin, his secretary, Stalin; after Stalin now, his secretary, Malenkov. Malenkov is said to have made a speech stressing peace. Hess comments laconically, "I know, I know. That's when the danger of war is greatest."

April 3, 1953   Today it suddenly came back to me how in 1942 the expansion of the armaments program almost ran aground on difficulties over the supply of screws. The historian easily overlooks such details. I must pay attention to such points. That is why I am noting it here.

April 11, 1953 Through a clandestine note from his son-in-law, Dönitz has heard the results of a survey by the Allensbacher Institut* in July 1952. He himself stands at the head of a list of formerly prominent personages whom the Germans still have a good opinion of. Dönitz has 46 percent; he is closely followed by Schacht with 42, Göring with 37, myself with 30, Hitler with 24 percent. Schirach and Hess lag behind with 22 percent. Seven percent have a bad opinion of Dönitz, 9 percent of me, 10 of Schacht, 29 of Schirach and Hess, 36 of Göring, and 47 percent of Hitler. "Because the German people cherish me in their hearts, I shall soon be getting out," Dönitz observed complacently as he stood beside me today washing his hands.

Nevertheless, the letter gave Dönitz no pleasure, for his son-in-law unforgiveably passed on the information that he is now as popular as Rommel. In a tone of sharp repugnance, Dönitz commented that Rommel had been nothing but a propaganda hero because he participated in the July 20 conspiracy. Then Dönitz stalked off.

For a moment I wondered whether I should defend Rommel, whom I at any rate always got on well with. But I refrained. Ample experience has shown that conversation on these questions is pointless with all my fellow prisoners, although Dönitz in his agitation had left an obvious opening when he commented bitterly that everybody still speaks of Rommel as the "field marshal," while he and Raeder are always merely called "the former grand admirals." "The thing is ridiculous—even under international law the rank of grand admiral is just as irrevocable as that of field marshal." I forbore to remind him that he had not come forth with this opinion when after July 20 his fellow officers had their rank revoked, and were in fact expelled from the army, so that Hitler could hang them.

April 14, 1953 Stimulated by yesterday's argument, I have been trying to call the other Dönitz to mind. For my memoirs, therefore, I have done a sketch of our first meeting in his Paris headquarters, when he was commander of the submarine fleet. He then had the reputation of being a calm, capable, objective-minded officer. His headquarters in a plain modern apartment building differed sharply in its sobriety from the pomp that Field Marshal Sperrle had displayed the day before in the Palais Luxembourg, where he gave a banquet served by liveried waiters. At the moment a horde of U-boats was attacking an Atlantic

* The most prominent German public affairs research institution.—*Translators' note.*

convoy. From Paris the submarines, thousands of miles away, were guided through every phase of the battle by shortwave radio.

Shortly before my meeting with Dönitz a British submarine had been captured. To everyone's surprise it was equipped with steel torpedo tubes. German U-boats were provided with bronze torpedo tubes, and it was taken for granted that no other metal could be used. After experiments with the captured vessel, German engineers declared that in the future we too could use steel tubes, which was highly important, because bronze was a serious bottleneck. Together with Dönitz, I finally persuaded Hitler to allow us to go ahead on this. Raeder then felt ignored in his capacity as supreme commander of the navy, and forbade Dönitz henceforth to have anything more to do with me. He also sent a reprimand to me through official channels, by way of the Navy High Command.

When Dönitz became Raeder's successor in the spring of 1943, I worked closely with him. He was always decent and reliable, and made an excellent impression on me. Despite the clouding of our relationship in the course of our imprisonment, I remember our collaboration with pleasure. I understood why he has held aloof from me, and respect his reasons. Moreover, he has been gripped by the psychosis of a prisoner who dashes his head against the wall of his verdict and sentence. Such refusal to accept often produces unexpected, uncontrollable reactions.

April 24, 1953   Every evening the medical aide goes from cell to cell with a large tray on which there are several bottles of medicine and innumerable tubes of tablets. He was accompanied today by Guryev, the Russian who at Christmastime had that clairvoyant impulse and found chocolate in Neurath's pocket. Shortly after the two disappeared into Funk's cell I heard noisy excitement in the corridor. The medical aide, Vlaer, shouted, "Then go ahead and try it!" Guryev's deep voice replied, "I declare all bottles confiscated." Then Vlaer, indignantly: "What, you want to search me? Don't you dare touch me!" Doors slammed; other guards came and went.

A few hours later Funk filled me in. "Yes, it's a wild story. What luck I had. The medical aide pulled a bottle out of his pocket in a flash and poured the contents into my cup. Cognac! The Russian was standing outside the door, but caught a glimpse of something. He snatched at the cup, smelled first with one nostril, then with the other, and ran after the medical aide. But due to habit he naturally locked me in first. So I was alone with my cognac! The cup almost full, a tremendous drink. I raised it to my lips and drank it in one draft. Down the hatch

It wasn't easy. But it had to be drunk up. My legs began to shake. But I immediately poured coffee from the other cup into the cognac cup. The whole thing took just seconds. Then the Russian was back at the door and in the room. Again he smelled the cup. Imagine his face! Coffee. He just sagged. A transmutation. He couldn't figure it out. Then off he rushed with the full cup."

Laughing, Vlaer joined us. "What luck I had. First he smelled all the bottles, then searched my pockets."

Where had the cognac bottle been?

"I always carry that in the rear pocket of my trousers," the aide replied slyly. "Nobody's ever found it there. I guess the Russians don't know anything about that."

April 26, 1953   The subject of the confiscated drink was presented at the directors' meeting. It was determined that the beverage in question was cold coffee.

May 2, 1953   In Coburg my friend's secretary is typing up the closely written pages I have smuggled out. Naturally my friend is reading the typescript. Now, in a letter that I received today, he complains because I have called Hitler a criminal. But there is no dodging that. Either I write the way I see things today, or it is not worth doing. Certainly I shall be losing a good many friends. And perhaps acquiring no new ones.

May 6, 1953   For a long time I have been marking the heights of my children on my door. The marks make cruelly plain how they are literally growing away from me. In today's official letter I learn that in the past year Ernst has grown twelve centimeters and now measures 1.35 meters; Albert is 1.77 meters tall, Hilde 1.69, Fritz 1.74, Margret 1.63, and Arnold 1.64 meters.

May 9, 1953   For his birthday Schirach drank half a bottle of cognac. I see him sitting dazed on his bed.

June 16, 1953   I have written to the children that I am transferring my parents' estate to them, to avoid confiscation. Each child will receive his share, but must use it to go to college. Supposing that education costs for each child come to about thirty thousand marks, as much again will remain as a reserve. The fund is in inflation-proof investments.

June 21, 1953   A few days ago sensational rumors about an uprising in East Germany. With a shock I realized today how uninterested I have been all these years in the Soviet-occupied part of Germany. Strange! Here we sit, all erstwhile leading men in a government that incessantly spoke of Germany, and we have almost never mentioned Weimar, Rostock, Dresden, or Frankfurt an der Oder, or wondered what life is like for people in that area. Not once have I tried to imagine how the presence of the Russians may have changed life there, whether they dominate the street scenes in the cities, whether people have adapted to their presence. Apparently not—given the German temperament with its bent for order, the fact that these people have attempted an uprising bespeaks an extraordinary degree of bitterness and despair.

In the garden Neurath and Dönitz became rather excited for a moment, saying that we take no interest, go on behaving as usual; it almost seems as though we do not want to talk about it.

I held my peace.

June 22, 1953   Today the melody of the song "I Had a Comrade" drifted in from some loudspeaker. There is not a murmur from any of the cells.

July 8, 1953   Heard today that at the beginning of the Russian month and two weeks after the uprising of June 17, Major Andreyev invited his three colleagues to a lavish dinner. The American director did not come.

July 16, 1953   A petition for a copy of my verdict has been denied on the basis of a Russian veto. When I remarked that every prisoner had a right to see his verdict, Brésard replied, "You have enough wires to the outside!" What does he know? Are all our secret communications not so secret after all?

July 22, 1953   Recently, by a decision of the directors we have had to wear the official prison dress of heavy brown corduroy even in spells of tropical heat. After years, shorts have suddenly been forbidden. Pease, who informs me of this decision, is surprised at how calmly I take it. "What's wrong with you?" he asks me. The truth is, it scarcely interests me.

August 2, 1953   In the early morning hours of July 28 Neurath had another attack of angina pectoris. A British and a French guard

I passed the time dashing
off a few pen drawings
which expressed my long-
ing for the small towns of
South Germany. In this
way I have actually suc-
ceeded in creating an
imaginary world.

For the first time in years I
have completed a design that
is fully worked out. Happy
about this activity, and also
about a new version of my upper-
middle-class house.

For Göring I designed an Office
of the Reich Marshal whose
model, in the back of my mind,
was the Palazzo Pitti in
Florence.

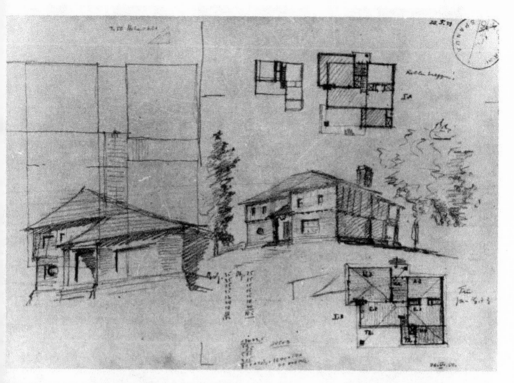

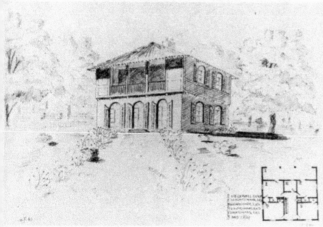

A few days ago I began developing the design of a medium-sized house. The Russian guards are delighted when I explain my sketches and ask them their opinion. Their response is always the same single phrase: *"Ochin khorosho"* ("very good"). Since I have not done any architectural drawing since 1942, the detailed drawings give me trouble. Although I have had enough of monumental architecture and turn my mind deliberately to utilitarian buildings, it sometimes comes hard for me to bid goodbye to my dreams of having a place in the history of architecture.

Sometimes I imagine my fellow prisoners in the days of their glory and recall my former meetings with them. Recently Funk has started a friendly talk with me every few days, but my own ineptness at small talk hampers things. Another obstacle is Funk's tendency to wallow in self-pity. But sometimes he gives even his laments an ironic twist. He also likes to mourn the loss of his onetime corpulence and recollect vanished sybaritic pleasures.

Raeder and Dönitz have their difficulties with each other. Raeder, who in the spring of 1943 was replaced by Dönitz as commander of the navy, is now seventy-two years old, and still vigorous. He still regards Dönitz, fifteen years his junior and his former subordinate as chief of the submarine forces, as an over-ambitious officer. Dönitz blames his predecessor for his policy of bloated surface vessels. Thanks to Raeder, he says, the German navy entered the war with only some fifty U-boats, of which only ten could be permanently operating in the Atlantic.

Dönitz, with whom I was once quite friendly in the line of our official duties, seldom talks with me, and when he does, usually makes covert nasty remarks.

In the last few months my relationship with Schirach has become more and more relaxed. In a conversation about Hitler he said: "Hitler's credulity was rather romantic in nature, the kind of thing we systematically cultivated in the Hitler Youth. After all, we had set up the idea of a sworn community; we believed in loyalty and sincerity."

Hermann Göring, the principal in the trial, grandiloquently took all responsibility, only to employ all his cunning and energy to deny that he bore any specific guilt. He had become a debauched parasite; in prison he regained his old self and displayed an alertness, intelligence, and quick-wittedness such as he had not shown since the early days of the Third Reich.

In the midst of the many dubious creatures, the numerous condottiere types, who peopled Hitler's court, Neurath seemed like a figure from another world. His world had remained that of the monarchy; as the representative of the conservatives, he atoned for the game they had played with Hitler.

As Hess and I walked together today he told me, with a touch of cunning, about his flight to England. "Have I already told you what Hitler's last words to me were, two days before I took off? 'But fly carefully, Hess!' He meant a flight from Munich to Berlin in the Junkers 52."

As late as the end of 1944 Göring emphasized to me that he must stand by the Führer. He added that what would come afterward was another matter.

Robert Ley, head of the Labor Front and Party organization chief, escaped trial by hanging himself; tearing the hem from his towel, he attached it to the drainpipe of the toilet.

Of course the twelve years in the aura of Hitler's power must have taken from me that spontaneity I surely had at times in my youth. I had better not tell myself that it was only the effect of the great personality and the historic tasks that weighed me down. It was also bondage in the commonest sense of the term, not only in the sublimated, psychological sense. After all, I was entirely dependent on Hitler's whim for achieving my ambitions.

Today I mowed for the first time with the new lawnmower. The machine's resistance, so I have calculated, corresponds to a difference in altitude of four hundred meters. In other words, it is as if I were climbing a medium-sized mountain in the Black Forest. In reality I mowed four thousand square meters.

The garden work is gradually becoming, as Hess disapprovingly observes, an obsession. At first I felt it as a liberation. But now I am sometimes fearful of the trivializing effect of such mechanical activity. If I go in persistently for gardening, I may become a gardener intellectually and spiritually. Survival in prison is a problem in balance.

Fiery heat in the garden today. Scarcely a breath of wind. Now and then I walk through the mist of water from the garden sprinkler. For a few hours today I hauled water for the fruit trees; I let the larger ones have three cans, the smaller ones either one or two.

In intense heat, every other day I carry fifty full watering cans, each holding ten liters of water, to the plants I set in the spring.

I can now do whatever I please in my part of the garden. In the spring I dug out the ground to a depth of about half a meter, and created a sunken rock garden; using thousands of bricks, I made a series of retaining walls twenty to forty centimeters in height.

When I lie on the grass in the rock garden, these brick retaining walls look like a small city. This garden, this ridiculous architecture in bricks, has the priceless advantage of being concretely tangible and still there every single morning.

I can hardly believe
it. A prison employee
has offered to smuggle
letters out for me.
Our toilet paper has
since acquired unimagi-
nable importance to me
and my family. What
luck that no one
thought of dyeing it
black. I keep the
sheets I have written
on in my shoes; such
padding has its points in
the present cold snap.

If this way to reach the
outside world actually
proves practicable, my
whole existence here
will have taken on
a new dimension. Up to
now I have operated on
the assumption that
in prison all I have
to do is to survive;
that I will not be able
to accomplish anything
meaningful until the
twenty years are up.
Now I am obsessed with
the idea of using this
time of confinement for
writing a book of
major importance: a
biography of Hitler, a
description of my years
as armaments minister,
or an account of the
apocalyptic final phase
of the war. That
could mean transforming
prison cell into scholar's
den. During the walk in
the yard I have to keep
a tight hold on myself,
not to talk about it.
At night I can scarcely
sleep.

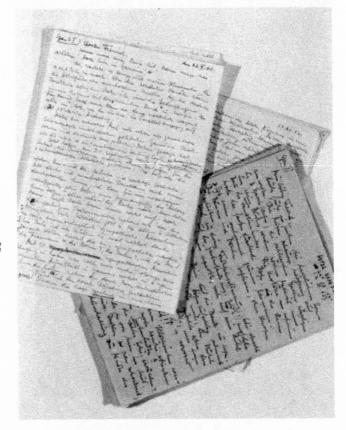

As Hitler's architect I worked my way up, in a relatively short time, to a secure and admired position. For Göring I designed an ostentatious Office of the Reich Marshal.

gave him first aid with cold compresses. After four days of bed rest he is better, although he is simultaneously suffering from violent bronchial catarrh, and running a temperature.

This morning, at his request, the three Western directors came to his bedside. Neurath asked them to inform their governments that they were keeping a helpless old man behind bars. A few hours later Monsieur Laudry, the French legal officer, appeared and rudely told Neurath that he was himself to blame for the bad state of his health. Neurath lost nine pounds in July because he cannot eat the monotonous Russian food.

August 5, 1953 During the past several days sensational news about Neurath has reached us. The three Western high commissioners are said to have taken up his case. But as Neurath sees it, the prognosis is not hopeful, because little is gained from the goodwill of the three as long as the fourth, the Russians, say no. I promised him to use my clandestine route to get to his daughter and learn whether anything is in progress. Now in his eighties, he is too nervous, uncertain, and helpless to write clandestine messages himself.

August 6, 1953 Today Neurath was told that the following sentence must be omitted from his letter of August 2: "A few days ago I had an attack of weakness. This time not in my head but in my legs. But I am already feeling better and hope to be quite all right again by the time you visit me." Neurath then asked to see the new British director, Cuthill, who merely observed in a terse, unfriendly tone, "Any information about your health should come from us."

In the evening Neurath had a fit of hysterical weeping.

September 2, 1953 I had been considering for a long time whether I should have the children come see me, especially since we have now been granted half an hour's visiting time each month. Finally I decided to do it, and day before yesterday Albert came, today Hilde. Their request to be allowed to come together was turned down; children over sixteen are permitted to visit only one by one.

Albert was ten, Hilde nine when I was arrested. Now, eight years later, mature young people sat facing me. I had to study their faces to recognize the familiar features. How inadequately photos and letters represent a person! Albert was in a state of high emotion, which took a lot out of me; Hilde was more composed. As we had agreed in our letters, we chatted about her American experiences. It was as though her joys were mine, although I am not participating in them.

Because my sweater is worn through at the collar, I put it on backwards for the visit.

September 3, 1953   Raeder has returned from his wife's visit. He told her that he gained six pounds during the American month. When she asked how much he had lost during the Russian month, the Soviet interpreter interrupted, "Stop! you're not allowed to say that." Neurath, during his wife's visit, reported that he was not feeling well. That time, too, the Russian interpreter interrupted, but Neurath went on undeterred. "As you see, everything is lies and hypocrisy here."

September 7, 1953   We heard the first results of yesterday's Bundestag election by half past six. By twelve o'clock the approximate results were clear. Dönitz did not comment, which prompted Schirach to observe, "He can't get over the failure of the right." Hess mused, "The party of the right did not obtain a single seat? You say it's the successor to the National Socialist Party? Did the people know that?" When I confirmed that they did, he added, shaking his head, "Then I cannot understand it." As for me, the news of Adenauer's victory gave me satisfaction.

September 9, 1953   After the meeting of the Directorate, Colonel Cuthill speaks to Neurath in an unusually friendly manner, but only, it turns out, to inform him of the directors' decision that even at visits he will not be allowed to give out information on his state of health. Neurath says tonelessly, "Next you will forbid me to think about my illness."

September 10, 1953   This evening I was able to give Neurath an affidavit, many pages in length, by Professor Erich Kaufmann. I received it from Neurath's daughter. Kaufmann was a highly esteemed professor of international law who fled Germany. He returned soon after the war and was frequently consulted on legal matters by the German Foreign Office. In this capacity he drew up an affidavit demanding Neurath's immediate release on formal legal grounds. Nevertheless, Neurath remains fatalistic. "Still, it sounds more affirmative than I ever would have imagined," he comments.

While Neurath is reading I have to stand guard, so that I can take the papers from him immediately in case of danger. He hears and sees poorly, and in addition might betray himself by agitation. So I am now acting as his permanent secretary. Neurath asks me to let his family know that his health has considerably improved since his last severe attack; that only his legs are still unsteady. But he asks them to refrain from making any petitions to the Russians.

September 30, 1953   Today the censor told me to inform my family that abbreviations for such words as *doctor* (Dr.), *and* (&), *especially* (esp.), and for first names may not be used in letters. If a letter exceeds the permitted number of words, it will be returned, he says. He also recommended that instead of the permitted 1300 words, they should keep to 1200, because sometimes opinions differ on the count. I should think so! For instance, is *Himmelkreuzdonnerwetter* one word?

The Eighth Year

November 2, 1953 I am organizing our news service. Twice a month I have my secretary send me a summary of the most interesting news. Today, for example, we have learned that the president of the United States has met with Messerschmitt and other German aviation experts. Heusinger has become Adenauer's military adviser. I well remember the man, usually pallid and reticent, from Hitler's military conferences. And I worked in close association with Messerschmitt. Curiously, during the last weeks of the war in order to protect his associates, he proposed building four-engine jet bombers with which to attack New York. In Norway, my secretary's bulletin continues, the last German prisoners of war have been released. A German-Allied pardon commission is examining all cases of convicted war criminals still imprisoned in Germany; but this does not apply to us. Nevertheless, in the official statement introducing his newly formed government, Adenauer expressed hopes that the efforts of the federal government on behalf of the aged and ill prisoners in Spandau will prove successful.

November 14, 1953 After Adenauer's statement to the Bundestag, Hess and Funk are redoubling their efforts to be considered seriously ill. Today Donaho told me in almost admiring tones, "Around noon Funk came back from seeing the doctor. He was sitting in the medical office whimpering softly to himself, 'It was terrible, I felt so weak!' Then he recognized me and started to his feet. 'You here? And alone? Give me a slug of cognac, Jack! Quick. Ah, that's good.' Suddenly we heard footsteps in the hall. Funk instantly dropped into the chair and in a dying voice continued his moaning. 'All this blackness around me. It's terrible, terrible! Won't somebody help me?' As soon as the intruder disappeared he said hastily, 'Now one more drink and then a cigar!' With deep satisfaction he took a few puffs and turned the cigar in his fingers like a connoisseur. Then came footsteps again. 'Hurry, the cigar into that glass and cover it with a towel!' And he started in to wail again."

Hess, too, is back in form. Immediately after Adenauer's speech he came down with total forgetfulness. About once a week he asks me to explain who Malenkov is or who Adenauer is. When Director Cuthill reproved him because he had not folded his blankets properly, he exhibited his poor memory by writing on the wall of his cell: "Fold blankets." He has also increased the force of his attacks. Tonight he groaned for hours, crying out again and again, "I can't stand it any longer. My God, my God, I'm going mad!" When I visited him in his cell this morning he gave the impression of being quite sound of mind, but remained lying on his bed and underscored his point in dramatic and rather moving terms: "One of my worst attacks. My end is nearing. I've lived like a man and will know how to die like a man. By the way, who is Adenauer?"

November 20, 1953 Hess has begun to regard me as his valet, and without a "please" or a "thank you" to order: "Bring me the broom!" Even our guards are noticing. "This grand gentleman over there," Major Brésard remarked in the garden a few days ago, indicating me, "is playing with fire. Brings Hess this, brings him that. We know all about it. We would have taken a strict line, but he crosses up everything. This grand gentleman!" A little later I was given an official warning because I brought Hess's coat into the garden when he was sitting groaning on a bench in this cold weather.

November 28, 1953 I have been informed from Coburg that there are already 350 typewritten pages filled. Three hundred and fifty pages in eight months; an average of a page and a half every day. For many events, however, I lack data and material from memoranda. After this version is done, therefore, there will have to be another, but only after my release.

I have not proceeded chronologically. From my youth I jumped to my years as a government minister. I plan to take up the decade as Hitler's architect last of all. Today I began the section on July 20, 1944. One of the consequences of that day was the appointment of Goebbels as Reich commissioner for total mobilization of resources for war. Funk, with whom I am again on a fairly pleasant footing, had good contacts with Goebbels, and from him I learn with what duplicity the "little Doctor" acted toward me, even during the years in which we thought we had common interests. "He never meant to be honest with you," Funk says. "Of course he knew that you had proposed him for the position. But he was so full of spite and resentment against you, against the place you had acquired with Hitler at the age of thirty, against your solid middle-class background, and perhaps against your fame as an artist—don't forget that he dreamed of a career as an artist himself, as a great writer—anyhow, he was so full of jealousy and animosity that not even common interests could really bring the two of you together."

Funk was lying on his bed; he had offered me his wooden stool to sit on. Obviously he was enjoying this opportunity of going back, at least in conversation, to the days of his power. He did not suspect that this talk was supplying me with background material. "Anyhow, why *did* you recommend him for the post of Reich commissioner?"

I pointed out that I had done so before July 20, when I could not have suspected that my name would figure on the conspirators' list of prospective Cabinet members, thus giving Goebbels his chance to come out openly as my enemy. Moreover, I was convinced that Goebbels was the best man to put across austerity measures on the home front.

Funk laughed. "You were always playing naïve. Whenever I saw you in the company of the Gauleiters and Old Fighters, you always looked like a Parsifal. In reality you were more cunning than all the rest of us. I realize now that you didn't want to strengthen Goebbels, but to have him take the blame for all the consequences of a total war effort. You wanted the people's irritation at shortages to be directed against him."

I was amused, and although the situation had actually been quite different, I said: "Exactly."

Funk reflected for a moment. "Maybe you underestimated Goebbels. He was even slicker than you, and I think it isn't impossible that he saw right through your intentions. Because from that moment on he turned openly against you, in the Führer's Headquarters, at meetings of Gauleiters, everywhere."

I knew that, and since Bormann and Himmler had also been hostile toward me at the time, I remarked, "Undoubtedly I would have been lost if Hitler had not continued to support me."

December 8, 1953   Last night I had the following dream: In a rather sizable group, sometime toward the end of the war, I declare that everything is lost, that there is no longer a chance and the secret weapons do not exist. The others in the dream remain anonymous. Suddenly Hitler emerges from their midst. I am afraid that he will have heard my remark and may order my arrest. My anxiety increases because Hitler's retinue displays extreme iciness. Nobody says a word to me. Suddenly the scene changes. We are in a house on a slope, with a narrow driveway. Only gradually do I realize that it is Eva Braun's house. Hitler comes to tea, sits facing me, but remains frosty and forbidding. He chews the corners of his fingernails, as he so often did. There are bloody places where they are bitten down to the quick. Looking into his swollen face, I realize for the first time that perhaps Hitler wore his mustache in order to divert attention from his excessively large, ill-proportioned nose. Now I am afraid that I will be arrested any moment because I have perceived the secret of his nose. Heart pounding, I wake up.

December 25, 1953   This year a special worship service was approved for Christmas Day for the first time. Christmas carols, and the sense that the family is thinking of me.

We will not receive our presents and letters until the twenty-seventh. The prison administration settled on that date.

Brooding, I recall the Christmas of twenty years ago. In order to show appreciation to Hitler for his first architectural commissions, I gave him a sketch by Karl Rottmann for a large landscape fresco of Cape Sounion in Greece, which the painter later executed for the Hofgarten in Munich. I had heard it said that Hitler thought highly of Rottmann. And in fact he showed friendly interest, but was quite cursory in his expression of thanks. Later he hung the picture—which at a thousand marks had been a sizable expenditure for me—on the upper floor of the stairwell at the Berghof. At Christmas of the following year, as a return gift, Hitler gave me a gold glass-domed clock. He handed me this commonplace object with its built-in alarm in a rather casual fashion; I placed it in my curiosities cabinet. After this experience

Hitler and I no longer exchanged any presents. From then on only printed Christmas cards with his signature came; during the war there would occasionally be a pound of coffee from a gift he had received from the Orient. I recall that it was much the same for Eva Braun. For her twenty-third birthday Hitler sent her, via his adjutant, an envelope containing a hundred marks. At the time I took it as a proof of his modest nature rather than a sign of his not caring.

At seven o'clock, just as I am about to go drearily to sleep, I hear a brief "caw." I respond in the same fashion. Donaho dashes into my cell, puts down a small bottle of cognac and a bar of Swiss chocolate. With lightning speed he does the same for the other prisoners, except for Hess who, as always, refuses. Just about as quickly I down the cognac and chocolate and return the bottle and chocolate wrapper. I feel as if I am soaring. Christmas!

January 3, 1954 Under the title of "The Seven Men of Spandau" *Empire News* is publishing a lurid series. Today, weeks delayed, we have had a chance to read the text, with the caption: "The Woman Who Got Behind the Iron Curtain." The heroine in question is Frau Funk, who thrust her fingers through the wire grating that separates us from the visitors in order to touch her husband's fingers. The Russian guard supervising the visit instantly put a stop to this. "What will the British newspaper reader say when he finds out that our wives are not even allowed to shake hands with us?" I asked Pease. All the Western guards feel embarrassed at seeing their prison thus exposed.

"The ship has a hole in it," Hawker remarked crossly today. "News leaks out and in." Probably Hawker read the very thing in the *Empire News* of December 27, 1953: "The authorities of Spandau know there is an organized two-way traffic of smuggled letters, which all countermeasures so far have failed to stop."

Suppose Hawker suspected that I have already smuggled many hundreds of pages out of the "best-guarded prison in the world." But countermeasures are not being taken. Whereas the administration assumes that the excessively large number of guards employed to keep an eye on us increases security, actually cutting back on the staff would make it harder for us to find intermediaries among them.

Do I feel too secure, and will I someday be caught? Or—a terrifying thought—is the secret mail tolerated so that it can be checked on and our secrets learned? I have taken this possibility into account for a long time. But if it were so, there would still be far more gained than lost.

January 4, 1954 For that reason, too, I am going on with my memoirs. I have by this time reached the description of the Ardennes offensive, which the Americans call the Battle of the Bulge. I was present at the military conference at which its final failure had to be admitted. The place was the headquarters near Bad Nauheim, which I had built in 1939. Hitler talked about a run of bad luck that meant nothing as far as the ultimate victory was concerned; he was planning new offensives that would soon change the fortunes of war. The generals remained icily silent. I can still see seventy-year-old Field Marshal von Rundstedt merely bowing stiffly to Hitler, who was virtually begging for assent. Hitler must have sensed the refractory attitude of the men around him, for he abruptly stopped discussing the Western theater of war, and began playing off Tito against his own field marshals. There was someone who had set an example, he said. He had raised fresh troops out of nothing, and with the most primitive weapons had held down twenty German divisions in Yugoslavia. "Are we to say we are incapable of what those Balkan Slavs can do? Then what would the Americans' technical superiority matter, *meine Herren?* What you have to do is fight with the same resolution, boldness, tenacity, and above all with the same iron obstinacy. Then the war can never be lost." But then, he concluded, Tito was a shoemaker with iron nerves, not a general staff officer.'

During the years before the war Hitler had sought the company of the upper middle class, and perhaps I owe my own rise partly to these social yearnings of his. By now he had come to despise that class, and the way he bawled out representatives of it on this occasion gave evidence of a deep-seated resentment. Now shoemakers were held up as models of vigor, energy, and ruthlessness. During the thirties he had hardly received the ruffians among his Old Fighters, preferring people from better society. It was no coincidence that at this point in the war Bormann reached the height of his power. And the vulgar drunkard Ley, who after July 20 had published an article screaming hatred of the nobility, now returned to the circle of intimates.

January 7, 1954 Again in Funk's cell in the evening. I turn the conversation to the last phase of the war and ask what his experience of it was. Funk grins and reaches under his mattress. He holds up a hip flask and says, "This! It was one prolonged drunk." I am disturbed by his carelessness, for he is imperiling our guards as well as himself. "Honest!" he says with a slightly dreamy expression. "During meetings in those last months I often didn't know whether or not I was dealing with people who were conscious of what they were saying. Don't you remember yourself the time in the spring of 1945 that we met for a conference with Terboven, the Reich commissioner for Norway, in his apartment at the Adlon Hotel?"

I remembered the untidy room, the man who sat on the sofa with his tunic open, surrounded by a clutter of wine and brandy bottles. Instead of discussing his problems with us, he cracked macabre jokes about the impending end. A few weeks later, Funk told me, Terboven sat down on a crate of explosives, empty bottles scattered all around him, and lit the fuse. That seems to be the classic pattern for an Old Fighter: taking to drink out of a feeling that the Idea had been betrayed, and then explosives.

January 9, 1954 Funk has been bedridden for days, so Hess is my bathing partner. He is concerned about the report in the *Empire News* that he is the future leader of a German nationalist party. In a troubled tone, he says, "That puts a heavy obstacle in the way of my release, coming as it does right during the foreign ministers' conference."

I ask innocently, "Would you rather be represented as a repentant sinner, like me?"

Hess hesitates. After some consideration he replies, downcast, "At the moment, yes. I'd like to get out. How and why, I don't care."

In the library in the evening Dönitz, too, shows concern over the ambitions ascribed to him to become chief of state after his release. "But the newspaper also wrote that I would like to establish a children's home," he says, trying to comfort himself. "My wife is trying to dissuade me from it because I'm too old. She may be right."

Hess assumes a false kindly tone. "Well, well! Too old for a children's home, but young enough for chief of state. Is that the idea?"

February 2, 1954 The first visit from little Ernst, our youngest son, has depressed me. He is ten! But I did not show how sad I was.

February 8, 1954 Immediately after the report in the *Empire News* that mail is being smuggled in and out, I again placed a piece of folded toilet paper under my bed and strewed dust on it to find out whether it is picked up and replaced to catch me. That was five weeks ago.

February 10, 1954 Have continued to work on the memoirs, although sometimes I regard the thing as a failure. Has it become more than a collection of historical anecdotes? At any rate I have not been successful in depicting the period as a whole. It is more an attempt at probing myself. But even if it doesn't become a work of history, historians may be able to put it to good use.

February 14, 1954 Today I read a sentence by Karl Jaspers stating that there cannot be any such thing as objective truth. Not even for the historian who undertakes to set down historical events dispassionately.
The sentence restored some of my peace of mind.

February 18, 1954 These memoirs depress me more and more. My longing for an unburdened period of my life, one that I might tell about with pleasure, is growing by leaps and bounds. So for the time being I will go back to writing the chapters on my youth.

February 28, 1954 Frederik is bringing in genuine Hennessy and Canadian Club in unlimited quantities. Temporary change of mood. The children will wonder about my exuberant official letter. Dönitz has written his Sunday letter in verse. This jollity should make an attentive censor suspicious.

March 1, 1954 Tonight, between two and three o'clock in the morning, Frederik let me read an incredible passage in Field Marshal Kesselring's memoirs, which we were recently discussing. As late as the spring of 1945, after the collapse of our armaments program, Hitler held out to Kesselring the prospect of new miraculous production achievements, even though in memos of January 30 and March 5, 1945, I had informed him in full detail of the breakdown of production. So he did not deceive the people alone; he lied even to his army commanders. I wonder whether they believed him. Or were they even grateful for such lies, which let them off the hook? Similarly, when Hitler had my associates from the armaments industry before him, he spoke of new offensive operations by non-existent divisions. In this way he used one group to deceive the others. Was he also deceiving himself?

March 3, 1954 Because it was raining this morning, I changed my pants and hung the wet ones over my chair. Returned to the garden. Meanwhile a French guard checked the cell. Not until this evening did I realize that the pages with my notes on Kesselring were in those pants. But nothing was found.

A few days ago I was in even greater danger. I had pushed the sheets of paper into their place, buttoned the top button, and gone to fetch my meal. On the way to the serving table I suddenly realized that I was wearing short underwear. The sheets were held by the waistband; that alone kept me from depositing them at the feet of the French director, who happened to be at the serving table. Luckily I have gained nearly ten pounds during these three Western months.

March 5, 1954   A three-man Soviet commission visited us today. To judge by the Russian director's obsequious air, the visitors must hold high ranks. Incidentally, they were the first friendly Russian inspecting team in seven years. They greeted us with "Good day, how are you?" and asked about our health and whether we were not too cold. But they dodged the question of the inadequate rations by asking the seemingly sympathetic question, "Have you a good appetite?" Then, commenting on my photos: "Ah, you have six children? How old? And these are your parents?" My slide rule also excited interest.

The inspection will change nothing.

March 25, 1954   Our hopes have once again reached a nadir—the Berlin Foreign Ministers' Conference on the question of Germany has been a bust. We had anticipated that if agreement were reached, there would be some positive effects on the problem of Spandau. Today, when Schirach and Funk were lamenting the failure to reach an understanding, I was disagreeable enough to remind them that only recently they were triumphantly referring to Hitler's prophecy that the coalition of wartime allies was bound to break up. Now all this friction grieves them, because it affects their personal destinies.

March 27, 1954   We were all equally surprised when Frederik slipped me an item from the *Frankfurter Allgemeine Zeitung* today. It states that formal negotiations are taking place among the four high commissioners on the fate of the prisoners in Spandau. Molotov is said to have authorized Ambassador Semyonov to discuss the question of Spandau. The report has produced restiveness and something akin to euphoria among us. In the garden none of us wants to undertake any kind of work. I too must keep a tight grip on myself to preserve my composure. This is the first sign that things need not go on forever unchanged. Some kind of movement is apparently beginning.

Standing together in groups, we hold one of our grand political bull sessions, which soon passes on to fundamental matters: Soviet policy toward Germany. But the basis for our discussion is only a few lines of a report, and we know virtually nothing about the motives and backgrounds of this policy throughout the past years. Schirach expounds the theory that the Soviet Union has been forced, after the uprising of June 17, 1953, to make some kind of gesture toward the Germans. That is very vague and identifies our personal welfare in simplistic fashion with the interests of the German people. But at least this much of it seems right to me: it remains astonishing that the Soviet Union is still averse to playing the German card. In Nuremberg I first heard of Stalin's statement that the Hitlers come and go but the German people will remain. At the time I thought this an outstretched hand, and although I did not for a moment believe in Stalin's magnanimity, I saw the statement as a sign of his tactical cunning.

After the First World War the Soviet Union made very strong efforts to win Germany to her side, probably out of the perception that hegemony over Germany would mean hegemony over Europe. But all her agents, all her attempts at putsches and revolts, failed. They were thwarted by the strength of the Social Democrats, by the old army, by the bureaucracy, by a still intact bourgeois society. Now all those forces for stability were gone, the large landholdings shattered, industry bombed out, classes eliminated, everybody leveled by misery. Whenever I saw people during the last months of the war and in the period thereafter, seeing their despair and total exhaustion, I thought: Whoever comes along now and shows them a future, speaks to them of hope, no matter how slight, would have an easy time winning them over. Never, it seemed to me, was Russia closer to taking hold of the German soul than during those months. And Stalin's statement indicated that he had realized that. But in that respect he was like Hitler—and perhaps all despots are alike in that respect. Just as Hitler, after his victory over France, wanted to take the French provinces, not win over the French people, so Stalin first garnered East Prussia, Silesia, and Pomerania, partly for himself, partly to be used as bribes for the other Eastern nations. Then he established his dominion over central Germany with tanks and satraps. And only then, after he had frittered away all his psychological opportunities, did he permit a shrunken and hopeless Communist party to court the masses. When Stalin took Königsberg, he lost Germany.

What was the reason? Was it the inveterate distrust of the Georgian

who had never risked everything on a single card? Was it the insight of
the realist who had never believed that Moscow would succeed in winning the German working class to the cause of world revolution? Or
was he too sure of himself in the face of a continent sunk in misery? In
any case, his behavior testifies to doubts of the power of the Communist
ideology. Significantly, after this war he did not, as in 1918, send the
Radeks and Levinés into Germany, but uncouth Soviet marshals.
Stalin's policy toward Germany was, strictly speaking, a farewell to
faith in the victory of communism as an idea.

March 28, 1954 On what I wrote yesterday: Perhaps I was
thinking in excessively political terms. By separating the eastern provinces from the German Reich Stalin threw away his chance to win
Germany in another sense. For in a cultural, commercial, and psychological sense those areas constituted Germany's link with Russia, and
with the East in general. It is no accident that all German policies of alliance with the East, whether instituted by Frederick, York, or Bismarck and right on up to the leadership of the Weimar Republic's army,
were made by East Elbians.* I shall never forget the impression it made
on me in my schooldays when I read, in the program notes for a play of
Gerhart Hauptmann's, that the writer's first collected works were published in Russian in Moscow, before a German edition appeared. Just
as the first Western editions of the great Russian writers were mostly
published in Berlin, if I remember rightly. Eastern Germany was the
great European gateway between the Western and Eastern mentality.
That is no longer so.

There is another element. Germany always distrusted the West, the
spirit of crass Enlightenment. Germany rejected that spirit as shallow,
overrationalistic. Stalin's policy forcibly drove Germany into the arms
of the West. The distrust has ended. Now Germany, which put up
such a prolonged resistance, will be conquered from within by the
West; and the Soviet Union is unwillingly and perhaps even unwittingly helping to bring it about.

Evening, after reading this over again: Much of it probably rests on
an insecure foundation. The fateful implication of what I have written
comes down to this—that I will be doing time here for a good long
while if I am right. To get out of here soon I would have to be entirely
wrong.

* The Junkers, who owned great landed estates east of the Elbe River.—*Translators' note.*

March 29, 1954 In my memoirs I have arrived at the end of March 1945. After the fall of Mussolini, Jodl said, the Fascist regime burst like a soap bubble. What figure of speech would characterize the end of the Hitler regime? Would it be too harsh if I said that the events of the last months were like the bursting of a boil?

March 30, 1954 Sometimes I envy my fellow prisoners. Their unbroken relationship to the past must make life easier for them. Outward forms continue to be preserved among us, of course, but they have their own world, to which I do not belong. When I approach, they fall silent and turn away. I can only guess what is in their minds. What I tell about us here is composed of occasional fragments of interchange in pseudoconversations, which have only a sham common ground. The prisoner is always an outcast from society; I am an outcast among prisoners. Göring's statement at the Nuremberg trial, "We should never have trusted him," still applies.

Naturally I do not enjoy standing to one side. I often feel tempted to give in. A few words and they would take me into their circle. That would make a good many things easier for me. But still, it would be a kind of capitulation. I simply do not belong to them; I remain the defeatist. But I must guard myself against making that into a question of moral superiority; perhaps it is only a matter of a loner's temperament. I have never quite belonged fully anywhere. Recently, when I took an English grammar out of the library, Dönitz remarked pointedly, "I suppose you want to get a job with the Secret Service."

March 31, 1954 Neurath, whom I really ought to except from my remarks of yesterday, came back from his wife's visit looking quite rejuvenated. "She made many hints." But an hour later he was skeptical again. "I'll not believe it until I stand on the other side of the gate."

When Funk is not bedridden, he walks back and forth in the garden with Schirach for a few hours. The American guard Felner recently called them "the two evil spirits." But nowadays Funk is in bed almost all the time. Today the doctor came, because Funk was supposedly on the verge of uremia and had almost lost consciousness. Dönitz calls that "an attempted escape." Raeder, too, is envious of Funk's chances of being taken to the hospital. When he was passing the cell today he punned to Felner, "Well, he doesn't seem to be in such a funk after all."

April 9, 1954   The judicial representatives of the four high commissioners are said to have sat conferring for five hours in the Control Commission building.

I would greatly miss Neurath. But Raeder and Funk are also ill. I wouldn't mind being without them. Although that would leave only four of us, and when Dönitz finishes his sentence two years hence there would remain only Schirach and Hess and myself. Not a very pleasant prospect.

Raeder reckons his chances at fifty-fifty and suggests that some of the others will find a few more illnesses. Funk remarks dully, in a low voice, "It's too late for me. Nothing matters to me any more." The poor fellow is painfully struggling to win the favor of the Russian guards. He addresses them with friendly smiles, but they do not react. And Hess, ordinarily so aloof, declares that his stomach cramps also should be taken seriously: "Terrible, waiting for the decision. I can't take it any more. It's been thirteen years now." Dönitz refers to his good conduct: "If a third of the sentence were properly taken off for 'good time' I should have been released nine months ago." I remind him that Kranzbühler has sent word that the old and the sick will come first. The rest of us should not do anything to upset this plan. Dönitz is indignant: "He never wrote that!" He slams the cell door behind him.

Schirach says maliciously to his retreating back, "And yet he's ruining everything for us with his bigshot playing president. He's stuck like a cork in front of a premature release for the two of us."

Since ten pages of blank paper have been pinching inside my shoe for days, I am starting on the remaining part of my memoirs, the period as an architect. Last week I concluded parts two and three with Hitler's death, thus completing the description of events from 1942 on.

May 2, 1954   Hilde and Margret have been here together twice, as charming in their conversation as in their movements. For half an hour they transformed the dismal atmosphere of the visiting room. Never before in the past nine years had I so completely escaped the world of prison. Although I have not seen Margret since the spring of 1945, she greeted me cheerily: "You still look just the same as you used to!" She was six years old at that time.

They want to get a dog from an animal shelter. When I promised to conjure up a dog for them, they laughed. This evening I wrote to my friend in Coburg to use a few hundred marks from the account to which architects and associates from industry have been contributing to buy the children a dachshund of good stock.

May 11, 1954   We are summoned to the chapel. The British director comes alone and announces to the assembly of seven sitting in front
of him that the directors have decided on a variety of ameliorations,
which he will now read aloud. He avoids pomposity, and emphasizes
two or three points with: "Probably that will please you."

From now on the light can be turned out at fifteen minutes to seven.
The ban on talking is abolished. Twice a month there will be half an
hour of classical music on records. In our letters we may now deal with
such topics as health and life in the prison. But these are mostly matters
that actually have been tolerated for some time. More important, we are
now allowed to exchange letters with our lawyers, although not on questions concerning the Nuremberg trial. With that same restriction, we
may see a lawyer and have wills or other documents prepared by him.
For Christmas an additional visit of half an hour is approved, and the
grating in the visiting room will be removed. But the visit will be
terminated at once if there is any physical contact, such as shaking
hands or embracing. Each of the four nations will now provide us with
a newspaper. The Americans are ordering the *Frankfurter Allgemeine
Zeitung,* the British *Die Welt,* the French the Berlin *Kurier,* and the
Russians the *Berliner Zeitung.* Each director is responsible for the censorship of his own newspaper.

So that is the result of the grand conference. Each time an improvement in our lot has been announced, our depression grows. Now I
no longer have any hope. Such a chance will not come again.

In 1942 at Carnac in Brittany I saw a granite block that our prehistoric forefathers had mounted on another in such a way that the upper
block could be made to rock by a mere touch of the fingertips. Who
will give the slight pressure needed to sway our petrified fate to the
other side?

May 14, 1954   The Russian guards reacted angrily even toward
their Western colleagues when the new relaxations were announced.
They slammed doors, clanked bowls, ran excitedly to and fro. Now
they have calmed down and are abiding by the new rules with stiff formality.

A blackbird sits on an acacia outside my window and sings while I
read Thomas Mann's *Joseph and His Brothers.* Two thousand pages. I
read thirty every day. I have time.

May 20, 1954   Our letters are returned because, trusting in what
Colonel Cuthill said, we reported on the innovations in our prison life.

Dönitz is the only one who does not have to rewrite his letter, because he is vexed by the ameliorations and did not mention them.

May 21, 1954 For several days we have been receiving the four uncensored newspapers. Our grand admiral librarian has been assigned the task of distributing them. He announces: "All four newspapers will be circulated together in one file folder. I shall paste a white slip of paper on this folder: each man will enter first the time of receiving it and then the time he passes it on. In addition, each man checks off when he no longer wants it."

"It will take too long for one person to read all four newspapers," Dönitz protests.

Raeder insists obstinately: "That doesn't matter. You've got plenty of time, after all."

May 24, 1954 Pease confided to me last week that there is no provision for releasing even the dying. In case of death the body will be buried in the prison yard, the chaplain performing the service. But it has been decided, Pease said, that members of the family will be permitted to come to the grave site. Dönitz has also heard this, but we have agreed to keep the news from Neurath. It is his great longing to be buried at home. But a few days later Neurath comes to me, and for once, contrary to his usual manner, is almost beside himself. "Dönitz just told me something incredible. They won't release me even after my death! What good is an old man's corpse to them!"

I am not the only one irritated with Dönitz about this. Schirach is also furious. For once he even confides in me. "I heard the grand admiral talking away at the old man, saying it was all useless, that nobody could be getting out of here before his sentence is over."

It's easy for Dönitz to talk. He will be going home in two years.

May 25, 1954 A unit of the same Guards regiment that does duty in front of Buckingham Palace is now guarding us. However, they have left their busbies at home. A few hours ago the lieutenant on duty made his round. In the van came a sergeant with shouldered rifle, followed by the goose-stepping lieutenant, who in turn was followed by two soldiers, one behind the other. At first I thought that the lieutenant was under arrest; but to my astonishment the other three obeyed his commands. Pease explained: "Do you know who that lieutenant is? The marquess of Hamilton, heir of the duke of Hamilton." In 1941 Hess flew to Scotland to see the duke.

May 26, 1954 Raeder has changed his system. The newspapers are distributed singly.

May 30, 1954 Although we are still forbidden books on contemporary history, we are being allowed to receive uncensored the series by Theodor Plivier on Hitler's last days in Berlin, which is being published in the *Welt am Sonntag.* The British director, who is solely responsible for censoring his newspaper, has no objections; and the Russian can interpose a veto only in the case of books.

The exaggerated descriptions of my active opposition during the last months of the war brought forth nasty remarks by most of my fellow prisoners. Raeder was personally incensed, because the account is written by the former sailor Plivier. Aside from Neurath, Hess is the only one who has not attacked me. Because of his flight to England he too is a "member of the underground."

July 6, 1954 The Russian director has again ruled that we must not work in the garden in our shirts. In spite of the July heat we must put on our corduroy jackets; that is the uniform, he says. Shortly afterwards he confiscates a cardboard frame around a photo Dönitz had in his cell, and a souvenir card from Frau von Bismarck in Neurath's cell. Both had been tolerated for years. Yesterday Funk had to rip out an embroidered "W.F." on his pajamas.

July 8, 1954 Again a Russian guard has found a piece of Western chocolate on Neurath; it was slipped to him to make up for the bad food in the Russian month. The Russian director interrogates Neurath. "Tell who gave it to you. We already know anyhow."

Neurath, wearily: "Then you know more than I."

The Russian threatens: "I'll have your cell searched every hour until you tell."

Neurath shakes his head. "Do whatever you like."

"I would make the Russians find Russian chocolate," Long says to me.

July 9, 1954 Last night at quarter past eleven eighty-year-old Neurath was wakened from sleep by the Russian Kovpak. His cell was searched and the bed was thoroughly messed up.

July 11, 1954 This morning all of us had to get up and go out into the corridor at a quarter after one. Funk alone was allowed to stay in bed. The cells and the prisoners were thoroughly searched, but nothing was found—even on me! Before going to bed I had slipped my notes under the loosened inner sole of my slippers.

July 13, 1954 Again we find ourselves standing in the corridor in pajamas or nightshirts at quarter past twelve, blankets draped around our shoulders. Guryev piles our bedding, blankets, and even mattresses in a disorderly heap and throws everything else on top. He searches Neurath's cell even more furiously than the others. The old men, Neurath and Raeder, complain this morning that they were so upset they could not get back to sleep.

July 15, 1954 General Dibrova, the Soviet commandant of Berlin, dressed in resplendent uniform and accompanied by the Russian, French, and American directors, inspected the prison today. When he entered my cell he gave a military salute. His director explained who I was; I caught the word *architekti* several times. Politely, the commandant asked about my wife and children, and looked at the book I was currently reading. He picked up my drawing roll, which happened to be blank, and leafed through my sketchbook. "Have you no requests?" he asked. I shrugged. He saluted, hand to cap; I bowed. That was all.

August 1, 1954 The food program in the Russian month has scarcely changed in the past seven years. Day in, day out, we are given ersatz coffee, barley and noodle soup, and in the evening stringy meat with boiled potatoes and a few carrots. This month the meat smells and tastes abominable. Schirach commented in disgust, "When I find a cat's whiskers in the goulash, the truth will be out." Some of the others suspect that it is horsemeat, or dog. For lunch, however, we have a delicacy: a piece of heavily salted herring, and plenty of bread, butter, and sugar. After Dibrova's visit, herring roe was provided as a variation.

Contrast that with the menu for the first day of this American month. For breakfast, two fried eggs with bacon, apple jelly. Lunch: tomato soup with rice, pork cutlets, green pepper and potato salad with mayonnaise, two slices of pineapple, half a liter of whole milk. For supper: roast turkey with beans, cheese, a slice of melon. At all meals coffee with cream and wonderful white bread.

August 2, 1954 Nocturnal searches slacken off. On July 20 at quarter past eleven, on July 23 and 24 at quarter past twelve, on July 30 at half past eleven.

August 10, 1954 For a week there has been a placard on Neurath's door, signed by the chief public health officer of the American sector of Berlin, by his deputy, and by the American director of the prison: "Complete bed rest from nine P.M. to six A.M. All guards are requested to obey these medical regulations." This is something new—up to now the Russians had insisted on the principle, within the complicated legal machinery of our prison, that only the four directors jointly could call off such measures as the prescribed searches of the cells. No more nocturnal shakedowns.

August 18, 1954 In a slump. No desire to keep journal. I am also letting the memoirs lie.

August 21, 1954 While lying awake the last few nights I reflected that Schirach and I, although he is by now forty-seven and I am forty-nine, will always remain the youngest, no matter how old we grow. The thought has something terrifying about it, but also something reassuring. We will not notice that younger men, new forty-year-olds, long ago stepped into our shoes.

August 22, 1954 This evening, beaming with pleasure, the helpful British chief guard, Letham, brings the 1953 bound volume of the magazine *Baumeister* and the 1951–52 volume of *Glasforum*. The library of the Technical University has offered to lend me any professional books I want in the future. That way, I shall be able to keep up with current developments. This comes at the right time!

August 24, 1954 Leafing through the architectural magazines today, I reflected once more on the buildings I designed, and my promising start in 1933. I was surprised to realize how few commissions I had accepted. I had made it a principle not to be working on more than three major buildings simultaneously. At all costs I did not want to establish an architectural factory.

August 26, 1954 For three months now we have been receiving newspapers. Reading them has proved to be a strenuous and confusing occupation. They bring us tidings of a world from which I have become entirely alienated, at any rate far more so than I previously imagined. Often I can no longer fit the details together into a coherent pattern; it is like a jigsaw puzzle with a good half of the pieces missing. It must have been like that for exiles, who could no longer form a conception of what things were like back home. I, too, lack a view of things in the round. Imagination cannot make up for the missing dimension.

The quick shift from one subject to the next comes surprisingly hard to me. Should newspapers be delayed by no more than a day, their contents become peculiar, uninteresting, even here in Spandau. If I were resolute enough to let the newspaper lie unread for twenty-four hours, I would save myself half an hour or more every day. Jefferson writes somewhere that in the years after his presidency he read newspapers only at considerable intervals, as a matter of principle. By so doing, he said, he saw political relationships emerging more distinctly.

First I read the *Frankfurter Allgemeine Zeitung;* it provides the most substantial information. After going through that one, which takes about twenty minutes, I attack *Die Welt.* Then I can run through the *Kurier* and the *Berliner Zeitung* (East Berlin) in three to five minutes each.

August 28, 1954 Surprisingly, Dönitz has come out strongly for Adenauer. "Granted, he's a thickheaded martinet, but by his obstinacy he holds the government together. Always better to have someone like that, rather than one of these intellectuals whose cabinet ministers go running in all directions."

All of us are struck by the fact that the newspaper from East Germany is constantly invoking such notions as "Fatherland" or "Germany." Today Schirach commented to Dönitz on Ulbricht's speech at a youth group meeting, a speech larded with quotations from Schiller: "You've got to read this! One of the best speeches I've seen. Simply tremendous!" And Raeder echoed him: "Simply tremendous!"

Incidentally, our wheelbarrow has been equipped with a pneumatic tire.

September 2, 1954 Around half past ten last night a guard hurriedly unlocked Neurath's cell and called the medical aide. Sounds of choking and gasping in the silence of night. Toni Vlaer dragged a respirator and oxygen cylinder to the cell. After half an hour the British doctor appeared, soon followed by one of his French colleagues. Both men labored over Neurath until the early morning hours. I sat up in bed, and finally heard someone saying: "He's better now." Utter silence returned to the cellblock.

This morning Neurath sat in his armchair, his face very flushed, his eyes lifeless, looking helpless and broken. He finds breathing easier in a sitting position. A few hours later an oxygen tent was set up over his bed. A likable British nurse came in to care for him. "He is very, very ill," she said to Pease. The British director asked Neurath whether his family should be informed by telegram and whether the chaplain should be called. Neurath said yes.

September 6, 1954 Day before yesterday Neurath's wife and daughter came for a visit in the infirmary. From what reliable guards have told us, the setup must have been humiliating. Eight persons were there—one American, three Russians, a Frenchman, and Colonel Cuthill representing the prison authorities; a British military doctor and nurse keeping the sick man under observation. The two visitors were not allowed to take the old man's hand; they were required to sit on two chairs at the foot of the bed, while the nurse kept taking his pulse. When he grew weaker, she gave him an injection. The visit was cut short after the prescribed thirty minutes. Even when leaving the visitors were forbidden to shake hands with the patient.

For two days after this visit Neurath lay under the oxygen tent with two British doctors taking turns watching him. Today he has been returned to the cellblock.

September 15, 1954 Yesterday Funk was transferred to the British military hospital to undergo an operation. This is the first time that one of us has been outside the walls. Four British jeeps filled with MPs accompanied the ambulance. The four directors of Spandau, the heads of legal departments, and other representatives of the Four Powers followed by car. Since each one had his own car, the column was almost a kilometer long, as one of the guards described it. Quite a bit of fuss for one old man. At the hospital a stretcher was waiting. Four strong men took hold of it and carried it on the double up one flight of stairs; Funk was in his room before he could look about him.

"If they had given Funk twenty-five pfennigs for the streetcar, he would have arrived on his own," Long commented dryly.

September 22, 1954 Only a week later, Funk is back in his cell, eating bread and butter with good appetite. "Has the operation been postponed?" Schirach asked him.

Funk shook his head: "A young American surgeon from the Frankfurt military hospital operated on me by a new method, using an electric wire; no incision of the bladder, and just local anaesthesia." He talked enthusiastically about his hospital stay, like a vacationer who has just returned to the office. "I was treated like a private patient. A sort of mixture between Napoleon and Al Capone. The guard in the anteroom was made up of two Russians and of sergeants from the Western countries. There were day nurses and night nurses. One was a nifty blonde. I received English officers' rations, ice cream in the afternoon, and even tea with cake."

September 26, 1954 Have just seen a photograph of my successor for the eastern part of Berlin, chief architect Henselmann, who has designed the Stalinallee. He was showing prominent visitors models of the future Berlin, just as I used to do. My impression is that this Stalin Boulevard follows the lines of our planned eastern artery. And in West Berlin the circular roads I had planned are being built. Perhaps they will even get around, sometime, to building the new South Station in simplified form, and installing a grand north-south avenue in place of the unused tracks. I have read in *Die Welt* that my old associate Hans Stephan is supervising the rebuilding of West Berlin. I hope he will manage to keep open the lines of the arteries we had in mind, for our skeletal city plan was not bad.

September 28, 1954 A foolish magazine article has had consequences. The photos, it was discovered, could only have been taken from close up. Suspicion fell upon Monsieur Gerhardt, another of the Alsatian Frenchmen. The man had attracted attention by his lavish spending on his mistress. The suspicions hardened when someone noticed that one of the pictures showed Raeder with his cane, which he uses only on Sundays. Moreover, in this picture a veiled sun in a rainy summer garden could be seen. With the aid of weather reports, they narrowed down the day the picture was taken, and the prison log revealed that Gerhardt was on duty that day.

The embarrassed French now want their revenge. Their director has issued orders that the slightest infringement of regulations by British or American guards is to be reported in writing. This makes for a nasty atmosphere. For example, it was reported that when Wagg returned from a vacation back home in the USA I greeted him in English, although German is the only authorized language of the prison. Another American was reported because he fell asleep at night. This denunciation is all the more petty because the Frenchman who made it has often had to be waked by us, the prisoners.

Funk, who must know the photographer since he was one of those snapped from close up, was prompted to state that no Frenchman took the pictures. Since no suspicion has fallen on any Russians, the Americans were questioned under oath by their military administration. They were also required to swear that they had smuggled no letters for prisoners. Undoubtedly there were a good many perjuries. Eyes wide with anxiety, Frederik told me that he may have to take a lie detector test. "I'm afraid, I'm afraid!" he said.

September 30, 1954 The condition of Neurath and Raeder, and the peril for my friend, weigh heavily on my mind. I have a new idea to make myself exercise regularly to the point of exhaustion: I have begun, along with the garden work, to walk the distance from Berlin to Heidelberg—626 kilometers! For that purpose, I have marked out a circular course in the garden. Lacking a tape measure, I measured my shoe, paced off the distance step by step, and multiplied by the number of paces. Placing one foot ahead of the other 870 times, thirty-one centimeters to a step, yields 270 meters for a round. If I had taken a different route, along the prison wall, I could have made my track 350 meters. But because of the better view, I prefer this other track. This project is a training of the will, a battle against the endless boredom; but it is also an expression of the last remnants of my urge toward status and activity.

Hess often sits on his garden bench for hours. For some time the guards have been letting him alone. Today I stopped briefly in front of his bench. Hess remarked, "By the way, I've stopped thinking that my food is doctored to give me stomach cramps. After all, I can take any one of the seven bowls that are standing on the table for all of us."

I nodded my appreciation. "Well, well, so you've got over your obsession at last."

Hess smiled. "No, of course not. If I did, it wouldn't be an obsession."

The logic of his reply so staggered me that I made a confession. "Oh well, I have my own eccentricities," I said. "Do you know that I'm collecting kilometers? Isn't that crazy, writing down the kilometers I've walked every day?"

Hess shook his head. "Why not, if you enjoy it?"

I insisted on my claim to having a screw loose: "But every week I add up the kilometers, calculate the weekly average, enter the kilometers for the week in a table with various columns, one column for the general average, another for the total number of kilometers."

"That just happens to be your pastime," Hess said consolingly. "Others have others."

I went on. "Besides all that, in addition to the garden work I have to reach seven times seven kilometers by the end of the week. If I don't achieve this goal, I have to make up for it the following week. And I've been doing this for ten days."

I asked Hess, since he was sitting so comfortably on his bench, to note each of my rounds on the walk to Heidelberg by drawing a line in the sand. He stood up, walked slowly over to our bean rows, and gave me thirty beans. "Put these in your left pocket, and after every round drop one in the right pocket. At night you can count them up. Clear?" Then he walked back into the building.

The Ninth Year

October 6, 1954   Brésard, it is said, was tripped up by his order to report to the four directors any misbehavior by British and American guards. His successor, Monsieur Joire, comes from the civil administration of the French sector and is not a military man. He immediately put a stop to this ridiculous reporting. Now peace and quiet are restored. Once more we are smuggling out our letters.

October 16, 1954   As I usually do when a Russian is on duty, tonight I wrapped the papers around my leg and secured them with an elastic bandage. As I slept the bandage slipped, and when I awoke the papers were strewn about the bed. But none had fallen on the floor, where the Russian guard could not have helped seeing it if he merely glanced through the peephole.

October 18, 1954   At home, the longhaired dachshund puppy has come. The children overjoyed. The censor declares strictly: "Photos of a dog have arrived. But you cannot receive them. According to regulations, only photographs of members of the family are permitted." I have therefore written home in the official letter that they are to have photos taken of themselves with the dachshund on their laps and the cat on their shoulders.

In one month I have covered 240 of the 624 kilometers to Heidelberg. My day's record so far is sixty-one beans, or sixteen kilometers.

October 26, 1954   At the Paris Conference it was decided to admit the new German army into NATO. *Die Welt* has a report on the structure of this new army and its methods of training. Dönitz took a critical view: "A mistake not to build the Bundeswehr on the traditions of the Wehrmacht. They are cutting off the limb they are sitting on."

And Schirach exclaims, "Outrageous! Saluting officers only once a day! And no more high boots! I can't understand it. The best part of the army."

Dönitz was more interested in what all this might portend for us. "I've never ventured to prophesy, but this time I predict that all of us will be going home next spring. The Western Powers simply cannot keep us prisoners longer than that. My naval officers simply wouldn't go along with it."

Neurath could not take part in this conversation. Since his last attack he has been sitting alone in his cell, reading in his armchair or staring into space. He is not allowed visitors, allegedly so that he won't be agitated. Nevertheless, some of the guards open his cell door to let us in for a talk with him.

November 4, 1954   This afternoon something incredible happened. Raeder did not send the newspapers around the cells in their normal order, but actually came dashing out of the library room into the corridor. "Come," he called excitedly, "read this! It's incredible." Lowering his voice so Neurath would not be able to hear, he explained, "It says in the paper that Neurath is going to be released." An uncensored AP item in today's *Die Welt* reports that Soviet High Commissioner Pushkin has proposed to his three Western colleagues that Neurath be released because of his age and his ill health. The final negotiations are to be carried out by the high commissioners.

Attracted by the noise, Guryev came up. When he saw that Dönitz was trying to snatch back the newspaper, he insisted on seeing it. He looked at the headline and, lowering the paper for a moment, stared stunned into space, then carefully studied the text.

Shortly afterwards an order came that Neurath must not be given the newspaper until after he had received a dose of Theominal in the presence of the medical aide. But Neurath took the news calmly. Again he remarked that he would have to stand on the other side of the gate before he would believe it. He is counting on at least three more weeks, he said, before the regulations for his life on the outside can be drawn up.

Hess displayed wild agitation. "You must explain to Neurath at once," he called out to me across the corridor, "that it is just a propaganda lie. I know the Communists' tactics!"

November 6, 1954 Saturday. Neurath was irritable today because his clothes locker was emptied overnight. "What right have the Russians to clear out my locker?" Later he noticed that his books had been taken away also. Angrily, he repeated again and again: "What right have they!"

At eleven o'clock I came back from the bath. In the corridor I saw the American chief guard Felner, who gave me a sign. But I did not understand what he meant. While I was standing there, Felner entered Neurath's cell. I saw the old man in his armchair slowly raise his head. "Come along to the storeroom," the American said. I went to my cell, and saw Neurath in his slippers shuffling unsteadily along behind Felner. At the end of the corridor the iron door closed behind the two. For a moment there was silence. Suddenly Charles Pease was standing beside me. "He's gone," he said dryly. That was all. No farewell, no ceremony, not even a handshake. Just this disappearance through the iron door. One of us was in freedom.

For hours afterward we all felt dazed. Dönitz's eyes were wet. In my case, too, my old trick of biting my tongue failed me. Hess, shaking his head, admitted, "I really never would have thought it possible."

November 7, 1954 Before the services the chaplain gave us messages from Neurath. It grieved him that he had been unable to say goodbye, the chaplain said. He had been led to the storeroom without explanation. There, instead of his moth-eaten suit, he had been given prison clothing without a number. Neurath's daughter had received her father in the visiting room and then, without identification papers or a certificate of release, taken him to the car waiting in the prison yard. No restrictions on his freedom had been imposed on him.

After Bruckner's *Te Deum* the chaplain read Psalm 126: "He that goes forth weeping . . . shall come home with shouts of joy." The chaplain prayed for Neurath. Then for our release.

November 8, 1954 This afternoon we read the reports on Neurath's release. That same evening Adenauer telegraphed his congratulations, and even Heuss wrote him. This concern of the representatives of new Germany has made a profound impression on all of us, even on Dönitz and Hess.

After the release Neurath asked a reporter worriedly, "What will become of my garden without me?"

In passing out supper, Raeder poured the coffee into the sugar bowl instead of his cup.

November 10, 1954 Still all worked up over Neurath's release. To calm myself, I walked eighty-nine beans, or 24.1 kilometers, today, at an average speed of 4.65 kilometers per hour. Funk watched, frowning. "I suppose you want to become a suburban letter carrier."

November 12, 1954 Two days after my walk I am lying in bed. My right knee is swollen, my leg in splints. How the sense of time is distorted by the mists of memory! I tell the medical aide that I last had trouble with my knee about two years ago; according to the medical record it is actually five. Unarticulated time is not measurable; strictly speaking, where there are no events, there is no time.

November 24, 1954 The newspapers in recent days have carried brief accounts on the back pages to the effect that the UN is still debating whether the Nuremberg principles are to be acknowledged as a basis for international law. Naturally Dönitz, Schirach, and Raeder have been making taunting remarks, as though this constituted a personal defeat for me. And in fact I admit that my view of myself is affected by it. For to me Nuremberg was never just a settling of accounts with past crimes. Rather, to this day I have drawn strength from the hope that the trial's principles would become international law. Now it turns out that evidently only a few nations are willing to accept it.

What can I do in the face of recriminations but remain silent?

November 25, 1954 In the eyes of my fellow prisoners, so far as they do not view me as a mere opportunist, I have developed a Dostoevskian guilt complex, a form of masochism that affects not just me alone, but the entire German people. Even when they do not say so— and they do say it often enough—they think I adopt such attitudes only to show off.

But is my position so unusual, so extraordinary? The concept of the "sound instincts of the people" has been thoroughly discredited after the disgusting way that idea was exploited in the recent past. But some such instinct really does prevail. Undeniably there exists, far from all legal strictures, an instinct among people for what is permissible and what is not. Everybody knows what isn't right—no matter how clumsily I am expressing it here. Sometimes I think that the simple feelings of the people offer a better guideline to decency than any laws.

Basically, Dönitz and Schirach and Funk are denying the obvious. An experience I had at the end of 1941 points that up. I was sitting through a boring lunch in the Chancellery that dragged on forever. In the course of the conversation Goebbels began complaining to Hitler about the Berliners. "The introduction of the Jewish star has had the very opposite effect from what we intended, mein Führer. Our idea was to exclude the Jews from the community. But the man in the street doesn't avoid them. On the contrary. People everywhere are showing sympathy for them. This nation is simply not yet mature; it's full of all kinds of idiotic sentimentality." Embarrassment. Hitler silently stirred his soup. We others who were sitting at the big round table were, for the most part, in no way antisemites, and would have preferred to hear about the advance in the East. Dönitz and Raeder really weren't either. But at the time we passed over that remark. At least it has stuck in my memory, and now it seems to me a kind of proof of the natural, almost innate sense of right that people have. That was what I thought in Nuremberg and that is what I still think today.

November 26, 1954 I have already been in bed for two weeks because of the swollen knee. The Russian doctor looks in every day. Striking display of sympathy by the others. Schirach brings me my meals and does the cleaning; Raeder comes by every day to exchange books; Hess pays sick calls and chats. Even most of the guards try to cheer me up. Only Funk and Dönitz seem allergic to sickness.

Sustained by eight aspirins daily, I have been writing approximately twenty pages of my memoirs every day. Still dealing with my time as an architect.

I wonder whether Hitler ever observed that in all the years before I became a cabinet minister I never uttered so much as one political phrase? I rather think he didn't even notice. Just as it was only after we had been acquainted for years that he learned with surprise, but with no particular interest, that I had been a party member since 1931. It was a matter of supreme indifference to him whether the artists he esteemed, from Breker and Thorak to Hilz and Peiner or Furtwängler and Eugen Jochum, belonged to the National Socialist Party. He regarded them one and all as politically feeble-minded. In a certain sense he must have applied the same standard to me. In 1938, a few days before the opening of the annual exhibition in the Haus der Deutschen Kunst, a small group of us sat in Hitler's favorite Italian restaurant, the Osteria Bavaria in Munich. Out of a clear sky Adolf Wagner, the Gauleiter of Bavaria, began to relate that he had recently discovered a Communist proclamation that had been signed by a large number of artists. The manifesto in question had been published a little while before the seizure of power, and among others had borne the signature of Josef Thorak.

I stiffened, for Thorak was more or less "my" sculptor, who frequently designed statues and reliefs for my buildings and in the past year had just created the group of figures for the German pavilion at the Paris World's Fair. Wagner went on to say that such a man could not be allowed to decorate the great buildings for the Nuremberg Party Rally, which for centuries to come would be an object of admiration and veneration. I was convinced that now Thorak would be lost to me. Had he occupied a party office, Hitler would in fact have immediately ordered his dismissal. But in this case Hitler replied disdainfully, "Oh, you know I don't take any of that seriously. We should never judge artists by their political views. The imagination they need for their work deprives them of the ability to think in realistic terms. Let's keep Thorak on. Artists are simple-hearted souls. Today they sign this, tomorrow that; they don't even look to see what it is, so long as it seems to them well-meaning."

November 28, 1954 Wanting to do something nice for Toni Vlaer, I today drew him a sketch of the main reviewing stand of the Zeppelin Field in Nuremberg. In gratitude, he told me what a great impression this building had recently made on him. And no matter how firmly I have taken my leave of the world represented by the site of the Party Rally, I am oddly happy that the Zeppelin Field has not yet been destroyed.

How close to me all of that still is!

The Party Rally of 1938 had just ended when Hitler summoned me to a post-Rally conference. He went over the events of the preceding week day by day, assigning praise or blame. "Several of the acts have by now reached their definitive form," he declared. "These include the Hitler Youth demonstration, the parade of the Reich Labor Service, and the night appearance of the party officials [the *Amtswalter*] on the Zeppelin Field. The memorial services of the SA and SS in the Luitpold Arena are also highly satisfactory. We must keep the procedures for these events fixed so that they will become unalterable rites while I am still alive. That means that no one will be able to mess these things up later on. I fear the urge for innovation on the part of my successors. Perhaps future leaders of the Reich will not be able to achieve the effects I can, but this framework will support them and lend them authority."

Up to this point I had taken the phrase *Das Tausendjährige Reich** as purely rhetorical, a mere claim to establishing something that would last more than a single lifetime. But when I saw Hitler virtually canonizing the ritual in this manner, I realized for the first time that the phrase was intended literally. I had long thought that all these formations, processions, dedications were part of a clever propagandistic revue. Now I finally understood that for Hitler they were almost like rites of the founding of a church. Two years earlier, for example, when he had worked out procedures for the memorial service for November 9 in Munich, the written record quite openly used the quasi-religious term, "a National Socialist pilgrimage."

I still remember how surprised I was that all this put a crimp upon Hitler himself. He actually began restraining himself in favor of the "rite," no longer displaying the full range of his rhetorical powers when he was in Nuremberg. Instead, he began moving the architecture and the massing of huge crowds into the foreground, so that the enormous scenery of the ceremony became, so to speak, the ceremony itself. Perhaps I was astonished because I could not reconcile so much seemingly modest restraint with the tremendous claim Hitler was actually making. It now seems to me more likely that he was deliberately giving up the smaller claim to the status of a celebrated popular hero in order to gain the far greater status of founder of a religion.

November 30, 1954 Memories keep flooding back. Today I gave long thought to the question of why it was Hitler picked on me to be his architect and gave me the assignment to build his sacramental backdrops. By background and education the high-flown, rather inflated world of Hitler was basically alien to me. He himself hinted that he

* This phrase, usually translated "The Thousand Year Reich," conveyed to the German era both the prospect of lasting for a thousand years and the eschatological awe inherent in the words "Millennial Kingdom."—*Translators' note.*

wanted only a talented young architect still enough of a *tabula rasa* so that he could form him. Probably I fitted that specification.

Today the British commandant of Berlin went from cell to cell. Something must be up! At the end of October the American commandant was here, although it was not the American month; and two weeks ago we had high-ranking Soviet visitors.

Hess maintained a wall of indignant silence toward the general. Schirach, intent on making a good impression, delivered himself of a perfect bow, with: "I thank you for your visit." Funk thanked the general for having visited him in the hospital. Dönitz made a plea for being operated on soon for his bladder ailment. When he called on me, the general confined himself to a few sympathetic words about my swollen knee. Raeder inveighed against Colonel Cuthill, who almost two years ago announced such ameliorations as visits from lawyers and letters from friends, pledges that were not carried out.

December 1, 1954   Today Cuthill angrily came to see Raeder and told him, "The general has looked into your complaints and finds them unjustified."

In protest, Raeder refused to stand up. "But I'm right nevertheless," he retorted.

Furious, Cuthill turned on his heel. "Impertinent, impertinent!" In the evening the American director informed Raeder that by decision of the four directors he was receiving a warning for having concocted a falsehood. But Raeder repeated undeterred, "Still I am right!" And in fact I was present when these promises were made.

Though I try to stay aloof from all this I am upset at the way they treat Raeder, scolding him like a troublesome schoolboy. If they aren't going to respect his military rank, at least a man decades younger than he might show respect for the dignity of age.

December 9, 1954   Very weak and feverish. Spitting blood. A young lieutenant of the Medical Corps insists I have bronchitis. Without an examination he has prescribed two aspirin every two hours.

Last night I suddenly could not catch my breath. At the same time I had piercing pains in the chest. I sat upright in bed; the uneasy Russian switched on the light every ten minutes, as though a feverish patient represented an increased danger of escape. Otherwise, he did nothing.

December 10, 1954   Today I tapped my chest myself. I could hear the same dull sounds of ten years ago. I wonder whether there is a

pulmonary infarction again? The lieutenant, at last alarmed by my
bloody sputum, also taps my chest. Although he notes the dull, thud-
ding sounds, he insists on his diagnosis of bronchitis. I am listless and
let matters take their course. I feel no fear, almost no vexation; rather
something akin to relief.

December 12, 1954   Yesterday Long became very grave when he
saw the traces of my bloody sputum. Two hours later a high-ranking
American doctor arrived, and immediately found fluid in my chest. An
X ray was taken with a portable apparatus from the American hospital.
The conclusion was: pulmonary infarction.

December 16, 1954   Days of torpor, no books, no newspapers, no
appetite. Dimly, as if through a veil, I became aware that my condition
had given rise to disputes. Cuthill put an end to them by ordering me
to be transferred at once to the infirmary, in spite of Russian objection.
Hawker supervised the transfer. Terray was beside himself. "Only all
four directors can decide that," he declared.

Unmoved, Hawker replied, "The only orders that count for me are
the ones from my director."

December 19, 1954   For three days I have been in the large
infirmary, seven meters by five, a bright room with two real windows. A
good sickbed.

December 24, 1954   Several times a day I have sat up for fifteen
minutes in the Chancellery armchair I designed. Good to be sitting in
it. You'll recuperate quickly now, the doctor said today.

I was rolled to the chapel on a stretcher. But I had to stay lying
down during the service.

Day before yesterday my wife was here. She visited me in the
infirmary and brought me a small private recording of a Bach sonata:
Hilde playing the flute, Albert the cello, and Margret the piano.

December 29, 1954   My estimate was pretty close. I wanted to
conclude the memoirs on January 1, and today I brought the book to a
conclusion as best I could. The end came rather abruptly, but it has become more and more apparent to me that this is only a first draft. Contrary to my original intention, I have ended it with Hitler's death. My
arrest, trial, and conviction are really an epilogue. It seems to me, too,

that the Spandau years do not belong at the end of that period in my life, but are the beginning of a new one.

This is the end of a laborious, sometimes upsetting task that has taken me two years. The retrospect in itself would have required a great deal of my strength. I think I have done pretty well to have persisted with it here, under these circumstances, with the constant fear of discovery. It's almost a miracle that everything has gone smoothly. From Heidelberg I hear that it mounts up to some eleven hundred typewritten pages.

January 6, 1955 Long before Christmas I had been thinking a great deal about how, as a father, to come closer to the children, who have no real concept of me. I considered what had particularly moved me as a child, and remembered the custom my father had of hanging a sausage from the Christmas tree for the family dog.

Just today a letter came from the children testifying to the success of this idea. They reported in full detail how the dachshund, in an excess of good manners, sat up and begged several times in front of the sausage before he at last believed their encouragement and snatched it. What moved me most was to learn that eleven-year-old Ernst, who really knows me only from letters, made a speech to the dog that Hilde happened to overhear. Did he know who the sausage came from? Ernst asked. It came from Papa, who'd written to hang it from the tree. So he must be grateful to Papa. For the first time I have had some influence on the children's Christmas celebration. That is a sort of sharing in it.

January 7, 1955 Back to the cell. Before entering, a last glance at the prison gate, which I had approached to within a few meters.

The first few hours in the narrow cell felt like a blow on the head. My heart pounded unsteadily, my pulse rate increased, frequently jumping to 120.

January 13, 1955 In spite of all the sedatives I have been receiving for days, today I lost my self-control during the British doctor's visit. I said he was violating his obligations as a physician; he had sent a sick man back to the cell; I couldn't stand it any longer. I grew more and more worked up, finally crying out that all people here could think about was punishment, that I simply had to return to the infirmary. The doctor listened patiently, and with evident concern, to my outburst. This was the first time in nearly a decade that I lost control of my nerves. My psychic state seemed to alarm him more than my physical condition. At any rate, henceforth I am allowed to take the tablets he prescribed for the next few days only under supervision.[1]

January 22, 1955 A friendly talk with another British doctor, who turned out to be a psychiatrist. "Your attack was the result of a shock," he said, "prompted by your transfer back to the cell and the state of your nerves, weakened by a long illness."

Hess, too, had a one-hour interview with him. I had a chance to glance at Hess's sickbook, and found the following entry: "His pains are probably hysterical. No psychiatric treatment necessary. To be treated gently, but firmly."

February 7, 1955 The first American professional guard has arrived. He previously worked in an institution for mentally ill prisoners. A former football player with a round, good-natured face. He laughs all day long and cracks those mournful jokes that produce their effect more by the joker's physiognomy than by any inherent humor. He has been nicknamed Moby Dick.

A Russian proposed the name Sancho Panza for this new man. But most of the Western guards would surely be embarrassed if they were asked where that name comes from. While they content themselves with detective stories and crossword puzzles, or merely sit half-dozing, the Russians study chemistry, physics, and mathematics; they read Dickens, Jack London, or Tolstoy and are remarkably well acquainted with world literature.

---

[1] The notation in the official health record of Prisoner No. 5 read:

"The prisoner was in a highly emotional state this morning. He complained bitterly that he had been moved back from his sickroom to the cell too soon and that, as a sick man, he was being unjustly punished. His emotional state was such that he was beyond reason.

"Later in the day he had quieted down considerably, apologizing for his outburst in the morning and complaining merely of lack of sleep, of worry and of palpitations.

"The impression gained was that he has an acute depressive anxiety state and that more than usual care be taken to see that he can in no way injure himself.

"1/14/55 Rather quieter this morning. To have 1) Tablets, [illegible] T l.d. 2) Medinal gr X nocte for 2 nights.

"The prisoner must not be left to take these tablets himself. They must be given to him and he must be seen to swallow them. If he were able to collect them and take a great many together it would be a simple way of committing suicide.

"To have porridge at night.

Signature (capt.)

"Make copy for Chief Warder's book. Tablets must be given by a warder or in his presence.

(Signature of the British director)"

March 5, 1955 During the noon pause Guryev brings the newspapers. Schirach takes the *Kurier*, the paper supplied by the French. He happily draws a line through his number and hands the newspaper back to the Russian. "There," he says, "finished with one newspaper already." Then he picks up *Die Welt*, likewise draws a line through his number, and beams. "Finished with this one too, already. Read those pretty quick, didn't we?" With the Russian-licensed *Berliner Zeitung* tucked under his arm, he returns complacently to his cell.

When a Western guard hands one of us the *Berliner Zeitung*, we make a deprecatory remark whenever possible, but if it is a Russian, we look interested. When Funk receives the *Berliner Zeitung* from Western guards, he usually says at once, "You might as well take this one right back with you." And he ostentatiously crosses out his number. But to the Russian guard he says in dulcet tones, "Oh, many, many thanks," and returns to his cell, seemingly delighted with the pleasure in store for him. Schirach has found the ideal solution. To the Western guard he says when the paper is handed over, "I only do the crossword puzzle; that's the one good thing about this yellow sheet." And he actually does do the puzzle. But to the Eastern guards he comments, "How interesting!"

Funk comes over to me with the *Berliner Zeitung*. "Why, this is wonderful," he exclaims. "Molotov's whole speech is in it; you really have to read that today!"

I pretend to be burning with impatience. "Let me have it; that really interests me, you know. The whole speech, you say?"

Dönitz, who maintains he is always straightforward and candid, remarked to Guryev a few days ago, when by oversight the *Berliner Zeitung* was offered to him for the second time: "No thanks, I've already read it through very carefully. Everything excellent." He recently had an embarrassing moment with the Westerners. Long was standing nearby when Dönitz said to Seminalov, "*Die Welt* has a bad reputation, so my wife tells me. It's wholly under English influence. One can't believe a word of it."

Long came over and asked sanctimoniously, "What's so bad about us?"

Dönitz whirled around, and for a moment writhed with embarrassment. Finally, he blurted out senselessly, "British democracy is the oldest of all." The moment Guryev was gone, he added, "And of course the best. That's my profound conviction." With that, he strode off. At his cell door he turned around and once again assured all and sundry, "I always speak my mind."

March 19, 1955 My fiftieth birthday.

By sheer chance, on this day I completed the last stage on the walk to Heidelberg. While I was still tramping my rounds in the garden, Hess came out and sat down on his bench. It consists of two brick pedestals with a narrow board laid across them. He leaned against two tomato stakes to keep his back from touching the cold wall. "Now I am setting out for Munich," I said as I passed him on the next-to-last round. "Then on to Rome and down as far as Sicily. Sicily's in the Mediterranean, so I won't be able to walk any farther." When I had completed the last round, I stopped and sat down beside him.

"Why not by way of the Balkans to Asia?" Hess asked.

"Everything there is Communist," I replied. "But maybe I could go by way of Yugoslavia to Greece. And from there through Salonika, Constantinople, and Ankara to Persia."

Hess nodded. "That way you could reach China."

I shook my head. "Communist too."

"But then across the Himalayas to Tibet."

I turned that route down too. "Also Communist. But it would be possible to cross Afghanistan to India and Burma. The more interesting route would be through Aleppo, Beirut, Baghdad, and across the desert to Persepolis and Teheran. A long, hot tramp, lots of desert. I hope I'll find oases. At any rate, I have a good program now. It should do me for the time being: it's a distance of more than four thousand kilometers. You've helped me out of an embarrassing predicament. Many, many thanks, Herr Hess."

With the hint of a bow, as though we were at a diplomatic reception, Hess replied, "Most pleased to be of help, Herr Speer."

This evening I have been vainly trying to recall the course of earlier birthdays. Only one of them was especially noteworthy: that was my fortieth, ten years ago. On that day I handed Hitler a memorandum that later was much discussed in Nuremberg.

Went to bed early and will, as I often do, pray for the happiness of family and friends.

March 25, 1955 My relations with Dönitz have continued to deteriorate. For his part, Dönitz has recently been trying to work things out with Raeder—the two of them, the onetime supreme commander of the navy and his successor, have managed to retain their former antagonism right up to the present time within these walls. On the other hand, Raeder's hate complex toward Hess, so fierce it is almost grotesque, is outlasting all changes of time and place.

April 16, 1955   Ten years ago today, four days before Hitler's last birthday, Lieutenant Colonel von Poser, my liaison officer to the General Staff, awakened me soon after midnight. We had arranged to drive to the Oder breach in order to watch the last decisive offensive against Berlin. Long ago I had picked out a hill on my property, an estate in the forest near Eberswalde, from which the territory along the Oder could be viewed. Before the war I had intended to build a small country house there. Instead I had had an observation trench dug on the land.

We drove for almost two hours through Berlin's eastern suburbs and then into the barren land, still marked by winter. Here and there we encountered horse-drawn wagons loaded with household goods and refugees. Once a dog trotted alongside a wagon, and stood still on the road as we approached, its eyes gleaming dully in the thin beam from the blacked-out, shielded headlights. We had expected to encounter a frantic bustle at the rear of a main line of resistance, with motorcycle couriers, supply columns, troop movements. Instead an uncanny stillness prevailed; we found nothing but emptiness and lethargy. Here and there we passed through dense, shallow belts of fog. Now and then we had to switch on the windshield wipers. As we approached the Oder, the sound of occasional artillery fire could be heard, but that soon stopped. Near my property we came upon the state forester; he had heard that the German troops were on the retreat since the early morning hours, and said that the Russians would surely be arriving soon. Strangely, we had not met a single one of the retreating units. Everything was unreal, ghostly; never had I so fully grasped the meaning of the word "no-man's-land." But the forester urged us to leave; we must not stay here, he repeated. Hastily, we packed up our shelter-halves and, avoiding the highways, drove through deserted woods back to the west.

April 20, 1955   "Do you know what day this is?" stocky Rostlam asked me today.

"Yes, the twentieth," I replied unsuspectingly.

He gave me an encouraging look, like someone who has a surprise in store. "Anything special about today?"

I still did not understand. At last I said, "Oh, of course, the British director has promised to call."

At this Rostlam nearly lost his temper. "Don't act so dumb!" he snapped at me. "You know perfectly well."

Only then did it dawn on me. But no matter what I said, he

wouldn't believe that I hadn't realized this was the tenth anniversary of Hitler's last birthday. As a matter of fact, now that I reflect on it, it also seems odd to me. I can't explain why the date slipped my mind. What is more, I'm not even interested in why it did.

Not so long ago—at Hitler's ceremonious birthday parade of 1939, for example—who among us could have imagined that some time later such a scene as this would take place between two of the most prominent guests? Hess takes a stake from Raeder's tomato plantings to use as a backrest for his bench. Raeder sees this and, swinging his cane, comes charging up to Hess, who sits there brooding, and begins berating him. Hess says, in an ironically soothing tone, "My dear Herr Raeder, your prison psychosis will go away once you are free."

Raeder grows even more furious. "Mine will, but not yours! You'll always be a nut."

April 23, 1955   Hess is hardly eating and complains of unbearable pains. No one pays attention to his groans. Today Schirach even mimicked him, to everyone's amusement, while Raeder and Dönitz took advantage of the general mood to virtually break off all relations with him. I suppose their military background has made them intolerant of Hess's whining, self-pitying manner, his muddled character and intellect. At any rate, if they come down on Hess, it is not just from nastiness. Raeder, at least, is not a mean person. But he insists on order, bearing, self-control, qualities that mean little to Hess. And so Raeder will try to bring me over to his viewpoint, as he did today while cleaning the hall. "He no longer does a thing. He simply lies there. Look at how lazy he is. I don't understand the guards. Everyone here has to work. But not Hess—sheer laziness. That's it. Stomach cramps. What a laugh. I have stomach cramps too." Broom in one hand, he waved a wet brush in the other. The whole thing was embarrassing, because guards were present.

Dönitz, attracted by his loud voice, came over and joined in the denunciation. "It's nothing but resistance. He could work if he wanted to." When Hawker turned away, Dönitz continued in the presence of Petry: "He still prefers to be the deputy. We do the work; he deputizes it to us." When nobody laughed at this feeble joke, Dönitz walked away, remarking, "Terrible mistake to give in to Hess. He has to be trained and treated harshly."

April 26, 1955   On the eve of his birthday Hess, after a build-up of about an hour, had a severe attack. His wailing—"Ach, ach, oh, oh!"

—gradually mounted to: "My God, my God, how can anyone endure this!" And in between, as though to banish rising madness: "No, no!" Raeder, from his cell, parodied Hess in the same rhythm: "Oh my goodness, oh my goodness!" A gloomy farce in the nocturnal stillness of the big building. Hess did not fall asleep until he had received an injection.

At breakfast I visited Hess in his cell. He seemed confused, his eyes strange, murmuring to himself, "I beseech God, the Almighty!" When I asked what he was beseeching God for, he said tonelessly, without looking at me, "To finish me off or let me go mad. Madmen don't feel their pain."

I can't tell whether he is merely playacting. Funk, to whom I confided my doubts, commented, "No, this is genuine. And our two grand admirals are the cause of these attacks. Do you remember how Raeder told him that he'd always be crazy? That sort of thing preys on Hess's mind, and sooner or later it comes out."

We then went to Hess's cell and congratulated him on his birthday. The others took no notice.

At the weighing it turned out that Hess weighs only fifty-seven kilos (125 pounds). When he refused to take lunch, the medical aide came with tube and syringe and threatened to pump milk into Hess's stomach. Two guards had already seized him before Hess finally yielded. "In that case I'd sooner drink the milk."

In the garden during the afternoon I sat down with Hess and let him tell me about his son, whom he adores. But finally he burst out, "I can't go on. Believe me, Herr Speer, I can't go on."

I tried to calm him. "Herr Hess, these attacks pass. They come perhaps twice every year."

Hess turned to me in surprise. "What's that? Have I really had them before? When?"

Then he turned to his obsession that the milk must be poisoned.

"Nonsense, Herr Hess," I said. "I drink the same milk."

Depressed, he replied, "I know you're right, Herr Speer. But I can't get the idea out of my head."

After supper Raeder proposed: "If Hess makes a fuss again tonight, let's all start in. Let's each of us let out bloodcurdling wails. What a racket that will make! And you'll see, he'll stop right off."

May 2, 1955 For several days the medical aides have been bringing Hess his breakfast in bed. Raeder, outraged, says to Roulet, "This on top of everything else! It's getting better and better. He has himself treated like a prince. His imprisoned lordship!" Agitated, Raeder adds, "After all, we're not here for our own amusement!" Then he realized what he had said, and gave a discomfited smile. And as if to cover up his slip he added in an explanatory tone, "You know he didn't wash again today. A great mistake, this giving in to him. Only strictness will do in a case like this!"

But Raeder is wrong. For since the authorities have yielded, Hess is eating normally again. In two days he has gained four and a half pounds.

May 4, 1955 Hilde and Arnold have come for a visit. Hilde looks very good. I have feelings of fatherly pride. Her long, slender hands are especially striking. We compare, and mine seem almost clumsy in contrast. She is nineteen now, a grown-up, independent person speaking to another adult. When I come out of Spandau, she will be thirty. We discuss problems of vocation.

On the other hand, I scarcely manage to talk to fifteen-year-old Arnold. Perhaps it is out of embarrassment that he seems more interested in the details of the visiting room. My efforts at contact are made in something of a vacuum. Unhappiness.

May 5, 1955 In previous years the British officers, in spite of their aloofness, would give us friendly greetings as they made their rounds in the garden. For the past three days they have been treating us frigidly. Today we heard that last week they were shown a film on the Nuremberg trial.

May 7, 1955 Months ago, through the approaches of Colonel Cuthill, the Berlin Memorial Library agreed to supply us with two books on architecture every month. In *Der Hochbau,* by Ebinghaus, I have come across the first ostentatious buildings of the postwar era on Düsseldorf's luxury boulevard, the Königsallee. The Benrather Hof is good mediocrity. The Trinkaus bank, designed by Hentrich, who used to be one of my architects, with its rectangular double columns inset with panels of glass, is reminiscent of the facade we planned for the High Command of the Armed Forces headquarters.

I also have an issue of the *American Builder.* With astonishment I note the many German names: Gropius, Mendelssohn, Neutra, Breuer, Miës van der Rohe. Naturally I know them all. When I studied under Tessenow in Berlin, many of them were working only a few halls down, so to speak, and now and then their designs, even if never carried out, created an uproar. As a matter of fact I always felt that a good many of these works were deliberately aimed at outraging the public—roofing the Alps with glass, building a theater in the style of a limestone cave, stalactites and all. Nor was anyone really surprised that most of these projects remained just that, sketches, ideas, plans. They seemed not even meant to be carried out, and simply ignored the social problems of the Depression years.

Now I see that something has evolved out of the extravagant experimental architecture of those years. If I can believe the magazine, something like a universal style is arising for the first time, a style extending from London to Tokyo, from New York to Rio. But what is altogether astonishing to me is that it comes from Berlin, virtually 'from the same floor of the Academy of Art. In the United States Miës and Gropius in particular seem to have had the kind of broad influence that they failed to win in Germany.

There is a spareness about this architecture, a reliance entirely on proportions, an achievement of effect strictly without ornamental additions, a primness and rationality of articulation that strikes me as very Prussian. Possibly I am mistaken, but I don't think so. It was always my ambition to be the legitimate heir of the Berlin classicists, and to this day it seems to me that the garden facade of the new Chancellery, together with the greenhouse, had that tempered emotionalism I have always revered in Prussian classicism. But circumstances condemned my course to failure. The German Miës van der Rohe, with his glass skyscraper on Alexanderplatz, the first in the world, was a long way off from my sort of thing. But the photo in the *American Builder* of works by the American Miës van der Rohe shows me that such work, too, has evolved out of the spirit of Schinkel. I agreed with Hitler that Miës van der Rohe's glass-and-steel constructions belonged rather to the world of technology than to the world of government, and were more suitable for a factory than for an opera house. Was I then thinking too narrowly, along far too traditionalistic lines? It is plain that at the age of twenty-eight I did not understand the Bauhaus. But even now, at fifty, I am deeply convinced that the glass high-rise is wrong when it is used outside the industrial realm. Whether what we had in mind was good or bad, I still think that people have a need for walled-up space, and that a house should be above all a house. It comes down to the question of whether our human need for dwellings is eternal or fluctuates with the times, and whether people's happiness is more dependent on the sense of shelter or the number of lux [the unit of illumination].

May 12, 1955 For a few hours Raeder had a speech impediment. Like Neurath during his last months, he is no longer allowed to work. He sits in the garden on his stool twice a day for an hour, staring into space, lost in thought. The rest of the time he is locked in his cell. In spite of all our differences these past years, I am deeply moved by the sight of this doomed old man. Raeder no longer wants to gloss over the state of his health; I can't understand why he has done so up to now.

May 15, 1955 Routine visit from the British general. He does not seem as pleasant as his predecessor. Raeder, who is feeling better, wanted to say something about his illness, but was so keyed up that he could not produce a word. The British director urged him to sit down. Luckily Schirach, instead of making any personal request, called the general's attention to the danger hovering over Raeder.

For no reason that I can see Colonel Cuthill barked at me to go to the back corner of my cell. "Stand here!" Tersely, the general asked whether I had any wishes. In view of the two men's attitude, I replied briefly, with a formal bow, "What every prisoner wishes. It's obvious."

They left abruptly, without a word.

May 24, 1955 Yesterday, on the tenth anniversary of our arrest, reporters and several of Dönitz's adherents are said to have waited outside the prison, for it was expected that Dönitz, whose ten years have expired, would be released. Schirach, for whom it is hardest to realize that life is going on outside, commented, "Only a few? What a miserable nation. Why aren't tens of thousands standing out there demonstrating?"

But today Colonel Cuthill informed Dönitz that by English law time spent in prison before trial is not counted. Dönitz protested indignantly. Schirach has made a malicious but not altogether unjustified comment: "All along he kept saying that his sentence was as unlawful as the entire trial. So he's being inconsistent now in asserting that his sentence has come to an end."

June 3, 1955 Nobody regrets the departure of the Soviet director, who was with us for many years. His successor is a friendly major who for months observed our procedures from the lower level, disguised as a chief guard. Today he announced his first change: from now on during the Russian month as well we will be allowed to walk in the garden on weekends for two hours both mornings and afternoons.

Additional professional guards have been sent here from American prisons; one comes from notorious Alcatraz. We welcome this, for by now we have discovered that professional guards have a good understanding of the cares and depressions of long-term prisoners. But they also react badly if they are not courted; dealing with generations of submissive prisoners has dangerously fed their sense of power.

June 17, 1955 Ill humor for days. Without asking our admiralty, I recently did my laundry a day earlier than usual. Even today, four days afterward, Dönitz and Raeder stood together discussing my behavior. "Another of his explosive decisions! An idea leaps into his head and he's got to carry it out right off. He doesn't ever pause to consider."

June 19, 1955 In beautiful sunshine and with a fresh breeze from the Wannsee, I took a Sunday walk of several hours. I covered the last kilometers to Vienna and looked down on the city lying before me from the top of the Kahlenberg. I imagined I saw the spot where after the Anschluss Hitler had a plaque installed stating that Vienna was a pearl to which he intended to give the proper setting. The Viennese at the time were outraged.

By steadily increasing the distance I do each day, I have made up for those weeks of confinement to my bed during the winter. My record for one day so far is 24.7 kilometers, my best pace 5.8 kilometers per hour.

My Coburg friend has obtained for me the figures for the distances I have still to cover: Vienna to Budapest to Belgrade, 615 kilometers; Belgrade to Sofia to Istanbul, 988 kilometers. I have decided to be in Istanbul on January 1. With the aid of my slide rule I have determined that in spite of winter and snow I must keep to a daily average of 8.3 kilometers.

On the stretch from Salzburg to Vienna I several times had to fight boredom; several times I was on the point of quitting the whole thing. Merely covering distance no longer satisfies me; it's too abstract just to count the kilometers. I must make it all more vivid. Perhaps I should take the idea of hiking around the world quite literally and conceive each segment in full detail. For that purpose I would have to obtain maps and books and familiarize myself fully with the segment immediately ahead: the landscape, the climate, the people and their culture, their occupations, their manner of life. That way I would be killing two birds with one stone. First of all, I would be introducing order into my rather indiscriminate consumption of books; and if I develop sufficient imagination in picturing what lies before me, I should even be able to feel something like enjoyment of the novelties in store. And

Extensive rebuilding was planned for Nuremberg, city of the Party Rallies.

Hitler intended to provide his home town of Linz with a new museum and a new opera house. He wanted to make the city a cultural metropolis.

The Party Rally of 1939 had just ended. We descended from the stands of the Zeppelin Field, which I had built. Hitler assigned praise and blame.

In the summer of 1941, three days before the attack on the Soviet Union, Hitler, his personal physician, Karl Brandt, and I went for a walk down the broad gravel paths of the Chancellery park. Behind trees to our left lay the long, yellow garden facade of the Chancellery, its large windows framed in gray limestone.

For health reasons Neurath has been issued an armchair. I could scarcely believe my eyes: it comes from the Chancellery and was designed by me in 1938. The damask upholstery is tattered, the sheen faded, the veneer scratched, but I still like the proportions, especially the curve of the rear legs.

Today I finished August Koehler's book on lighting technology; he cites me as one of the fathers of light architecture. If my own view is correct, I took the first step in that direction on the occasion of the Paris World's Fair by bathing the German pavilion in dazzling brightness at night by means of skillfully arranged spotlights. The result was to make the architecture of the building emerge sharply outlined against the night, and at the same time to make it unreal. Nevertheless, it was still a combination of architecture and light. Somewhat later I did without constructed architecture altogether. At the Party Rally I experimented with antiaircraft searchlights; I had 150 of them pointed vertically into the night sky, forming a rectangle of light. Inside the rectangle the ritual of the Party Rally took place—a fabulous setting, like one of the imaginary crystal palaces of the Middle Ages. British Ambassador Sir Nevile Henderson was carried away by the unearthly effect and described it as a "cathedral of ice." I feel strangely stirred by the idea that the most successful architectural creation of my life is a chimera, an immaterial phenomenon.

Sometimes Hitler paused and praised
my bright-red pillars of the portico and
the greenish capitals trimmed with
gold.

On my flight to see Hitler for the last
time on April 23, 1945, I wanted
once more to walk through the
Chancellery I had built. I left behind
not only the ruins of my building, but
the best years of my life.

Thorak was more or less "my" sculptor who was to decorate the great buildings for the Nuremberg Party Rally, which for centuries to come would be an object of admiration and veneration. One day Gauleiter Wagner told Hitler that Thorak, a little while before the seizure of power, had signed a communist proclamation. But Hitler replied disdainfully: "We should never judge artists by their political views. Today they sign this, tomorrow that; they don't even look to see what it is, so long as it seems to them well-meaning."

My friend Arno Breker was Hitler's favorite sculptor. After the conquest of France, Breker introduced me to his old teacher Maillol, who in the early decades of this century led French sculpture to a new flowering.

Up to this point I had taken the phrase *Das Tausendjährige Reich* as purely rhetorical, a mere claim to establishing something that would last more than a single lifetime. But when I saw Hitler virtually canonizing the ritual in this manner, I realized for the first time that the phrase was intended literally. I had long thought that all these formations, processions, dedications were part of a clever propagandistic revue. Now I finally understood that for Hitler they were almost like rites of the founding of a church.

Only in the perspective of
Spandau do I fully realize
how relaxed, how familial
the atmosphere at Obersal
berg was—more like the
summer residence of a pro
perous industrialist than th
mountain castle of the inaccessible Führer who had
so painfully adopted the
statesman's pose, and who
even in my memory is in-
creasingly assuming the fe

tures of a historical abstraction. On the terrace we would stand around informally while the ladies stretched out on the wicker reclining chairs with cushions covered in red-and-white gingham. The ladies sunned themselves as if they were at some spa, for being tanned was the fashion. Liveried attendants, select SS men from Sepp Dietrich's Bodyguard Regiment, with perfect manners that seemed a shade too intimate, handed around drinks. Hitler appeared in civilian dress, in a well-tailored suit that was somewhat too loud. His color was not healthy; his slight paunch gave his whole appearance a portly, comfortable cast.

On certain days the SS
opened the gates of the
Obersalzberg property. A
column five yards wide,
consisting of thousands
upon thousands of
admirers, filed past
Hitler, who stood in a
raised place, visible to
all. People waved; women
shed tears of exaltation.
Hitler would point out
one child or another
to his chauffeur, Kempka,
and an SS man would then
lift the child above the
crowd.

Once Hitler took the trouble of letting my daughter show him her first efforts at writing. For a few minutes our eldest son looked on with some interest, but ran off abruptly when Hitler tried to draw him in also. The children tried to go off by themselves as quickly as possible—a normal reaction, but an unusual experience for Hitler.

Sometimes Hitler invited Bormann's children and mine for chocolate and cake. They were washed up, dressed in their best clothes, and instructed to be cordial and friendly. But they would not let us crack the whip; they acted uninhibitedly, and Hitler did not win them over. He did not have the knack of winning children's affection; all his courting of them met with no response.

It was one of those dismal Obersalzberg days, with west winds driving low-lying clouds from the plateau of Upper Bavaria down into the valley. These clouds piled up against the surrounding mountain slopes, producing steady falls of snow. In spite of the noon hour, it was dark, but at least the gusts of snow had let up. We walked down the path, which had been newly cleared. To the

right and left were low walls of snow; in the background the Untersberg. The clouds had dissipated; the sun was already low in the sky, casting long shadows, and the Alsatian dashed barking through the snow. An old man, a man who was really already defeated, walked in the snow impotently squeezing out his stored-up bitterness, his toxic resentments.

How many New Year's Eves
I spent in Hitler's private
clique at Obersalzberg.
Heinrich Hoffmann took the
obligatory group photo-
graph, which was sometimes
published in the newspapers.

Today I found in the garden one of the notes that Hess makes for his talks with Schirach.

Since I have no paper, I am writing on a leaf torn from the calendar that hangs in the cell.

From the Steel Works we drove a few kilometers eastward to the Nibelungen Works, the largest tank manufacturer in our armaments program, to inquire about progress in the building of the seventy-ton Porsche Tiger, with which Hitler intended to initiate the offensive near Kursk a few months later. So convinced was he of the superiority of these tanks that he counted on a few dozen of them to turn the tide in the summer campaign of 1943, and thus win this greatest of all wars.

Of course my job as minister of armaments used all my reserves of strength. I had to throw myself into the job with an excess of personal involvement in order to make up for my lack of overview, my inadequate knowledge. From morning to night, even during hasty meals, I held important talks, dictated, conferred, made decisions. From conference to conference the subjects jumped around from one problem to the next; I frequently had to find temporary solutions, make decisions of vast import. I suppose I stood the pace only because I would take a trip every two weeks, spending a few days visiting bomb-damaged factories, headquarters on the military fronts, or building sites, in order to gather fresh impressions, to come into contact with practical activities. These tours represented more work, of course, but they also gave me fresh energy. I loved to spend myself to the very limits of my strength. In this I was basically different from Hitler, who regarded the constant activity imposed on him by the war as a terrible burden; he was forever longing to return to the easygoing pace of earlier years.

In discussions about armaments, industrialists were given the floor only to speak on special technological problems. No military, let alone political questions were even discussed in their presence.

I have realized the dangerous, criminal nature of the regime and have publicly acknowledged it. Yet here in this wretched cell I am repeatedly plagued by fantasies in which I imagine how I would have been one of the most respected men in Hitler's world government. Maybe it

is the coming of spring after a hard winter in this prison that puts such a disturbing notion into my head. But when I consider that under my direction as armaments minister the bureaucratic shackles restricting production up to 1942 were removed, so that in only two years thereafter the number of armored vehicles almost tripled, of guns over 7.5 caliber quadrupled, that we more than doubled the production of aircraft, and so forth—when I consider that, my head reels.

In the middle of August 1942 several industrialists accompanied me to Vinnitsa, Hitler's headquarters in the Ukraine. This was the period of the tempestuous German advance toward Baku and Astrakhan. The entire headquarters was in splendid humor. After one of the conferences, Hitler sat on a bench at a plain deal table, in the shade of the trees surrounding his frame bungalow. It was a peaceful evening; we were alone. In his low voice, hoarse from all the talking, Hitler began: "For a long time I have had everything prepared. As the next step we are going to advance south of the Caucasus and then help the rebels in Iran and Iraq against the English. Another thrust will be directed along the Caspian Sea toward Afghanistan and India. Then the English will run out of oil. In two years we'll be on the borders of India. Twenty to thirty elite German divisions will do. Then the British Empire will collapse. They've already lost Singapore to the Japanese. The English will have to look on impotently as their colonial empire falls to pieces."

In the summer of 1944 Field Marshal Keitel, Chief of Staff Zeitzler, armaments manufacturer Röchling, Porsche, and I sat with Hitler to discuss the crisis caused by the knocking out of the German fuel production plants. "Soon we can begin the attacks on London with the V-1 and the V-2," Hitler declared exultantly. "A V-3 and V-4 will follow, until London is one vast heap of ruins. The British will suffer. They'll find out what retaliation is!"

Gloomily, I brood about the last three Christmases of the war. At the time I thought it my duty to spend the day with the Todt Organization crews; in 1942 on the Biscay coast, where bunkers were being built; in 1943 by the Arctic Ocean in northern Lapland; and the last time on the German-Belgian border. The Ardennes offensive was still going on, and the Todt Organization was assigned to restoring shattered bridges.

Architecture I loved, and I hoped to make my name live on in history by building. But my real work consisted in the organization of an enormous system of technology. Since then my life has remained attached to a cause that at bottom I disliked.

In the middle of 1941 Hitler could easily have had an army equipped twice as powerfully as it was. For the production of those fundamental industries that determine the volume of armaments was scarcely higher in 1941 than in 1944. What would have kept us from attaining the later production figures by the spring of 1942? We could even have mobilized approximately three million men of the younger age-groups before 1942 without losses in production.

Schirach shook hands with me in parting, we wished each other all the best for the future. A black Mercedes was waiting. Out of habit I went to take my place in the front seat beside the driver, as I had always done in the past. Flächsner pushed me to the rear door; after all, I had to leave the prison at my wife's side.

At the stroke of twelve, both wings of the gate were opened. Suddenly we were bathed in blinding light. Many television spotlights were directed at us. In front, phantoms in the glare, I saw British soldiers running around us. For a moment I thought I recognized Pease in the tumult, and waved to him. We passed through a thunderstorm of flashbulbs; then we turned away. The prison lay behind us. I did not dare look back.

Family photos had accompanied every letter from Heidelberg. I held them in my hand again and again, comparing them with older pictures—at least in this way I could follow the children's development. In the past I had looked forward with pleasure to this period in the lives of my children. Now I felt more and more intensely that I had lost the children forever, not just for the duration of my imprisonment. How were the natural feelings going to begin again after twenty years? Sometimes I feared that if I were to reappear prematurely, it could only disturb the process of growing up. In the course of such brooding I sometimes wondered whether it might not be better if I never went home again. What were they going to do with a sixty-year-old stranger?

Fourteen quiet days in Schleswig Holstein. We had rented a house by the Kellersee, and for the first time the whole family was together. Every day I woke at the accustomed time, and I continued to feel the urge to tramp out my kilometers. A harmonious atmosphere prevailed, and everybody tried his best with me, but the family observed my eccentricities with some astonishment. Every so often I had an inkling that there were things I would not be able to adjust to.

the other advantage would be that my stupid tramping around and around would cease to be so mechanical. Playing Hess's bean game would finally come to an end. These are efforts at survival!

After a prostate treatment Raeder had violent chills and fever for days. We thought he was nearing his end. But today he seems somewhat recovered. Evidently he is quite a bit better. When Hess again started his nocturnal wailing, the old fellow joined in, although with a feeble voice: "Oh, my goodness!" Alternately, and from different distances, I could hear "Oh, oh!"—"Oh my goodness!"—"Oh oh!"—"Oh my goodness!" But after about five minutes Raeder's voice grew weaker and weaker. In the end Hess won the contest.

July 6, 1955   The new Russian director announced in a friendly manner that my application to have my children allowed six extra half-hour visits has been approved. A considerable help.

July 27, 1955   After the aborted Geneva Conference the green salad disappears from the Russian meals. But we continue to have tomatoes with onions.

August 1, 1955   First day of the American month. In the garden Funk suddenly became conspiratorial and said to Schirach, "Now you watch the soldier on the left tower. When he goes to the other side, give me a sign." And turning to me: "You post yourself a little more to the right. There, now the soldier on the other tower can't see me. And where is the guard? Ah, he's busy with the admiralty back there." Then, in a low voice, he called out, "Schirach! What is your man on the tower doing?" Schirach gave the agreed sign. Funk took a deep breath. Then he reached into his pocket, saying, "Well then, cheers!" With a groan of pleasure Funk took a long drink, then passed the bottle on. It was quickly emptied. "First rate," Funk moaned. "From my wife. Eighty proof—real aged rum. Now we know what we're missing. We manage to get used to doing without other things, but not this!" He looked around. "But what are we going to do with the bottle?" We dug a deep hole and buried the bottle in it. The label read, "Tussamag Cough Syrup."

August 4, 1955   Funk has created a kind of arbor by planting many sunflowers in a square. Today the order came to remove these sunflowers because they interfered with observation. The order produced something like a nervous breakdown in most of us. Funk, outraged, formally resigned his office as chief gardener. Schirach lopped off his flowers, which were in no way being threatened, and Dönitz destroyed his beds of beans. Rostlam watched us, stunned. He seemed really troubled. "Like children! In our prisons you'd get one week of solitary confinement on bread and water." The incident shows how fragile our equanimity is, and how thin-skinned we have become.

August 6, 1955   Shimmering heat waves over the *puszta* as I covered the stretch from Budapest to Belgrade, a few kilometers away from the Danube. The roads were sandy, there was seldom even a single shade tree, and the flies were a plague. From the nearby Havel I heard the sound of tugs, which I transformed into ships on the Danube. I plucked a stem of lemon balm from our herb bed and crushed the leaves between my fingers. The strong odor intensified the illusion of foreign places, tramping the roads, and freedom.

August 28, 1955   Apparently it's still the custom in English prisons, Hawker tells us, to speak of "corpses" when referring to prisoners. Perhaps that explains some aspects of Colonel Cuthill's behavior.

September 17, 1955   This morning when I was in the medical office with Raeder, the British doctor paid his routine visit. Raeder received his daily medicine, vitamins, and Theominal. "But today I need to have my hair cut, I have a visit tomorrow," he said. Then he went to the library to register the newly arrived books. Seminalov watched him go with an appreciative nod. "Number Four always work. All time. Won't ever stop working."

Fifteen minutes later the British doctor returned to the cellblock and went in to see Raeder. "Didn't you say something about dizzy spells? Come along to the medical office for an examination." Both men vanished from the cellblock. The iron door closed behind them with a metallic clang.

After an hour, while lunch was being passed out, and Raeder was not yet back, we looked at Pease. Nobody said a word; none of us dared to ask. But as though he guessed what we wanted to know, Pease said simply, "Yes."

Later in the afternoon Vlaer tells us that Cuthill received the astonished Raeder with the words: "You are completely free and you may go wherever you want." But Raeder wanted to return to our cellblock. He said he must hand over the library to his successor, and he didn't even know who that would be. But this request was refused. He sent his regards to us by way of the medical aide.

I felt sorry for Dönitz. Raeder's release has taken a good deal out of him. For the first time in many months I have walked with him and tried to buck him up. Schirach joined us.

Once free, so he confided to Schirach, Raeder plans to attack two persons chiefly: Hess, because it was psychological torture to be forced to live with him for years, and the British director, because of his total lack of feeling. "Oh, hell," Dönitz said, "that may be what he had in mind. But his wife always gave the orders. Of course he has to attack me."

September 28, 1955 In the newspapers we see pictures of Raeder's first steps in freedom. Like Neurath when he was released, Raeder too seems entirely changed by his civilian dress and by his relaxed features. Curious, how one of us looks in freedom. But it isn't really all that exciting.

September 29, 1955 Raeder's release has revived hopes in the rest of us. A few days ago in Moscow Adenauer negotiated the return of all captive Germans, including the generals and party functionaries sentenced to maximum penalties. Now we are all deliberating whether the concessions he won may have any bearing on our case. One of the new Americans, Charles Hardie, says he recently heard on American radio that the Russians have no objections in principle to the release of the Spandau prisoners. I did not sleep last night.

Still and all, today I set out new strawberry beds. When Dönitz saw that, he asked, "For whom are you setting out strawberries?"

I shrugged. "I don't know. Maybe for myself."

Dönitz frowned. "How come? Are you counting on being here still next year?"

Bent over the bed, I did not answer.

These strawberry plants will not be ready to harvest for two years!

The Tenth Year

October 18, 1955 An item in the *Spandauer Volksblatt* of October 5 states that a delegation under Attorney General Brokhungof of the Soviet Union has arrived in Berlin to seek information on questions that may lead to a settlement of the Spandau problem. This delegation is part of Moscow's effort to close the books on the past, the article says. Schirach and Hess, it adds, are prominent Nazis and are therefore to be turned over to the German judiciary; but the other prisoners will be released.

Is it chance that just at this time the prison administration is replacing the wooden watchtowers by stone ones, is having the washroom painted, and is issuing new headgear? Depending on mood I am hopeful or skeptical.

October 19, 1955 Today I wrote a clandestine note home describing how I imagine my release: Flächsner comes for me, gives me seven hundred marks, so that I can buy clothes and the plane ticket. The family meets me at the airport in Frankfurt. I asked them for the Heidelberg telephone number.

October 20, 1955 I am growing more cautious in order not to jeopardize whatever chance I have for release. As a warning signal, when I suspect danger, I say the word "valerian" to the medical aide. When I need paper, I ask him for "charcoal tablets." This morning, for example, while my knee was being radiated, I said to Vlaer, "I have an upset stomach. Perhaps you could ask the doctor whether I might have charcoal tablets." He gave me an understanding look: "Not necessary, Number Five. That's no problem. What do you think, would four of them do?"

In addition, I have asked Vlaer to be short and rude to me. He has fun with this game. Today, when I forgot my medicine, he barked at me, "Can't you keep your mind on things? We're not your servants! Here's your medicine."

October 22, 1955 Great excitement! Our notebooks have been confiscated. Now of all times. We immediately speculate that the authorities want to find evidence against us.

Schirach reveals that for years he has kept a diary—nine hundred pages in the last twenty months alone. But nobody will be able to read it, he says, because he kept it in English but in German script. I assume that the notes contain material for the psychological study he means to write someday on the Spandau prisoners. His guilty conscience is unmistakable. Stooping forward and moving with rapid, jerky steps, he walks back and forth along the wall of the yard, the same stretch every time. It seems to me that as he walks he is watching us out of the corners of his eyes. At the end he is almost hopping, and at the same time he begins whistling cheerfully. It's unbearable! Nobody who is really light-hearted behaves so light-heartedly.

November 2, 1955 Visiting times have been doubled again. Fritz has come twice, irritating me by his grave manner. I realized as we sat facing one another, smiling and groping for topics of conversation, that none of my words were reaching him. Probably I queried him in a highly clumsy way, pallid, conventional questions for which there are scarcely any answers. The hesitant course of the visit, the boy's obvious embarrassment, paralyzed me more and more. I suppose I might have asked him how he is doing in English in school, how the plans for the bicycle tour of the Black Forest are coming along, whether he has made up with his girl friend, which of the children the dog is most devoted to. None of these things occurred to me. And while the pauses in the conversation grew longer and more painful, it dawned on me that I have been betrayed in my fatherly hopes that with the years communication with the children would become easier. In fact, the children have been slipping away from me. And suddenly it became desperately clear to me that the walls of Spandau are robbing me not only of my freedom, but of everything. Or should I say, have already robbed me?

November 10, 1955   Only an hour and a half every day in the small inner yard. The garden is closed to us because for the last three weeks masonry work has been in progress on the massive watchtowers. There is no saying when this will end.

Plump Seminalov, who is being relieved soon, suddenly comes up to me in the yard and sits down beside me. He asks, "How are things with you?" Evidently he wants to show friendliness once more before he leaves. "Only four more days," he says. "Then I home." His good-natured seal's face throws a startled look at me as he realizes that I will stay right here; and abruptly he points a stick at a few patches of moss on the wall. "What glowing colors. Beautiful. Green like back home!" Again the startled look—he realizes that he may have caused me pain. I reassure him, saying, "Yes, Russian forests very beautiful." We communicate by means of pantomime about animals he has hunted, since he cannot think of their names in German: rabbits, partridges, and foxes. Then, again frequently resorting to gestures, we talk about his family. If I understood rightly, his sister has had a baby. At some point he begins to laugh; his whole huge body shakes, but I cannot find out what it is about. Nevertheless, I laugh along with him. Who is dispelling whose boredom here? At the end it suddenly occurs to me that conversation with him has gone easier than with my son.

November 15, 1955   Today the Russian commandant of Berlin, General Dibrova, came on an inspection. He began with Hess, who complained about his health. Dönitz treated him with coolness, for he and his comrades are responsible for Dönitz's still being held here. The general asked the admiral, "Who is that in this photo?"

"My son," Dönitz replied tersely.

"What does he do?" Dibrova asked in a friendly tone.

"He was killed in the war."

Dibrova pointed to another photo: "And this one?"

"My second son."

"And where is he?"

"Also killed."

Thereupon, so I am told, the general bowed sympathetically.

He then came in to see me. "Ah, the architect." In the background were the four directors, two guards, one chief guard; at the general's side a young interpreter. "Do you recall that I visited you once before?" he said genially. "Have you done any new drawings since then?"

"No, the light is too poor," I replied. "I want to spare my eyes. I hope to be needing them soon."

His smile indicated that he had understood. "Well . . ." Dibrova obviously wanted to continue the conversation, but I said nothing more. "How do you mean that about better light?" he resumed.

"When I'm in my studio—once I am free."

With a very friendly smile in his eyes, he asked, "And when do you think you will be free?"

I evaded that. "Every prisoner has his hopes."

He considered, then turned to the photographs. "Six children? You are fortunate to have so many children. Children are the best capital!" A parting bow. The general said a word that the interpreter translated as, "Very pleased."

Confused, my composure distinctly shaken by the unwonted cordiality, I replied, "I thank you for your visit."

Followed by his escort, the general went in to Schirach and asked tartly, "Have you any complaints?"

I heard Schirach say, "No."

Dibrova sounded disconcerted that this time Schirach had nothing to complain about.

"Why aren't you complaining?" he demanded in an unfriendly tone. I wondered whether he was familiar with the contents of Schirach's diary.

In the afternoon Funk went over his grand scene again and again for our benefit. "How are you, Herr Funk?" the general asked, and at once answered the question himself: "I can tell you this, better. You look like a young champion."

Thereupon, said Funk, he had brought the general up to date on his three incurable diseases, for probably he had not even been informed of the precarious state of Funk's health. Funk has seized the opportunity to explain to the commandant that his being here was a rank injustice. The American prosecution in Nuremberg had forcibly extracted the crucial testimony against him by mistreatment of one of the German witnesses, he said. Although he was still alive, he did not hesitate to call the whole thing a judicial murder; at least that was how it would turn out if he were held here much longer.

"You must write all that down," the Soviet general said, smiling.

"I replied to the general that I've already done so," Funk told me. "Several times, in fact. I said I'd written to the Control Commission."

Dibrova shook his head. "You must write to the Soviet Ambassador. The Control Commission no longer exists. You have the right to bring up your case. Insist that it be dealt with by a special committee." In parting the general had wished Funk a good recovery. Funk is so sure of the effectiveness of his presentation that he again has hopes of a release soon. He is setting himself deadlines again.

November 18, 1955 Today I read in Vallentin's book on Leonardo da Vinci that the artist, after his patron Duke Ludovico's flight from Milan, wrote merely: "The duke lost the State and his property and freedom, and brought none of his works to completion." The author comments: "That is all that Leonardo da Vinci has to say after his fate was intimately bound up with that of the duke for sixteen years. It is like an epitaph composed by an indifferent hand."

November 22, 1955 These have been days of careening between hope and despair, and in the midst of these shifting moods comes a letter from General Speidel, the first German officer to hold a high post in NATO. The letter comes from Washington, addressed to my wife, and informs her that through contacts with an important figure he has been able to do something about a release in the near future for me. Speidel recalls my conduct after July 20, 1944, when he was being held in the cellar of the State Security Office. It moves me to read that in spite of my own difficulties I "selflessly, courageously and in a truly friendly way" did my best for him and his wife, "aiding by word and deed."

November 26, 1955 Fresh signs of a turning point in our affairs. We have been told to make lists of our belongings. Three days in which to do this. This same evening, paper is handed out to us. This time Schirach is optimistic. "What would be the sense of it if our release weren't imminent?" I myself begin worrying about the foreword and epilogue of my memoirs. Outside I shall no longer have so much time for that.

November 30, 1955 This morning we were informed that Cuthill will be coming in an hour to deliver an important message to us. Funk became weak with excitement; Hess began hastily cleaning up his cell; I tried to control my nerves by putting my drawings in order and numbering them. At ten o'clock all the cell doors were opened.

Then Cuthill appeared, accompanied by Letham and the chief Russian guard. Like a tank clanking up, he posted himself in each cell door, one after the other, and said tersely to Letham, "Go ahead." Mechanically, Letham ran through the following litany: "Number One. We hear that you have been entertaining hopes. The requested lists are a purely administrative measure. All anticipations that you will soon be released are absolutely unfounded."

Before the first man had grasped this, Cuthill merely said, "Next door." There the scene was repeated. Five times, exactly the same.

Evening. Still feeling dazed. Throughout the day not a word was spoken. All of us were totally dashed. I saw Funk sitting on his stool with arms dangling feebly, sobbing without a sound. Schirach sat staring into space, repeatedly shaking his head and suddenly looking like an old man. The many signs and seeming signals of the recent past had so fed our hopes, no matter how hard we tried to preserve a skeptical attitude, that today's communication has struck us all like a second sentencing. For a moment in the depression of this afternoon the thought flashed through my mind that perhaps all this meant nothing, that Cuthill, irritated by the restiveness and breakdown of discipline, merely wanted to recall us to order in his rather rough fashion. Who knows?

December 2, 1955   The second visit from my youngest boy, after more than a year. He is now twelve. He looks at me curiously; he answers my questions like a well-brought-up child speaking to a stranger. My wife, who accompanied him, looks overworked and tired. Grief. Numbness.

December 8, 1955   Made a start on an entry. Sat for half an hour over this sheet of paper. Searching for thoughts. What am I to write?

December 14, 1955   Months ago I drafted a petition for leniency, then dropped the idea. But today I have handed it in after all. What prompted me was my boy's sad eyes. Hitherto I have always been opposed to such a petition, on grounds of dignity—out of contempt for all those who slipped out of their responsibility, either by suicide or by whimpering evasions. Above all, it seemed to me inconsistent first to assume responsibility and then to ask for mercy.

From the vantage point of ten years in prison, I wonder sometimes at my recklessness in assuming responsibility for the whole policy of the regime. But still, for me that was an attempt to make a decisive break with the spirit of the past. During the past two weeks of brooding, however, even this certainty has left me, at least at times. Was my stand in court really an intelligent repudiation of the high-flown bathos of those years? Was it not rather only a different kind of blind self-sacrifice, one more piece of romantic mania for self-surrender, mindless youthful emotionalism? And sometimes the thought alarms me that Hitler himself, for all that I so strongly disavowed him and all he stood for in court, would have been keenly delighted by the role Albert Speer played as a defendant. The emotional atmosphere from which my self-accusations sprang was wholly Nazi—I had learned my lesson well. Only the content differed: "You count for nothing; your guilt counts for everything."

Two hours later: In rereading this I am filled with a profound distrust, wondering whether all these intellectual acrobatics are not meant merely to justify my change of heart. But let it be; the petition is handed in. I am relieved.

December 15, 1955   Another comment on yesterday's entry: I am reading in Martin Buber that one "obtains power over the nightmare by calling it by its real name."

December 24, 1955   After the despair of the past weeks I have resumed my tramp. This morning I left Europe and crossed the pontoon bridge to Asia. I have trouble picturing the magnificent panorama: mosques and minarets in the midst of a tangle of small houses. How many towers does Hagia Sofia have? Also, I keep confusing the Golden Horn and the Bosphorus. Problems of the imagination.

Before going to sleep read the Apostle Paul's Epistle to the Romans. In spite of all the spiritual aid, I have been living for many years in a kind of spiritual isolation. Sometimes I think about death. But it is rather because I have had enough of life. Only the thought of the children . . . And then the book! That is gradually displacing architecture. It is becoming the sole task I can still see ahead. Otherwise, I expect nothing more.

December 25, 1955   Had the light turned out last night at seven o'clock in the evening.

January 14, 1956   No entry for three weeks. The stone watchtowers have been occupied; we are back in the big garden. Protracted listlessness. Still reliving Cuthill's scene.

February 20, 1956   Another five weeks without an entry. After all, what happens? Is it worth mentioning that Dönitz has his favorite broom and is furious if someone else uses it? Is it worth recording that for years we have been sweeping the hall in precisely the same order?—first Schirach and I do the sides, he always working from the left and I from the right toward the center, while Dönitz takes care of the center. Subsequently the heaps swept up by Dönitz are picked up by Funk and Hess. Hess comes with a pail and dustpan; Funk always has the broom. Wordless motion. How well we have adjusted to our surroundings!

March 15, 1956   A high point in Spandau social life: In spite of the revocation of the Four Power status, Dibrova has invited the three Western commandants of the city to the prison mess. Because of this we had to wait for several hours in our neatly cleaned-up cells. Then at last our food came too. The Russian director presented himself in full dress uniform. But he was obviously in bad humor. Hess was barked at because he had cramps and did not want to fetch his food, I because a button of my jacket was open. Later we learned that the host, Dibrova, had not appeared for his own dinner; his three Western colleagues, refusing to let his absence trouble them, calmly went ahead and dined without him. At three o'clock they had peaceably driven away again. Presumably this is the reason we were not presented. We have, incidentally, long since become accustomed to being the living inventory of a waxworks. Guests being conferred special distinction are shown a few old men in their cells: "This is the admiral . . . This is the architect . . ."

March 18, 1956   We made three fireplaces in the garden today and burned leaves. Hess kept a fire going, but most of the time he stood in front of it staring into the flames. Fifty paces from him Schirach poked around in another fire. I too am burning leaves. As I watch the flames I suddenly no longer know whether I still want freedom.

March 28, 1956   Among the new Russians, Fomin is the only one who insists on being treated as a person of consequence. We frequently have the impression that he enters the cellblock or the garden without the slightest pretext, merely to receive tribute. In the garden today I saluted him by raising my hand to the visor of my ski cap. "Number Five, you did not salute me correctly." I looked at him in astonishment and repeated the salute a shade more formally. "No," Fomin said, "not that way. Go back and then approach me." I did as requested. When I again came up to him and raised my hand in the military salute, Fomin shoved his own cap to the back of his neck in surprise. "He doesn't know! Number Five, why no salute correctly? The cap off. Down from head. Once more!" This description, as it stands here, seems slightly comic, as though I had retained a degree of ironic superiority. I had not. One never grows used to humiliations.

May 5, 1956 Today friendly Bokov said to me as I stooped over the flower beds, plucking weeds, "What, always *rabotte, rabotte?* Why work? Now always ten minutes work, fifty minutes rest." Then he laughed heartily: "That's Communist work. And Communist work better than German work." Stimulated by the cordiality of a few Russians, Funk has by now discovered a Slavic grandmother. A Russian great-great-uncle turned up a little later; gradually he is undertaking, with growing boldness, a genealogical displacement to the East. Schirach commented spitefully, "I suppose it's pure chance that your family happened to drift to Germany." But Funk stuck to his cheerful cynicism. Good-naturedly, he slapped his knee with his paperback Russian vocabulary and said, "Now I'm going to learn a bit of the mother tongue."

May 12, 1956 My chestnut trees have grown to a height of two meters—above my head. Exactly a week ago the hard winter shell of a bud seven centimeters long cracked and began unfurling downwards. Only yesterday the lowest of the three-stage structure within had the shape of a sugar tongs; the tip resembled an Egyptian capital. Now, like a well-organized building exhibiting complementary rhythms, the bud has articulated sixteen chestnut leaves, each of which is divisible into seven individual parts. One hundred twelve units. The leaves droop slackly, as if tired by their rapid growth.
One doesn't need a royal water lily to be lost in admiration.

June 12, 1956 Through Hilde I have received a copy of a letter from John McCloy to my wife, dated May 21. He promises to get in touch with the State Department, and continues: "I have a very strong conviction that your husband should be released and I would be very happy if I could do anything that would tend to expedite such release."

June 14, 1956 Our hall is being repainted, this time by prison employees. We are left with the job of cleaning up the floor. Under the leadership of the grand admiral, we have introduced a simplified procedure. Shouting "Swab the decks!" we splash buckets of water on the floor, then mop it all into the cold-air returns of the new hot-air heating system. Pease and Bokov had taken off their tunics and were helping us when suddenly, as though he sprang from the floor, Colonel Cuthill was standing behind them. Hastily, the guards put on their tunics. "Who came up with that idea with the water?" Cuthill asked sternly.

No answer. "It will run down and out," I tried to reassure him. "The system isn't watertight." Cuthill snapped at me, "You're not going to tell me it isn't watertight when it's airtight?" No prisoner dares to contradict so much logic backed by superior authority.

June 15, 1956 My disinclination to keep this journal is constantly increasing. Only rarely, and as though I were fulfilling a burdensome obligation, do I take up notepaper and pencil in my cell. I don't really have anything more to communicate to people on the outside, and now that I have finished the draft of the memoirs, the past is over and done with also. The books I am reading are merely a pastime now. I long ago forgot my plans to write a big book on the function of windows in building, or on the unbuilt architecture in Giotto's paintings. I have abandoned my projects for learning languages, for keeping abreast of technological developments in architecture. What have I set down on paper during the past few months? If I remember rightly, aside from the epilogue to the book, there are only a few silly anecdotes: stories about Funk's grandmother, irritations with the guards, Hess's stomach cramps. Am I suffering less or more?

If things go on this way, I fear I am doomed. I might really become a convict. But although I see that clearly, I am too tired, too slack, to make any decisions. In three months Dönitz will leave us. There have been many tensions between him and me, but even these tensions have helped keep me alive. From October on I'll be alone with Hess, Funk, and Schirach. What a thought! If I want to keep going, I shall have to make a new start by that time at the latest.

July 15, 1956 Nothing. For four weeks, nothing.

July 17, 1956 Today Hess sat doubled over on his stool in the shade of the nut tree, groaning pitiably. Obviously he is feeling worse again. Since December a notice signed by the American doctor has been attached to the door of his cell, ordering: "Number 7 must work at least half an hour in the garden under supervision of the guards every day." This order was confirmed during the following three months by the signatures of the British, French, and Soviet doctors. Since then Hess has been twice penalized, "to cool him off," as Cuthill once remarked. Today, too, Letham ordered Hess to go to work immediately or he would be transferred to the punishment cell. It took him five minutes to walk the hundred meters to the patch of sweet corn. Stooped, doubled over, he paused after every second step, began hoeing with groans and laments, took long pauses, leaning on the hoe, and wailed continually. After ten minutes he painfully settled to the ground, drew up his knees, and laid his head on them.

A guard came over. "You have to go on working. Come on, stand up!"

Whimpering, Hess shook his head. "I'm having a heart attack. Report me, punish me, kill me if you like." Three guards stood around him with indifferent expressions. We kept away. We have long since grown used to scenes of this sort, and let them pass. It took fifteen minutes before Hess yielded to the guards' persuasion. Painfully he rose to his feet and with contorted features resumed his work. When he had completed his half-hour, he staggered to the stool and sat there hunched over, his head on his knees again. At his request I brought him his jacket.

July 20, 1956   The new Russian general for East Berlin, Chamov, has inspected the prison. In contrast to the rather amiable Dibrova, he merely had the interpreter ask, "Have you any complaint?" When we said no, he behaved rather strangely: in each cell he fixed his eyes on the ceiling for some time, then departed without another word.

July 21, 1956   This afternoon I happened to be standing in the corridor when Hess came out of his cell, relaxed and cheerful. When he caught sight of me, his expression changed in the fraction of a second. I was startled. Suddenly a tormented, suffering man confronted me. Even his gait changed abruptly. His springy step became stiff and faltering, like an invalid with an amputated leg.

I shall not say a word about it, neither to Hess nor to others, but I am profoundly disturbed. He has been keeping up this sham for fifteen years. What an expenditure of energy! What consistency in doing violence to his own body! But also what confusion of mind!

July 23, 1956   In his cell this morning Dönitz was reading a French book, half aloud, as is his habit. Fomin knocked on the small window in the door: "Not read aloud. *Verboten!* Read to yourself."

Dönitz said obediently, "Yes, sir." Silence. Fomin, who for some time has been somewhat friendlier, is having a relapse.

August 1, 1956 Dönitz had a half-hour conference with his lawyer, Otto Kranzbühler. "Negotiations are in progress with the three Western Powers to find a procedure for my dismissal that will not attract attention." Once again he is all "head of state," obviously delighted that the three powers are conducting negotiations on his account. He genially informs us that discussions are to be held soon on the dissolution of Spandau; basically, the prison has been kept up this long because the British have grudges against him. Somewhat haughtily he adds, "But that doesn't mean for certain that you others will be released." Then he says, "Admiral Ruge, the new inspector-general of the Navy, happens to be one of the officers I trained. He literally hangs on my lips. Even now." Once again he is talking about "my officer corps," as though the navy were his family business. Sometimes he reminds me of a naval lieutenant who has won his promotions too quickly.

August 2, 1956 For several days Funk has been sick with jaundice. He had previously complained of gall-bladder pain and had been vomiting frequently. In the prison infirmary he is being kept in quarantine, since jaundice can be contagious. Apparently complications have developed.

August 6, 1956 Recently my newspaper reading has been taking me less time. It is the same for the others. There is no longer any bickering when someone forgets to pass the papers on. Interest in events outside is diminishing, has almost entirely ceased. I often catch myself merely leafing through the pages for items that might have some bearing on our fate.

August 12, 1956 This noon all the cell windows were provided with mosquito netting. For the first time I can sit reading by the open window until ten o'clock in the evening, while listening to the gnats vainly buzzing outside the netting.

August 13, 1956 Funk has been in the British hospital since yesterday. Possibly the guards are trying to keep the transfer secret from us. Letham sets his lips when I point to the empty cell. But Fomin, that simple soul, says in all innocence, "Number Six taken to hospital."

August 16, 1956   This morning Rénard came and announced, without a trace of feeling, *"Le numéro trois est mort."* We were stunned. Neurath dead. Our respect for the old nobleman had steadily increased since his release, especially in these last months. He was the only one who never lost his self-control. Older and sicker than the others—and perhaps also less guilty—he had set a standard for the way this period, with all its harsh disappointments and humiliations, was to be endured with a stiff upper lip—in fact, with dignity. I had hoped to see him once more.

I can scarcely assess the role of Neurath in German foreign policy. But in the midst of the many dubious creatures, the numerous condottiere types, who peopled Hitler's court, he certainly seemed like a figure from another world. It is really incomprehensible that he should have condescended to collaborate. That was where his guilt lay—precisely because he always despised this camarilla around Hitler, and never made a secret of it. His world had remained that of the monarchy; as the representative of the conservatives, he atoned for the game they had played with Hitler.

August 23, 1956   In the evening I see in the *Frankfurter Allgemeine Zeitung* a photo of Kars, a mountain town in Turkey that I passed by months ago on my way to the Persian border. I have drawn a sketch of the citadel of Kars. Opposite it is an imaginary meadow, on which my tent is pitched under three rather tousled firs. Wild mountains in the background. Outside the tent, two men at a fire. Do I have a guard as my constant companion? The way my drawing combines Anatolia and the Allgäu in South Germany makes me smile.

August 24, 1956   Schirach's only reaction to a picture of Neurath's funeral in *Die Welt*: "Did you see Papen's morning coat? Perfect fit; he must have a first-class tailor. Probably done by Knize in Vienna."

August 26, 1956   Good news about Funk. The British director tells us that Funk has undergone an operation and is recovering nicely. In two weeks he will be "all right" again. So that means: return to the cell.

August 28, 1956   I have begun with my "History of the Window" after all. This project, for which I have worked through dozens of books and taken a great many notes in the years past, is intended as an investigation of the style-shaping influence of windows in various eras, giving consideration to various climatic conditions, modes of construction, and aesthetic concepts. First of all I calculate the proportion of window surface to area in the Renaissance palaces. This subject of windows has also reawakened my passion for collecting. I look through every book on history for pictures of old windows.

August 30, 1956 Waking up from sleep at midnight, Dönitz had an attack of dizziness. Everything spun around him; he had to vomit. The professional guard Pemberton commented, "I've seen this. Circulatory diseases very frequently appear among long-term prisoners shortly before their release." During the noon break I while away the time by dashing off a pen drawing that expresses my longing for South German small towns. In this way I actually succeed in creating an imaginary world. Feelings of liberation.

September 2, 1956 Two hours before the visit from Margret and Ernst a new indictment is slipped to me. My case has come up in the Berlin Denazification Tribunal. But by now my nerves are somewhat recovered; that the visit went relatively cheerfully was proof of that. Ernst wants to be a geographer; I talked about my world tour. Toward the end of the visit I mentioned the possibility of his watching the Scots changing the guard, with kilts, tassels, and all the traditional trimmings. "No, I don't want to see that," he declared very determinedly. Then Fomin said, "One more minute." The boy fell silent at once. In silence we sat facing each other. Then goodbye.

September 4, 1956 A spider has spun a web between two trees. A few days ago Schirach spent half a morning finding another spider to place in the web. He was expecting a sharp battle; but when at last he had found a spider he couldn't bear to take hold of the creature. Long thereupon placed it in the web, but the alien spider was peace-loving, and left the web by the shortest route. Schirach and Pemberton then threw moths into the web for the spider, then grasshoppers, and observed how the spider stunned them and after several skillful windings fastened them to the web. Since then the feeding of the spider has become Schirach's mania. Everything here goes to extremes. Not only with the prisoners. Today all of them on their knees in the grass, an American, a French and a Russian guard, and Schirach, jointly pursued a grasshopper.

"Recently each of us has developed his own particular craze,"

Dönitz commented. "Schirach has to be talking or singing all day long, and now he's catching spiders. You twitch your mouth when you walk." I think what he says is true.

September 7, 1956   Before going out into the yard this afternoon we had to wait for Hess. When he arrived at last, Dönitz said to him, "If I had a mark, Herr Hess, for every quarter-hour I've had to wait for you in the past eleven years, I'd be a rich man." Hess retorted without hesitation, "And if I, Herr Dönitz, had only a single pfennig for every useless word you've addressed to me in these eleven years, I'd be much richer than you."

Recently Dönitz has been showing his irritation with the preferential treatment of Hess by speaking of him as "Herr Baron." Lately he has formed the habit of posting himself ten paces in front of Hess and staring at him for minutes at a time. Sometimes I then post myself beside Hess and stare back, which makes him stop his rudeness.

September 14, 1956   While I was working in the garden, the British director, followed by his deputy, Letham, put his ritual question to me: "All right?" Only as he was going away did he casually take two sheets of paper from his pocket: "These are for you." They are the documents concerning the opening of settlement proceedings in my case. The letter is dated August 18; so it has taken twenty-seven days to travel a distance of a few kilometers. Hardie commented dryly, "A retired turtle would envy it."

September 17, 1956   In these last weeks of his stay at Spandau the pressure is lifting from Dönitz. He frequently sits on a bench with guards. Stories, jokes, recollections.

September 18, 1956   Today I ended the second year of my walking tour. I have walked 3326 kilometers; counting the winter, that makes a daily average of 9.1 kilometers. As long as I continue my tramping, I shall remain on an even keel.

September 22, 1956   Shortly before waking I dreamt that Funk had returned. Weakened, he leaned against the wall, grown curiously small and wrinkled.

I could not believe my eyes when, half an hour after I was up, four British soldiers carried Funk into his cell on a stretcher. In the van came our medical aide in a white smock, followed by Mr. Letham and a British sergeant.

Shortly afterwards, Funk was already standing in front of Schirach's cell, talking away. Dönitz was drawn in. Funk did not bother about Hess. Or me either.

September 23, 1956   In the afternoon I am provided with paper so that I can write to my lawyer, Flächsner. It torments me to have to go through everything all over again after a decade of imprisonment. What's the point of it all? I don't really exist any more. Let them have the bombed-out property in Wannsee for all I care.

September 28, 1956   Only three days more for Dönitz. A curious high tension prevails, since there is always the possibility that the release will be advanced in order to avoid demonstrations at the prison gate. The guards, too, share the uncertainty. Almost all the Western guards today shook hands with Dönitz and wished him luck; even Bokov crossed the garden to him to bid goodbye. This is the first time that one of us is being released after serving his sentence.

September 29, 1956   Funk and Schirach are now standing around with Dönitz almost all the time. Schirach shows traces of his former gentlemanly bearing. He takes one of the sticks that are used as tomato stakes, transforms it elegantly into a light cane, and with inimitable panache twirls it rapidly from his wrist. During the afternoon chatting session today Schirach used the stake as a support for his backside. The only time I've seen this in the past was with upper-crust movie characters watching a horse race. I noticed Schirach vehemently urging some point on Dönitz. Since early morning the program of the radical rightist DRP, which was in the papers today, has been causing a rumpus. In passing I heard our grand admiral say, "This is clear, at any rate: it is the only high-class party program." But tomato stakes are not high-class bamboo canes; the stake broke and Schirach took a tumble.

Toward me Dönitz has been constrained. Probably he is expecting me to address him; but he is going and I am staying, and it is up to him to do so.

September 29, 1956   Thirty cars full of reporters are said to be waiting outside the gate because of persistent belief in Dönitz's premature release. "Once I'm outside, the first thing I'll do is discuss with Kranzbühler how all of you here can get out," Dönitz declares generously. He seems to have forgotten completely that his connections were not a bit of help to him personally, and that he has had to serve his sentence down to the very last day. So I tell him, "There already are several important persons among the Allies who are working in my behalf. Any effort on your part could only do harm."

Dönitz is taken aback. During my walk he keeps out of my way. I, too, make no further attempt to talk with him. In the afternoon Cuthill announces the sibylline decision of the four directors, that Dönitz will no longer be in Spandau on October 1.

September 30, 1956   Dönitz's last day.

Once again the same scene. Dönitz engaging in a long conversation with Schirach and Funk, I on my long hike, and Hess sitting alone on a stool by the nut tree. Dönitz has not exchanged a single conciliatory word with him.

Abruptly, Dönitz turned to me. "There's something I'd like to ask you," he said.

I expected that he would at last say a friendly word, that just before his release he wanted to dissipate the prolonged hostility of these past years. Readily, I responded, "Yes, gladly. Let's go over to the bench."

When we were seated side by side, Dönitz said, "You once told me that during your last visit in the Führer's bunker you recommended me to Hitler as his successor. You said there was a discussion of his testament and my appointment. Just how did that come about?"

"It wasn't quite that way," I replied. "Rather, Hitler asked me probing questions about how you were doing as his deputy for the northern region, and I said you were doing very well indeed. Of course I was fairly certain that Hitler had specific intentions in mind when he asked this question. But as his way was, he didn't let on. When Göring was deposed a few hours later, I had the feeling that now your turn to take over was coming. Who else did he have left? Therefore your appointment didn't surprise me very much. But it wasn't I who proposed you."

Dönitz nodded. "That was what I wanted to know. Because when I write my memoirs I have to know clearly how my appointment came about."[1]

[1] In his *Memoirs*, however, Dönitz states, contrary to the true facts: "Later, in the winter of 1945–46, Speer told me that on that occasion he happened to be present when Hitler was considering the terms of his will. He himself had then suggested that Hitler should appoint me as his successor. Hitler, he said, had then become very thoughtful, as he always did, when he had something particular on his mind. From what Speer told me, it seems to me that it may well have been his suggestion that first put the idea of considering me as a possible successor into Hitler's mind." (*Memoirs. Ten Years and Twenty Days*, by Admiral Karl Doenitz [Cleveland and New York: World Publishing Company, 1959], pp. 441–42.)

For a moment we sat side by side in silence, staring into space. I made an effort to recall the scene in the bunker, but could not. Suddenly I heard Dönitz saying in an entirely changed, cutting voice, "Because of you I've lost these eleven years. You're to blame for it all. That I was indicted like a common criminal. What did I have to do with politics? But for you Hitler would never have had the idea of making me chief of state. All my men have commands again. But look at me! Like a criminal. My career is wrecked." He stood up, stared hard at me, and went on in the same hostile tone. "One more question: Was that remark about Kranzbühler your last word? Kranzbühler is leading the whole operation in behalf of those condemned for war crimes. He often sees Adenauer. And I have some influence too. After my release I want to be able to say, 'Let the four in Spandau go free.' Am I to restrict it to 'Let three of them go free'?"

I shook my head. "I don't mind your speaking of all four. But perhaps you have a moment to listen to what I have to say?"

Dönitz made a permissive gesture and said tersely, "By all means."

"For ten years here you have slandered, disparaged, and ostracized me," I said. "Long ago Neurath advised me to ignore that, simply to keep silent. Imprisonment itself was bad enough, he said. I followed that advice. Even though you constantly blamed me for having acted dishonorably during the last months of the war and in the Nuremberg trial.[2] But at least once I want you to hear this: You and the others here have endlessly talked about honor. Every other word you or Schirach utters is dignity, bearing. This war killed millions of people. More millions were murdered in the camps by those criminals. All of us here were part of the regime. But your ten years here perturb you more than the fifty million dead. And your last words here in Spandau are: your career! No, I don't want anything from you and your Kranzbühler. Of course I want to get out of here. But if it depends on that, I'd rather stay here another ten years."

Dönitz had listened rigidly. Then he said casually, "All right, as you like!" He returned to the others. Both of us had raised our voices. They were waiting for him in suspense.

After the Sunday walk the cells were searched—idiotically, Dönitz's

[2] Ten years later, in an interview in *Christ und Welt*, October 7, 1966, Dönitz revised his opinion. He was asked: "In regard to the Nuremberg trial you declared that it was not the best solution but that at any rate it was an effort at purification and as such better than no effort at all. Was this an affirmation on the part of the defendant, which you were at the time, to the trial, or rather to the basic idea underlying this trial?" Dönitz replied: "Yes, exactly, insofar as the crimes against humanity are concerned."

as well. Meanwhile we paced back and forth in the cellblock. By way of conciliation and to show Dönitz that my morning outburst was partly the product of shattered nerves, I made fun of the thoroughness of the guards. Dönitz entered into that amiably. At least outward peace has been restored.

After supper Dönitz asked for a Theominal tablet and then, shortly before we were locked in again, went over to Hess. "*Auf Wiedersehen,* Herr Hess. I wish you all the best."

"*Auf Wiedersehen,* Herr Dönitz," Hess returned equably. "All the best, and rest up your nerves."

The farewell to Funk and Schirach lasted somewhat longer. And then he came over to me after all, visibly moved. "*Auf Wiedersehen,* Speer, keep well."

I shook hands with him. "*Auf Wiedersehen,* Dönitz. Good luck." I turned away quickly.

Dönitz through the door window: "I forgot—give my best regards to your wife."

From the cell I said only, "Thanks." Dönitz sounded distraught; he was weeping.

Outside, they say, people are waiting with bouquets of flowers.

The Eleventh Year

.

October 1, 1956 The rules were enforced up to the very last minute. As he does every evening before sleeping time, shortly before ten o'clock Godeaux asked Dönitz for his glasses. Even Dönitz's request to leave the light on was not granted. The unyielding reply was that all cells had to be dark at ten o'clock. In the silence I could sometimes hear Dönitz pacing back and forth in his cell.

Shortly after eleven Pease said encouragingly to Dönitz, "Only a half-hour more." Soon afterwards, about twenty to twelve, Cuthill had the cell door opened. Dönitz was handed his civilian suit, which Vlaer and Mees had spent three days trying to clean, the dust had settled in so. And while Cuthill was leaving, I heard Dönitz say, "Is this search really necessary?" Then he asked, "Can I go now?" Evidently he had changed clothes.

"Why, no," Letham's voice replied in honeyed tones. "There are five minutes more, five minutes more." Again I heard Dönitz pacing.

"Is my wife already here?"

"Yes, she's come. Just wait another five minutes."

The last five minutes passed in a friendly exchange. "Does your suit still fit after so many years?" Letham asked. "We thought it might have become too tight." He laughed.

"It fits just as well as it used to," I heard Dönitz answer good-naturedly. "We military men never lose our waistlines." There was silence again. "Does my driver know——" Dönitz was beginning to say, when suddenly footsteps could be heard. Cuthill returned.

"The time has come." Then the voices grew fainter; the first door slammed shut, then the second. Shortly afterwards I heard a car starting abruptly outside; a second followed. A few shouts, then silence again.

In the distance a thunderstorm was brewing; it finally crashed down on Spandau.

This morning I stood for a long while in front of the poplar Neurath planted, with the help of Dönitz, nine years ago. It has grown to fifteen meters, and for me is probably the most terrifying symbol of all the time that is running out for me here. Pease was probably trying to banish my black thoughts when he told me, "After the delivery of his possessions, the Russian director said to Dönitz, 'Sign here, Number Two.' Then he went straight on to say, 'So that ends that, Admiral Dönitz.'"

October 3, 1956   I read in *Die Welt* that Dönitz has held a press conference in Düsseldorf. He said that for some time to come he will have to hold his peace, until he can form some opinion on various problems. He is most concerned, he said, with the fate of his fellow sufferers, and his thoughts are constantly returning to them.

October 6, 1956   Day before yesterday we divided up the cleaning chores on a new basis. A bitter quarrel arose between Hess and Schirach, because Hess categorically refused to clean the guards' toilet two days a week. When I tried to mediate, Schirach and Funk furiously turned on me, saying that my everlasting indulgence had brought Hess to this point.

In the service the chaplain preached on the text of Galatians 5:13: "For you were called to freedom, brethren. . . . But if you bite and devour one another, take heed that you are not consumed by one another."

November 9, 1956   In Hungary the uprising against the Soviet occupation has been finally crushed. For two weeks there was scarcely any other subject of conversation here. It divided Spandau into three camps. During this period the battered front of the Four Power prison authority collapsed completely. The Russians were embarrassed until the British and French undertook the landing in Egypt. And suddenly we, for the first time, were in a more solid position. Today Schirach said to the American guard Rostlam, "By the way, since when are aggressive wars permitted? Didn't I hear they had been banned?" The American did not know what to say.

Funk, who had overheard Schirach, came over and said, "There we have it again. It's always the victors who decide what morality is."

Schirach agreed. "How can they go on holding us here?"

I was standing by and said nothing. But it seemed to me too that the claim of Spandau to represent morality had been undermined. How are they going to justify our imprisonment henceforth? Only now, as I write this down, do I fully realize that I must be on guard against all such balancing of accounts. But from now on it is going to be harder to be here.

November 18, 1956   A few years ago, I reflected today, events like those in Budapest or Suez might have given us hope. Now we are all resigned. With the dramatic events of the past days, the world has other things to do besides worry about a few forgotten "Nazis." What is more, we have become an embarrassment to the world. Any discussion on the continuation of our imprisonment can only provoke, in the respective countries, the question: "Why only those four? Why not Bulganin? Why not Eden? Why not Mollet?" Today Funk said in a whimpering tone, "I have never before felt so hopeless."

December 1, 1956   Still feeling depressed about Hungary and Suez. All of us downcast. Even Schirach refrains from his usual irritating remarks. With him subdued, the last animating factor has vanished. Now we really have the quiet of a graveyard. Schirach only addresses the most essential words to me; "good morning" is not among them. His satellite Funk has also ceased all conversation with me. Hess occasionally orders me around, rudely and imperiously: "Come over here!" or "Tell me what's in the paper today." Recently he called out to me: "Hey, you!" That was too much for me. No need for him to let his domination neuroses out on me. I told him so.

December 2, 1956   Today I am 353 kilometers from Kabul. If no snowstorms intervene I count on arriving in the capital of Afghanistan in the middle of January. I am hoping I won't have to walk all the way to Calcutta, but I thought that a year ago about Kabul.

December 3, 1956   A few hours ago my wife came on a visit. I can no longer summon up the force to say encouraging things. She was very far away. We exchanged monologues.

December 4, 1956   Flächsner was here today. We greeted each other heartily. He commented, "You haven't changed at all in these ten years." He himself has put on considerable weight. We talked about the denazification hearing. He recommended delaying tactics; he could justify postponements on the grounds of my imprisonment. In saying this he inadvertently blurted out, "If that works, we've first of all gained many years." Is there then no hope at all? Is he so certain that I shall have to stay here to the end?

Nevertheless, I feel much revived by the three-quarters of an hour. I could have gone on talking for hours. All I need is a subject. And my only subject is my past.

December 24, 1956   Today I marched my rounds all alone in the twilight; a Christmassy snow was falling. From the direction of Spandau the bells were ringing; scraps of music from a brass band could be heard. After supper I had myself locked in with two books; I wanted that feeling of shelter and comfort. In a book on Schinkel I found the lithograph *Prediama Palace,* a copy of which was given to me by Daniel Krenker, my professor in art history, after a report I made on architecture of the ancient Teutons. Lying on the bed, I thought of how often as students we had sat in the Romanische Café near the Gedächtniskirche—at the small iron tables with white marble tops which were also occupied by people like George Grosz and Käthe Kollwitz, Dix and Pechstein, Lesser Ury and Liebermann. It was the custom to scrawl ideas onto the marble. How often we twenty-year-olds used to glance, with some shyness, at the adjacent tables. For us it was exciting to be sitting in the same room with such famous people, around whom controversy swirled; but what they were doing really did not concern us. Prediama Palace was very close to us; Dix's *Trench,* on the other hand, worlds away from us. What impressed us was not the picture but the scandal it gave rise to. When I look at the newspapers now and see the triumph of all the art that is after all the art of my generation, I realize in hindsight how little I was a contemporary of those others. I never wanted to own a Pechstein or Kirchner; I could not afford a Blechen; and it would have been my dream to possess a painting by Caspar David Friedrich. I gave the Rottmann to Hitler not because Rottmann was one of his favorite painters but because it suited my taste. And only now, as I leaf through the drawings in this cell, do I fully realize that everything I did turned romantic in my hands, and that a revolution in art passed me by without leaving a trace on my work.

The new French guard, Godeaux, was just here. As soon as he knew he would not be observed, he entered each of the cells, in silent embarrassment shook hands with each of us, and gave us a small package of biscuits.

December 26, 1956 Last night I was going over things in the darkness. There was the Christmas of 1945 in the Nuremberg cell. In the midst of the trial. Then Christmas of 1946, after the sentencing. In 1947 it was already Spandau; at that time it was very hard for me. Then followed 1948, probably not much different from 1947. And 1949, the same. And 1950. And 1951. It's a long series when you say it aloud to yourself. And 1952. I have never been fully conscious of how often it has been repeated. And 1953. And 1954. And 1955 . . . and 1956 . . . How many more times?

Late morning walk in the snow. I put on my old ski boots. Colonel Cuthill was just going on his round. Funk wished him "Merry Christmas" in English, and the director said he wished him a better Christmas next year at home. Schirach bellowed out his "Merry Christmas" like a command, and Cuthill replied politely and aloofly, "Thank you very much indeed." I kept in the background, so that there was no more, for all the friendliness, than the usual "All right?" and my thanks. Hess behaved likewise.

As a Christmas present the directors approved a new record player for us. The chaplain brought us two new records, the great Schubert C-major Symphony and Beethoven's Violin Concerto. To the surprise of us all, for the first time Hess responded to the chaplain's friendly invitation and came to our concert; hitherto he had always listened from his cell. And then came the day's real sensation: in the evening he took the New Testament out of the library. Funk asked him in astonishment, "But Herr Hess, what has given you that idea?"

Hess smiled mockingly. "Because I thought you would ask that."

As long as Neurath lived, he sent us greetings through the chaplain every Christmas. Raeder and Dönitz remain silent.

December 27, 1956 Funk has aged alarmingly since his operation; at sixty-six he might be taken for a man of eighty. He also seems unwontedly apathetic. At a friendly word his eyes easily fill with tears these days. He has almost lost interest in life. Most of the time he lies on his cot as if it were a sarcophagus, staring at the ceiling.

December 28, 1956   Schirach in the garden. Absently, with sudden, inexplicable movements of his arms, he paces hastily back and forth along the path. Sometimes he stops, then abruptly goes on, whistling a few bars of music aloud. His behavior reminds me of some of the rather eccentric characters in E. T. A. Hoffmann. Instead of the improvised cane he has now acquired a staff in size and thickness exactly like the batons carried by British officers. The stick does not rest for a second, and like a seismograph registers the degree of his inner tensions. Today, when in spite of the cold Funk was out sitting on one of the garden benches, Schirach stood in front of him, hopping continually and whipping the baton, talking furiously away at him. Patiently, head half drooping, Funk sat there and let it all pass over him with no show of emotion. His strength really seems at an end. Sometimes I try to penetrate into his inner world; but it seems to me that there is no longer any access.

December 31, 1956   Today, New Year's Eve, I received the news that Willy H. Schlieker, my former associate, spent an evening in Washington with Bob Murphy, undersecretary of state. Murphy told Schlieker that in the middle of January he hopes to put through a decision in the State Department to abolish Spandau. Since the Soviet Union seemed inclined some thirteen months ago to release Funk and me, an affirmative decision may actually be imminent.

Schlieker. As I read the smuggled letter I thought of our many conferences during the last months of the war. At the time everything was coming to an end he was thirty-two years old. My principal associates, who were usually suggested to me by the industrialists and with whom I organized the Reich's armaments program, were all unusually young: Ernst Wolf Mommsen, Josef Neckermann, Stieler von Heydekampf, Hans Günther Sohl. They were sometimes called "Speer's kindergarten."

January 1, 1957   A new year, a new song. Yesterday Schirach must have discovered the words for "Lili Marlene" in a songbook. Since seven o'clock this morning he has been singing it almost without a pause in his cell, reeling off all four stanzas. When he stops, it is only to blare out an imitation trumpet variation on the same theme.

January 8, 1957   I have conducted a kind of opinion poll to measure our prestige among the guards. The special aspect of it is that none of those involved knows anything about it—neither those whose popularity is to be measured, nor those who are being polled. My procedure is this: the order in which we fetch our meals is decided by the guards. They are aware that each of us, oddly enough, would like to be first. The degree of their liking decides whom they will let out of the cell first. I give the first man three points, the second two, the third one, and the last none. After a week, Funk leads with forty-nine points, and Schirach is just ahead of me with thirty-nine points. I have thirty-six points, whereas Hess is credited with only two—only once was he let out second, otherwise always last. For the first time I realize that this troublesome, sick man has been getting his meals last for ten years.

January 12, 1957   McCloy has written to a business friend of mine that the State Department is sympathetic to my release. He thinks that in the reasonably near future, by constant pressure on the Soviets, my release can be "effected." Why doesn't this excite me more? Why, today too, am I silently and sullenly treading my rounds as I do every day?

From across the way "Lili Marlene" keeps coming.

January 13, 1957   Only a few months ago Hess was able to give me the names of his associates, Klopfer and Friedrich, which I needed for my denazification trial. Today, sitting on his garden bench, he said to me in his imperious tone, "Tell me, Funk has just mentioned a Herr Leitgen. Who was that again?"

For a moment I was really dumbfounded. "But that was your adjutant, of course!"

Hess seemed to think hard. Then he dropped into his whining tone. "But that's dreadful! I no longer know that? For heaven's sake, how is such a thing possible? Can you explain it to me? My adjutant. Really? Then I must have lost my memory." His eyes held a cunning expression.

"Don't worry about it, Herr Hess. In Nuremberg, during the trial, you also lost your memory. After the trial it came back."

Hess pretended astonishment. "What's that you say? It will come back?"

I nodded. "Yes, and then it also goes away again. The same thing happens to me."

Hess was irritated. "What, to you too? What don't you know?"

I looked at him thoughtfully, as if I were trying to figure something out. Then I shrugged resignedly. "At the moment I simply cannot remember who you are and what you are doing here."

For a moment Hess was perplexed. Then we both began to laugh.

January 23, 1957   A few weeks ago I asked one of the directors to let me have canvas and oil paints. I learned this morning that the request has been refused. Obsessed with the idea of painting, I have put two imaginary paintings down on paper; strictly speaking, two sketches in the romantic manner, symbolizing my escape world. With the utmost concentration I conjured up the colors of the painting before my eyes and noted them down on the drawing by the numbers of a paint catalogue. The effort was so intense that I thought I saw where I went wrong, and, operating solely with numbers, repainted certain bits.

February 12, 1957   For weeks Funk has been evading his strict diabetic diet, in unsupervised moments pouring almost the entire contents of our sugar bowl into his cup. To cover up, he adds coffee. I have just checked with the slide rule: almost two hundred cubic centimeters. He drinks this repulsively sweet brew at night before a urine sample is taken. Frequently I help him by standing between the guard and the sugar bowl.

The French chief physician has detected a swollen liver in Funk. "My jaundice is coming back," Funk said mournfully. "My arm is already yellow, and my eyes also." This humorous man has often helped us through depressive states in Spandau with his clownish mixture of jollity, opportunism, and plaintiveness; but all the comic elements have gradually faded away. Now he is merely a sick man who knows his end is nearing. And yet he poisons himself, on the slight chance of going home a little beforehand. Like a dog that wants to die in its familiar corner.

March 18, 1957   We have heard from Mees that the Soviet doctor is putting together a summary of Funk's case history from the three patient registers containing our medical records of the past ten years. So his case is being discussed. But today the Soviet director came to see Funk, accompanied by a doctor. Funk immediately began to expatiate on his various illnesses. The Russian snapped at him, "Don't put on an act! And will you be so good as to stand up! You make a ridiculous impression, Number Six."

Funk shouted angrily back, "Then go ahead and shoot me. Why are you letting me live?"

Suddenly I heard Funk begin to sob. Then there was a moment's silence, until the Russian director said icily, "You are a prisoner with a life sentence and must behave like one."

After the two had left the cell, Funk began again. "Go ahead and kill me, go ahead and kill me!" Vlaer recently told me that nervous crises of this sort are typical of diabetics.

The Russian director then went to see Hess. I heard another angry exchange, but out of the confused babble could only once make out the Russian's loud voice saying, "If you do not eat everything, you will be punished."

March 19, 1957   This morning outside my door, at the morning unlocking, the representatives of three nations were present: Godeaux, Pemberton, Bokov. Godeaux counted slowly and rhythmically: "One, two, three!" and then the three called out in chorus, with a low bow, "Happy birthday!" It was hard for me to hide my emotion.

The congratulations were continued in the washroom. Hess came up to me. "*Ad multos annos!*" he said, adding: "Though not necessarily in Spandau." Later Funk came up; he wanted to say something, but before he could bring it out his eyes filled with tears and he choked up. He no longer has his feelings under control. Schirach brought me a newspaper. He did say "Good morning" this time, but then vanished at once after clearing his throat and managing a "Hmm." He cannot jump over his own shadow, but it does not bother me. What petrifaction of the personality. But each of us has evidently undergone personality changes: Hess has become hysterical, Funk lachrymose, Schirach unsociable. And I?

March 26, 1957   Hess has spent five days in the isolation cell because he has not cleaned the tables in the corridor and the washroom, as provided for in the work schedule. He endured his punishment stoically. No sooner was Hess back than Schirach ran to Fomin. "Number Seven hasn't cleaned the washroom today." Hess was threatened with fresh punishments.

Meanwhile Funk, sallow and trembling, continues his gamble with life. He has asked me to fill his cup half full of sugar at every meal from now on; he has become too nervous to do it himself, he says.

April 6, 1957   Funk has been bedridden for two days. Now he has inflammation of the bladder, and the doctors have again diagnosed a swollen liver also. He pursued this "sugar cure" of his for three months. Now he has stopped it.

With Funk ill, Schirach has nobody to talk to. Together with Fomin he seeded a round bed with red and white lupines this morning, in such a way that the flowers will form a Soviet star. I asked Hess, who was sitting in the opposite corner of the garden, "What do you think of that? Your Reich youth leader is decorating a flower bed with the Red star." Hess just smiled.

April 7, 1957   During the winter months I was unable to keep up my calculated daily average of ten kilometers; I was left with a deficit of 62.9 kilometers to make up. During the past three weeks I have worked off 43.3 kilometers, doing 99 kilometers in the last week alone. At present I am merely walking the route mechanically and stubbornly, hardly trying to visualize the region I am tramping through. I am already deep in India, and according to the plan will be in Benares in five months.

For several weeks Funk's wife has been alluding in each of her letters to the not-distant future when she will be with her husband again. "It's really strange that the Russians don't censor these remarks," Funk commented. "Either they are no longer interested in me or they're sure I'll die soon." Occasionally he resumes his sugar cure. Recently, in spite of intense gall-bladder pain, he has asked Schirach or me to slip him large cubes of leftover butter.

Have read a great deal recently. As early as 1904 Chesterton, in *The Napoleon of Notting Hill*, dealt with the frightening consequences of a mass psychosis. In this story a pseudoking arbitrarily picked out of the London city directory succeeds in playing on the emotions of a whole people—as Hitler was to do—bringing about the most absurd actions and reactions. Such books are always read only after the fact.

This evening I have been thinking about Chesterton again. Strange how such Caesarean demagogues, who really need a splintered society in which to work, were nevertheless foreshadowed in the orderly, strictly hierarchical, stable-seeming world of the *fin de siècle*. I thought of how often Hitler used to talk enthusiastically about Kellermann's *Tunnel*, likewise the story of a demagogue, as one of the major reading experiences of his youth. Significantly, the laws of mass psychology were also being extensively investigated by the turn of the century. Le Bon's study has not been surpassed to this day, I believe. He did not need to observe the great demagogues from Lloyd George to Lenin, Mussolini, and Hitler in order to fathom the mechanics of the mass psyche.

I wonder how Chesterton was read in his time—as a kind of prophecy or as entertaining fantasy? After half a century, at any rate, it is clear that, with the nervous attunement of a great artist, he sensed what the future would be. This much seems certain: Art has no need of reality in order to bring to light the truth about an era.

May 8, 1957   A copy of a letter from German foreign minister Heinrich von Brentano has been smuggled in. The German side, he writes, has for a considerable time been endeavoring to obtain an amnesty for Funk and me.

May 17, 1957   Last night Hardie said that for the past three days special meetings of the directors have been taking place. There were similar meetings shortly before Raeder's release. The guard went to Funk to tell him about it, too.

For a long time I could not fall asleep, for I felt that this could affect me too. This morning I looked in "Watchwords" and found: "It is a precious thing to be patient and to hope for the help of the Lord." Silly, to take any stock in that.

At nine o'clock we walked in the garden; Funk remained locked up. After fifteen minutes, however, he appeared with Pease, but did not come over to us; he sat on a chair alone by the prison wall. As if turned to stone, he stared at his shoes. I went over to him, but he sent me away because Fomin might see us. Funk was so nervous that his hand shook continually.

A few minutes later Fomin came up to him and ordered him to come along. Hesitantly, with uncertain footsteps, not looking around, Funk followed the Russian. We others stopped our work on the opposite side of the garden and watched. Nothing about this incident was unusual, but all of us felt that something was up. Two hours later, Godeaux told us that Funk was first locked in his cell. He collapsed on his bed, looking utterly done for. After three-quarters of an hour, however, he was called to the medical office, where Cuthill, Letham, and a doctor were waiting for him. He was given a sedative; then Cuthill asked him to sit down, they had something to tell him: He was a free man.

His clothes and valuables were already laid out in the visiting room, Godeaux reported. Funk at once put on his ring, and tucked his gold watch into his vest pocket. His wife was waiting in a car in the yard.

The American guard Hardie, on duty at the gate, was the last person to whom Funk waved from the moving car. No reporters were present. The news was not given out, in fact, until hours after the release, whereupon, senselessly, two cars full of German police turned up at the prison several hours too late.

I am happy for Funk, but also depressed. Now months will pass before people again become concerned about Spandau.

May 17, 1957 Now there are only three of us. I am really alone. Schirach and Hess do not count.

What I dreaded has now come about.

May 21, 1957 New hopes. There is said to have been an article in the *Stars and Stripes* about the dissolution of Spandau; allegedly the radio carried a similar report. All three Western newspapers have two columns on the first page cut out. I have stared fixedly at the gaps for a long time. This time even Hess believes there will be a change. I have been occupying myself with all the details of organizing my returning home—a plan covering two closely written pages.

But I am not sending it off.

May 23, 1957 Today, on the morning of the twelfth anniversary of my captivity, Vlaer brought me the newspaper items that were cut out of the papers two days ago. There are plans afoot for transferring Hess to a mental hospital, Schirach and me to the German penitentiary of Tegel. Trying to fathom the reason for my panic at this report, I realize that in spite of everything, Spandau has become a kind of home for me. If I am not going to go free, I want to remain here.

In the afternoon I planted a small lilac bush in the vicinity of the rock garden. It will not bloom for three or four years.

June 4, 1957 Visit from the new American general. Preparation for transfer to Tegel? The inspection was remarkably brief and impersonal. Opening of door, entrance of general. "This is Number Five, Speer. This is the new general." Brief bow and door closed. Two seconds. On the double to the chapel. Another two seconds. One minute in the garden. Then forced march to the officers' mess. The three guards were scarcely able to unlock and lock up fast enough.

June 18, 1957 Most of the guards show more sensitivity than one would think. Without our having said a word about it, they have observed what the departure of Funk means to us even after a month, and above all for Schirach. We too realize how dependent we now are on one another. Of late we have taken to walking a few rounds together every day. However, I have to persuade myself every time, because my craving for solitude is greater than my need for company. Moreover, I worry that the many depressions and anxieties from which Schirach suffers might prove contagious.

Nevertheless, his cross-grained and difficult character actually stimulates me. The way he looks at things is in almost every case different from my way. But this brings out a streak of contradiction in me, whereas when I am reading I am apt to agree with whatever book I am reading at the moment.

I realize once again that no book can replace a living person. In Schirach's case there is probably the additional factor that I am full of reservations about him. Often I am obviously disagreeing not so much with the argument as with this person for whom I have no liking.

Somehow we began to talk about the fact that both of us had actually fallen from grace before the Reich collapsed: Schirach after a visit to the Berghof in the early part of 1943, in the course of which he had a violent argument over the persecution of the Jews; and I since the beginning of 1944. We discussed what part intrigues might have played in both cases, and then came round to Hitler's credulity, which so strikingly contrasted with his general distrust.

"Do you think it was just his vanity and conceit that made him not want to see how he was being deceived?" I asked.

"Not so," Schirach replied didactically. "Hitler's credulity was rather romantic in nature, the kind of thing we systematically cultivated in the Hitler Youth. After all, we had set up the idea of a sworn community; we believed in loyalty and sincerity, and Hitler believed most of all. He was really inclined to poeticize reality."

I was taken aback for a moment. This was something I had never thought of. But then I remembered Göring with his mania for costumery, Himmler with his folklore craze, to say nothing of myself with my fondness for ruins and idyllic nature. "Not only Hitler," I said. "All of us, really."

"Very well," Schirach said, somewhat annoyed because I had interrupted his train of thought. "But when Hitler suspected an opposing opinion, that was the end of his credulity. The time I sponsored that exhibition of 'Young Art' in Vienna was just such a moment."

I remembered the dinner in the Chancellery, to which Goebbels had come with the catalogue of the exhibition in his raised hand, remarking smugly, "Degenerate art under the sponsorship of the Reich and the Party! This is really something new!"

I told Schirach that Hitler had leafed through the catalogue, and with increasing irritation had exclaimed: "The title alone is all wrong. 'Young Art'! Why, these are all old men, idiots from the day before yesterday who are still painting this way. The Reich youth leader ought to check up with his own young people to find out what they like, not make propaganda against us!"

Schirach knew what had happened. His father-in-law, Heinrich Hoffmann, Hitler's court photographer, had been present at the dinner and telephoned Schirach immediately afterwards. "That didn't finish me off," Schirach resumed the thread of the conversation. "But thereafter my opinions on art no longer counted." During those years he had been officially hailed and showered with literary prizes, Schirach went on, but he had never been able to win Hitler's interest in himself. He did not even know whether Hitler had ever read a single one of his volumes of poetry. "He didn't care much about literature," Schirach concluded. "You were better off in that respect. He was absolutely obsessed with building."

June 20, 1957   While I was trying to summarize my conversation with Schirach, it occurred to me that I actually never once heard Hitler talk about any of the representative writers of the Third Reich. Nor can I recall his ever having attended a session of the *Reichsschrifttumskammer** or associating with such prominent writers as Erwin Kolbenheyer, Hans Grimm, or Hans Friedrich Blunck. On the other hand, he took Breker with him to Paris; he spent hours in Troost's studio; each year he opened the Grand Art Exhibition; and from the early twenties to the early years of the war he never missed a season in Bayreuth. Literature was truly an alien art to him. How odd that this never struck me before!

I wonder why this was so. Perhaps the chief reason was that Hitler took everything as an instrument, and that of all the arts literature lends itself least to the uses of power politics. Its effects are always unpredictable, and the mere fact that books are meant for private consumption must have made him suspicious. The audience for every other art could be swayed by showmanship—but not the solitary reader within his four walls. In addition, for him art was always connected with sensationalism, a *coup de théâtre*; he loved smashing effects, and

* The Nazi writers' organization.—*Translators' note.*

literature did not smash. And yet everything Schirach had said was wrong again, persuasive as it sounded at first. Including that point about romanticism. Hitler had no sense of the dualistic nature of romanticism, its inner conflicts and decadence. Nor did he understand its serenity. He knew only its dark side, its destructive urge and its popularized debased forms: its Boy Scout quality. Wilhelm Hauff, Richard Wagner, and Karl May.

June 23, 1957   Schirach informed me today that in the last sentence of her letter his sister wrote, "I'm chilling the champagne." Since she is planning a trip in August, his release must be expected earlier. Everything is already organized for Schirach's reception.

July 14, 1957   Our prison roof, whose boarding is partially rotted, is being repaired—the work has been going on for weeks. That does not suggest a transfer to Tegel.

Because the workmen can see into the yards and the garden, we are not admitted into the garden until six o'clock in the evening. Heat wave. But a fresh breeze blows from the Berlin lakes. The smog hanging over the city seldom descends upon us.

For the first time in ten years I am experiencing evenings in the open air. Colors I had already forgotten: the greens become stronger, the blues and reds of the flowers livelier, and the area of the garden seems much bigger. The sun's last rays illumine comically shaped leaves that gleam now like copper, now like red gold against a dark-blue night sky. Leaves like stylized ferns.

How I would like, just once, to go walking in the moonlight.

July 30, 1957   On his second visit Flächsner gave the impression of being confused. Perhaps because the documents he meant to pass on to me were taken from him before our discussion.

August 2, 1957   Ever since the press chief of the Federal Republic declared that relations with the Soviet Union have reached a nadir, our goulash consists of offal, only a few grams of which are edible.

August 10, 1957   Last April Hess was examined by an American psychiatrist, soon afterwards by a French colleague, and three days ago by another American psychiatrist. These various examiners, Vlaer has assured me, agree that Hess suffers from hysterical disturbances, but not sufficiently to justify his transfer to a mental hospital.

Schirach is not happy about this diagnosis. By his reasoning, Hess's transfer would increase his own chances for release.

August 12, 1957   Tonight, I don't know why, I could not help thinking of the forecast of a fortuneteller at a wartime bazaar at the end of the First World War. I was thirteen at the time, and she told me, "You will achieve early fame and early retirement." When at the age of thirty I became virtually Hitler's chief architect, my mother reminded me of that prediction one day when I was visiting Heidelberg. I still remember how the whole table laughed at the second part of the forecast. I no longer laugh.

August 16, 1957   A strange dream tonight. While eating I break a tooth, reach into my mouth, and am suddenly holding a sizable piece of rotten jawbone in my hand. I look at it curiously as though it did not belong to me.
Schirach commented pithily when I told him the dream: "Loss of the jawbone means misfortune."

August 17, 1957   I am still marching my rounds, and have by now passed Benares. Now there are only 780 kilometers to Calcutta, where I'd like to arrive on October 23. That will simultaneously mark the completion of my ten thousandth kilometer. Bokov has told me that the railroad distance from Berlin to Vladivostok is twelve thousand kilometers.

August 21, 1957   Last night I woke at three o'clock. The guards in the corridor were laughing and shouting, pounding boisterously on the table, as though they were in a beer hall. I made out Fomin's voice, and Godeaux also seemed to be present. Sleepy though I was, my fury mounted. I pressed my button, and heard how the sound of the dropping flap silenced the noisy crew. Together, they came to the window in my door. "What do you want?" Fomin asked harshly.
"Unlock the door; I have something to tell you."
"I have to go get my keys," Fomin replied. After a while the door was unlocked. Fomin, Hardie, and Godeaux stared at me.
I began: "Don't make so——"
Fomin broke in. "Number Five, why don't you salute?"
I bowed formally to each of the three noisemakers. "Good morning, good morning, good morning! Don't make so much noise. It keeps me awake. If you don't stop, I'll file a complaint."

They stared at me, deflated. Godeaux looked unhappy, Hardie gave an embarrassed laugh. Fomin was the first to recover. "Go back into your cell at once, Number Five."

But from then on they talked only in whispers.

August 22, 1957   For weeks I have been reading *Lehre von der Schöpfung*, one of the volumes in Karl Barth's dogmatics. Bokov picked up the book curiously. "What kind of book is this?"

I explained that it was a theological book.

"Is theology something realistic?" he asked.

I said it was not.

"Then why read?"

"There are things outside of reality," I said.

Bokov shook his head. "Is there anything new in the book?"

I smiled. "No, not necessarily."

He looked at me in astonishment. "Then why read?"

Would a prerevolutionary Russian have asked such a question?

September 3, 1957   Margret, now eighteen, visited me before she leaves for a year in America. We had agreed beforehand to omit any show of farewell grief. It cost no effort.

September 17, 1957   Several guards have been changed in the last few months. Recently Petry came to my cell to say goodbye. In his agitation he repeated the word "freedom" again and again. How many years has Petry actually been here? A problem that I vainly try to settle.

His successor, a professional boxer in the middleweight class, has been in a good many fights; and to judge by his face and cauliflower ears, he cannot have done very well. But as is frequently the case with such men, he is soft-hearted and full of sympathy. A few days ago the newly arrived Russian, Naumov, on his first tour of duty nonchalantly extended his hand to me in greeting. I hesitated to take it, so that Bokov had time to call his attention to the regulations. Rostlam, who was observing the scene, still doubles up with laughter at the idea of anyone's shaking hands with a prisoner. To what an extent the inmate becomes merely a number to the professional guard!

Yesterday, after a two-year interval, I began a three-week sleep "vacation." I have had oppressive dreams lately.

September 30, 1957   Colonel Jerome Cuthill, the British director, has had a stroke. He is in the hospital suffering from a coronary thrombosis. He is said to be better, though no one is expecting him to return.

He has always been candid and straightforward. To the point of being wounding—but you knew where you were with him. As I belatedly learned, he held the First World War's second-highest decoration, the Distinguished Service Cross, which approximately corresponds to our Pour le Mérite. I asked Pease to give him my wishes for a good recovery. He returned thanks.

The Twelfth Year

October 5, 1957   Huge headline in today's newspaper that the first satellite is circling the earth. For a minute I lay on the bed with pounding heart. Some events really hit me hard. During the first forty years of my life I admired technology. When Wernher von Braun told me about his future projects, such as a flight to the moon, I was fascinated. But Hitler, with his technologically based dictatorship and his assembly-line extermination of the Jews, shocked me so deeply that I can never again be naïve about technology. Every advance nowadays only frightens me. News like this account of the first satellite makes me think of new potentialities for annihilation, and arouses fear. If they fly to the moon tomorrow, my fear will be all the greater.

October 12, 1957   Today a letter from Hilde which alarmed me; it sounds very alienated. For a long time I have been unable to conjure up any image of her. No member of the family knows what it means to be imprisoned. They cannot imagine how much effort it costs me with every visit, every letter, not to depress them.

By chance an elegiac drawing that I made some eight years ago or so has fallen into my hands. It accurately reproduces my feelings of that time. Lost on the peak of a mountain three thousand meters high, and absolute stillness around me.

October 15, 1957   Funk has sent a clandestine communication to Schirach saying that in October the Four Powers will meet in Berlin to make preparations for the dissolution of Spandau. Schirach is convinced that Spandau will cease to exist after December 31; only recently he maintained it would be all over in August. Hess pretends pessimism: "Idle nonsense. Spandau will stay."

A few of the guards are trying to nip all our hopes in the bud. Rostlam asked me today whether he should order the sweet corn seed for the spring. When I replied that it wasn't all that certain that we would be here next spring, he replied without emotion, "You'll still be here. And nine years from now too. You can be sure of that."

October 31, 1957   Today Letham assigned the friendly Bokov, who hardly understands German, to escort duty in the visiting room. The Russian was pleased: "I see your wife!" For the first time at one of my wife's visits there was no Soviet interpreter keeping a record; and the directors were missing too. Our first natural conversation in years shows me that it is not so much alienation as the intrusive supervision that makes all contact so difficult. In high spirits, contrary to all the rules, I introduced Bokov to my wife. "This is a particularly friendly Russian guard." Laughing, I added, "When he's on duty at night he often disturbs us by his loud snoring." Bokov replied good-naturedly, "If you free soon you write story of Spandau. And of Bokov's snore."

November 1, 1957   My wife's second visit—again the Soviet interpreter didn't show up. On the other hand, after a few minutes the American director arrived, sat down at my wife's side, and boldly studied her expression.

November 7, 1957   Today—I could scarcely believe my ears—Schirach suddenly began whistling "Lili Marlene" again. He had let up on it for some eight months. If only this isn't a new outbreak!

November 17, 1957   During the walk Schirach told me about extracts from Raeder's memoirs, which he has managed to read. Raeder is now creating legends about Spandau, he says. Among other things, he speaks of his friendly relations with Dönitz and Neurath during their imprisonment. In fact, bitter enmity prevailed between him and Dönitz for many years. Schirach now confides that Raeder frequently chided him when he talked with Dönitz, saying, "You should not even speak to him."

Actually it was Schirach who cheered Raeder when he was suffering from depression, helped him when he was ill. On his own initiative Schirach had several times petitioned the commandants of Berlin for the release of Raeder during the admiral's severe illnesses. But in hindsight Grand Admiral Dönitz and the diplomat Neurath are the only ones with whom Raeder wishes to have associated in Spandau; anyone else would harm his reputation. The foreign minister and the naval chief are in his class, so to speak; the others are mere convicts. Schirach now says bitterly, "That's how it is. As soon as someone is outside, he puts as much distance as possible between himself and those he left behind."

December 4, 1957 Another visit from Flächsner. Although in the past the Russians have been particularly interested in visits from lawyers, this time none of them was present. A British and a French guard supervised our meeting. I asked Flächsner when he would be coming in his car to fetch me. "I wish it could be tomorrow!" he replied. Sadot, a lively fellow, interjected, "Very good, very good." He put in a word quite often. I was able to carry out a full hour of conversation without noticeable exhaustion.

After the visit the new Russian chief guard, Yeshurin, who speaks German fluently, asked, "Are you satisfied with the visit? Did you discuss your release?"

I said no.

"You ought to put in a petition for amnesty. After all, at the end of the war you were the one who prevented Hitler from wrecking everything."

When I told him I had already submitted a petition, he suggested skeptically, "But possibly it wasn't passed on. In our country that often happens."

Actually, I seem to have been forgotten. Word of efforts to bring about my release reaches me more and more seldom. My few friends have resigned themselves. Soon I shall have reached the end of my strength. Once the decay begins, I need make no more plans for the future.

Today Schirach puzzled over six cakes of soap that his sister had sent him. "Even if she assumes I can use up a cake in only two weeks, that would last until March." Shaking his head, he returned to his cell.

December 17, 1957   Colonel Procter, chief of protocol to the British commandant of Berlin, has been appointed as Cuthill's successor. A man with manners, which could not have been said of his predecessor. The new director is continuing in his post under the commandant, so he will carry out his Spandau duties just by the way. No great burden, I should think.

December 24, 1957   Coming and going in the corridor. The guards hum Christmas carols, but that no longer bothers me. Services in the evening. Since Funk's release there has been no one to accompany on the organ, so we no longer sing chorales. Instead, at the end of the service we are permitted to hear records for half an hour. But today we refused the offer of records of Christmas music. My motive was not really fear of collapsing into sentimentality; rather, the holiday sentiment no longer touches me.

December 25, 1957   As a kind of Christmas present, a guard let us know that the directors have proofs of the existence of illegal channels to the outside. A short time later Schirach was summoned to see them. A Bavarian court had sent to the prison administration a document signed by him and asked for confirmation of the signature. With icy composure Schirach denied that the signature was authentic. On his return he said merely, "Thank God I was prepared."

December 26, 1957   Yesterday Toni Vlaer drove into the East Sector to visit his mother-in-law. Two of our Russians asked him to take them with him to Karlshorst. At the house where he left them off he was bluntly asked to come along. Then for several hours he was interrogated by officers of the NKVD. Finally they came out with what they wanted: they were looking for an agent to work for them, and since he had always got on well with the Russians in Spandau, they had decided to recruit him. When he tried to back off, they spoke more forcefully and presented him with a prepared letter in which he agreed to collaboration and silence. Out of fear, Vlaer finally signed it. Now, so he informed me, on the fifteenth of January he is supposed to carry out his first assignment. He is bewildered and desperate.

December 29, 1957   Yesterday I advised Toni Vlaer to inform the Allied authorities, in spite of his fears for his mother-in-law. He accordingly made a report to the British military police and the Dutch consulate. They advised him to leave Berlin and return to Holland. They said there had been too many kidnapings of late. Now he has given notice and will leave in a few days. He has helped me keep going these past ten years.

December 30, 1957 The last year has been the hardest so far. More than any of the others, it was filled with disappointed hopes. More and more often the fear sweeps over me that I will not be able to hold out much longer.

The letters from home show that the holidays passed as they used to in my childhood, only somewhat plainer, less elaborate. But on the whole I felt, as I read about it, transported back to those years. Several of the children left to go skiing over the New Year. Margret will spend New Year's Eve with friends. These plans, too, evoke the familiar atmosphere of the past. How strange!

Toward the end of the war, when the outlines of the collapse were becoming apparent and it could be seen how far more than a mere defeat it was, my feeling was that not just this regime and this Reich were falling to pieces, but a whole world. To define the all-embracing character of the process, people justifiably spoke of a catastrophe. Everything seemed over; everything had lost its innocence. We were utterly sure that not only the functionaries of the regime would step from the stage, but also the old strata who formed the sustaining element of society. A whole world with its culture, its claim to property, its authority, its morality—in short, its power—would simply cease to exist. We saw before us a time of leveling, of poverty and humility. Romantic as always, I even fastened some hopes of moral and intellectual renewal to such a prospect. Automobiles, planes, technological comfort would cease to exist for Germany after this breakdown; music, poetry, and art would take their place. As after Jena and Auerstädt,* Germany would rediscover her cultural mission.

But the revolution we all expected, which seemed so certain at the time, has evidently not taken place. I cannot pretend to judge whether there has been an intellectual and moral upsurge. But it seems to be undeniable that the forms of life, the whole middle-class ritual, have returned in full force. Every letter from home indicates it, whether it speaks of student balls or the Heidelberg Rowing Club, of the chil-

* At the Battles of Jena and Auerstädt on October 14, 1806, Napoleon shattered the Prussian army. The defeat became the stimulus for the revival of German cultural as well as military life.—*Translators' note.*

dren's friendships or Christmas observances. Even hand-kissing and "*gnädige Frau*" are said to have come back. Most surprising is the extent of prosperity that already has returned. Criticism of it seems to me the chief and favorite theme of contemporary literature. The division into social strata and substrata is, if I see the situation rightly, rather greater than in the Third Reich; it evidently resembles the Weimar conditions that I was already trying to break out of in those days. Technology, too, has returned, more dominant than ever; all the warnings against its dangers have been repressed. Sometimes the newspapers actually give the impression that the whole Federal Republic is a single industrial area, incessantly producing the stuff of prosperity. Settling accounts with the past has not, I think, been undertaken with a view toward the future. Rather, a step backward has been taken. The period of the Republic has been restored. How tenacious conditions can be!

January 1, 1958   New Year's Day. I have copied out a quotation from Cocteau: "People have made me a man whom I do not recognize. . . . Dreadful, to meet this being in the street."

January 12, 1958   Weeks ago I crossed the Ganges. Now my walk is taking me over a high, wild mountain range. There are still four hundred kilometers to Mandalay in Burma and one thousand one hundred to Kunming in China. I am planning a side-trip to Pagan, a small village with more than two thousand pagodas and stupas of considerable size. The town served exclusively for the veneration of the Buddha; it was built between the eleventh and the thirteenth centuries. As I was reading about it recently I could not help thinking of our plans for Nuremberg. The Party Rally terrain was also intended, in the course of generations, to grow into a district given over to spiritual ceremony. The rally area itself was only to be the first stage and the nucleus of the whole. Oak groves had already been planted or staked out. All sorts of buildings of a religious nature were to be erected within them: monuments to celebrate the concept of the Movement and its victories; memorials to outstanding individuals. Today it strikes me as an act of immature self-glorification that I secretly decided to place my own tomb by the grand processional avenue, just where the avenue crossed the artificial lake. I had even discussed this with Mayor Liebel of Nuremberg. But I had not yet said anything to Hitler about it. Once my plans had been carried out, it seemed to me at the time, I would be famous enough to speak of such a matter.

Today I covered thirteen and a half kilometers. I have quite a few to make up, because last week I did only fifty-seven. Without this rigid pedantry, I would be giving up this game, considering my current depression.

January 25, 1958 Several hundred starlings have settled down in the garden, evidently having missed the fall migration to the south. Flying in squadrons they perform such precise turns that any air force commander would pale with envy. Today, during the concert on records, they clustered on the branches of an acacia. It looked as though they were regarding us curiously through the window.

Nothing more has happened. For four weeks.

January 29, 1958 Battling the monotony, in the last two days I have written up thirty pages of notes on the history of the window.

Window surfaces of Lever House (1952) amount, by my calculations, to 16 percent of the surface area to be illuminated. But more than two hundred years ago Fischer von Erlach achieved substantially higher proportions. In the Count Starhemberg Palace in Engelhardstetten (1694) the window area amounts to 27 percent; in the Gallas Palace in Prague (1713), the same percentage; in the great hall of the Imperial Library in Vienna (1719), actually 34 percent. Of course such coefficients of illumination in the baroque palaces were made possible by the tall windows of high-ceilinged rooms.

But such proportions did not apply only to the homes of the gentry. David Gilly, the Prussian director of buildings for Pomerania, toward the end of the eighteenth century designed simple burgher houses that had 18 to 22 percent window areas. Even in his houses for peasants and foresters, or in homes for cotters in Pomerania, the figures were at least 8 to 13 percent. But these statistics are not what really interest me. I have gathered the figures solely as material for my real question: What is the relationship between the growing craving for light in a society and the spirit of the age? At the start it seemed to me that there was much to suggest a relationship between window area and rationalism. But by now I have come a long way from this view. Like all too plausible theories, it seems striking at the very first, but does not stand up. The merchant architecture of the Dutch cities in the sixteenth and seventeenth centuries often had facades that were totally dominated by glass. And in spite of all Protestant rationalism, this development preceded rationalism by a good century. Gothic, on the other hand, seems to have had no marked craving for light, although it possessed the technical means to achieve it, as, say, the Sainte Chapelle shows—

where such extreme window area values as 160 percent of the floor area were reached. For the vast Gothic windows did not simply bring the light into the nave of the church; rather they actually excluded it, or transformed it into a mystical atmosphere. In addition the colors of stained glass were intended to shield worshipers from the outside world; those windows were really glowing walls.

Another field for investigation would be the place of the crystal palace in myth, literature, and legend. For example, Wirnt von Gravenberg fantasizes about such a crystal palace in describing the dwelling of Queen Guinevere, the spouse of King Arthur. A castle in *Herzog Ernst* and the palace of Queen Candace of Meroë also consist entirely of transparent material. In every case, this much seems to me certain, these medieval fancies have nothing to do with the glass skyscraper that Miës van der Rohe planned for Berlin in 1921, nor with the "Crystal house in the mountains" designed by Bruno Taut—"entirely built of crystal," which would awaken "reverence, inexpressible silence in the region of snow and glaciers." Taut, as his drawings show, conceived of buildings several hundred meters in height.

March 2, 1958   Another month gone by. That's all.

March 21, 1958   After an interval of nine months I can at last work in the garden again. I had to rescue my plantings from under a wilderness of weeds. The work gives me the excuse to hold somewhat aloof, unobtrusively, from Schirach. Only now and then do I walk a few rounds with him. His persistent ill humor and everlasting querulousness make me nervous. I am glad I no longer need to listen to all that. It ruins the day. I am trying to protect myself.

April 4, 1958   Months ago I wrote asking my wife to beg a magazine not to run a projected series on Spandau. But no use. Now I have recently had four issues in my cell. The cover for the first issue was a horrifying photo of me taken in Spandau. In the text were innumerable lies, such as, for example, that the rule of silence was strictly enforced, that the guards issued orders rudely, that daily personal searches were conducted, and so on. Funk and his friends have told atrocity stories. Letham and Terray, who have been very concerned about us, particularly in difficult times, are maligned. I myself come out quite well. The magazine quotes Telford Taylor, the American chief prosecutor in Nuremberg, as saying, "I would be inclined to favor the release of Speer. Schirach, in my opinion, richly deserves every year he was sentenced to." And Louis P. Lochner actually says, "Above all, Speer is the man who long ago deserved release." That will not make the Russians any kindlier.

As a result of this series of articles, three hundred birthday congratulations are said to have arrived in Spandau for me. Of course I do not receive them.

April 19, 1958   Today we heard a record of Gregorian chants. Although primarily an expression of the piety of the early Middle Ages, they are at the same time, in their slightly monotonous quality, evidence of the unspoiled capacity for emotion that people had in those times. Stronger stimuli were not needed. In the painting of the age, also, small gestures sufficed to express drama. And recently I read that people fainted when they first heard early polyphony. Thus progress can also be understood as impoverishment.

May 9, 1958   Toward evening I observed two partridges; also saw an earthworm. Perhaps the partridges will find the earthworm and devour it. But then the hawks are already hovering above the partridges.

May 12, 1958   Today I found a few hawk feathers in the garden. I have pinned them to the wall of the cell.

May 22, 1958   A long time contemplating the hawk feathers. They are composed of innumerable tiny parts that grow according to a complex plan. To produce the precise curve, the difference between two adjacent parts of the feather must be a minute fraction of a millimeter. These curves are geometrically complex structures; only with the aid of an electronic calculator can we determine them. Who decrees such growth?

July 11, 1958   Visit from the Soviet general. An ugly scornful laugh was the reply when, in response to his question, I expressed the wish to be released. In conjunction with the inspection a dinner was given for the four commandants of the city in the prison's officers' mess. Occasions of this sort always astonish me. It seems to me that a dinner in such a place ought not to be allowed, as a matter of psychological sensitivity.

July 13, 1958   Last night I dreamed I was in Spandau, but not as a prisoner. Rather, I was the one who gave orders, made decisions, directed affairs. Impatiently, I telephoned the German Embassy in Moscow to insist on my release. The operator connected me with the person in charge of the matter. In an unpleasantly tinny voice he answered, "Brinckmann speaking." In response to my request he replied tersely, "We can do nothing for you." I went on talking, but there was no reply. Brinckmann had hung up.

September 7, 1958   Another two-month interval of nothing happening.

September 8, 1958   Today Hess sat almost a hundred meters away from me at the opposite end of the garden. Schirach was making himself useful in the library. I was weeding, guarded by Hardie.

Three men came out of the adjacent area and at first walked past me. I gave them a friendly greeting, and to my surprise they replied pleasantly. Suddenly they stopped, had a brief discussion among themselves, then approached. One of them, gray-haired and with a finely carved head, removed his hat and had his escort formally introduce him: "David Bruce, ambassador of the United States—Herr Speer."

The ambassador spontaneously extended his hand, shook mine for a long time, and said that he wished to convey regards from McCloy. "You aren't forgotten," he said in English. He explained that the difficulty of achieving anything in my case was due to the obstinate attitude of the Russians. With emphasis, he repeated, "You aren't forgotten, you aren't forgotten!"

I asked him to look over my petition for amnesty, but to my amazement he had already read it. He asked about conditions, and I said they were bearable. "I can survive in Spandau, I hope." He was shocked by the few opportunities I have to see my children. Cordially bidding goodbye, he asked me whether I had any message for McCloy. I asked him to thank McCloy for his regards, and for the hospitality he had shown to my daughter in America.

Ordinarily the four directors are present during such visits. But while they were waiting impatiently in the office, the American chief guard had unobtrusively let his ambassador into the garden through a side door. Now a curious cavalcade poured out of the building: directors, deputy directors, chief guards, and guards. As Hardie told me right afterwards, the ambassador was informed that shaking hands with prisoners was forbidden; also, addressing them by name was not allowed. Bruce said coolly that he had no such intention. Then he greeted Hess and Schirach, who had come over, with a nod of his head, and went back into the building.

September 14, 1958   Hardie told me today that a macabre scene occurred in the course of Bruce's visit. As the high point of the inspection, the ambassador was led into the prison office, where a gray machine stood on a table. Then Letham took one of Hess's notebooks, which had just been brought in, and inserted it into the machine. He pressed a button, and it began to chatter. Triumphantly, he displayed the shredded bits of paper to the astonished ambassador. This, I now hear for the first time, is the road that all our official notes have taken for the past ten years. No better symbol can be found for the uncanny, E. T. A. Hoffmann-like absurdity of this huge, almost empty building.

September 18, 1958   Yeshurin, the Soviet chief guard, has again allowed the half-hour visiting period to go on twice as long. There is talk about this among the Western guards. Since Yeshurin has done this of his own accord, I asked him to keep to the official visiting times, so that he does not run into trouble one of these days.

September 20, 1958   Hilde has had discussions with Adenauer's state secretary, Dr. Globke, in the matter of my release, and also with Pferdmenges, the banker, who is the chancellor's friend, and with Undersecretary Berger of the Foreign Office. All promised support. Hans Kroll, the German ambassador in Moscow, will even try to interest Deputy Premier Mikoyan in my cause.
I am touched, but skeptical.

The Thirteenth Year

October 10, 1958 Once more no entries for three weeks. Only a few notes for my thesis on the window. In addition, continuation of the senseless hike. In the interval I have crossed the Chinese border.

November 14, 1958 Now five weeks without an entry. Time is becoming unreal. Sometimes I have the feeling that I have already spent decades, even a whole life, here.

November 16, 1958 Knee trouble; this time my left knee is swollen. I am in bed; the Soviet doctor has prescribed two aspirin tablets a day. I am not allowed to fetch my food and must wash in bed. My fellow prisoners are helping. In his daily tidying of my cell Schirach shows a real fanaticism for cleanliness.

I asked Badanov, the Russian, who is a veterinarian on the side, how a horse with a swollen knee is treated. "If horse cheap, shoot dead," he said. "If good horse, give aspirin."

November 17, 1958 Two months ago Ambassador Bruce raised the question of the lighting in my cell after he had been informed that

I have given up drawing because of lighting conditions. Today a "mercury vapor mixed light lamp" with a rating of over three hundred watts has been installed. Schirach and Hess rejected the offer of this advanced lighting for their cells.

November 28, 1958   A speech and note of Khrushchev on Berlin. He demands that the Western Powers withdraw their troops from Berlin within six months. The one firm Four Power agreement on Berlin concerns, so I read today, Spandau Prison; on everything else the arrangements are vaguely formulated. Thus Spandau has become a kind of juridical Rock of Gibraltar for the Western Allies. They cannot give it up under any circumstances. Schirach remarked bitterly, "Maybe the city of Berlin will actually make the three of us honorary citizens." Hess offered, "We'll be that in any case someday."

November 29, 1958   In spite of Khrushchev's speech I am not really in despair. Perhaps I long ago decided that the situation was hopeless. Not because I am a pessimist, but because skepticism is a kind of shield. Prison would be harder to bear if I always felt I was on the verge of being free.

December 14, 1958   Today, while tramping the round in the garden, I told Hess that I have been keeping a journal for some time, but that by now I no longer have any suitable material for it. Hess remarked that I had really chosen the wrong moment for a diary. I agreed. "Back when we were in Hitler's entourage we should have kept a diary! At the time, in the Chancellery or at Obersalzberg, there was often talk that someone ought to do it."

Hess shook his head, smiling: "But that would be painful reading for you today. Your new friends certainly wouldn't have enjoyed it."

Schirach, who had joined us, agreed. "Probably all the things that impressed you then are those you no longer want to admit today. You would have zealously set down every trait that tended to make a hero out of Hitler."

Evening. I must admit that at the time I certainly regarded Hitler as a great man, of the stature of Frederick the Great or Napoleon. Recently I copied out two sentences on Napoleon from Eduard Mörike's *Maler Nolten*; they seemed to me to fit Hitler perfectly: "He was sober everywhere except in the deepest recess of his heart. Do not take from him the only religion he has ever had, the worship of himself or of fate." A year before the outbreak of the French Revolution

Schiller wrote prophetically in his *History of the Revolt of the Netherlands* that people whom fortune has surprised with a reward for which there is no natural reason flowing out of their actions are easily tempted to lose sight of the necessary relationship between cause and effect. They introduce into the natural order of things the higher power of miracle and end up by recklessly trusting to their luck, like Caesar.

Some time ago I noted that we always read such sentences too late. That was wrong. What I meant was: We understand them too late.

December 15, 1958 I'll accept yesterday's Schiller quotation, since I have it down. But it appalls me to see that once again I have placed Hitler at the side of Napoleon. That was what I was trying to avoid.

December 17, 1958 My wife's Christmas visit was early this year. I bent every effort to seem on even keel. It was very difficult.

December 25, 1958 Christmas. I have been sitting for endless ages, so it seems, over this blank sheet of paper. I can think of nothing to write. I have no thoughts; I do not want to hold on to feelings.

December 28, 1958 Hilde has sent me a newspaper clipping from the Christmas issue of the Ludwigshafen *Acht-Uhr-Blatt* with the banner headline: CITIZENS ASK AMNESTY FOR ALBERT SPEER. Twenty-five hundred citizens of Heidelberg—professors, clergymen, artisans, factory workers, clerks, and students—have addressed a petition to the four heads of state asking for my release. They will not even receive an answer.

January 1, 1959 This morning I knocked on Hess's door and asked with ironic formality, "May I pay you a New Year visit, Herr Hess?"

He made a gesture of invitation. "Do sit down."

We had a lively chat. We talked about the past year, and Hess once more told me about the good treatment he had received in British captivity. From that he went on to Wolfgang Wagner, who in the autumn of 1939 fell into Polish captivity with his hand shot up. The only reason his hand was saved from amputation, Hess related, was that as the composer's grandson, he received the very finest of medical treatment.

And so we went from one thing to another. Hess has amazingly detailed memories when he wants to. Thus, he described vividly how after Unity Mitford's attempted suicide on the day the war broke out, Hitler arranged for her to be taken to the best hospital in Munich. Hitler paid all the costs of her treatment out of his own pocket, and visited her in the hospital right after the Polish campaign. Then Hess went on to talk about the time Hitler, during a period of high tension in foreign affairs, flew into a frenzy of rage on a drive through Munich when he discovered that his favorite old movie house, the Fern Andra, had changed its name.

I sometimes think Hess's amnesia is merely the most convenient way to turn a deaf ear to the world. I too feel rather the same way, although with me it doesn't take so blunt a form. In regard to dreary, gloomy Spandau my recollection is likewise severely curtailed, whereas the events and circumstances of the years with Hitler remain very much alive in my memory.

After about an hour Hess gave me a sign that the conversation was over. He had once more become the Führer's deputy, dismissing the visitor. Aware of the irony of the situation, we bade farewell with slightly exaggerated bows.

January 17, 1959 Gromov, the new Russian guard, has studied the rules, which are now a decade old. He insists that we may only sit on our beds during the daily rest period. During today's noon rest he entered my cell. "Not sleep, Number Five. You must sit up! Up, up!"

I played stupid. "Who says I'm sleeping? I just have my eyes closed. But I'm lying awake."

He shook his head. "The rules say no lying."

I turned my face toward the wall. "Let me be. You've come ten years too late."

To my surprise, in spite of this, he has been pleasant for the rest of the day.

January 18, 1959 In today's *Berliner Zeitung* I have read, flabbergasted, an article captioned: BATHS ARE BEST WITH NEW TECHNOLOGY. A coal water-heater with, the article states, an "interior mounted one-handled mixing faucet, reversible flexible shower-head and ceramic slow-burning stove built in at the bottom" would represent a construction step forward in socialist competition. But although nine thousand three hundred such water-heaters have been delivered so far, many hundreds suffer from "functional inefficiency of the one-handled mixing faucet." The article continues: "The Berlin

Heating Apparatus and Armature Works is competing in a neck-and-neck race with the German Bureau for Testing of Materials and Goods to see who will bring to fruition the extremely urgent technical improvements of coal water-heaters."

On January 12, a week ago, a meeting took place under the leadership of a Party secretary between the representative of the Bureau for Testing of Materials and Goods, the manufacturer, and the supplier of mixing faucets. It was finally determined "that a good many improvements still remain to be made on this coal water-heater, both in terms of construction and of manufacture. Even relative trivialities such as a better bracket for the hand-shower or a more practical shape for the knob must still be attained. For it is precisely in this that scientific technological progress consists; such progress not only eliminates complaints, but also helps to create products that represent peak technical achievements."

It is really incredible. Not long ago factories of this kind were headed toward a new technological age. Here in Germany the world's first jet engines ran on the testing stands; here the world's first rockets were tested; here the first plastics were developed! And now in the same city, commissioners are stewing over problems that were solved by handcraftsmen at the beginning of the century: a coal water-heater with a mixing faucet!

February 15, 1959 Since the Soviets have denounced the agreements on Berlin, the Western commandants of the city have regularly been demonstrating their interest in Spandau. Today, following the American and British generals, the French commandant likewise inspected the prison. In any comparison the French officers always outshine their colleagues. They know how to produce an atmosphere of elegant casualness. In a conversation in French the commandant said courteous things to me about the photos of my family, while I repaid him with compliments about *"la bonne cuisine française."* The Soviet director, who was observing attentively, looked irritated, since only German is permitted in Spandau. His American colleague remarked as he was leaving, "He'll give us hell for that at the next meeting."

February 20, 1959 The French director, Joire, informed me today with some embarrassment of the decision at the last conference of directors: I was officially warned. My using a foreign language was a violation of the prison regulations.

March 21, 1959 Now we have a one-man parish in Spandau. For weeks Schirach has sent his excuses to the chaplain, though he gives no reason for his absence. And so I sit opposite the chaplain alone. It is equally embarrassing to us both that he, standing two paces away, preaches down at me. He was therefore relieved when I proposed today that he deliver his sermon sitting. Not that this helps very much. In this situation the solemnity of divine worship simply will not come.

March 23, 1959 At intervals of several days I have been reading the memoirs of Dönitz, which are just coming out. Where he discusses military operations and questions of armaments, the book is interesting, and probably also reliable. His political attitude, on the other hand, his relationship to Hitler, his childish faith in National Socialism—all of that he either wraps in silence or spins a veil of sailor's yarns around. This is the book of a man without insight. For him the tragedy of the recent past is reduced to the miserable question of what mistakes led to the loss of the war. But should this surprise me?

March 24, 1959 The longer I read these *Memoirs,* the more incomprehensible it is to me that Dönitz should systematically obscure his personal relation to Hitler. He took part only in the armed forces conferences, he writes; he was consulted by Hitler only on naval questions; he never bothered his head about other matters. He alleges that he wanted to win Hitler's confidence only in order to secure greater attention for the navy. He does occasionally mention that he had lunch with Hitler, but then the curtain falls and nothing is said about the content of their conversation. Why has he concealed his cordial relationship to Hitler? Why does he omit the fact that Hitler at one time held him in higher esteem than almost any other officer in the services? Hitler frequently remarked, "There's a man whom I respect. The way he is knowledgeable on all matters! From the army and the air force I receive only vague information. It drives me to despair. With Dönitz I know where I'm at. He is a National Socialist through and through, and he also keeps the navy free of all bad influences. The navy will never surrender. He has implanted the National Socialist concept of honor in it. If the army generals had had that spirit, they would not have abandoned cities without a fight and pulled back front lines that I had strictly ordered them to hold."

After July 20 I once heard Hitler, at the Führer's Headquarters, follow up a long tirade against the army generals by saying: "Not a single one of those criminals belonged to the navy. There won't be another

Reichpietsch there!* The grand admiral would come down with an iron fist if there were a trace of even the slightest defeatism. I regard him as my best man."

Nothing of all that. Even on trivial matters Dönitz pretties up the picture. For example, he asserts that he always kept far away from central headquarters and always stayed in command posts close to the fronts. The facts are that he first had his headquarters in an office building in Paris, then on Steinplatz in Berlin, and later in the building of the Naval High Command. By maintaining that he was constantly close to the front he suggests that he had no share in the responsibility for all that went on.

March 25, 1959 Today I came upon the passage where Dönitz asserts, after all, that I proposed him as Hitler's successor. The very evening before his release from Spandau I told him just the opposite. But probably this story of his is supposed to strengthen his claim that he really had no personal relationship with Hitler. Incidentally, Hitler's testament argues against Dönitz's version, for in it Hitler hails the spirit of the navy as the model for German soldierly virtue. That was a tribute entirely to Dönitz.

And how Hitler protected him during the last half year of the war! Dönitz maintains that he had no inkling of Hitler's esteem for him. Hadn't it ever struck him that he was one of the very few men awarded the distinction of an armored Mercedes weighing some five tons? Or that during the last months of the war Hitler forbade him to use an airplane? That he was not allowed to leave the territory of the Reich because of the increased danger of assassination? All these were precautions that Hitler, for one example, did not think necessary in my case. Sometimes, when I was in Hitler's bunker during the heavy air raids in the last months of the war, I heard him telephone Dönitz and with considerable concern ask whether he had already gone to his shelter.

March 27, 1959 Finished reading Dönitz's book. Probably we should not read the memoirs of a person whose slightest emotions and thoughts we have become familiar with in the course of ten years.

April 14, 1959 About two years ago, in response to Cuthill's invitation, I systematically set about landscaping our garden, making a park of it. I graded uneven ground into interesting terraces, sowed lawns,

* Reichpietsch was one of the leaders of the sailors' uprising in Kiel on November 3, 1918, which initiated the revolution in Germany.—*Translators' note.*

planted forsythia, lavender, hydrangea bushes, and roses. In addition I set out twenty-five lilacs of my own raising. Along the paths I have laid out beds of iris two and a half meters wide and fifty meters long. Today seedling pines, birches, and lindens were delivered. With such a wealth of plant materials I can begin to lay out a landscape garden.

No one interferes. During the past few weeks I have made many sketches, trying to visualize my park in its completed form. But I know that no landscape gardener has ever seen in nature what was present to his mind's eye. Trees, bushes, flowers, and grass take too long to grow together into a landscape. But I want to see at least the beginnings of the thing I am working for here day after day with such obstinate passion. And so I must hope to remain here long enough to witness nature's realization of my plans; but at the same time I fear that very thing. Spandau has become a meaning in itself. Long ago I had to organize my survival here. That is no longer necessary. The garden has taken full possession of me.

Today, toward the end of the working day, the Russian director asked me with a friendly smile, "Would you like to stay out a while longer?"

Letham, the Scottish supplier of my flowers and plants, could rightly say to me in English, "Now, after all these years, you've brought him round."

I agreed: "After years, and by defiance."

April 15, 1959 Mowed today for the first time with the new lawnmower. The machine's resistance, so I have calculated, corresponds to a difference in altitude of four hundred meters. In other words, it is as if I were climbing a medium-sized mountain in the Black Forest. In reality I mowed four thousand square meters.

Schirach hardly participates at all in the garden work any more. Nor does he show any desire to enlarge his tiny private garden. More and more he tramps around aimlessly, but with head held high and swinging his cane—an elegant guest at a spa walking in a park that is kept in order by me, the gardener. He is becoming solitary and peculiar.

April 30, 1959 In my last letter I had to omit the following sentences because it is against the prison rules to write about our everyday life: "And so I am working hard in the garden. I have developed a taste for it and will go on gardening at home."

Schirach, to whom I mentioned this, commented haughtily, "What, you write about such things? My letters never deal with such banalities. On principle I never mention my life in prison."

May 2, 1959   As a late birthday present my wife has brought me a shirt of a strong blue. John Musker declared, in the presence of Yeshurin, "That is a fascist shirt."

I disagreed: "But they were black, you know."

"Not so," the Briton insisted. "I saw the blue shirts myself in Rome in 1936."

Yeshurin mediated the dispute: "Blue is the color of the shirts of the Free German Youth." Naïvely he added, "In our German Democratic Republic."

June 8, 1959   Of late the Soviet director has developed a knack for appearing just at the wrong moment. Today the French cook was serving breast of chicken in mayonnaise, but the Russian came up and protested. In the afternoon Schirach was sitting in the garden with Pemberton, in the shade of one of the big, beautiful walnut trees, when the Soviet colonel again appeared.

June 9, 1959   The American director has already expressed his disapproval to Pemberton. He stated: It is all right for guards and prisoners to stand together; there is also no objection if the guard sits and the prisoner stands in front of him. But if the prisoner sits and the guard stands in front of him, that must be regarded as an impertinence on the prisoner's part. Furthermore, it is quite impossible and contrary to all order for both to be sitting together on a bench.

Basically, of course, the director is right. But when prisoners and guards live together for a decade, it is impossible to maintain the strictness of regulations.

June 10, 1959   A pair of wild ducks have nested in the garden and with six ducklings in a row go marching aimlessly up and down the grounds. Occasionally they swim in the little pool I created out of a discarded bathtub. They feed on the new shoots of water lilies that came to us courtesy of the Berlin Botanical Garden. A few days ago they tried to walk to the prison gate—although the high walls around the building block the view—because the nearest lake lies in that direction. No one opened the gate for them. Now guards and prisoners together are undertaking a duck roundup in order to drive them to the gate again and release them.

June 13, 1959   The chaplain informed me today that Karl Barth was delighted to hear that I am reading his treatise on dogma. The volumes, incidentally, come from the library of Frau Gertrud Staewen, the sister-in-law of the onetime cabinet minister and SPD [Social Democratic Party] deputy Gustav Heinemann, and bear friendly dedications by the author.

I have by now read six volumes of Barth's *Dogmatik*. There is much that I still cannot comprehend, chiefly because of the difficulty of the terminology and the subject. But I have had a curious experience. The uncomprehended passages exert a tranquilizing effect. With Barth's help I feel in balance and actually, in spite of all that's oppressive, as if liberated.

I owe to Barth the insight that man's responsibility is not relieved just because evil is part of his nature. Man is by nature evil and nevertheless responsible. It seems to me there is a kind of complement to that idea in Plato's statement that for a man who has committed a wrong "there is only one salvation: punishment." Plato continues: "Therefore it is better for him to suffer this punishment than to escape it; for it sustains man's inward being."

July 13, 1959   Arrived in Peking today. As I came to the Imperial Palace, some kind of demonstration was taking place in the great square outside it. Two, three, four hundred thousand people—who can say how many? In that constantly surging crowd I quickly lost all sense of direction; the uniformity of the people also frightened me. I left the city as quickly as I could.

In recent weeks the gardening has left me little time for my long hike. It took 415 days for the 2,280 kilometers from Kunming to Peking, but that still makes a daily average of 5.4 kilometers a day. Since the beginning of my pilgrimage to the continent of Asia four years and ten months ago I have covered 14,260 kilometers. If anyone had told me, at the beginning of my walk to Heidelberg, that my way would lead me into the Far East, I would have thought him crazy, or that I was going to be. Now I have the distance from Peking to Vladivostok before me, and have requested books on that route.

July 14, 1959   The joke about Peking was no joke, of course. Today, in the course of my daily round, I tried to figure out what had given me the idea of leaving so precipitately. For naturally it was a flight. Presumably it has to do with that profound irritation that overcame me when, in the course of my preparatory reading, I learned that the imperial metropolis boasts some of the very things I had in mind to build in Berlin. The Palace of Heaven, the huge square, the great axis, the mighty hall of audience—momentarily all that seemed to me a realization, adapted to Far Eastern style, of long vanished dreams.

That was one aspect. In addition was the fact that in Peking an urban architectural ensemble, marked by an unerring feeling for proportions and a classically controlled form, aroused the impression—in spite of its extreme size—of great serenity and lightness. Such a sense of style is always the consequence of a tradition many hundreds of years old. We wanted to force everything; we set ourselves deadlines where others trusted in time; we were hectic and megalomaniacal. I did not want to expose myself to this comparison.

I fled from Peking because I did not want to admit that we were parvenus.

July 16, 1959 Perhaps I went too far. A tradition of megalomaniacal building extends from antiquity up to the time of the French Revolution. The French Revolutionary architecture of Boullée, Ledoux, and Lequeu exceeds anything that was ever turned out on my drawing board. A town hall, for example, has an area of 280 by 280 meters and rises to a height of 80 meters. A church is 920 meters long, the dome 550 meters high, if I may base my scale on the people shown in the renderings. In other words, solely from the viewpoint of the dimensions, our plans certainly had their forerunners. So perhaps I really went too far in what I wrote day before yesterday. Probably what ultimately decides the value of our projects is not magnitude, but the question of quality. I must also be on guard against my tendency to self-accusation.

July 19, 1959 For several weeks I have been building a new walk, twenty meters long and eight meters wide. It leads from the prison exit to my avenue lined with flower beds, which in memory of the planned Berlin grand boulevard is aligned in a north-south direction. The walk was actually already finished, but today a windstorm blew away its surfacing. Now I am once again carting up sand, watering it, and tramping it down more thoroughly.

July 23, 1959 Received eight hundred pipe cleaners from home. I wonder what they were thinking when they packed them!

July 24, 1959   Last night the rabbits ate the first buds of my pinks. A newspaper item has given me the idea of repelling the rabbits with moth flakes. I should think the pungency would be highly unpleasant to the animals' sensitive noses. I had better sprinkle it where it's not seen, because it has not been approved by the Soviet director.

August 12, 1959   Recently a book was smuggled into my cell. *The Army Air Forces in World War II*, a semiofficial history by Craven and Gate, on which George Ball collaborated. In spite of the amplitude of the material, it seems to me the book misses the decisive point. Like all other accounts of the bombing that I have so far seen, it places its emphasis on the destruction the air raids inflicted on German industrial potential and thus upon armaments production. In reality the losses were not quite so serious, although in 1943 I estimated that the air war was costing us—in terms of production for the Eastern Front— the equivalent of more than 10,000 heavy guns of more than 7.5 centimeters caliber, and approximately 6000 medium-heavy and heavy tanks.

The real importance of the air war consisted in the fact that it opened a second front long before the invasion of Europe. That front was the skies over Germany. The fleets of bombers might appear at any time over any large German city or important factory. The unpredictability of the attacks made this front gigantic; every square meter of the territory we controlled was a kind of front line. Defense against air attacks required the production of thousands of antiaircraft guns, the stockpiling of tremendous quantities of ammunition all over the country, and holding in readiness hundreds of thousands of soldiers, who in addition had to stay in position by their guns, often totally inactive, for months at a time.

As far as I can judge from the accounts I have read, no one has yet seen that this was the greatest lost battle on the German side. The losses from the retreats in Russia or from the surrender of Stalingrad were considerably less. Moreover, the nearly 20,000 antiaircraft guns stationed in the homeland could almost have doubled the antitank defenses on the Eastern Front. In the territory of the Reich those guns were virtually useless. Over the attacked cities they did little more than provide a kind of reassuring fireworks display for the population. By that time bombers were operating from such high altitudes that the shells of the 8.8-centimeter flak guns reached the planes at too slow a speed.

August 16, 1959   In intense heat, every other day I carry fifty full watering cans, each holding ten liters of water, to the plants I set in the spring. This amounts to moving a load of five hundred liters, or half a metric ton. I can be content: of the sixty plants I set out in the spring, only two have died.

Our sprinkler, which I am allowed to have for my garden every other day, turns fast or slow according to the water pressure, but at any speed it produces beautiful images of swirling, intersecting jets of water. The pressure can be lowered so that it stops turning, though continuing to sprinkle. Badanov takes delight in this change of pace. He plays with the sprinkler. "Now slow. Now fast. Now full stop."

The water pressure in Spandau happens to be unusually high, and when the Russian makes his fountain race around, I open the faucet at a tap fifty meters away. When that makes the sprinkler stop, I turn my faucet off again. Immediately, the sprinkler begins to race madly. Shaking his head, Badanov stops it again. Finally, this time very slowly, he turns his faucet on. Just as slowly, the sprinkler begins to turn. Badanov is astonished. I turn my faucet on again, and once more the thing stands still. Badanov is even more astonished when I shut it off and the sprinkler once more turns. Now Badanov puts it on slow, but I promptly close my faucet. The sprinkler races. Open again. The sprinkler stands still. And so on, until Badanov, baffled by the whims of technology, leaves the garden.

Strange that this should be the content of my days, months, and years. Sometimes I think of all I could have done in these years. Now I produce paths in the prison garden, meditations on crime and punishment, or silly nonsense.

August 17, 1959   The American director, this time only a captain, regularly asks everybody, "Have you any problems?" With the same regularity, I say I have not. In order not to seem impolite, today I made a few remarks about the heat. He felt addressed in his official capacity and reacted with: "We can't do much about that."

September 14, 1959   Today Sadot spoke enthusiastically about the triumph of the Russians, who have just landed a rocket on the moon. "It's all the more amazing," I said, "because we happen to have only a half-moon now."

Sadot, without thinking, replied, "Of course, that makes it even harder. Good heavens, at the moment that didn't even occur to me.

These Russians!" Only after he was already a few steps away did he give a start and pause thoughtfully; then he abruptly stalked off.

September 18, 1959   I had a heap of notes in my trousers pocket —all rather silly episodes, like the bit about the sprinkler. Today I burned them. Reading them, I felt uncomfortable. For I am falling to a level that I must not allow myself to sink to.

But just this one item: The rabbits pay not the least attention to the moth flakes.

The Fourteenth Year

October 22, 1959 The new Soviet director doesn't seem so bad. I said so to Naumov. But in reply he quoted a Russian proverb to the effect that you do not know a man until you have used up a *pood* of salt with him.

I looked that up. A Russian *pood* weighs thirty-four pounds.

November 12, 1959 The censorship continues to suppress every newspaper item on Spandau, but the many well-meaning guards keep us informed on everything. Four times in the last few days I have been told about an article in the *Sunday Times*. This morning, under seal of absolute silence, a fifth guard actually let me read the newspaper myself. After lunch it was brought to me again, and in order not to betray the fact I had to study it once more, with all the signs of joyful surprise, including loud "ahs" and "ohs." The article is headlined: LAST NAZIS MAY QUIT SPANDAU.

November 14, 1959 Our chaplain has surprisingly been called away; another has undertaken the long journey from French headquarters in Baden-Baden in order to officiate at a one-man service for the single interested Spandauer on this Saturday. But he knows only French. Musker interrupted him in the middle of the liturgy: "Excuse me, but only German is allowed to be spoken here."

I translated. The chaplain was aghast. *"Mais je suis français: je ne sais que dire: 'Guten Tag, guten Abend.'"* Nevertheless the service was stopped. But there was no objection to the *Te Deum* in Latin on the recording. During the music the chaplain covered his face with his hands, murmuring: *"C'est impossible, impossible!"* In bidding goodbye he painfully groped for German words: *"Gott mit Ihnen! Bei Tag und . . . bei Nacht!"**

November 22, 1959   For some time Hess has been tormented by attacks. He is suspected of having used small quantities of laundry detergent to produce artificial stomach cramps. For this reason all washing and cleaning materials may henceforth be used only under supervision.

November 23, 1959   Hess has been groaning and wailing day and night lately. He stares at the walls and is entirely apathetic. Within seven weeks he has lost almost fourteen kilos; 1.75 meters tall, he weighs only forty-five kilos at the moment. At the bath he reminds me of the grotesque figures conceived by Hieronymus Bosch. He can no longer take the few steps to the washroom without help. Today I have written in his behalf to the president of the German Red Cross.

November 26, 1959   Excitement in the corridor today, constant coming and going in Hess's cell. For the first time in a long time I have to stay inside the cell. Feelings of great uncertainty.

November 27, 1959   This morning I succeeded in visiting Hess. He was lying on his bed, his wrist wrapped in bandages. When I entered, he looked up with waxen face. Nevertheless he gave the impression of a child who has carried off a prank. With something like cheerfulness he at once began: "When you were in the garden yesterday and there was no guard in the vicinity, I quickly smashed my glasses and used a piece of glass to open the veins in my wrist. For three hours nobody noticed a thing," he went on rather happily. "I lay in the cell and had plenty of time to bleed to death. Then I would have been freed of my pain forever. I was already feeling very weak and pleasant.

* "God be with you! By day and . . . by night!"

But then, from far away, I heard noise. It was that wretched Soviet medical colonel on his round. He saw me lying there and immediately sewed up the cut." Hess looked at me mournfully: "Don't I have hard luck! Admit it!" But I congratulated him on his failure, which he took as a friendly gesture.

At noon Hess devoured piles of food: milk, porridge, custard, bouillon, cheese, oranges. In the evening, too, he ate with the best of appetite. I have the impression that he has broken off an "operation." Through my friend I sent a telegram to Hilde asking her to call off any Red Cross intervention.

December 11, 1959 In just two weeks Hess has gained fourteen kilos. Only a man with an iron stomach could endure such a fattening diet after several weeks of fast. Hess is in fact a bit embarrassed: "Everything is crazy here, including the scales."

Although some of the Russians call the suicide attempt sabotage, most of the guards have been treating Hess with great civility. Everything revolves around his health. Obviously a good many of the guards have been thoroughly scared. They seem to be telling themselves: Two millimeters deeper and we'd have been out of a lifetime job. So Hess has unexpectedly become a precious object. He rather likes that.

December 18, 1959 Hilde's efforts are making progress. Herbert Wehner and Carlo Schmid have been supporting my release. The new Federal president, Heinrich Lübke, has received Hilde and promised to do everything humanly possible. I follow their efforts gratefully, but indifferently. I have already been here too long.

December 31, 1959 Christmas lies behind me. Nothing happened, nothing felt, nothing noted. Wasn't it like this last year also? The Christmas sentiment, which in any case always has something artificial about it, like a dog trained to sit up, tends to disappear when we have no Christmas for a while.

January 1, 1960 On February 1 I shall have served two-thirds of my sentence. I wonder whether that opens up any new chances.

I look at the new wall calendar without excitement.

January 11, 1960 Albert's visit was a good beginning to the new year. We discussed the problem of his studies; he wants to be an architect. Before we could turn to personal matters, the half-hour was up.

February 12, 1960 Two days ago one of the Russian guards told me about his wife and mentioned that they have two children. Then he suddenly brought his fingers to his lips in alarm. Does this mean he is not even allowed to communicate such matters?

March 19, 1960 My fifty-fifth birthday.

Funk used to remember my birthdays. This time only the chaplain congratulated me. He brought me Bruckner's Fourth Symphony as a gift. I had once mentioned to him that in April 1945 I asked that it be played for the last concert of the Berlin Philharmonic. Together, we went to the chapel, which is the prison music room. The chaplain and I sat down at a distance of five meters from the speaker, on different sides of the room, because the Russian director would object if we sat too close to each other. Schirach remained in his cell with the door closed. "I have so many melodies in me; I need no concerts," he said when I invited him. Hess lay on his bed with his door open.

March 24, 1960 During the last few days Hardie has let me read *Hitler's Table Talk*, which has been published by one of Bormann's assistants, Dr. Henry Picker. I vaguely recall Picker, a young, inconspicuous administrative assistant at the Führer's Headquarters. He always sat at a side table with a group of adjutants, but I used to think that he did not really belong in their circle. One day Julius Schaub told me that the young man owed his confidential position at the court solely to the fact that his father, a Wilhelmshaven senator, had entered the Party in the early days and invited Hitler to his house back then. It is curious now to read what this largely ignored young man had been taking down.

This *Table Talk* does not give an altogether accurate picture of Hitler. By that I mean not only that Picker more or less filtered his torrent of speech and subsequently smoothed and styled it. Rather, I mean that Hitler, too, tended to falsify himself when he sat at the table in the Führer's Headquarters. I was always struck by the choiceness with which he would express himself in a group of officers and other cultivated persons, sometimes to the extent of using a distinctly stilted style. This was a different Hitler from the one I knew in the private circle; again, he must have been altogether different in the company of his Gauleiters and other Party functionaries, when he relapsed into the jargon of the period of struggle and comradeship. In ordinary conversation, when he was being straightforward, he was far more primitive than he is in Picker, coarser and rougher, but also more forceful. The flow of Hitler's speech was also quite different. He had a clumsy style; he would blurt out his sentences, which were by no means shaped or ready for the printer. He jumped from one subject to the other, frequently repeating words like "fundamental," "absolutely," "unshakable." Then, too, he had a special fondness for phrases and words out of the days of beer-hall brawls, such as "club down," "iron perseverance," "brute force," or "beat up," as well as scatological words like "shithead," "crapper." In moments of excitement he also tended to phrases like: "I'll finish him off myself"; "I'll personally put a bullet through his head"; or "I'll fix him."

Picker's transcript also fails to convey the slow, painful process of gestation which could be felt in the way phrases were formed. Hitler would often begin a sentence three or four times over, repeatedly breaking off and then starting out again with almost the same words, especially when he was angry or embittered. But as far as the ideas are concerned, nothing in the book has been falsified. Almost all of what Picker puts into Hitler's mouth I likewise heard Hitler say in the same or similar phrases. Only much of the superstructure has been dropped, and vivid monologues have been produced out of agonizing long-windedness. In this manner a correct text can give a false picture.

April 11, 1960   Tears in bidding goodbye to Hardie, one of my few friends.

May 2, 1960   Still 139 kilometers to go to Vladivostok.

May 5, 1960   Hess outraged at an article in today's newspaper, which in his view overestimates the abilities of Field Marshal Manstein. But when I told him that distinguished generals even during the war regarded Manstein as a splendid strategist, perhaps the best of the Second World War, Hess exploded: "Nonsense! Blomberg told me before the war that Manstein was only a second choice."

"Who was the first choice?" I asked.

I ran through a list of all the possible candidates from Fritsch, Jodl, and Brauchitsch up to Halder and Beck. At last Hess said, with a know-it-all smile, "My dear fellow, it's no use. You won't ever think of it. I'll tell you: Blomberg said to me in so many words: 'I certainly know nothing about art, architecture, and politics, but I do know something about strategy, and I must say without jealousy that the Führer is the best man Germany has, the greatest strategist alive at this time. In the area of strategy,' Blomberg told me, 'the Führer is absolutely a genius.' "

May 6, 1960 Someone ought to write on Hitler's dilettantism someday. He had the ignorance, the curiosity, the enthusiasm, and the temerity of the born dilettante; and along with that, inspiration, imagination, lack of bias. In short, if I had to find a phrase to fit him, to sum him up aptly and succinctly, I would say that he was a genius of dilettantism.

He also had a profound sympathy for all dilettantes; and although I am on somewhat shaky ground here, I am inclined to believe that there was something extremely dilettantish about Richard Wagner. Then there were those nonacademic scholars such as Houston Stewart Chamberlain and Walter Darré, not to speak of Rosenberg—they were all dilettantes. And so was probably the greatest dilettante of all—Karl May.

Hitler would lean on Karl May as proof for everything imaginable, in particular for the idea that it was not necessary to know the desert in order to direct troops in the African theater of war; that a people could be wholly foreign to you, as foreign as the Bedouins or the American Indians were to Karl May, and yet with some imagination and empathy you could nevertheless know more about them, their soul, their customs and circumstances, than some anthropologists or geographers who had studied them in the field. Karl May attested to Hitler that it wasn't necessary to travel in order to know the world.

Any account of Hitler as a commander of troops should not omit references to Karl May. Hitler was wont to say that he had always been deeply impressed by the tactical finesse and circumspection that Karl May conferred upon his character Winnetou. Such a man was the very model of a company commander, Hitler would say. And he would add that during his reading hours at night, when faced by seemingly hopeless situations, he would still reach for those stories, that they gave him courage like works of philosophy for others or the Bible for elderly people. Moreover, Hitler would say, Winnetou had always been his model of a noble spirit. After all, it was necessary to have such a heroic figure who would instill in young people the right concepts of nobility of mind; youth needed heroes like their daily bread. There you had the great importance of Karl May, Hitler would say. But instead of such reading, those idiotic teachers hammered the works of Goethe and Schiller into their unfortunate pupils.

This evening a hopeful report from Hilde. But the hopes are hers. Not mine.

May 7, 1960 Sunday. A blackbird bathed in the bathtub pond and afterwards sang above my head in the walnut tree. A young sparrow lost its way underneath the garden bench. Meanwhile five hawks practiced stunt flying in the wind. One of them settled down on a water faucet a few meters away from me, flew onto the lawn to drink from the bathtub, and because it is still young and clumsy, almost fell over on its face. Finally a young wild pigeon came and perched on the lowest branch of the walnut tree, under which Hess and I had already been sitting for an hour in silence. Into the stillness Hess said, with almost a touch of embarrassment, "Like paradise."

Will I later miss these quiet days with books and gardening, free from ambition and vexation? Sometimes I have the feeling that time is standing still. When did I come here? Have I always been here? In the evenness of the days, which simply flow by, time can fall into oblivion. Perhaps this was what life was like in the monasteries of the Middle Ages. Isolation not only from people, but also from the bustle of the world. Sitting on the garden bench today, for a moment I saw myself as a monk, and the prison yard as the cloister garden. It seemed to me that my family alone still links me to the outside. Concern with everything else that makes up the world is more and more dropping away from me, and the idea of spending the rest of my days here is no longer frightening. On the contrary, there is great peacefulness in the thought.

Is this submission a weakness or resignation? In any case it makes things easier. The thought in fact has already occurred to me that it may be another, novel form of dealing with my fate. After language studies, architecture courses, book projects, and an around-the-world tour, it may be the last and perhaps the wisest way to give meaning to my lot. It is a matter not of seizing fate by the throat, to use Beethoven's famous phrase, but of willingly putting oneself into its hand.

May 10, 1960 An American reconnaissance plane, a so-called U-2, has been shot down deep inside the Soviet Union. This morning the newspapers report that Khrushchev now considers the Paris summit conference wrecked before it has started. Schirach is once more in despair.

I have taken the news without the slightest emotion; it hardly reaches me. What strikes me is that the effort of hoping has lessened. All these fifteen years I have wanted to hold out and have organized my life in terms of a future. But with the passage of time the future has quite literally shrunk and the present has stretched out. In earlier years I was scarcely able to conceive how Charles V at the height of his power could renounce the world and choose an existence as a monk. Today that thought is more familiar to me than any other. The day of release, to which I look forward with longing, has by now come to be mingled with feelings of uncertainty and anxiety. Will I still be able to cope with the world? Or instead will I cry out, like that Pope Celestine whom they fetched from a hermit's cell and brought to Rome, "Give me back my desert!"

May 12, 1960   Fetched out my notebook and reread what I had copied from Goethe's *Elective Affinities:* "There are situations in which fear and hope become one, mutually cancel each other out, and are lost in the dark absence of emotion."

June 2, 1960   My wife's visit taken up with family problems. We had no time for anything else.

Shortly after the visit, the Russian director had my cell unlocked. "When I entered the visiting room you remained seated when you greeted me. That is improper. You are to stand up when I enter. I am issuing an official warning to you."

I smiled at him.

July 4, 1960   I have had to rewrite a petition to the directors because I omitted the proper form of address: "To the Directorate of the Allied Prison." The Soviet director angrily bawled me out: "This is the last time!" What punishment he is threatening remains his secret. But a few hours later in the garden he was genial again. I was plucking sprigs of lavender, which I mean to give to some of the guards I like. The director sniffed at the bag filled with the flowers and had his interpreter ask me whether they promoted the growth of hair. As the question was asked, he smilingly lifted his military cap to show me how badly he needed some such measure. With equal friendliness I lifted my ski cap to show him how ineffective lavender is in that respect.

July 5, 1960   Together with Schirach, Hess, who months ago was complaining of acute circulatory weakness with unbearable cardiac pain, has been tramping for hours around the garden at a brisk pace and without a pause. Both men have again made contact with each other, and Schirach has since seemed somewhat more relaxed. With

Hess he feels superior; taking the lead with Hess suits his disposition. But Hess, too, seems more balanced. Sometimes I think that something like a friendship is slowly developing between them. If so, it would be the first that has come about in Spandau.

July 6, 1960 At the bottom of my pool, the old bathtub, a stray goldenrod had rooted itself. When I emptied the pool, the stem bent with the dropping water level. In other words, the plant gave its stem only the degree of sturdiness necessary to keep it upright in water. I transplanted it, and after a few days it was as strong as other goldenrod stalks and stood erect in the wind.

July 7, 1960 For weeks I have been occupied with a senseless project. I want to continue the north-south boulevard to the northern end of the garden. Since I have obstinately decided to keep my roads running strictly horizontal, I have already raised this one half a meter above the normal ground level, so that it is a kind of elevated walk. The embankment gives me a pretext to build a continuous rock garden on the eastern side of the walk. Since the width is four meters, I have had to wheelbarrow up large quantities of sand and cinders.

These are days of hard work. The happy result of them in medical terms is: my blood pressure, which in recent years has been 110, has risen to 130/75, whereas for my two sitting or promenading fellow prisoners it is only 100/65. True, Schirach and Hess have recently been occupying themselves in the garden again, but only when they expect the Russian director to come by. Their gardening area in any case amounts to only a thirtieth of mine.

At the moment they are leveling out a small lawn area there. This morning Schirach claimed to have invented a new leveling device. We watched in suspense as he tied three tomato stakes together, then spread them apart at the bottom, creating a three-legged stand. "There! The cord wants to be somewhat shorter, and weighted with a stone." We watched attentively.

"What now?" Hess asked, frowning.

"Now," Schirach said proudly to us, "now I make the stone swing as a pendulum."

We looked at him, stunned, and Hess murmured an encouraging "Aha! So that's how it goes." First he rocked his head from side to side, then nodded rather vigorously.

Schirach went on, "Yes, and in this way I determine the horizontal and can proceed to level. Very simple."

Soon afterwards they paused in their walk and stood beside me with condescending looks. "What's up? What have you two got to say?" I asked Hess.

Hess hesitated somewhat, but finally came out with it: "Schirach just commented that in mental hospitals they usually set the feeble-minded to gardening. . . ."

July 10, 1960 This morning Hess came stalking up to me. Obviously he intended to pass on an important communication.

"Today is Sunday. I have just decided that in the future I shall spend a half-hour in conversation with you every Sunday."[1]

And so we are walking together. His walking pace is breath-taking; it seems to give him pleasure to demonstrate his physical powers. It delights him when I get out of breath. "And yet you're a good ten years younger than I, Herr Speer," he says happily.

July 12, 1960 In recent months I have written an essay on "Hitler as a Military Commander." But ultimately I had the feeling that I was working in a vacuum. I have more and more been losing the desire to cling to the past. I also notice to my surprise that it really no longer interests me in general whether Hitler or his marshals or somebody else was responsible for misguided decisions.

August 4, 1960 A long spell of indifference. Battles and flower beds—both have become equally unimportant to me.

August 18, 1960 Great excitement in the prison. Today for the first time the Russian woman, who came to Spandau some while ago, was in the cellblock. She holds the rank of captain and is in charge of the censorship. "We must not let her know that we think her ugly," Schirach remarked today. Yet I cannot at all agree with his opinion, for I find her looks highly attractive. Hess and I call her "Pretty Margret."

We think that she is putting pressure on our Russian director to adhere strictly to the regulations, which for a long time have been taken lightly. Weeks ago the directors approved the performance of a recording of Mozart's *Don Giovanni*. But when the time came, Pretty Margret put in a protest: "That's an opera about love, and everything that has to do with love is not permitted the prisoners." As a substitute

---

[1] This agreement was kept for more than six years, until the end of my imprisonment.

the prison administration sent us Beethoven's Ninth Symphony. But for me the "joy, god-descended daughter of Elysium," was spoiled.

August 20, 1960   The weekly conference of the directors, normally a routine matter that takes only a few minutes, dragged on for hours yesterday. Now the discussion has been concluded. The American director informed me today that "apparently" operas may not be played because of "some technical difficulties." When my face showed my astonishment, he explained, rather incoherently, that in operas music was more or less a secondary matter. What was really in the foreground was the plot, and unfortunately most of the plots had to do with subjects that "apparently"—there was that word again—might contribute to making us restless.

August 21, 1960   Pedantic as I am, today I calculated how much music on discs we have. Beethoven leads off, with 290 minutes, followed by Mozart with 190, Schubert with 150, Bach with 110. Tschaikovsky comes next with 90 minutes, Haydn with only 50, Chopin and Verdi with 40, Handel, Schumann, and Prokofiev with 30 minutes, Reger, Bruch, and Stravinsky with 25, and far in the rear are Brahms, Hugo Wolf, Richard Strauss, and Frank Martin, of whom we have only small pieces. Taken all together, we possess 1,215 minutes of music, or some twenty hours. We are now permitted to hear music three hours a month; consequently, we need seven months to play through our stock.

August 22, 1960   Globke has been turned down again. He writes that the American ambassador indicates his understanding of the desire, on the part of the government of the Federal Republic, to see some progress in my case, but he considers the present time highly unsuitable. The Eichmann case, he points out, has at the moment called the world's attention far too much to the crimes of the Third Reich.

As a matter of fact, the desire for release strikes me as almost absurd.

August 24, 1960   When I consider it, Eichmann precisely sums up the problem. In the past several years, especially when Raeder or Dönitz would go on at great length about the injustice of their convictions, I often recalled Napoleon, who with his insatiable hunger for power likewise plunged Europe into a blood bath and who nevertheless was the hero of his nation twenty years after his death. Would anything similar happen with Hitler? This is the question I ask myself.

The misdeeds committed in the attaining and consolidating of his power, the murders of Röhm and others, the breaking of so many treaties, the war, and even the determination to subjugate Europe—all these things were in the tradition of European history. Desire for power and lack of scruple cannot surprise anyone really acquainted with conditions on this continent. Even the regime's antisemitism was nothing unusual; throughout the nineteenth century the governments in St. Petersburg and Vienna provided many examples of antisemitism; and in Paris the Dreyfus affair revealed that something like "official" antisemitism existed even in western Europe. In all these matters Hitler remained within the norms of European tradition.

Where he did really go beyond the norms was the way he took seriously his insane hatred of Jews and made that a matter of life and death. Like almost all of us, I thought Hitler's antisemitism a somewhat vulgar incidental, a hangover from his days in Vienna. God only knows why he can't shake it off, we thought. Moreover, the antisemitic slogans also seemed to me a tactical device for whipping up the instincts of the masses. I never thought them really important, certainly not compared with the plans for conquest, or even with our vast projects for rebuilding the cities.

Yet hatred of the Jews was Hitler's central conviction; sometimes it even seems to me that everything else was merely camouflage for this real motivating factor. That perception came to me in Nuremberg when I saw the films of the death camps and became acquainted with the documents; when I learned that Hitler was even prepared to risk his plans of conquest for the sake of that mania for extermination.

Going over it all in Spandau, I have gradually understood completely that the man I served was not a well-meaning tribune of the masses, not the rebuilder of German grandeur, and also not the failed conqueror of a vast European empire, but a pathological hater. The people who loved him, the German greatness he always talked about, the Reich he conjured up as a vision—all that ultimately meant nothing to him. I can still recall the astonishment with which I read the final sentence of his testament. In the midst of an apocalyptic doom it attempted to commit us all to a miserable hatred of the Jews.

Perhaps I can forgive myself for everything else: having been his architect is excusable, and I could even justify my having served as his armaments minister. I can even conceive of a position from which a case could be made for the use of millions of prisoners of war and forced laborers in industry—even though I have never taken that position. But I have absolutely nothing to say for myself when a name like Eichmann's is mentioned. I shall never be able to get over having served in a leading position a regime whose true energies were devoted to an extermination program.

How can I make that clear to anyone? I am not speaking of Schirach and Hess. But how would I be able to explain it to my wife? To my daughter Hilde, who with all the ardor of her twenty years writes letters and appeals, tries to mobilize sympathy, goes to see people, and tries to obtain intervention, in order to free her father. Will they ever be able to understand that I want to get out of here and yet see a meaning in my being here?

August 26, 1960 Some time ago one of the Britons vanished into the hospital with a severe liver ailment and from there was sent on to a sanatorium. Now Terray, who was always so decent, has likewise broken down. He too is suffering from a severe liver illness. Both of these men were in charge of the mess for guards and directors during the English and French months, and also administered the stock of liquor. Many guards have suffered from ill health. One is a severe diabetic, another has circulatory disturbances, two suffer from high blood pressure, most of them are subject to obesity. Several have already died. The causes: a too easy life, cheap alcohol, tax-free cigarettes, food too good and heavy. We prisoners, on the contrary, are comparatively in good shape; most of our illnesses probably have psychic causes.

September 15, 1960 Recently, when the Soviet director came into the garden, he saw the usual Spandau idyll: Schirach and Hess seated in the shadow of a walnut tree, Pease mowing the lawn in the summer heat. As the embarrassed Englishman put on his uniform jacket, the Russian called on the two others to go to work. Although the rules say that we are not permitted to remove our heavy corduroy jackets, I stood in shirt and trousers before the director. But he tactfully turned away until I had put on my jacket; only then did he give a friendly response to my salute. As soon as he left, Pease went back to his mowing, I took off my jacket, Schirach and Hess resumed their conversation under the tree. I recalled the remark the American commandant of the city made recently after an inspection, although he intended it rather differently: "Spandau, what a great farce!"

The Fifteenth Year

October 1, 1960   After today's service Hess sat on his bench in the garden and read the newspaper. When I asked him what he was studying so intently, he replied, "The church. But keep that to yourself." Shortly afterwards, Schirach joined us, and Hess, stimulated by his reading, asked us whether we could recite the Ten Commandments. I managed five, Schirach pushed it with difficulty to eight, and Hess alone fluently rattled off all ten. As far as I recall, this was the first time in all these years that the three of us have sat together on one bench.

October 22, 1960   *Die Welt* recently published an item to the effect that a second book by Hitler has been found and will shortly be published. Schirach laughed scornfully and remarked that they've really been somewhat late in hitting on this particular swindle. Hess, too, denied that any kind of continuation of *Mein Kampf* exists; and as Hitler's secretary he really ought to know, he said. But I myself recalled that when money ran out for the rebuilding of the Berghof, Hitler obtained an advance of several hundred thousand marks from his publisher on an existing manuscript that for reasons of foreign policy he did not wish to be published as yet. Hess stuck to his opinion. It was possible, he finally conceded, that the work involved might be a lengthy memorandum, perhaps in connection with the preparations for the Harzburg Front.* Schirach rejected that too. In order not to disturb our rare harmony, we dropped the subject.

November 30, 1960   Albert's visit has given me a lift. I congratulated him on receiving his engineer's certificate by clasping his hand, for no one was sitting by to enforce the regulations. Accustomed to being under constant observation, I no longer know what it is like to conduct a natural conversation.

As I afterwards heard, Albert was admitted on his pass without the signature of the Soviet director. When he left the building, he ran into the Russian. "What is he doing here? Is he waiting?" the Russian asked the American guard.

"No, the visit has just ended."

I hear that the Russian colonel looked completely flustered and strode away without another word.

December 6, 1960   Kroll, the German ambassador to Moscow, has candidly told Hilde that he sees scarcely any prospect for my release before completion of my sentence.

December 12, 1960   Today the Soviets presented a formal protest against infraction of the rule that all four directors must sign a pass. Pretty Margret, the Soviet censor, finds my handwriting illegible; she insists that I recopy my last letter.

December 25, 1960   A guard tells me that yesterday, Christmas Eve, three men delivered packages for us at the prison gate; of course we will not be allowed to have them. Then they set up a tape recorder, but before they could start it they were led into the guardroom, their papers were checked, and the apparatus was confiscated. The tape began with the "Prisoners' Chorus" from Verdi's *Nabucco*, then came Christmas carols, and finally a nationalistic address to the three prisoners. The guard on duty finally let the three young men go their way.

Pease brought Hess and me the Christmas presents from our families. Schirach received nothing. In November, in an access of defiance, he wrote home that this year he did not want to have any

* A temporary union of Nationalists and Nazis in 1931, which soon broke up.— *Translators' note.*

presents. Now, as he admits, he is dismayed that his children took him at his word.

No Christmas greetings from Dönitz, the only survivor among those who have hitherto been released. For Funk died at the end of May, and six weeks ago Raeder too, unnoticed by the world and by us.

January 1, 1961   Last night, in preparation for midnight, my cup was filled with smuggled Pommard. Amid the bell ringing, the booming of cannon, and the rising rockets, I drank to each member of the family and to my friends, one by one. Then I climbed up on the bed, rested my elbows on the windowsill, and watched the fireworks over the city: without anguish, rather, feeling curious about what the outside world is up to.

Never before have I got through critical November, the holidays, and the beginning of the New Year with so little emotional turmoil.

March 2, 1961   During the past two months I sometimes sat over the paper and wrote a few sentences. But the pointlessness of all these notes for fifteen years paralyzed me. I stopped and burned what I had written.

March 6, 1961   New Russian director, about thirty-five years old, but already a lieutenant colonel. He is a former schoolteacher, speaks German fluently, and is markedly obliging toward Schirach and me. He has already been here for several weeks. The full extent of my sulkiness, my distaste for writing, is plainly evidenced by my not even caring to note the mere fact of this change.

March 12, 1961   Visit from my wife just an hour ago. Once again three supervisors take their places in the visiting room. On my new, deep-brown corduroy suit the number "5" on both knees stands out in sharp white; I have somewhat reduced the effect by rubbing the numeral with a thin coating of brown shoe polish.

March 17, 1961   I am forever reading in the newspapers about the "golden" twenties; this seems to be one of the fashionable subjects these days. Yet my memory of the twenties is quite different. I thought those years overcharged, eccentric, excessive, quite demented. "Golden" would certainly be the last adjective I would hit on if anyone asked my opinion. On the other hand, perhaps that has to do with the fact that I was a student and subsequently a more or less unemployed architect;

on the other hand, it may well be connected with the fact that the particular social group where the money of those years glittered so brightly was relatively alien to me. I did not attend the avant-garde exhibitions, nor the midnight revues and spectacular premieres. I also had no particular eye or ear for the corrosive brilliance of big-city journalism. In general, the lively, clever, cynical wit of the era meant nothing to me. I felt like a latecomer. But I did not regard this as a deficiency—on the contrary, my whole sense of being came from my feeling of belonging to a different age. Not that I felt hostility or resentment toward the contemporary scene; it was too alien for me even to feel aversion toward it. Undoubtedly I was aware of its modernity, and I think that even then I had a sense that it represented the spirit of the age. But did it necessarily follow that my own position was illegitimate? Has the straggler, the heir of the past, no claim to contemporaneity? If not, what justifies him?

March 28, 1961   A hasty letter from Hilde reached me today. Six days ago she and Frau Kempf, my secretary, were invited to the American Embassy, where George Ball received them. Ball declared that he would discuss with Nitze and McCloy, and with Bohlen also, what can be done. He said he had already obtained the consent of the British and meant to bring the French around at his forthcoming discussions in Paris. If necessary he would call the attention of the president of the United States to my case.

Oh, sure!

March 30, 1961   Once more on my being a straggler. Of course the two great architectural forms, classicism and romanticism, which I always loved and as an architect unhesitatingly embraced, ultimately became a problem for me to a visibly increasing degree. I came to see their dangers more and more clearly—the dangers of perversion and of imitative atrophy. Romanticism ultimately turned into mere antagonism for civilization, a weakness for the pseudoprimitive, while classicism ended up in empty heroic bathos. But does that mean that in the end they were completely discredited?

Nowadays, when I call to mind my own designs, I realize that I too did not escape those two dangers. It took effort to hold on to the grand lines of form; and the forced character of this link with venerable traditions cannot be overlooked. But I have always favored renaissances; and my sympathy for the resumption, the recreation of what had seemingly been left behind, was extremely strong. During my trip to Italy with a few friends, for example, I did not seek out evidences of early, original art, but late and tradition-soaked things, like the examples of the Hohenstaufen renaissance in Apulia and Sicily, of the Florentine renaissance, and of Palladio's discovery of antiquity. The Führer's Palace, the germ of which came to me on this trip, attempted to combine Pompeian architecture with the massiveness of the Palazzo Pitti. Nowadays, as I constantly read, our buildings are condemned for being eclectic, but at the time I was quite conscious of their eclecticism. Not that this is a refutation. But Schinkel still seems to me right in his liberal borrowings from antiquity, the Gothic, and the Byzantine. An indisputably original style can arise out of the combination of various historical elements.

If I were asked why I turned back to this reservoir of forms, I could scarcely think of an adequate answer. People cannot and do not have to justify a love. But from the historical perspective, it seems clear that all this was a last attempt to defend style against industrial form. The exaggerations, the megalomaniacal character that resulted show that this endeavor was vain and doomed to failure.

For similar reasons we had a great love for sculpture. It was my ambition to restore sculpture, so long relegated to the halls of museums and the homes of collectors, to its rightful place in the squares and boulevards of cities. It sometimes surprises me that nowadays the only thing that is noted about those runners, bowmen, and torchbearers is the martial gesture. At the time, we thought we were bringing the human figure back into the cities, whose human quality was being threatened by the onrush of technology. That was the reason for the fountain with figures in my big Round Plaza; that was the reason for the boulevard lined with sculptures in my plan to turn Grunewald into a park.

Even there I preferred classical forms. As for the type of painting that Hitler's adviser Heinrich Hoffmann annually gathered in the Haus der Deutschen Kunst, my attitude was one of amused condescension. It never would have occurred to me to buy a Ziegler or a Padua for my own house; the genre touches in these south German academic painters were not to my taste, and somewhat embarrassing. On the other hand, I took great interest in the latest work of sculptors, many of whom were also my friends. I can still recall how often, while making the rounds with Hitler of the Haus der Deutschen Kunst, I would stop before a new Breker, Klimsch, or Thorak. I had even succeeded, with no great effort, in rehabilitating Georg Kolbe and Richard Scheibe, both of whom had fallen into disfavor after the seizure of power—Scheibe because he was well known to be a liberal and in addition had designed the memorial to Friedrich Ebert in the Paulskirche in Frankfurt; Kolbe because he had been the designer of the Heinrich Heine monument in Düsseldorf and the Walther Rathenau memorial, both of which had been smashed by the SA after 1933.

When I read the art pages of the newspapers nowadays, I see that this whole school has come to nothing. But am I mistaken when I sometimes think that these works were doomed not for their intrinsic faults or for their lack of contemporaneity? The crimes of the regime are also charged to the account of the artists whom it patronized. In the verdict on my buildings, or on the sculptures of Breker and Klimsch, or the paintings of Peiner, there is always some element also of the judgment on Hitler.

To look at art that way is false and unjust, but I understand the impulse.

April 3, 1961   For months, only some twenty meters away from us, on the other side of the north wall, a new building has been rising. Hence we are allowed into the garden only on Saturdays and Sundays, or after work stops on weekdays. The idea is to prevent the workmen from observing our behavior and passing on information to reporters. Today I was in the garden in the early darkness. I could see Venus!

April 4, 1961   The precautions were useless, for the *Daily Express* has published excellent photos taken from the scaffolding. The directors have strictly forbidden the guards to show us the pictures—with the result that the number of our informants has been reduced from eleven to six.

In the few remaining gardening hours I have been trying to put my grounds in shape. Today the American director objected that I had been out in the open longer than an hour. "Today is Sunday schedule." In spite of the fine weather I had to return to my cell. This is the reality, not the intercessions of cabinet ministers and undersecretaries.

May 30, 1961   Often I sit down near the multiflora rose, which in the course of the years has spread over many square meters. There is a kind of alcove in it where today our new Russian guard, Sharkov, sat down on a stool. Absorbed, paying no attention to us, he read Gogol's *Dead Souls.*

"An idyll," I remarked to him.

"Ah, Russian *idyllia.* Yes, *idyllia,*" he replied dreamily.

June 8, 1961 News from Hilde: Adenauer has sent word to my wife that "once again everything is being undertaken" to obtain my early release. At the same time, Martin Niemöller has informed the family that he intends to appeal on my behalf to the president and the premier of the Soviet Union.

June 10, 1961 Days ago my wife sent me new underwear. Russian director Nadysev said sternly, "That isn't so simple. The matter has to be decided at the directors' conference." Today French director Joire finally informed me, "Your old drawers, all torn, and your new pair lay on the conference table as exhibits in evidence. It has been decided that you may receive the new pair." I performed a semblance of a military salute.

June 14, 1961 Totally exhausted. Earlier, I sorted the many illegal letters to the family and could not find the one to Hans, Margret's fiancé. I sorted them a second, then a third time without success. Uneasy, I searched all my pockets, unfolded my handkerchief, but could find nothing. The thought flashed through my mind that I might have lost the letter in the garden. I imagined its being found and presented to the directors. I searched between the mattresses, because I sometimes hide clandestine communications there, then shook out the blankets. Still nothing. Perhaps between the pages of the art book? I leafed distraught through that; nothing fell out. My anxiety mounted. Once again I sorted the notes, searched everything. Perhaps the sheet of paper had fallen under the bed. Or behind the heating pipe. Nothing to be found. I took the mattress off the bed, searched in my underclothes in the wall locker, once again went through the book, in a kind of panic shook out the blankets for the third time, and finally, heart pounding, sat down on the tumble of bedding and clothing. Exhausted and despairing as I was, my eyes filled with tears. I threw myself down on the bed—and saw the letter lying beside the stool.

At intervals of perhaps five or six months such groundless panics overpower me. After such fits I know what it must be like to succumb to madness.

Tomorrow, therefore, I shall begin one of my three-week sleep cures. The incident shows that my nerves have reached the breaking point.

July 1, 1961 After my vacation I feel better again. I have read once more Romain Rolland's *Michelangelo*, which made such an impression on me at eighteen. Also a volume of German painting of the nineteenth century, with good reproductions. Meeting again some of my favorite painters, such as Joseph Anton Koch, Philipp Otto Runge, Marées, Feuerbach, and Kobell.

July 3, 1961 My "Project 1961," the second sunken rock garden, is making progress. I have dug a pit ten meters long and six meters wide by one and a half meters deep and brought in humus. I need some two thousand bricks for the terrace of the rock garden and am obtaining these from the ruins of a small shed just being torn down. Seated on a stool, I pound the mortar from the bricks like a *Trümmerfrau.* *

July 5, 1961 We have a hedgehog; it must have passed through the prison gate, the only opening to the outside world. It lets me come close. Some disease decimated the wild rabbits weeks ago; the flowers have been spared.

July 19, 1961 New painting of the prison rooms. Even the morgue in the cellar is being fixed up.

July 20, 1961 Still 3300 kilometers to Bering Strait, and still 433 to Okhotsk. But of late I have been dropping behind; on the average I do only three kilometers daily. For more than a year now I have been tramping northward from Vladivostok. Endless forests of larch and fir, with gnarled silver birches in the highlands. Grass often over my head, which slows progress. Arctic foxes, beaver, and seals occasionally give me a friendly reception; probably they have not yet had any dealings with men.

July 22, 1961 The directors have again refused to recognize the second engagement in our family, Hilde's with a young *Germanist,* as a family tie within the meaning of the regulations. But of course I will be permitted to write a letter to my new son-in-law a week before the wedding, as Pretty Margret, in whose department this matter falls, explained to me today. Thus it would arrive in time for the wedding.

I have never written a letter for a wedding. I leafed through collections of letters by classical and romantic writers in the hope of finding

---

* *Trümmerfrau,* literally "rubble woman," was the name given to the women who kept body and soul together, and made a vital contribution to reconstruction, by toiling in the ruins of German cities after World War II, cleaning the old bricks so that they could be used in rebuilding.—*Translators' note.*

some suggestions, but discovered nothing. But when I began writing, I wrote without hesitation, although with misted eyes.

August 5, 1961   Under an alias I have used my Coburg personal account to have a bouquet of red roses sent to my wife and thirty pink roses to my daughter for the wedding.

August 10, 1961   The American director has made a fuss about the uncut grass. When I was allowed to work regularly in the garden again, starting in May, the grass was already too high for my hand lawnmower. Ill-humored and ill-natured as always, he now insists that I get the grass trimmed at once, no matter how. But however I try, I cannot break through. Then he orders Rostlam, a giant of a fellow and considerably younger than I am, to demonstrate that I am showing ill will rather than physical inability. Rostlam works up a sweat, making frequent pauses, but finally tells his director, panting, that it can be done. Pease, shrugging, commented, "That's what happens once a general has said that the garden looks good. You've brought this on yourself by going to all that trouble."

August 11, 1961   Pease and I have traded opinions about all the guards; our assessments matched perfectly. Of the six guards from each country, four of the Frenchmen, three each of the Russians and Englishmen, and two of the Americans are likeable and helpful.

August 12, 1961   My request for approval of a supplementary visit from Hilde and her husband has been turned down, the American director informed me grumpily today. I reminded him that the rules provide for extra visits in special circumstances. He was not persuaded by my argument, and commented disagreeably, "No, marriage is no unusual event." When I ironically inquired what was regarded as unusual, he murmured under his breath, "I don't know."

August 30, 1961   Two weeks without an entry. The days drag by. Very listless.

September 1, 1961   Ulf, my new son-in-law, was here yesterday. After only twenty minutes we reached a kind of intimacy.

Hilde came today. The first thing she asked me was how I had liked Ulf. For her visit she wore her simple wedding dress.

September 16, 1961   The second rock garden is finished. A regular, almost symmetrical system of tiers for flowers. Schirach, in passing: "Like the walls of Nineveh. Or a Party Rally area for garden dwarfs. Colossal!"

September 26, 1961   For days there have been persistent rumors that the Russian director, together with his American colleague, is drawing up a tougher work schedule. Today Pease let me into the chief guards' room, where the new schedule is posted. Like the minute-by-minute program for a state visit. It will be hard on Schirach and Hess, because from now on they will have to work; on me, because the additional cleaning jobs inside the prison will cut my garden work from twenty-four to seventeen hours a week.

September 27, 1961   Abruptly, Schirach has aggravated his ailments, while Hess laconically declares, "A work schedule! Don't make me laugh. The doctors have all certified my illnesses. That doesn't apply to me at all."

September 30, 1961   After conferring together, we have decided that the American director may want to arouse our resistance in order to be able to introduce stricter regulations. . . . After fifteen years!

The Sixteenth Year

October 28, 1961   In the month since the work ordinance was issued it appears that only the American guards insist on its being carried out. Today Sharkov sat stolidly in the guards' easy chair and listened as Rostlam lectured us on the principles of prison cleanliness. At last Sharkov asked dryly, "Why? General coming today?"

Yesterday there was a somewhat similar scene. The Russian Colonel Nadyzev came up to Schirach, who was indifferently poking around with the rake, and said genially, "A little work? Yes?" Ten minutes later Kargin told Schirach it was about time he started taking his walk. Shortly afterwards, Kargin asked me in astonishment why I was working so hard. "Too much, too much! Germans always work. I say: too much!" The American was visibly irritated.

Since the English and the French are also ignoring the new schedule, we remain unmolested in our cells during the prescribed cleaning periods. Cleaning is done only when an American is on duty.

October 30, 1961   Shortly before going to sleep, Hess said, with somewhat exaggerated politeness, "Good night, Gospodin Sharkov."

The Russian laughed. Whereupon I said to Hess, "Good night, Gospodin Hess." The Russian laughed even louder. "Good joke. Gospodin Hess always lots fun."

November 1, 1961 Today the Soviet contingent relieved the French contingent. Accompanied by a large staff of officers, Soloviev, the Soviet commandant of East Berlin, took part in the ceremony. The French commandant was also present, surrounded by his aides. Subsequently they dined in the prison officers' mess, in spite of—or perhaps because of—the tensions that have arisen as a result of the building of the Berlin Wall.

November 2, 1961 We recognized our Soviet director Andrysev in a photograph in which he is shown conducting negotiations at Checkpoint Charley with American officers; the tanks drawn up on both sides show how tense the situation is. From the caption it is evident that he is really chief of the military police in East Berlin. According to the declarations of all sides involved, we are almost on the brink of a war; but in the prison mess the antagonists meet every few days and toast one another.

November 4, 1961 Our Russian guards are anxious. Kargin interrupted me today: "If war, everything *kaputt!* Wife *kaputt*, children *kaputt*, houses *kaputt*, Kargin *kaputt!*" Spitefully, he added, "Kennedy *kaputt* too, Khrushchev *kaputt*. Ha, ha, ha!" I laughed along with him. Turning suddenly serious, he asked, "Why you laugh?"
I said: "Prison *kaputt* too."

November 12, 1961 Visit from my wife today. Pretty Margret, the Soviet censor, did not appear, and Sadot, the Frenchman on guard, discreetly stepped out of the visiting room. For the first time I was alone with my wife. After more than sixteen years. The separation is now almost exactly as long as the time we were together in our marriage. We were both so taken aback that I automatically obeyed all the rules. I could have held her hand, could have embraced her. I did not do so.
Sadot risked more than his job. All that was needed would have been for a director to happen by.

November 13, 1961 Schirach told me that yesterday he instructed his daughter that none of his sons is to serve in NATO. Germany must withdraw from NATO as soon as she can. Moreover, he wants his sons to learn Russian. "I said that," Schirach concluded with a meaningful expression, "in the presence of Pretty Margret, as you call her." Margret had smiled, he said, and allowed his daughter to hand her father a few lilies of the valley. But Long, the British guard present, had put a stop to that. The world topsy-turvy!

November 27, 1961 Colonel Soloviev, who according to the newspapers may not set foot in the Western sectors as a matter of principle, was in Spandau today. Three weeks ago I sent in a petition asking for increased visiting opportunities and the showing of cultural movies. Soloviev asked pleasantly, "Have you ever had such movies?" Nadysev answered for me that we had not. Afterwards he sent word to me that he in person had called the colonel's attention to my petition. Schirach remarked to the colonel, "I am quite satisfied with the treatment, especially on the side of the Soviet Union, and have no requests."

December 18, 1961 A few days ago Albert came on a visit. After we had said goodbye, the Russian censor switched out the light and left the room with Pease. Albert seized the opportunity and swiftly held out his hand. At this moment Pretty Margret opened the door again and caught us. Naturally she reported the incident. The Russian director queried Pease, who pretended that he had seen nothing because it was dark. Today the American director appeared, followed by his interpreter.

"You have shaken hands with your visitor. This violation of the rules is all the more serious since you took the initiative, as I have been informed by witnesses. Four years ago you were already given a warning for the same offense; this time you will be punished. On Sunday you will not receive a letter and will not be permitted to write one home. If it happens again, you will be deprived of four visits."

I replied angrily, "It is against regulations to punish the family!"

But the director simply left me standing there.

This evening Jack handed me the copy of a letter that Charles de Gaulle had addressed to Pastor, now Church President, Niemöller. It was in answer to a request to support efforts for my release. De Gaulle declares that he is quite prepared to support my release, but that all recent efforts have been ignored by the Russians.

December 21, 1961 The new work schedule has meanwhile been finally abandoned. But an unexpected boon has come out of it: whereas in the years past garden work stopped from November until spring, it is now permitted in winter also. I have obtained permission to prune the neglected walnut trees.

December 24, 1961   Christmas Eve. For weeks we have had severe winter weather. Deep snow, blue sky, and hoarfrost. The night frosts have formed large crystals on the snow; in the slanting winter sunlight these crystals assume reddish hues. The walls are coated with hoarfrost, which also lies on shrubs and bushes. The sprinkling of white on walls and cornices makes even our prison look like a fairy-tale castle. The trunks of the trees stand out, deeply black, against the snowy background.

Just as the bells of the city began to ring, a short circuit in the central fuse box cut off the lights of the building for an hour. It was an unwonted pleasure to lie in total darkness. My Christmas present.

December 26, 1961   The censor has cut a sentence from my Christmas letter. She objects to: "My letter of December 17 was unfortunately canceled because I shook hands with Albert."

December 31, 1961   Last day for the American director. He makes his final round with his successor, a lieutenant colonel. Among most of the guards as well as the prisoners the prevailing feeling is one of great relief.

January 1, 1962   I almost slept through the beginning of the new year, but the boom of cannon in the adjacent British military area woke me up.

Years ago, at the start of our imprisonment, we forty-year-olds often envied the older men among us because it was easier for them to bear the humiliations and various deprivations of prison. Now I myself will be sixty in a few years, and I can feel how much more even tempered I am becoming. Recently I read Jules Romains's novel *Le Dieu des corps* and had the impression, as I read the passionate scenes, that they did not concern me. I regard this new calm as a gain, although I always feared it. But I also know how much of a loss it signifies.

This evening Jack brings smuggled lobster with mayonnaise and British ale.

January 2, 1962   Today I was once again thinking how Hitler corrupted not only classicism, but everything he touched—a reverse King Midas, who transformed things not into gold but into corpses. There is only one exception to this rule, and I note it with astonishment: Richard Wagner. Enthusiasm for the work of the Bayreuth master seems to me as great as it has ever been, although it may well be that the Wagner put on nowadays is different from the one we knew. Such astonishing vitality is in the final analysis probably due to the iridescent, many-sided, forever new and adaptable nature of the Wagnerian oeuvre. I remember my last visit to Bayreuth with Hitler. Young Wieland Wagner said that he had decided to become a painter and would go to Munich. In response to a question from Hitler he began talking enthusiastically about the kind of art that was in those days regarded as "degenerate." Hitler listened to this talk with barely concealed irritation, and on the drive back his full anger erupted; it was compounded half of disappointment with this boy who as a child had sat on his lap, half of despair at the decline of the Wagner family. He could not suspect that already, in Wieland Wagner, the foundation for a Wagner renaissance was being laid, with the result that today the works have been brilliantly resurrected.

January 21, 1962 Have again been reading a great deal. Among other things have read for the second time one of the momentous books of my younger years: Thomas Mann's *Buddenbrooks*. Nevertheless, I now read the novel differently. Today the problem of the artist, which is focused in Christian as well as in Hanno, has receded for me. What now strikes me as more important and what has moved entirely into the foreground is, instead, the problem of decadence. It is true that the book deals with the history of a family's gradual exhaustion, its biological decline over three generations. But this time it struck me that the narrative could also be read as a parable—as an account of the disintegration of the German bourgeoisie's moral fiber.

I think of my own father, and of his father. For them there were still wholly unassailable values. They had no doubts whatsoever about right and wrong, good and evil. It is unimaginable to think of my father or grandfather with Hitler and his cronies at Obersalzberg on one of those dreary movie nights. How brittle all aesthetic and moral standards must have grown before Hitler became possible. I still recall my father's reaction after he had intensively studied, with the architect's eye, our plans for the new capital of the Reich. After some moments of silence he said merely, "You know you've all gone completely crazy." And left.

January 28, 1962 I am writing this as a profession of faith: I believe in a divine providence; I also believe in God's wisdom and goodness; I trust in his ways, even though they may seem matters of chance. It is not the mighty of the earth who determine the course of history. They think they are the movers, and they are moved.

March 2, 1962 During my wife's visit yesterday the Soviet and American directors appeared together. As always I half rose to my feet and wished them "good day." Twenty minutes after I was returned to my cell, the new American director came along and said, in a not unfriendly manner, "I'm sorry, but you did not salute correctly."

I stared at him uncomprehendingly. "But I did stand up."

He shook his head. "You know what I think about that. But let me give you a piece of good advice: Next time stand up like a soldier."

In a tone of despair I replied, "But I never have been a soldier."

He looked at me with a touch of concern. "You must understand that this is a military prison."

March 4, 1962 Today Sadot read to me from the prison journal: "Number Five will be punished for improper behavior during a visit: for one week not permitted to read books or a newspaper. In case of repetition a harsher punishment will be imposed."

Schirach remarked spitefully, "Undoubtedly the American director, not the Russian, is responsible for this penalty."

But Pease said sympathetically, "I don't understand it. You know you saluted them just the way you have always done in recent years. But maybe it has something to do with Schirach, who always sweeps his cap right down to the floor."

March 5, 1962 No books or newspapers. But the guards come, one after the other, into my cell and tell me what's in the papers. Nobody takes the punishment quite seriously.

March 6, 1962 After his report on the latest news Sharkov today told me about his experiences with SED* functionaries. They seem to have given him a real fright by their discipline and abstemiousness. "Germans under Hitler uncanny," he said, "and Germans under Ulbricht also. Always everything perfect. Always everything orderly." And then, with a surprising reference to me, "You with your garden also."

March 9, 1962 Relations with Schirach have again reached a nadir. There is perpetual friction between us, and I have long been ask-

* SED = *Sozialistische Einheitspartei Deutschlands* (German Socialist Unity Party), the ruling party in East Germany.—*Translators' note.*

ing myself what it is about him that so irritates me. Certainly it is not only a matter of differences in temperament and character, nor our differences of opinion about the past, that keep us so far apart. Probably the more decisive factor is that he does not possess what I am inclined to call a line of retreat, without which no human being can be at peace with himself. For me that was and is architecture; for Dönitz and Raeder it was their military craft; for Neurath his background and diplomatic vocation. Schirach really has nothing. As a schoolboy of fifteen or sixteen he met Hitler, and soon after, at the beginning of his university studies, he centered his existence entirely upon Hitler. He learned no profession and never practiced one; he was merely a functionary.

Sometimes I think about what importance his writing, his poetry, had for him. He was always considered one of the leading lyric poets of the Third Reich. But is he writing anything at all here? I've never heard him talk about it. And yet, as the history of European literature teaches us, prison promotes creativity. How many great works all the way on to Dostoevsky owe their genesis to imprisonment! In Schirach's case it rather seems to me that his poetry was merely doing his functionary's job; that no artistic temperament or desire to give form to reality lay behind it, but a craving to venerate. And once the object of his veneration ended, the poetry ended also; his creativity died with Hitler.

When I consider the matter rightly, this must be what comes between us. Both of us, after all, think of ourselves as artists. But in the stricter sense, he probably is not one.

March 10, 1962 Rather stunned when I read over what I wrote yesterday. Doesn't everything I say ultimately apply to me as well? Why don't I draw? The argument that all the designs I might make here could not be built will not wash. Boullée, Ledoux, and even my beloved Gilly frequently worked only for the drawing pad. What sort of an oeuvre might I have been able to create in these past sixteen years of imprisonment? Since I am not going to go down in architectural history for buildings, I might at least have defiantly won a place for myself with grandly conceived plans. Am I, too, lacking in original desire to give form to reality? In the passion to produce something out of myself? Was I, too, made creative only by Hitler?

March 12, 1962 The punishment week is over. The Soviet guards were reserved at the beginning, but soon displayed extreme helpfulness. Today the American and British directors paid me a joint visit. Even Andrysev came to the cell today, after the completion of the punishment. I was lying on the bed at the moment eating a piece of illegal chocolate. "Don't get up, please don't get up," he urged me, simply overlooking the chocolate. A week ago I was punished because I didn't get up. Only Rostlam reacted spitefully: "There are so few rules in Spandau; you might as well obey those."

During the punishment period I decided that the reading of four newspapers is an unnecessary strain on the nerves and a waste of time. Henceforth I shall cancel the *Kurier* and the *Berliner Zeitung* and restrict myself to *Die Welt* and the *Frankfurter Allgemeine.*

March 14, 1962   To return once more to the question of Schirach and me: Possibly it is after all due to the paralysis of incarceration that I have done no designing except for a few country cottages for guards: no theaters, no schools, no administrative buildings. I must admit that what stand in my way are not external circumstances, for after all I have written thousands, if not tens of thousands, of notes. It must be the inner, psychic pressure to which I am exposed here in Spandau, and which has less to do with my punishment than with the consciousness of guilt.

But if that is so and if I am therefore exonerating myself, then in a certain sense I must exonerate Schirach. Is my understanding always limited to myself alone?

March 19, 1962   For breakfast today I had some pastry sent by Hilde which Ulf did not take out of the oven in time. It is terribly hard; chewing it makes such a noise that I dare to eat it only when a plane is flying overhead.

March 25, 1962   A few days ago my friend Jack brought me a pocket transistor radio. In the cell I keep it in my back pocket, concealing the earphone under my ski cap. Only a few centimeters of white wire can be seen, but since I lie on the bed and spread out the newspaper, I am quite covered.

The pocket set, a Japanese Sony, is technically splendid. I can easily hear Stuttgart, my "home station," only an hour's drive from our house. For the first time in seventeen years I participated in a musical event today, listened to the murmur of the audience, the voices of the instruments, to that wonderful sense of solemnity and expectation which precedes a musical offering. I thought it was the Berlin station, but it turned out to be Salzburg.

Loud conversations in the corridor. Quickly, I packed away the apparatus. The American director had the guard open the cell door. "The directors have decided that you must return the shoes you received for your birthday. They are unsuitable with the uniform. We will provide you with another pair." This is the reality.

April 3, 1962 Whenever the weather has been bad these past months I have busied myself with doing up our chapel. I want it a deep dark blue like the mosaics in the tomb of Galla Placidia, with a rich, ochre-colored altar cloth, dark-red furniture, and an almost black floor—a kind of catacomb in which the candles would provide the light. But my conception was wrecked today. Director Andrysev ordered it painted sky blue.

April 12, 1962 In my dream tonight I swung myself athletically over the high prison wall and found myself in the midst of a wonderful landscaped garden not at all inferior to the Generalife in Granada. Great vistas of roses, flower beds, and fountains. I had never expected to find such gardening wonders on the other side of the wall. As morning was beginning to dawn I wanted to return to the prison, but became lost in a system of corridors and suddenly found myself on the outside, completely unobserved. Full of uncertainty and fear, I tried to find the way back into the prison, but kept losing myself. Panic-stricken, I began to run. Finally I found the wall, but it was insurmountable. I woke with pounding heart.

April 16, 1962 A velvet altar cloth in reddish gold that I chose harmonizes with the yellow candles of a pair of heavy candelabra that President Scharf of the German Evangelical Church has donated for our newly furbished chapel. Two beautiful vases have also arrived; in summer I can fill them with flowers.

The chapel has become the showpiece of the prison. No director fails to take a look at my architectonic achievement when he pays a visit.

April 17, 1962 Solitude, deep snow, taiga. I am several hundred kilometers north of Okhotsk. Endless forests surround me; in the distance are smoking volcanoes with glaciers snaking down them. I have been passing hot springs with violets already in bloom around them. Approximately two thousand kilometers more before I must make the crossing at Bering Strait, where I ought to arrive in about sixty weeks.

April 20, 1962   Margret, our second daughter, married a young Orientalist today. I have listened to Mozart's *Coronation* Mass, followed by Bruckner's *Te Deum*. Punctually at ten minutes after five Law comes in with a big glass of rum, and tells me that on his own hook he wrote to Heidelberg telling the family that everyone there should toast the new couple at fifteen minutes after five on the dot, and that I would be joining in.

May 30, 1962   After an interval of more than two months I am again reading our four newspapers. I missed the theater and concert reports, and news about reconstruction and city planning. The *Berliner Zeitung* is a sad but also salutary supplement.

July 12, 1962   In the *Frankfurter Allgemeine* the Schirach family announces the engagement of one of their sons. Our fellow prisoner signs his name Baldur Benedict von Schirach. Hess comments, "Schirach told me that all male descendants of the family have received the name Benedict for ever and ever; all females are named Benedicta." Then he adds sarcastically, "Did you know that? In the past he withheld from us this Catholic appendage to the Aryan Baldur."

August 9, 1962   Today an American soldier called down in English from the tower, "Mr. Speer, I like your garden. It's wonderful."

August 14, 1962   Months ago Hess had a violent disagreement with the British dentist. The dentist wanted to pull his last six teeth, since it is too much trouble to make new partials and bridges every time another tooth is lost. This prompted Hess to appeal to the directors in a petition. He succeeded in obtaining a ruling that no operation on any part of a prisoner's body may be performed without the prisoner's written consent.

After the French dentist had also decided that all the teeth must be pulled, a young female Soviet dentist examined Hess's mouth. Her verdict: "Those teeth must come out." At this point Hess demanded that an American dentist be consulted. Accompanied by three assistants, the American turned up in the infirmary yesterday with a portable X-ray apparatus. He finally determined that the six teeth were sound, and declared: "My principle is to make extractions only when necessary." Now this man is in charge of our dental work. Hess has won. Today he reveled in his victory and declared proudly, "One dentist for every one and a half teeth!"

September 13, 1962 A curious dream.[1] Shortly before Hitler is coming for an inspection I myself, though armaments minister, take broom in hand personally in order to help sweep up the filth in a factory. In conjunction with this I find myself in an automobile and try in vain to get my arm into the sleeve of my jacket, which I had taken off while sweeping; my hand repeatedly lands in the pocket instead of the sleeve. The drive ends in a large square surrounded by government buildings. On one side of it is a memorial. Hitler goes up to this memorial and lays a wreath. We enter the marble entrance hall of one of the buildings. Hitler says to his adjutant, "Where are the wreaths?" The adjutant turns reproachfully to an officer. "Why, you know that he lays wreaths everywhere nowadays." The officer is wearing a light, almost white uniform made of a kind of glove leather; over his jacket he has a smock ornamented with lace and embroidery, rather like an altar boy's. The wreath comes. Hitler goes to the right side of the hall, where there is again a memorial before which many wreaths have already been laid. He kneels and begins a plaintive song, rather like Gregorian chant, repeating again and again a long drawn out "Jesus Maria." Many other memorial plaques are aligned side by side along the wall of the high-ceilinged, long marble hall. In ever swifter succession Hitler lays down wreath after wreath; the wreaths are handed to him by bustling adju-

---

[1] See the interpretation of this dream in Erich Fromm, *The Anatomy of Human Destructiveness* (New York: Holt, Rinehart and Winston, 1973), p. 334. "This dream is interesting for many reasons. It is one of those in which the dreamer expresses his insight into another person rather than his own feelings and desires. These insights are sometimes more precise than the dreamer's conscious impression of another person. In this case Speer clearly expresses in a Chaplinesque style his view of Hitler's necrophilous character. He sees him as a man who devotes all his time to paying homage to death, but in a very peculiar way his actions are entirely mechanical, leaving no room for feelings. The wreath-laying becomes an organizational ritual to the point of absurdity. In juxtaposition, the same Hitler, having returned to the religious belief of his childhood, is completely immersed in the intonation of plaintive tones. The dream ends by stressing the monotony and the mechanized manner of his grief ritual.

"In the beginning of the dream, the dreamer brings to life a situation out of reality, from the time when he is still a minister of state and a very active man who does things himself. Perhaps the dirt he is sweeping is a symbolic expression of the dirt of the Nazi regime; his inability to put his arms into the jacket sleeve is most likely a symbolic expression of his feeling that he cannot participate further in this system; this forms the transition to the main part of the dream in which he recognizes that all that is left are the dead and the necrophilous, mechanical, boring Hitler."

tants. His plaintive singsong becomes more and more monotonous; the succession of memorials seems to go on forever. An officer ventures to smile and is reproved by the escort.

September 19, 1962 My apple harvest, some thirty apples, was stolen before the apples ripened.

The Seventeenth Year

October 1, 1962 Henry James in *A Most Extraordinary Case:* "Next to great joy, no state of mind is so frolicsome as great distress." Twenty years ago I would not have understood that sentence, or at best read it as mere literary cynicism. I would always have thought that a prisoner's real unhappiness lay in the loss of freedom, in being at the mercy of inferiors who serve as guards, in the constant sense of one's helplessness. It now surprises me that the outer as well as the inner lack of event is the real source of despair. Protected by a certain aloofness, one is ultimately actually grateful for the harassment of guards; for this heightens the feelings and at least creates the possibility of events. The good-natured, tepid atmosphere that on the whole is the prevailing tone here leads to gradual psychic breakdown. I observe how necessary man's emotions are to him. The deepest despair is full of secret satisfactions. That is the truth of Henry James's sentence.

October 26, 1962 Kennedy has ordered the total blockade of Cuba. An army of 100,000 men is being massed in American ports.
   This crisis, too, interests us only in its application to Spandau—my

conversation with Schirach and Hess this morning made that plain. World history, which we once upon a time wanted to move, has been reduced for us to the fate of a prison. What we worry about is this: in a few days it will be the Russians' turn to take charge of Spandau. Today Schirach elaborated on what might happen. One night they break open the garden door leading to the cellblock. A small squad of commandos under the leadership of a lieutenant overpowers the Western guards. Within minutes we are loaded into a Russian bus; the bus drives through a forested area to the crossing to the Russian zone at Staaken, only two kilometers away. It would all be done in a twinkling, and the Western governments, concerned as they are about Cuba and Berlin, would scarcely do more than send a feeble protest note to Moscow.

Subsequently we discussed this anxiety with some of the Western guards. Long, the first to whom we described our fears, turned pale. When I tried to soothe him by reminding him of the telephone and the alarm system, he gave a distraught laugh. "Alarm?" he said. "The bell rings in the sentries' rooms. That would only bring some more Russians."

Sadot had meanwhile joined us. I asked him, "What would you do if two Russian soldiers enter the hall and aim their submachine guns at you?"

Sadot grinned. "I've thought of that before. You know what, I'd act like de Gaulle at his meeting in Algeria: raise both hands in the air and cry out: '*Je vous ai compris!*'"

One of the well-meaning Russians had obviously seen that something was preying on our minds, for he said, "Politics not good, hey?"

October 28, 1962   Although everybody here tries not to let it show, the extreme high tension we all feel is almost palpable. The monotony of the past weeks has been wiped away; once again there are other things besides getting up, breakfast, cleaning cells, garden work, walk, and so on until sleep—the eternal, unchanging round. I thought again of Henry James. This Cuban crisis, which is threatening the very life of the world, provides a certain element of life for us. Of course we are also extremely upset by the confrontation. But our very nervousness gives us a center of gravity.

Today, for example, for all my relief I was nevertheless a little disappointed as, lying under my blanket, I heard on the transistor radio that Khrushchev had agreed to withdraw the rockets from Cuba. A short time later I ran into Gromov in the corridor, who said to me, "Very good news on radio. Peace! Very good." In the evening I listened to Schumann's Fourth Symphony, conducted by Furtwängler, on the earphone.

November 1, 1962   Yesterday Ernst came for a visit, but it was a bust. As happened years ago, aside from a few phrases he answered all my questions with a terse "Yes," "No," or "I don't know," in a very low, almost inaudible voice. It was obviously not so much indifference as a kind of paralysis. Today I told my wife how surprisingly communicative Ernst had been. Was I trying to help him or myself get over the disappointment? And what will the boy think when he hears what I said?

November 3, 1962   Willy Brandt has received Hilde. He has promised his help.

November 17, 1962   A few days ago I recommended to Kargin the novel *Man Does Not Live by Bread Alone* by Dudintsev. Only today did I read the epilogue stating that the book has recently been banned in the Soviet Union. I therefore corrected myself, and told Kargin, "Please not take Dudintsev out of library," involuntarily falling into Russian German. I added, "In Moscow big discussion. Now result: Book no good."

I could see plainly how my solicitude touched Kargin. He made an involuntary gesture as though he wanted to shake my hand, but repressed this at the last moment. Moved, he said, "Many, many thanks. When book no good, reading no good." He shook his head and walked off quickly.

November 20, 1962   I could not help thinking again of Kargin's alarm and gratitude when I saved him from Dudintsev. That was one of the rare occasions when I, who for years have been dependent on help from others, have been able to help someone myself. It gave me a remarkable degree of satisfaction. At the same time I am a little amused by the frank horror with which he reacted to the danger he had escaped.

In such experiences there is an element of condescension, and in this case there may well be the added factor that the prisoner is paradoxically the freer person. Strangely enough, it only now occurs to me, as I write this, that I felt no sense of infringement when authors and books were banned in the Third Reich: Thomas Mann, Franz Kafka, Sigmund Freud, Stefan Zweig, and many others. Quite the contrary, accepting such prescriptions actually gave many Germans a feeling of elitist specialness. An element of that attitude of renunciation that underlies all morality is certainly operative. One major secret of dictatorships, from Stalin to Hitler, lies in their ability to provide moralistic dressing for coercion and so transform it into a satisfying experience. It may be assumed that Goebbels, lover of modernity in literature, felt no real sense of loss when he obeyed the regime's policy toward the arts and renounced his former gods. He gave up literary pleasure in return for the charms of moral rigor.

November 21, 1962   Colonel Nadyzev has forbidden me to wear my bright-colored sweater and Schirach his silk shirts. He himself approved them several months ago. Now he declares: "Write home that gifts such as expensive shirts, sweaters, pipes, soap and so on will be sent back. From now on only plain things are permitted."

November 22, 1962   Colonel Nadyzev continued his hard-line policy today. He threatened stern punishment because I had spoken with a guard. I feel that this is illogical, for after all the guard represents the executive arm; he could himself have cut off the conversation.

In the afternoon the American, Bray, joined me during my walk in the garden. For half a round I tried to explain to him that he had better walk alone, because the Russian soldiers in the watchtowers might report his conduct by telephone. Sure enough, a few hours later Colonel Nadyzev bawled the guard out so loudly that all of us could hear it: "Guards are forbidden to talk with the prisoners. You know that! You're not a prisoner. What are you thinking of? How dare you talk with them?"

The American guard, usually quite courageous, replied evasively, "He joined me. What was I to do?"

Sadot has also been attacked by the Russian director. "You were talking with the prisoners!" Sadot proved more courageous: *"Tout le monde parle ici!"*

November 24, 1962   It goes on. Today Nadyzev ordered that Hess's and Schirach's doors have to remain closed during the divine services. Only those who go to the chapel will be permitted to hear music in the future, he said.

After the service Sharkov, who is back from leave, came up to me in the garden and wanted to tell me his impressions of Kiev. But I walked away from him, and he looked quite bewildered at this unfriendly reaction. An hour later, back in the hall, I explained my conduct: "Soldier on tower see, telephone! Director come right away." He thanked me warmly.

November 26, 1962   Because the Soviets have given up their headquarters in East Berlin, in place of the city commandant two colonels came from Karlshorst headquarters today. They proved to be jovial, but found fault with our new tiled bath as too luxurious.

Nadyzev immediately demonstrated what a puppet even a colonel and prison director is. Because of the friendliness of the visitors from Karlshorst he suddenly seems another man. Genially, he asked me, "The food is good, isn't it?" With a good deal of constraint I replied, "I can't exactly say that." Even the supper showed improvement.

December 2, 1962   Schirach has been ill for several days, and so I have been taking longer walks with Hess. But it soon turns out that we lack any interesting conversational material. After all, what do we have to talk about—after sixteen years? Starting with daily trifles we almost invariably arrive, by way of long pauses, at the past. Today I told him about my occasional unauthorized acts as armaments minister—only innocuous incidents, of course, to spare his feelings and not imperil the laboriously achieved harmony. I spoke of the tragicomedy of the jet fighter, the only plane that might have stopped the American bombing offensive against our fuel production plants; or of the switch of our atomic research to a uranium-powered motor because Heisenberg could not promise to complete the bomb in less than three to five years.

That I had acted without authority stirred Hess to excitement. "You mean to say you didn't send up a query about the atom bomb?" he interjected, dismayed.

"No, I decided that on my own. At the end it was no longer possible to talk with Hitler."

In the style of an official Party reprimand, Hess reproved me: "Herr Speer, that is an impossible proceeding. I really must point that out. The Führer had to be informed in order to be able to make the decision himself." After a pause he added, "What things came to after I left!"

I said, "But please don't tell this to Schirach. It will only create hard feelings."

Hess agreed, but remarked that only yesterday he had had to promise Schirach to conceal some incident from me.

"I find it strange," I went on, "that you of all people should be surprised. After all, plenty of acting without authorization went on in the Party, too."

Hess pondered. "Yes, yes," he admitted after a while, "but still I kept things under control."

This time I did not want to let him off so easily. "You may have," I said. "But not Hitler." Hess looked at me questioningly. "Or did you by any chance ask him before you flew to Scotland?" I added pointedly.

Hess was actually taken aback. "You have something of a point there. But from the higher vantage point I did act in a fully National Socialist sense—you'll have to admit that." Hess put on one of his impenetrable expressions. Was I mistaken when I thought I could discover in it, for a brief moment, a smile?

December 4, 1962 This morning, on orders from the British director, Letham officially asked Schirach why he stayed away from the chapel service. "Such matters are my private affair," Schirach replied sharply. "I refuse to talk about it. No one has the right to ask me about that."

December 20, 1962 A few days ago I became somewhat obsessed with the idea of painting the dark bricks of the window embrasure white. The iron bars would be sky blue, the cell door again white, the bedstead and furniture dark red, the floor almost black, the walls pea green up to waist high, with a dark-green line for a border; the upper part to be done in water paint, an off-white with a good dash of ochre. I could then have two yellow bath towels sent to me; as a tablecloth they would make an effective accent in this rather strange play of color. Maybe the directors would even approve a vase for flowers from the garden. "If you let me do it, before long it will look like a room at the Hilton," I said to the American director three days ago. But he has brought word that my request has been denied; the directors were worried about the impression my cell might make on visitors.

Curious, the only idea I have of the "Hilton" comes from the newspapers. How my imagination seizes on material from a world I do not know. All those odd little scraps, particles that I put together from newspapers, conversations, books and letters, form a picture of the outside world that is close and coherent. For the past few years I have been noticing how this picture is gradually replacing the reality familiar to me, even in my dreams. I no longer see the ruins I left, but the skyscrapers I have never seen.

I wonder how, when I am released, the imagined reality will relate to actuality.

December 24, 1962   A sweater, a shirt, a cake of Pears tar soap, and a pipe have passed across the luxury threshold, perhaps because of the holiday. However, Albert first used caustic on the expensive Stanwell to take away the high gloss; and the slippers were rejected as too elegant. Hess received a pair of pajamas and a Christmas star of larch wood, which came bedded in pine twigs. Schirach's sweater, knitted by his sister-in-law, was likewise felt to be too luxurious, as was a pair of underdrawers; these were made of excessively fine wool. Along with a miniature Christmas tree, he was left with a pair of socks and a cake of soap.

At six o'clock in the evening walked up and down the hall with Hess; we chatted about everyday matters and did not mention Christmas. At half past eight to bed.

December 31, 1962   It snowed overnight. The cold continues, 21°F and an east wind. In the garden I took the snow shovel and shoveled our circular path clear for the other two. "What do you say to my zeal, Herr Hess?" I asked when he came along with Schirach.

"It is highly praiseworthy," he replied. "But I have an idea for getting rid of the snow more easily. I've already asked for a petition form; maybe you would help me with the drawing. We simply set two boards at an angle to one another, so that the snow is pushed to either side. In front we fasten a rope, and behind a steering pole." Hess looked triumphantly at me as if he had just invented the wheel. Afire with an inventor's excitement, he went on to the practical aspects: "Up ahead, at the rope, Schirach and you will pull. I'll follow along behind and control the steering."

When Schirach and I laughed, he pretended to be piqued and said, "All right, as you like. Then I won't put in the petition."

Toward noon all the directors, one after the other, came through the cells and wished us a good New Year. At half past two I went into the garden. I decided to march about ten kilometers, but by quarter after four I had done thirty-six rounds, or 16.1 kilometers. That was also my record distance for 1962, and I was pleased. Another five hundred kilometers through the snowy wastes to the Bering Strait still lie before me, all to be done in almost total darkness. However, wonderful northern lights, such as I saw in North Lapland at the end of 1943, continually transform the scenery. Staring raptly into space, I lost myself in the course of my rounds so completely in my phantasmagorias of snow, light, and glittering void that at the end I was stunned to see before me the gloomy facade of the prison.

When I look back on this year, I am not dissatisfied with it. Albert has had his first success in an architectural competition; Hilde has good marks in the philosophical faculty; Fritz has passed the preliminary examination in physics; Margret has begun on her doctoral dissertation; Arnold is making good progress at the university; and at the end of the year Ernst surprised us with a whole slew of excellent marks.

January 19, 1963   The order issued by the Soviet director two months ago, that only churchgoers would be allowed to hear music, has been rescinded. Gromov had orders today to open all doors before the beginning of the concert on records.

February 7, 1963   With the temperature 10°F I today shoveled the circular path clear. To harden myself, I worked without a coat. Since Schirach and Hess are again treating me very haughtily, I dug the path only one track wide; they will have to deal with the second track themselves. But they preferred walking one behind the other, heavily wrapped up; Schirach's shawl hung out from under his cap and to either side, like a burnoose.

February 8, 1963   Hess is growing more and more unfriendly. Today, when we met in the garden, I stopped and asked, "Well, Herr Hess, shouldn't we have a little conversation?"

Hess frowned. "You know," he said, "at the moment I am rather quarrelsome. But if you need to talk, I am glad to oblige." More seriously, he went on, "Incidentally, there we have a subject for a quarrel right off. Why have you been avoiding me every morning?"

I replied that I was not avoiding him, but that I had noticed that of late he had not been responding to my greeting, and so I stopped offering it, since, after all, he wasn't Louis XIV.

"But you've stopped putting the broom in front of my door in the mornings," Hess replied. "You must admit that that is avoiding me."

There was not much I could answer to that. So I took a more principled tone. "Herr Hess, we live in two different worlds. That is the real reason. And for that reason every discussion between us seems to bring on misunderstandings and offense on both sides. Better to avoid it."

Hess insisted: "But after all, you're friendly with several of the guards."

I tried to explain to him that everybody needs a few contacts in order not to be destroyed by loneliness. As if seized by a sudden fit, Hess snapped, "But they are our jailers. I hate them. All of them. I hate every one of them!" He repeated this several times.

"What about Bray, who gave you chocolate for Christmas?" I asked.

"Him too," Hess said. "Maybe somewhat less, but him too. Absolutely!"

I left him there. When I had gone on half a round, he began following me at a rapid pace. I had the feeling that he wanted to close the gap in order to say something more to me. But I did not feel like talking, and accelerated my steps. Hess, too, speeded up, so that in the end we were almost running, each chasing the other and each chased by the other. In this way I covered 7.8 kilometers in an hour. Not until I was back in the cell did it occur to me that Hess, if he had really wanted to say something more to me, merely needed to stand still.

February 9, 1963   This morning Hess came up to me. "Herr Speer, I've thought it over. I was wrong. I would like to formally apologize to you."

At once relieved and irritated, I immediately accepted. "Then I also apologize to you if I said anything insulting in the heat of argument."

Together, we then tramped eight and a half kilometers in one and a half hours. Yet only recently Hess was claiming that he had a heart ailment.

February 14, 1963   The conversations between Hess and Schirach are, if I correctly interpret the fragments I overhear, typical exiles' conversations. That is, everything that happens in the world left behind, all the political and social developments even to such matters as taste, fashion or family life, are regarded as bad and corrupt. Every fault is noted with eager satisfaction.

When Hess and I converse and Hess does not receive the echo he is accustomed to from Schirach, he immediately begins to whistle shrilly and out of tune to indicate that he is not interested in continuing the conversation. "Why are you whistling, Herr Hess?" I interrupted him today with pretended naïveté.

"Why indeed?" he said slowly. "It's become a kind of habit with me lately. Yes, yes. And imagine, I don't even notice it myself when I whistle."

I replied, "I'll be glad to take the liberty of calling your attention to it from time to time."

Hess gazed into space and smiled inscrutably.

February 23, 1963   The Foreign Office has offered to pay the expenses for my wife to go to Moscow. A friendly gesture. If no press item appears, the trip will do no harm and cannot spoil anything.

February 24, 1963   In the immediate vicinity of Bering Strait, still craggy, hilly country, endless view of treeless, rocky landscape, as rough as the storms that prevail in this region. Sometimes I see creeping past me one of those arctic foxes whose habits I have recently looked into. But I have also encountered fur seals and the Kamchatka beaver known as *kalan*.

Bering Strait is seventy-two kilometers wide and frozen until the middle of March. Ever since I heard this from Bray, who comes from Alaska, I raised my weekly stint from fifty to sixty kilometers, for if I arrive in time I might be able to cross Bering Strait. I would presumably be the first central European to reach America on foot.

Today, a Sunday, I approached the goal. I walked the last kilometers with Hess. During the second round I said into the stillness, "Another hour to Bering Strait. In twenty minutes we should be able to see the coast."

Hess looked at me in astonishment. "What's that you're saying?"

I repeated what I had said, but he did not understand. "Then I'll give you a hint, Herr Hess," I said. "The cue word is 'beans.'"

He looked at me a shade less comprehending than before. "But I don't understand," he said with a slight note of concern. "What are you talking about?"

I reminded him how years ago he had advised me to count the rounds I walked by transferring a bean from one pocket to the other. At that time, I recalled to him, we had talked about organizing the daily walk as a kind of hike, round after round. "Right now," I went on, "we are in the middle of the seventy-eight-thousand-five-hundred-and-fourteenth round, and there in the mist we can already see Bering Strait."

Hess abruptly stopped. His face now took on a really concerned expression. "You mean to say you've kept that up all this time?" he asked.

"Including leap years, up to today exactly eight years, five months and ten days," I replied. "Up to this point I have covered twenty-one thousand two hundred and one kilometers."

Hess seemed visibly relieved to have come across blatant madness in someone else, but also slightly irritated at seeing his own obstinacy outdone. "My respects, my respects!" he said thoughtfully.

"My only regret," I added, "is that I've lost, so to speak, the distance I covered from July 1947 to September 1954. Given the same average that would have come to seventeen thousand seven hundred sixty-seven kilometers and thus enabled me, with the approximately nine thousand kilometers that I may still cover, to have done forty-seven thousand kilometers, or, in other words, circled the globe at the equator."

Hess now had a somewhat pained look. He said: "Doesn't all this worry you? You know, it really is a kind of mania."

I disagreed. "I have just been reading a biography of Elizabeth of Austria. The tale is told about Ludwig II that he would often go to his stables in the evening, order his adjutant to reckon out the distance, say, from Munich to Linderhof Palace, mount one of his favorite horses, and ride round after round along the track all night long. His adjutant had to keep calling out to him: 'Now Your Majesty is in Murnau, now in Oberammergau; Your Majesty has just arrived in Linderhof.' So you see, my dear Herr Hess," I continued, "if it is a mania, at least it's a royal one that I've picked for myself."

Hess shook his head. "Well, well! So that's how you look at it. But have you forgotten that Ludwig II went crazy shortly afterwards?"

That was a full year later, I said.

"And you have already been doing this for eight years! Tell me, how do you feel?"

I laughed and spontaneously shook hands with him. "We've just reached the coast of Bering Strait. Now the crossing begins."

Hess gave a rather worried look around, as if afraid someone might have overheard our conversation. Then he said wryly, "Congratulations, Your Majesty."

Back in my cell now and checking my calculations I have discovered that I made a mistake of one kilometer. So while I was innocently chatting with Hess I was already out on the ice of the Bering Sea. One really has to be damn careful!

March 3, 1963   In the course of the last inspections Hess put in a request for political literature, especially the memoirs of important politicians, and handed in a list of twenty books. Fourteen of these have now been delivered to him. Hess was taken aback. "Another one of their lousy tricks, giving me so many books at once," he complained.

But I remarked, "You're only irritated because you no longer have any reason for irritation."

Hess is deeply impressed by the *Spiritual Exercises* of Loyola, which he has found in the appendix to a biography of the founder of the Jesuit Order.

March 6, 1963   Today a blond muzhik gaily greeted me from the watchtower, although that is strictly forbidden. "Not too cold?" he called down, because I was working without a coat. He told me that he has to serve in the army for another two years, but that he would much rather go home right now.

March 7, 1963   Bray, the American, today gave me a guide to Alaska. It lists hotels and restaurants with their specialties, such as reindeer steak, bear cutlets, and smoked salmon. I began working out a route for myself.

March 9, 1963   Today I reckoned out that if I make my twenty-one-year imprisonment equal to a year, I would today have arrived at October twenty-seventh. If I equate it with the twenty-four hours of one day, 11.1 seconds pass every day. It is now only eight seconds beyond 7:58 p.m. That is, the day has already gone by, but the evening and the night still lie before me.

March 11, 1963   Today I read in Turgenev's *Fathers and Sons* a sentence that strangely paraphrases my recent bout of calculation: "In prison time is said to flow even more quickly than in Russia." How time must have been slowed down in Russia in those days!

March 19, 1963   Waking this morning, I reminded myself that today is my birthday. I lay awake for a good hour, letting my thoughts drift aimlessly, and arrived back in my childhood. I set myself the task of rediscovering my earliest important impressions. I thought of our nannies and of a few folk melodies they taught us; I thought of a vague smell of coffee and cigars; I saw my mother, elegantly dressed, stooping over my crib. I also dredged a few poems out of memory. And then the first specifically preserved experiences. It was, I think, in 1912 when I sat with my parents in the central stands of the Mannheim racetrack. My mother had come in grand toilette, my father in a dignified dark suit; we children wore fashionable woolen jackets and had on odd light-brown felt hats, as I can still recall from a photo that the family kept. A

French pilot and the German flyer Hellmuth Hirth, holder since 1911 of the world altitude record of 2,475 meters, displayed their flying skills. Their planes looked like Paleolithic grasshoppers; before they took off, every part of them rattled, and a quivering ran through the wires that were to assure stability until they could free themselves from the ground and perform their loops in the air. And these heroes of aviation behaved like normal human beings on the ground after their adventure; they joked and laughed only a few paces away from our stand. Barely a year later my parents stood with me and my two brothers at the cog railway station below the Heidelberg Schloss—to this day I could point out the spot. The great white Zeppelin, more than a hundred meters long, sunlit against a blue sky, was passing by on its flight from Baden-Baden to Frankfurt. Its noiseless, gliding motion had an overwhelming, literally unearthly effect upon me, a boy of seven. And then there is an evening at the theater, to see Schiller's *The Maid of Orleans*. I no longer recall the cast, but it was a tremendous experience. And Max's aria from *Der Freischütz*; with our parents we had driven to the opera in the family's new Benz touring car (16/40 hp). And amid all this, always returning to the house near the Heidelberg Schloss, with the valley of the Neckar far below us.

As I lay on my cot trying to sort out the throng of memories and determine which ones had been decisive impressions, I discerned a pattern. It consisted always of romantic elements paralleled with technical elements. When I consider the matter, these elements, with all their contradictions and frictions but also with all their interactions, are what have governed my life as a whole. Here I am not so much thinking of the dualistic nature of my position in the Third Reich, which indeed did neatly fit into both my romantic and my technologically oriented needs. Rather, I am referring to the perfectly commonplace experience of divided feelings that I have whenever I read a newspaper. All the new technological achievements fascinate me. I admire the mind that has made the earth subject to itself and now is beginning to reach out into the universe. But faced with the inexorable transformation of the world into modern technological ugliness, I am filled with panic and grief. A still further contradiction is that I have experienced in myself all the perils of the romantic relationship toward the world, all the blindness, the obscurantism, the reckless enthusiasm, and potential inhumanity of it—and still I love it and cannot part with it.

The contradiction extends even further. I thought of the fact that both my worlds, the romantic and the technical, have been brought together in a kind of synthesis by several artists approximately of my generation: by Lyonel Feininger, for example, or by Moholy-Nagy, Oskar Schlemmer, and Fernand Léger, as well as some of the Cubists—and yet I have never been able to get anything out of them, but have continued to take refuge in sylvan solitudes, castle ruins, and cavorting nymphs of the early nineteenth century. What a tangle!

April 4, 1963   Today at breakfast Schirach and Hess refuse to eat their eggs because the shells are cracked. They demand replacements, which amazingly enough are provided. In response to my question as to what the fuss is all about, Hess informs me: "Water on the inside of eggs is unhygienic. Think of all the people who may have handled the egg. Then all that penetrates through the crack into the egg, enters the stomach when consumed, and naturally has devastating effects. Now do you understand?"

I nod, at once grateful and intimidated. At noon Long whispers to me behind his hand that the rejected eggs are served in chopped egg salad—which Schirach and Hess devour with pleasure.

April 24, 1963   Unfortunately we are losing Badanov and Kargin, two of the most sociable Russians. They have long wanted to return home. One of their two successors has already arrived. Today I asked Kargin what the new man is like. Without hesitating he informed me, "Good, good man. No bother you." Evidently I can rely on this opinion; for when the second substitute showed up an hour later and I asked Kargin the same question, he merely shrugged.

May 12, 1963   It would have boded well had the Soviet Embassy given my wife a visa for the trip to Moscow. But the visa has been refused.

May 13, 1963   Today Hess vouchsafed his first praise for my gardening: "Keeping all that in shape is quite a feat. But for me dandelion remains the only beautiful flower here. Along with the nettles, of course; but then you had to go ahead and weed those out last year." He laughed with averted face.

May 14, 1963   A few days ago I received permission, over the objections of the Russian director, to go into the garden as early as half past eight in the mornings and half past one in the afternoons. But Schirach and Hess cannot be persuaded to come along. Today, when I wanted to start my garden work at half past one, Pelerin snarled at me,

"All you want is to make us dance to your tune. There's no entry about it in the book. Anyone could come along and demand special hours."

I referred to the permission already granted and threatened to inform the director. He flushed. "It's not for you to threaten me. What kind of tone is this you're taking with me!"

Luckily for me, as we stood furiously confronting each other, Joire, the French director, came by and, after listening briefly to the reason for the dispute, decided that I was right. Outside my door Pelerin commented indignantly to Rostlam, "Now he's running the whole show here. He's carrying on worse and worse. The directors do whatever he asks. Next thing you know they'll be handing him the keys."

May 16, 1963   Today after eighteen years I stopped smoking. I did so to test my strength. Perhaps also to get myself into condition for life on the outside, for I have come within three years of that.

June 3, 1963   Whitsunday. Operas are no longer banned; Pretty Margret lets them pass, although with a fierce expression. Today Mozart's *Cosi fan tutte*, acquired years ago, was played for the first time.

June 12, 1963   To combat the monotony I have decided on a change in my sleeping habits of many years. I am now again lying with my head on the window side. Mornings I no longer look into the bright light which hitherto has always waked me. From above a current of fresh air reaches my lungs. However, the constant draft around my head will not be bearable in the long run. So I shall introduce a summer and a winter sleeping position.

June 16, 1963   Summer weather. Tanned as a vacationer. Sometimes these days I wear nothing but gym trunks in the heat of the sun. Years ago that was strictly forbidden—now nobody notices. The lawn sprinkler runs day and night; everyone too phlegmatic to turn it off.

June 18, 1963   After the good four-week spell I have given myself, today I handed pipes plus tobacco pouch into the baggage storage, where they will lie with 481 of the pipe cleaners that were sent to me years ago. My original idea was to hand in all seven pipes at once, but I rejected that because it would have been making my renunciation too easy for my taste.

At the end of the sixteenth century a dour observer of the fashion of

pipe smoking, which Sir Walter Raleigh had introduced, wrote: "A repulsive, stinking smoke, repugnant to the nose, injurious to the brain,
harmful to the lungs; it produces effeminacy, leads to flabbiness and
weakness, destroys courage." I wonder whether ladies have a special liking for smokers because smoking has taken from the men some of their
toughness.

June 19, 1963   The lists of the Spandau library's new acquisitions
were handed out this evening. We are to write down which books we
want. Hess asks me: "Check some for me, so that I don't have to read
through the whole thing." I picked out for Hess a few titles such as: *A
Manual of Oratory, How to Become a Politician,* and *Lais, the Art of
Love among Corinthian Women.*

July 26, 1963   Fiery heat in the garden today. Scarcely a breath
of wind. Now and then I walk through the mist of water from the garden sprinkler. For a few hours today I hauled water for the fruit trees; I
let the larger ones have three cans, the smaller ones either one or two. I
carried fifty-six filled watering cans an average of forty meters; that
comes (as I determine compulsively) to 2.2 kilometers.

In the evening it was eighty-four degrees inside the building.

August 3, 1963   Since the chaplain is on vacation, instead of divine services we receive two-hour recorded concerts. For today I asked
for the Brahms Violin Concerto and Schubert's Seventh Symphony. In
turning over the apparatus to me, Felner told me that by a new decision of the director the records must be played very softly, with the volume turned way down.

"That's nonsense," I burst out excitedly. "Then I'd rather do without it altogether."

Bray gave me a good-natured and simultaneously amused look
through his horn-rimmed glasses. "Whatever you do, don't strike! Make
some positive proposal. Request earphones. You have to show goodwill." He is after all an old prison hand.

This evening I heard Schirach say triumphantly to Hess that the
new order had been issued in response to his complaint. He said that so
loudly that I could not help hearing it.

August 12, 1963   Arrived in Fairbanks. Now I set out on the
great arctic highway to the south.

August 16, 1963 At my request the administration has placed a mark on the volume control to indicate how high I may turn it up without violating the new ordinance. The volume is exactly what it has always been. Schirach's action has failed.

This evening I received the news that Margret has given birth to my first granddaughter, Annegret. The youngest of my children was born almost exactly twenty years ago.

September 2, 1963 Beitz has informed the family that an effort must be made, through the Soviet ambassador, to talk with Khrushchev in person; there is no point to any other course. Herr Smirnov must find it odd to be approached in succession by such very different persons as Lübke, Brandt, Beitz, Mommsen, Carlo Schmid, Kroll, Niemöller, Carstens, and others in connection with my case.

September 28, 1963 At the moment I am preoccupied with a curious chain of disasters that have been pursuing Rostlam of late. It began several weeks ago when his son had an automobile accident on a rain-slick road. But he escaped without serious injury. Shortly afterwards Rostlam and his wife went out to do some errands because the family was to sail home on the *America* a few days later. When they returned, their son was lying in bed dead; it seemed he had swallowed the wrong way and suffocated. When they left, therefore, they departed with the body in a coffin. Barely arrived in America, they heard that a nephew had fallen from a scaffolding and been killed. A few days later Rostlam's father-in-law died suddenly. Some time ago one of Rostlam's brothers had been killed in a hunting accident; another brother had then assumed the place of the father for the orphaned nephew and then, shortly after Rostlam's arrival in the United States, was murdered by two escaped convicts who wanted to steal his truck. His body was found only after a lapse of many days. Rostlam himself was appointed one of the pallbearers. On the way to the grave the coffin was dropped and broke open because one of the pallbearers suffered heatstroke.

What stuns me about such events is the absence of any causal connection. Not even a moral significance can be read into them; there is no guilt. Unlike the tragedy of the House of Atreus, where at any rate a compensating principle seems to have been operating, throwing a cast of moral necessity upon the events, here the virtually complete extermination of a family is due to nothing but blind chance. There is no way to face such meaningless events but to assume that some fault not detectable in the moral realm is present in the metaphysical sphere.

The Eighteenth Year

October 1, 1963 Yesterday half an hour with Ulf, today with Hilde. Such visits after a gap of a year remain strangely unreal and at the same time painful. By strict control, I try to keep down any expression of emotion, for that would make me lose my composure entirely. Afterwards, when the children have gone, I feel exhilarated every time, however badly the conversations went. I pour out on the guards a veritable torrent of words. This is something I note with astonishment.

October 5, 1963 Today I spoke to the chaplain about my feeling of having lost all touch with the children forever. When he asked me how often I am able to see them, my eyes filled with tears of grief. I told him that the worst of it was to have to tell myself, after each meeting, that now I would not be able to see my child again for an entire year. Then I walked away quickly.

October 7, 1963 Today in the garden I found some of the jottings Hess uses for his talks with Schirach: "Bantus produce more children than goods," the note read. Also: "Lübke congratulates the USSR on the anniversary of the October Revolution." And finally this: "Ultrasound (English) 250 g distance. Hard or soft surface. The premier of Schleswig-Holstein endorses special taxes on tobacco and alcohol."

At first this scrap of paper with its curious hodgepodge of subjects amused me. Then I felt taken aback. How depressingly empty our prison world must be if such inconsequentialities have to be noted. In fact it is my experience, too, that lack of events does not increase but diminishes the importance of the few subjects we have to discuss.

October 20, 1963 Solin, the nice new Russian, today picked a few raspberries still left on the everbearing canes here and there, and brought them to me on a rhubarb leaf.

Letham returned to Schirach his petition asking that the library purchase the novels of Fontane and Hamsun and the dramas of Hebbel. "You cannot write 'as soon as possible,' and worse yet, underline it," he told Schirach. "That's just too arrogant." When Schirach protested, Letham told him to rewrite the petition.

"But I'm always the one who writes the friendliest notes to the directors," Schirach commented, taken aback. Glancing at the petition, I noticed that it was signed "respectfully yours." Hess, on the other hand, usually signs his communications to the administration "Number Seven," implying that it would be a pity to waste his proper name on requests of this type.

October 22, 1963 Hilde has transmitted an offer from the Berlin publisher Propyläen Verlag for an option on my memoirs. To be sure, between one and two thousand pages of memoirs and about the same amount of supplementary essays and insertions are already written, but do I really want to get myself talked about? Whatever plans I have to begin a new career as an architect or executive would suffer from publication, that is beyond doubt. So what I say to the publisher more or less involves the decision on my future course.

Therefore I am asking the family to procrastinate politely. Still and all, I am tempted by the thought of having my memoirs published under an imprint familiar to me since my days as a graduate student, when I read the Propyläen history of art. In any case, the publishing house that wanted to bring out the memoirs would also have to be ready to publish my projected treatises on the architecture of the Third Reich, on armaments, on architecture in painting, and perhaps also the treatise on windows.

What plans! Will the third phase of my life be that of a scribbler?

November 2, 1963   Fabian von Schlabrendorff, one of the few surviving army officers of the active resistance, has offered to take over my case. He must be informed that according to the new Penal Code of the Soviet Union the maximum penalty has been fixed at ten, or in especially grave cases at fifteen, years, as I learn from the *Berliner Zeitung*. The law explicitly provides that the new maximum penalties also apply to persons who have already been sentenced to longer penalties. In my case the fifteen years were up two years ago.

November 15, 1963   Hess is planting strawberries. "Too late, Herr Hess," I remarked. "They won't have time to take root." Whereas Schirach merely looked on during the Western months, he has been pitching in since the beginning of the Russian month.

November 19, 1963   Schirach's request was approved today: Hebbel's collected works, Cervantes's *Don Quixote*, and novels by Theodor Fontane and Knut Hamsun have been bought for the library. To this day I cannot grasp what the reason for the purchase is, since we can obtain any book from the city library. Buying some reference works would have seemed to me far more sensible.

Meanwhile I am reading Jean Paul Sartre's *L'Age de raison*. Like much of today's writing, this startles and perturbs me. What is going on? Perhaps in prison I lead a more sheltered, more protected life than people on the outside. Sartre's characters are obviously more isolated in their loneliness than we here in our cells. Moreover, their isolation cannot be ended; they will never be free. At least I have a hope; perhaps it is only an illusion, but it is something I can cling to. I also ask myself whether this novel describes actual conditions, or whether it is the description of anxieties. In general I am struck by how little modern literature reflects the reality of outward life. From the novels of Balzac or Tolstoy or the great English novelists of the nineteenth century it is possible to form a pretty exact picture of the people of the time and the society in which they lived. Today, it seems to me, literary characters are like phantoms, and the society is present only as something talked about, but not really there.

November 25, 1963   I feel that Kennedy's assassination is not just an American tragedy, but a tragedy for the world. And I could not help thinking that here only one confused loner was at work, so it seems; he conceived the plan and the assassination was successful. But the attempts on Hitler's life—how many undertakings there were, planned with the precision of a General Staff operation by circumspect, cool-headed people, year after year, and never did they succeed—that is the real tragedy.

December 1, 1963   During the garden period I talked with Hess for a full hour about family, about excavations in Baghdad, and, as always with him, about the past. He spoke with special enthusiasm about the regime's achievements in cultural and social matters, about Professor Bier's theories on mixed forests, about Göring's regulations on hunting and nature preserves, and on the "philosophy of the beauty of the highway" developed by Todt, which was ultimately made a reality in the Autobahnen. In talking about this he mentioned such points as the idea that Autobahnen must be kept clear of all disturbing structures, that the bridges were to be built of the natural stone of each region, and that directional signs should be kept as small as possible. Landscape architects had supervised the plans, he said, to insure that the course of the road should conform to the landscape. When we parted shortly after four o'clock, a rich orange-red sky announced a cold night. I drained the water from the garden pool.

Now, evening in the cell, I have been thinking back on the regime's interest in beauty, which in fact was very marked. The ruthlessness and inhumanity of the regime went hand in hand with a remarkable feeling for beauty, for the virginal and unspoiled, although that feeling quite often degenerated into the sentimentality of a postcard idyll. Today I sometimes read statements to the effect that all this was merely camouflage, a calculated maneuver to distract the attention of the suppressed masses. But that was not so. Of course the regime's craving for beauty also had to do with Hitler's personal taste, with his hatred for the modern world, his fear of the future. But there was also an unselfish social impulse at work, an effort to reconcile the unavoidable ugliness of the technological world with familiar aesthetic forms, with beauty. Hence the ban on corrugated iron roofing for farm buildings, hence Autobahn maintenance buildings in half-timber style, hence birch woods and man-made lakes at army camps. As chief of the Beauty of Work Office I was responsible for a part of this program, and I still take unabashed satisfaction in what we accomplished.

But I do also see the dubious aspect of such efforts. I still recall how Himmler in 1943, after we had dined together in the Rastenburg bunker, talked glowingly about the future border villages for German peasants in the East, the *Wehrbauerndörfer*. There would be village ponds, village greens, window boxes of geraniums at the farmhouses;

there must certainly be a village linden tree, and oaks lining the streets. The new settler was to feel at home immediately in a kind of ideal German landscape. Hitler saw eye to eye with him on all this. In this connection it occurs to me that among the paintings submitted for the Munich art show he preferred to pick out the works that were "beautiful" in the traditional sense, and only reluctantly took note of the dutiful paintings glorifying the regime.

December 2, 1963 Pretty Margret, the Soviet censor, paid her farewell visit to the directors yesterday. I wonder whether her successor will be any better. She was not unpleasant, not inclined to harass, but had that exaggerated energy, that lack of calm, which women in responsible positions often exhibit.

December 3, 1963 The monotony of my days can scarcely be conveyed in these notes. The forever unchanging sameness of more than six thousand days cannot be recorded. A great poet might possibly be able to express the numbing evenness, the emptiness and helplessness, in short the intangible horror of imprisonment. Compared to what should be said, the diary remains nothing but a catalogue, usually of trivialities.

December 4, 1963 At half past two today I went into the garden to prune the chestnut trees. When I came along with the big pruning shears, Hess remarked, "What are you up to with that murderous weapon? Don't leave it lying around anywhere. The thing exerts a suggestive effect on me."
Schirach is limping badly today: the American doctor came in the afternoon to look at him. Toward evening Pease brought word that Schirach has an embolism in a vein. Pease said he has already been given an injection to inhibit clotting of the blood. Now, watched by Mees, he has been put in the infirmary for the night. His temperature and blood pressure are being taken every four hours, so I have just heard. The doctor in the hospital is on call. Tomorrow morning Schirach is to be X-rayed. George Reiner, the new guard, a German-American, frequently comes to my cell to discuss Schirach's illness, as does Long.

December 5, 1963 For the past several days I have been reading the works of Schiller, in some cases for the second time during these years. In spite of the persistently high-pitched, adolescent emotionalism of his language, which often makes me smile, his world of noble thoughts and strong feelings repeatedly captivates me. In this respect he seems to me entirely un-German. Wherever he touches, nothing remains narrow and provincial; nothing retains that smugness so frequently characteristic of German literature. Instead, everything becomes great. Even when he is dealing with petty relationships, as in *Kabale und Liebe* or *Die Räuber*, he always aims for the absolute. The dishonoring of a young woman, for example, does not remain limited to the superficial and personal realm, but promptly expands into an ethical problem for all mankind.

It strikes me that in the theater it has always been only this tone and this complex of problems that have truly interested me. Unless the scene opened out into a matter of political or humanitarian importance, it would strike me as virtually inconsequential. [Schiller's] *Wallenstein* always meant more to me than [Hauptmann's] *Rose Bernd*, *Hamlet* more than Gorki's *Lower Depths*. Am I wrong when I think that the literature of the theater during the past hundred years has tended to concentrate more and more on small familiar disturbances? All these petty-bourgeois tragedies about illegitimate children and problem drinkers elicit my full sympathy in the social realm, but in the theater they seem to me to yield nothing but boredom. An aid-to-dependent-children allowance or a withdrawal cure paid for by social insurance—and the whole lovely tragedy becomes pure melodrama.

Tomorrow I shall begin *Maria Stuart*.

December 6, 1963   Yesterday, at half past five, shortly after supper, Godeaux came rushing into my cell with the news that Schirach is going to the hospital at once. I asked Hess whether I should go to see Schirach and say goodbye. "His reaction to such unexpected gestures is to assume right off that his last hour has come," Hess replied. "Besides, your visit would give him no pleasure." But Hess visited Schirach and brought him news of the impending transfer. Schirach had actually known nothing about it. A few minutes later, however, Godeaux denied the report: "Nothing has been decided. The Russian hasn't approved yet." Probably Godeaux was only trying to cover his tracks.

At seven o'clock Bray informed me that Schirach had been driven away with all the fanfare of a potentate. Since Funk's trip to the hospital, something like protocol for the ceremony exists: The four directors together hand the patient over and come to claim him when he is to be sent back.

December 8, 1963 Cold, foggy air. Twelve rounds with Hess. "Today we see how wonderfully quiet a life for two in Spandau would be," Hess commented. "No loud talking, no singing, no whistling."

December 9, 1963 Yesterday's bulletin on Schirach in both the *Frankfurter Allgemeine* and in the *Daily Telegraph,* which Pease showed me, was: "Satisfactory."

December 14, 1963 Yesterday and today my wife's customary pre-Christmas visit. Shortly before her arrival the Russian on duty informed me: "You are not permitted to say that Number One is in the hospital, nor tell her anything about his illness." I was too weary to explain to him how foolish his warning was. Probably he doesn't know that all the newspapers are full of the story.

December 17, 1963 This morning I went to the infirmary to greet Schirach, back from the hospital but still bedridden. We shook hands for the first time in years. He extended his as though he were granting a boon.

December 20, 1963 In the past few days Hess has been spending hours in the infirmary. Now Schirach has harshly told him not to come any more. Hess was put out. "I like that! When he needs company he'll send for me in the future! Who does he think he is?"

Charles Pease reported: "In fact, he actually threw him out."

Have read Schiller's *Wallenstein* for three evenings—the play that made so lasting an impression on me as a schoolboy. In those days I did not yet know about the banal conditions in the circles of the mighty. Once again, what tremendous intensifications of reality in Schiller! Stripped of all unprepossessing and accidental features, the characters as well as the conflicts emerge with far greater sharpness. As a schoolboy I took sides with Wallenstein, the half rebel. Today I know how immature that was. In reality I was probably less impressed by Wallenstein than by Schiller himself, who mobilized the very constellations in order to provide grandeur and background for divided humans' inability to make decisions.

December 25, 1963 For days Hess has been trying to get medical attention by putting on from four to six bouts of cramps a day. Mees told the doctor, "Please don't call on Hess; if you do he will feel that attention is being paid to him and will get even sicker." Last night, Christmas Eve, toward midnight, I could hear the sounds of a prolonged attack from Hess's cell. Wails and moans, just like years ago. The medical aide was fetched from a Christmas party. As always, Hess fell asleep after an injection of distilled water.

This afternoon the American director personally brought the gifts from our families to the cells. For the first time they were still in their Christmas wrappings. I received four records, a shirt, a pair of gloves, socks, soap, and a black headband such as skiers wear.

From the infirmary, where Schirach is still in bed, a music box bleated "Silent Night" steadily as I unpacked my gifts. Evidently a Christmas present. It played perhaps twenty times. I thought of "Lili Marlene."

January 1, 1964   When the guards were relieved at eight o'clock, Pelliot came into the cellblock singing. Shortly thereafter Hess turned up at my cell and commented, "He's now visited me four times to wish me a Happy New Year." While Pelliot slept it off in the chief guard's room, Sharkov took over the task of conducting prisoners into the garden. Amused, he said, "Colleague is sick."

During the past few weeks I had built up a stack of prunings nearly two meters high. Today I placed the Advent wreath on it. At twilight, around half past three, I lit the pile. It blazed up several meters into the air.

Toward evening Schirach was transferred back to his cell. Rostlam remarked sarcastically, "Back home again!"

January 2, 1964   Today there were twenty centimeters of crisp powder snow, sunshine, dry air, snow-covered trees. During the past week several of the guards rebelled when I wanted to use the full working period of three and a half hours. Naturally I understand that the guards prefer to read their newspapers in the warmth. But today Solin was chief guard; without pity for his freezing colleague Rostlam, he let me work in the garden at five degrees Fahrenheit.

In the evening I finished Ernst Kantorowicz's *Frederick the Second, 1194–1250.* I remembered the tour I undertook a few months before the outbreak of the war, attempting to follow the traces of Frederick through Sicily and Apulia. My wife and I visited the castles, fortresses, and chapels built during the age of the great Hohenstaufen emperor. There seemed to be a certain deliberate intention behind the way the Fascist government was allowing these monuments of so important a German to crumble from neglect. Even the famous tomb of Frederick

II in Palermo cathedral looked untended; scraps of paper and cigarettes lay all around it. After my return I proposed to Hitler that the bones of Frederick II in their beautiful, classical marble sarcophagus be moved and placed under the grand tabernacle in our Berlin Soldiers Hall. I said the Duce might not be unhappy to have this reminder of a period of weakness in Italian rule outside the country. Besides, after all, he had presented Göring with the much more valuable Sterzing altar.

Hitler listened, smiling benevolently.

January 5, 1964 The thousand-day barrier has been broken. Now only nine hundred and ninety-nine days remain, assuming that I have to remain here until the last hour. With this as a pretext I have tried to arrange a small party. I managed to have half a bottle of champagne brought to me and drank it down, lying on my bed. Then, on the transistor radio, I heard a festival performance of Richard Strauss's *Ariadne auf Naxos*.

January 8, 1964 Today Hess took a brisk walk with Pelerin, the former lightweight boxer who in a few years of doing nothing in Spandau has eaten himself into the heavyweight class. Pelerin now weighs 220 pounds and is forever worrying about exceeding that limit. Soon the Frenchman gave up, breathless. Hess remarked in a victorious mood, "After eight rounds I knocked him flat morally and physically."

"But you weigh little more than a hundred and ten pounds," I replied. "Pelerin has to carry around twice as much as this bag of fertilizer weighs." We tried out the meaning of this increased weight by carrying the bag to the flower beds. After a hundred meters we too were breathless.

January 30, 1964 Thirty-one years ago today Hitler took power. In our small Mannheim apartment I listened on the radio to the description of the historic torchlight parade that was marching past Hindenburg and Hitler; I never suspected that I might be playing a part in the new era. I did not even take part in the small victory celebration put on by the Mannheim Party organization.

A few months later I met Hitler by chance. And from that moment on everything changed; my whole life was constantly lived under a sort of high tension. Strange, how quickly I gave up everything that had been important to me up to then: private life with my family, my leanings, my principles of architecture. Yet I never had the feeling that I was making a break, let alone betraying anything I cherished; rather the feeling was one of liberation and intensification, as though only then was I coming to my proper self. In the following period Hitler accorded me many triumphs, acquaintanceship with power and fame— but he also destroyed everything for me. Not only a life work as an architect and my good name, but above all my moral integrity. Condemned as a war criminal, robbed of my freedom for half a lifetime, and burdened with the permanent sense of guilt, I must in addition live in the awareness that I founded my whole existence on an error. All my other experiences I share with many; this one is my own.

But is it true that Hitler was the great destructive force in my life? Sometimes it seems to me as though I also owed to him all the surges of vitality, dynamism, and imagination that gave me the sense that I was soaring up above the ground on which everyone else was condemned to stand. And what do I mean when I say he took away my good name? Would I have had any name at all but for him? Paradoxically, I might actually say that this is the one thing he did give me and never again will be able to take from me. It is possible to thrust a person into history, but then no longer possible to push him out of it. I could not help thinking of that recently when I read Grabbe's *Hannibal*. The Punic general has likewise reached the end of all his hopes. Before he takes the cup of poison from his Negro slave, the slave asks what will come after the drink. "We will not fall out of the world; we are in it once and for all."

So then I ask myself: Would I like to fall out of history? What does a place in it mean to me, slight though it may be? If thirty-one years ago today I had been confronted with the choice of leading a quiet and respected life as city architect of Augsburg or Göttingen, with a house in the suburbs, two or three decent buildings done a year, and vacations with the family in Hahnenklee or Norderney—if I had been offered all that or else everything that has happened, the fame and the guilt, the world capital and Spandau, together with the feeling of a life gone awry—which would I choose? Would I be prepared to pay the price all over again? My head reels when I pose this question. I scarcely dare to ask it. Certainly I cannot answer it at all.

February 19, 1964 No entries for more than two weeks. But I have kept pursuing the question I recently set. In the interval there has been something of a shift inside me. Was it really the ambition to enter history that drove me on? This is the question I ask myself now. What really was the determining impetus of my life, the driving force of all my actions? One thing I know for certain: Unlike most of the members of Hitler's intimate circle, I did not have a crippled psyche. I was free of corrosive resentment. That fact also immunized me against Hitler's ideology. I was no antisemite; the racial ideas always seemed to me a crotchet; and I also never thought much of the Darwinistic theory of struggle and killing with which Hitler was obsessed; and finally the whole Lebensraum program was alien to me, much as I too wanted to see Germany big and powerful.

Then what was it actually? First and foremost there was the personality of Hitler, which for a long time exerted a hypnotic and compelling effect upon me. But it was not that alone. Almost as strong, if not stronger, was the sense of intoxication Hitler engendered in me, the tremendous intensification of my confidence in my abilities, and which I soon needed like an addict his drug. Then, during the war, as armaments minister, I noticed for the first time that power also meant something to me, the ordinary ambition to belong among the actors in historic events. I remember when Hitler gave me the assignment to build the Atlantic Wall, a system of fortifications from North Cape to the Pyrenees, what feelings of exultation filled me when my signature could mean the expenditure of billions of marks and direct hundreds of thousands of people to the construction sites. Only in retrospect do I become aware that as an architect at Hitler's side I was also seeking the pleasures of power.

Yet I am fairly certain that I was artist enough to have given up all the power in the world without regrets if a single perfect building had been granted me, perfect as the Pantheon, the dome of St. Peter's, or one of Palladio's temple-like mansions. To enter history with such a building—that was the ambition that impelled me. That is why I told Hitler, at the height of the war, at the height of my successes as armaments minister also, that I wanted nothing but to be an architect again.

February 27, 1964 I still have music in my coat pocket! Today I heard *Die Frau ohne Schatten*, conducted by Karl Böhm. A few days ago, moreover, I heard a production of *Parsifal* under Knappertsbusch that moved me deeply.

March 3, 1964 My request for the delivery of larkspur, stock, and clematis, as well as fifteen birdhouses, has been approved. Letham, it is true, asked, "Aren't fifteen houses too many?" Actually I had expected that the directors would allow only part of my request. We decided five would do.

March 16, 1964 Hess has listed several hundred titles of books he would like to have. Today he was told that he is no longer permitted to list more than a hundred titles. His interests center in general on sociology and political economy, but in particular on the ills of civilization. He has long been pursuing the connections between such phenomena and liberal democracy. Again and again he comes to me with examples of overconsumption in the United States. He happily notes reports of misguided investments in the market economy, collects examples of land speculation, criminality, bad posture in children, and health damage caused by canned foods. Out of frequently ridiculous and atypical items he is putting together his vision of doom, against the background of which he will presumably see arising, one of these days, the figure of the savior once more.

March 19, 1964 My fifty-ninth birthday—the nineteenth in prison—began with spilled salt. That was at breakfast. Afterwards I had my hair cut. Then everything as usual.

March 24, 1964 Since the beginning of the Russian month, March, I have noted down how often we have the same dish. The result: cabbage salad ten times, beets twenty times, canned tomatoes eight times, goulash forty times, boiled potatoes forty-eight times, carrots thirty-five times, and finally butter, bread, and ersatz coffee fifty times.

Pointless statistics, I know. Also pointless that I am writing them down here. What makes me do it, then?

March 26, 1964 Today, from five o'clock in the morning on, a blackbird concert. It woke me up. When I clambered to the window to look at the bird, the thought came to me that these are the selfsame notes that prehistoric men, the Neanderthals or the cave painters of the Dordogne, heard. What a strange link runs across the ages!

At six o'clock the bird's concert was replaced by Schirach. Once again while washing he lamented the disappearance of "Martha, Martha," but soon passed from the fickleness of women's hearts to the bright bank of the Saale, where in the slow coming of dawn he was at last liberated by an early death:

> *Morgenrot, Morgenrooot,*
> *Leuchtest mir zum frühen Toooood. . . .*

Nine o'clock. Hess had received several books from his wife, but wants to send one of them back. "Of course it was on my list, but it turns out to be a novel and I don't read novels on principle," he declared. Then he instructed the Russian chief guard: "The book is being returned to my wife. I'll bring it to you right away." He seemed oddly excited as he spoke, and his agitation increased when he knocked at my open door, book in hand. "Has this book been read or not?" he asked hurriedly. "Just look at it: has it been read or not? I ask you: I've read it up to this point. And the pages show it. But from here on it's unread. Yet my wife wrote me—do listen to me, Herr Speer!—that she and my son had read the book. In addition the censor must have read it —all together three persons. And do you know what conclusion follows from that?" he asked nervously, his eyes darting about uncertainly. "Now we have definite proof at last! Ha, ha!" He wrapped his knuckles on the cell wall. "Ha, ha! It isn't even the book my wife sent me. It's simply been exchanged. Ha, ha!" I looked at him speechlessly as he cavorted before me. "Don't you understand?" he cried out. "The Directorate bought another copy of the book. What do you say to that?"

I shook my head, mute and irritated. Hess, who will be seventy next month, froze, then straightened up proudly and said over my head, "I understand, you prefer to keep silent." Then he turned abruptly and stalked stiffly out of the cell.

April 4, 1964   Schlabrendorff is back from Washington. He was received by Soviet Ambassador Dobrynin, who is said to have spoken with him frankly. Among the detailed conditions for my release the Russian side have specified: that in the future I will not engage in political activity—which I will gladly pledge; assurance that I will have a sound financial basis; release of Communist prisoners in the Federal Republic; and then a deal with the firm of Krupp to trade with the USSR.

April 26, 1964   Today is Hess's seventieth birthday. I wished him all the best. The cook had taken notice of the event and declared, as he set platter upon platter on the serving table, with pretended annoyance, "And that too, and that, and that, for their lordships the prisoners!" It really was a kind of banquet: baked trout, guinea hen, cake with whipped cream, fruit, chocolate custard, and then nonalcoholic drinks. In the afternoon the American and British directors came together to Hess's cell to congratulate him. But before they had a chance to speak up, Hess said stiffly, "My thanks for that accidental good meal."

June 12, 1964 Today a festival concert for the centennial of Richard Strauss's birth was broadcast by the Dresden Staatskapelle, with which the composer had his greatest triumphs. For the first time I heard the Metamorphoses for String Orchestra in F major, which was written in 1945, shortly before the end of the war. A staggering musical document of the days of the collapse, composed on the basis of the funeral march of the *Eroica*. Lamentation, despair, wailing in the face of the apocalypse that has descended upon the Fatherland, and then in the end a dubious, hardly intimated hope. Strauss was eighty at the time, had placed himself at the disposal of the Third Reich as president of the Reichsmusikkammer, and shared many of the most common illusions about the regime. In this work, it seems to me, he unburdened himself of the things that weighed on his spirit: the sense of being in a blind alley, the perception of his own guilt, the knowledge of all that had been irrevocably lost. Then came the Concerto for Horn and Orchestra no. 1, and finally the symphonic poem *Also Sprach Zarathustra*, that soaring music associated in my mind with mountain solitude, prophetic verse, and Sils Maria. For a few seconds after the final chords the audience kept still from sheer emotion. Then came the applause.

June 22, 1964 Today one of the guards smuggled in a Minox camera with which I took three rolls of color film, mostly of the garden. I was able to shield the little camera with my hand, except for the lens. At home these pictures will give them a notion of what my world looks like outside of the visiting room. Most of my pictures are of my flower beds; they will see from that how proud I am of them. After all, those flowers, along with these notes, are the only things that have steadily engaged my attention all these twenty years.

If the shots turn out well, my wife and the children will see lovely pictures of iris, pinks, stock, and lupines—all things, of course, that they can find in the nursery garden around the corner.

June 23, 1964 I am more and more measuring the remaining time of imprisonment on my "Spandau clock." It has by now reached 27 seconds after 9:26 p.m. I am disappointed, for I thought it would be considerably later. The smallest unit of time, a second, corresponds to two hours and ten minutes in Spandau.

June 24, 1964 This morning awoke with severe toothache. Sharkov had a look at me, for it is up to him to sign the pass for the American dentist. Laconically, he declared, "Toothache no catastrophe." But, he added, he would telephone his director by the direct wire between the prison and Karlshorst.

The dentist, who holds a colonel's rank, X-rayed me a few hours later; in the afternoon he pulled one tooth, while another broke during extraction. My jaw was transformed into a mine; the remnants were removed with hammer, chisel, and drill in a session lasting more than an hour. Just in case, a French physician was on the scene.

July 23, 1964   Another five weeks without an entry. Worked a great deal in the garden, read little. Apathetic.

July 25, 1964   Some days ago I asked Bray for the name of a good American dictionary. A few days later he arrived with a fat new Webster's. "This is for you. My goodbye present." He is leaving us in a few weeks because the prison atmosphere is repugnant to him. "I'll put the book in the library right away," Bray said. "Nobody will notice. But it is for you!"

I had a better idea, and filed a request to have my family send me a French and an American dictionary. After that was approved, Hilde delivered Bray's Webster's and a *Petit Larousse* to the administration. Then, during one whole nighttime duty period, Sharkov leafed through the two big volumes to make sure that no secret message was marked in them. I find this concern ridiculous but also reassuring. For they would not go to the trouble if they knew anything about my illegal communication with the outside. Andrysev turned up this morning and said amiably, "Unfortunately a few passages have to be cut out of the dictionaries. Do you consent?" I said I did.

A few hours later both volumes were delivered to me. Five or six places were cut out, three of them under the letter H.

July 27, 1964   Seven-eighths of my whole sentence have been served. I reckon out, for example, that after Ernst's next visit in October, he will come only once more. I will also not bother creating a compost heap in the fall. This time I'll burn the leaves and use the ashes to improve the soil. I'll start wearing out my shirts and underclothes and will ask them at home to send me only recordings of single-instrument performances for Christmas and my birthday; for there is a stereo set at home and only the records of single instruments do not forfeit some of their sonority.

August 4, 1964   Schlabrendorff's call on Khrushchev's son-in-law, Adjubei, who happens to be visiting the Federal Republic, has gone well. The Russian dropped promising hints in regard to my case. After his return there was something in *Izvestia*, of which he is editor-in-chief, about "elimination of some remnants of the consequences of the war," if the German side were prepared to be obliging.

August 9, 1964   I have again been reading a great many professional books of late. If I am released and want to work again, I have to keep abreast of current developments.

Now that I have been giving rather more thorough study to the reconstruction since 1945, I am struck by how enormously the whole look of the country has changed. I will find the cities that I left as ruins largely rebuilt, but I will also find them greatly transformed. From the accounts I have read and from newspaper pictures, it seems to me that the formerly distinct character of German cities has been lost in the fever of rebuilding. The everlastingly stereotyped form of commercial buildings as well as residential units has obliterated the difference between a north German commercial metropolis and a south German episcopal seat. It has also given to the profile of German cities a quality of international facelessness.

But above all what surprises me is the undifferentiated triumph of high-rise architecture, from the inner cities all the way out into the countryside. In my time the rule held that high-rise was aesthetically permissible as well as economically feasible only in downtown areas. The extraordinary costs of foundations and the high construction and maintenance costs made the high-rise profitable only where top prices per square meter could be asked, and the highest rents exacted, as in New York, in the City of London, or in Berlin C 1. But now I see in the newspapers that high-rises have been built not only in middle-sized cities such as Ulm, Freiburg, and Giessen, but also in the picturesque small towns of the Lüneburg Heath and on mountain roads. Sometimes it seems to me that a second, and this time self-inflicted, devastation of Germany is taking place. How jealously the country always used to guard its national individuality; how much its special sense of being a cultured nation meant to it—even to excess. In the light of that, how much goodbye and giving up there is in this new trend. To someone of my nature, with my sentimental feeling for tradition, it would have been painful enough if this second and undoubtedly final transformation of Germany's architectural look had been undertaken by Miës van der Rohe, Taut, Hilbersheimer, or Gropius. But what in fact has happened is that the inferior producers of cheap ready-made goods have held the field, as always. In general it strikes me that aside from a few people like Eiermann, Scharoun, or Schwippert, no architect of strong character has been able to set his stamp on the development of building during these twenty years, whereas the first decade after the First World War did see an eruption of genius. It seems to me that a deeper underlying idea is expressed by that fact. In all these years I have repeatedly read of how glad builders have been to take leave of the architectural doctrines of the Third Reich. But couldn't it be that they passed over more than our historical classicism? It may well be that all striving for form ceased. That would mean not only the end of one or more styles, but perhaps the end of architecture itself.

Viewed from such a perspective I see, with some surprise, Scharoun and Le Corbusier, Poelzig and Mendelssohn ranged beside me, while on the other side stand the engineers of the twenty-first century's assembly-line mode of building. And all of us, no matter how opposed we were to one another, would then be figures of a departing era.

August 15, 1964   A second grandchild has arrived. Outside, time moves on.

September 18, 1964   Five weeks without an entry. Today I celebrate the completion of the tenth year of counted kilometers. I have covered 25,471 kilometers!

September 30, 1964   Throughout almost the whole of the past year, the eighteenth of my imprisonment, I was despairing and frightened. The approaching end, coming closer and closer, brought me neither equanimity nor relief.

The Nineteenth Year

October 1, 1964 A few days ago, at the end of the British month, Musker could not make his morning tea. Angrily, he made the following entry in the prison journal: "Overnight the tea was stolen. The Russians Sharkov and Solin were on duty." The Russians took this accusation in bad part. Since yesterday they have stopped greeting; their director is alleged to be ill. The Western directors then proposed sending their sick colleague a bouquet of flowers. But his deputy, Sharkov, icily rejected the gesture. "He's not as sick as all that."

Today the incident was cleared up. During the night in question, Pelliot discovered that the British guards at the gate had no tea, so he brought Musker's tea canister out to them. That was all. Today there was uproarious laughter about it in the cellblock.

And tomorrow, no doubt, the Russian director will have recovered from his illness.

October 2, 1964 Karl Piepenburg, my former chief of building operations, who in 1938 did so much toward completing the Chancellery on schedule, owns a large building company in Düsseldorf. He has sent word that I can count on him should I be looking for commissions after my release. And Otto Apel, formerly my closest associate, is also numbered among the successful architects. He recently built the complex of the American Embassy in Bonn. He too has offered to take me in after my release. This news has reassured me somewhat, but at the same time it intensifies the doubts I recently tried to formulate. By that I don't mean only that it will be difficult for me, as a man of sixty, to find a foothold in the offices of my now established associates. I mean also that their plans and buildings, which impress me favorably on the whole, do confirm my feeling that my time is really past. I also ask myself whether I can resign myself, after designing domed hall and Chancellery, to building a gym in Detmold, an auto laundry for Ingolstadt. Luxurious doubts, God knows!

October 3, 1964   I have been reading in *Die Welt* about Miës van der Rohe's recent visit to Berlin. At eighty-seven he is to build the Gallery of the Twentieth Century by the Landwehr Canal, not too far from the spot I had assigned to the Soldiers Hall, our Pantheon. The Berlin Senate seems a bit disturbed that the architect shows so little interest in considerations of cost. I read that with amusement, but in my mind I wholly take Miës van der Rohe's side. It is in fact a commonplace that great architecture demands great sums. I have always asked myself whether economical democracy can possibly be in a position to provide the country with proper architectural expression. To this day I understand Hitler's indignation over the fact that in the twenties every bank and insurance company could spend more on its administration building than the government could on its public buildings. But Miës also declared that he could scarcely find his way around shattered Berlin any more. How will it be for me?

October 15, 1964   Khrushchev has fallen. They will be disappointed at home, because once again a connection has been broken. I myself am almost without feeling. In earlier years I put on a skeptical pose; but behind it I cherished my illusions, like everyone here. Now they are really gone. The French have the word *assommer*, which means both "beating to death" and "boring to death." This word describes my condition.

October 24, 1964   For several months Hess has been fighting for the right to make good-sized extracts from his reading. He asked for large batches of writing paper for this purpose, but so far his requests have been turned down. Today he made his request to the French general virtually in the form of an ultimatum. "I have no objection to my papers being censored," he declared in an angry tone, "and I would even allow the extracts to be burned later on. But I want to keep all my notes together for a fairly long time, so as to be able to go over them. That is not possible with these few small copybooks."

When Hess's tone become vehement and excited, the general abruptly left the cell. But he stared stunned at the director when the latter confirmed that all our notes are collected from time to time and destroyed by machine. "Is that so?" he asked, surprised and disturbed, and turned away, shaking his head.

November 10, 1964   Cut back the roses today and raked leaves. Nutall started a fire with several issues of the *Daily Telegraph*, and I kept it going with rose canes and leaves. The sun shone; our newly installed thermometer showed thirty degrees in the shade, forty-six in the sunlight on the south wall. The thermometer in the sun helps some of the guards not to feel the cold so keenly. Schirach, meanwhile, walked around whistling "Ol' Man River."

November 11, 1964   The American director, who has been with us for many years, said goodbye and introduced his successor, Eugene Bird. The new director assured us that everything would go along as before; he is incidentally also responsible for clubs and entertainment of American troops stationed in Berlin. Recently the *Kurier* carried a picture of him acting as master of ceremonies; he stood on a platform introducing a beauty queen. As early as 1947 he was assigned to Spandau sentry duty as a lieutenant, but I cannot recall him.

November 12, 1964   During the noon recess today I was having a lively, hour-long chat with Godeaux when Schirach suddenly made his signal flap drop. Indignantly, he demanded quiet; he wanted to sleep, he said. His lordly tone offended the Frenchman, who told Schirach that it was not the prisoner's business to decide when and how the guards should converse. Schirach self-righteously referred Godeaux to the prison rule forbidding guards to speak with prisoners. "Very well, then shut your trap now!" Godeaux replied; he added that singing and whistling were also, incidentally, against the rules. But Schirach refused to be intimidated. "If you don't stop talking with Number Five right this minute, I'll report you to the Russian director," he threatened.

We would not let him bully us, but all the fun had gone out of our chat. Soon we ended it.

November 18, 1964 Today Hess was visited by his lawyer, Dr. Alfred Seidl, for the first time since Nuremberg. Since he has refused all family visits, this is the first outside person he has seen in the nearly twenty years in Spandau. Afterwards, Hess seemed very much worked up. For hours he was lively and accessible. "Seidl was pleased that I looked so well," he said, beaming. "But he hit on the wrong man. First thing I did was to run through a list of all my ailments." Airily, Hess went on: "And then, you see, my son would like to have a look at me. Does that make sense to you?" And when I nodded, he continued: "Yes, as a reward. As a reward if he passes the civil service examination for government architect with a mark of 'good,' he'll be allowed to see his father."

I was stunned. "As a reward?" I repeated. "But he's no longer a small child who has to be rewarded."

Hess smiled proudly to himself, as is his way. "Schirach has the same opinion. But that's the way it's going to be. I've already counted one, two, three."

I did not understand. "One, two, three—what's that all about?" I asked.

"When the number 'three' is spoken," Hess said, "a decision is irrevocable, you see. Then there's nothing more to be done about it."

I said that if I were in his son's place I'd try to fool him. If necessary I would report a false mark in order to have the visit.

"I've already thought of that danger," Hess answered. "I wrote my son some time ago and told him that if there was any trickery he could be certain of not seeing his father. He'd just have wasted the expense of coming to Berlin."

"Was that also true in the old days?" I asked. "Once you'd made a 'one-two-three decision,' you couldn't revise it if a new situation arose?"

Hess shook his head bleakly. "No, never. That wouldn't do."

Afterwards I recalled hearing Hitler mention that even when they were in jail together in Landsberg Fortress, in the course of a discussion Hess would sometimes exclude all concessions by using this formula.

November 18, 1964 While I was writing a letter today, I heard Letham in the corridor. I hastily and nervously stuffed all the paper into my underwear. Then, while fetching the meal, I had the unpleasant feeling that Letham was staring right at the bulging spot. Back in the cell, I uneasily stowed the writing materials between the mattresses and put a handkerchief into what had been the bulging spot on my trouser leg. When I brought the mess things back, Letham paid no attention at all to me. I felt almost sorry about that. For I had already imagined how he would point suspiciously, but with fake geniality, at the bulge, how I would feel the spot, reach in and pull out my handkerchief, exclaiming: "I've been looking everywhere for it."

November 19, 1964 Hess's complaints to the French general have unexpectedly produced results. By decision of the Directorate, we are entitled to a copybook of 190 pages for our notes. This corresponds in size, as Hess has reckoned, to twelve previous copybooks. He now spends hours every day transcribing the contents of his old notebook, which in turn consists of excerpts from earlier writings.

November 20, 1964 A windstorm has blown a sheet of paper with the instructions for the guards of the four nations down from the watchtower to the garden. Use of firearms is permitted only if outsiders penetrate the garden by force; in case of self-defense, only if the prisoner and his accomplices are a threat to the soldiers' life and limb; in case of an attempted escape, only if there is no other way to frustrate it, and even then the guards must try merely to immobilize the prisoner. In no case is killing him permissible.

November 22, 1964 I have been reading Petronius's *Satyricon*, a work of the first century A.D. And I ask myself whether this depiction of excess, corruption, and baseness provides a fairly accurate picture of Roman mores in the time of Nero. For after all, the Empire went on for a good many brilliant centuries before its ultimate disintegration. The same profound pessimism and the same deprecatory verdict on their own particular times can also be found in Horace, Martial, Persius, Juvenal, and Apuleius. There seems to be a kind of law that each generation must see its own mores as corrupt and glorify those of the past. Yet viewed in terms of successive generations, the corruption should have assumed incredible proportions. This is something to hold in mind. It is doubly important in my case, since I know nothing of an outside world. Thus I ask myself whether the contemporary novels I have been reading through these years, the lamentation literature that runs from Böll to Walser, has given me even a halfway reliable picture of present conditions, and whether the dominant aspect of the outside actually is that morass of vice, conformism, Nazi mentality, and mediocrity that has been presented to me.

November 24, 1964   Today I read a story in *Die Welt* that Attorney General Bauer of the state of Hesse has offered a reward of 100,000 marks for the capture of Bormann. There are said to be indications that he is in South America. As I was considering what would happen if I had to confront Bormann, my former bitter enemy, in a trial, short, round-faced, stocky Sadot opened my cell and with an obviously sly note in his voice asked: "By the way, how long do you still have to serve?" Sadot knows perfectly well, of course. When I did not react, he continued, "It says in the papers that your friend Bormann is still alive and that new crimes have been discovered. What did he actually look like?"

Trying to put together a picture of Bormann in my mind, I looked thoughtfully at Sadot. Abruptly, I had an inspiration. As though struck by a sudden illumination, I said with pretended excitement: "No, really, is such a thing possible? Why—why it's absolutely unbelievable! You call yourself Sadot?"

He looked blankly at me. Then he regained his composure. "Certainly, Sadot is my name, Number Five. What's this all about?"

I put on a knowing, somewhat demented smile. "But of course. The very face, the stocky figure, the same size. Fits perfectly. Only the hair, that's been dyed." After a short pause during which he looked expectantly at me, already a bit intimidated, I gave him a jovial poke in the chest. "Man, what a brilliant idea! How did you ever hit on it?"

Sadot gave me a stunned look. "Hit on what, for God's sake?"

"*You're* Bormann! There was always something familiar about you. I can't help telling you it's a stroke of genius. Really, nobody would ever suspect you'd be here. In Spandau!"

For seconds it seemed almost as though Sadot was panic-stricken. Then he flushed furiously and slammed the cell door. I imagine I'll be spared his jokes for a while.

December 1, 1964   Visit from my wife. Only two more Christmases of separation.

December 16, 1964   In turning over my compost heap I found a curled-up hedgehog who had settled down to hibernate there. I carefully put him into the wheelbarrow and transferred him to another compost heap at the other end of the garden. Now I will pile leaves on top of him.

December 19, 1964   Today a photo was handed to me. I couldn't decide which of my sons it was, and became altogether confused. Then I read Ernst's letter and learned that this was a picture of myself as a boy.

December 21, 1964   Today I passed Seattle on the West Coast of the United States. In sixty days, despite cold and high winds, I have covered 560 kilometers. Recently I broke my day's record and in five hours and forty minutes covered twenty-eight kilometers.

By now my tramping has infected several of the guards. Some days four or five persons can be seen on the track, with determined looks on their faces. "I'll tell you the difference between you and me," Hess said to me today. "Your follies are contagious."

December 24, 1964   A few days ago Colonel Bird casually asked me about the customary Christmas dinner in our family. This evening, in accordance with my reply, there was boiled ham, potato salad, horseradish, and asparagus. For dessert, as at home, chocolate ice cream. The asparagus was a mistake, but one I may introduce to the family. The colonel was present when the food was served. As I heard later that evening, he bought all these special things himself and paid for them out of his own pocket.

January 12, 1965   Rather stunned to read an article in *Die Welt* deploring the fact that all former defendants in Allied military tribunals are exempt from further prosecution due to a "transition treaty" between the three Powers and the federal government. Meanwhile the newspapers are full of reports on the Auschwitz trial, and I have the impression that the past, which seemed already sunk in oblivion, is once more being revived. Suddenly I feel something akin to fear of the world out there, which I no longer know and which is beginning to rediscover with so much new passion the things that have been slowly fading for me since Nuremberg, by dint of my conscious acceptance of atonement. And suddenly Spandau seems to me not so much the place of my imprisonment as of my protection.

It would certainly be harder for me if I had once again to face indictment, or even merely charges. Back in Nuremberg everything seemed comprehensible. Good and evil were unequivocally separated from one another. The crimes were so ghastly and the criminals who had taken refuge either in suicide or patent evasions were so abysmal that given only a moderate sense of justice, humanity and dignity, my attitude took shape of its own accord.

In the meantime twenty years have passed. In those twenty years all of the Great Powers who then acted as judges have at least once, and some more often, sat in an imaginary dock: Russian tanks in East Berlin, Indochina in flames, street-fighting in Budapest, Suez, Algeria, and again Indochina, which is now called Vietnam, and then millions of slave laborers in many parts of the world. . . . How much more difficult it has become to accept within oneself the guilty verdict pronounced by those judges. Moreover, the many years of brooding, of dialogues with myself, have dissipated my former guilt feelings. For at bottom every confrontation with one's own guilt is probably an unconfessed search for justification, and even if that were not the case, no human being could go on asserting his own guilt for so many years and remain sincere.

And now this trial! I must seize upon what is being written in the newspapers about Auschwitz now as a kind of support. That can restore the almost lost meaning of these Spandau years, and at the same time help me recover moral clarity.

January 27, 1965 This morning Schirach told British director Procter that he could no longer see anything with his right eye. A few hours later the British senior medical officer drew a sketch in the case history showing two-thirds of the retina not functioning. An eye specialist from headquarters in Mönchen-Gladbach confirmed the diagnosis; Schirach is suffering from a detached retina. An hour later he was transferred to the infirmary.

January 28, 1965 Last night Schirach was taken to the hospital. Colonel Nadysev was shocked because in spite of all the secrecy television crews appeared at the gate with searchlights mounted precisely at the minute Schirach was to leave.

January 29, 1965 Beautiful winter day, snow and sun. In the garden we hung out titmice rings, peanuts spitted on a wire. Pease sewed a few almonds to a thread and fastened the whole thing to a branch. At first the birds tried to snip through the thread with their beaks. When they could not manage, one of them pulled the thread up a few centimeters and put its foot on it; it repeated the maneuver twice more, and the first almond was in reach. Sitting on the wall, the crows watched the titmice, as we did the crows. Who was watching us?

In the evening Mees told me that Schirach was done with Spandau. He would not be returning. And in fact it also seems to me that the loss of one eye would impress even the Soviet Union as a good enough reason for releasing him. Schirach, Mees thought, would not regard the price as too high.

February 3, 1965   The silence in the cellblock is growing more and more uncanny. I almost begin to miss Schirach's nervousness, his restlessness, his singing and whistling. I go walking with Hess more often, but it quickly becomes apparent that I cannot replace Schirach. Once Hess even forgot whom he was walking with. "Did you read," he asked triumphantly, "that they have painted swastikas on a Social Democratic Party shop?"

February 7, 1965   After a ten-week delay, Dr. Seidl has given the newspapers a report to the effect that he has visited Hess and found him in good condition. There could be no question of any mental confusion, he said. Presumably this statement is intended to dispel any plans to transfer Hess to a mental hospital. The lawyer simultaneously announced that his client explicitly rejects any petition for leniency because his sentence is legally invalid. As I see it, this bars all efforts to obtain a release for Hess. The Russians in particular will regard the statement as an affront. But Hess, our Don Quixote, is very pleased with his lawyer's statement.

February 10, 1965   Yesterday Hess officially informed the French and British directors that in the future he will have no more cramps and no pain. He has also sent word of this to the doctor.

In the meantime his son has passed the examination, but has not sent along the report. I asked Hess whether his son knows what "reward" is awaiting him. Hess said no, that he had not written home about this because if he did they might try to trick him.

February 11, 1965   Last night an unexpected snowfall. Out of a pure desire for something to do, by evening I shoveled a path 482 meters in length. Back in the cell I undertook the following calculation: given a path 55 centimeters wide, the height of the snow 20 centimeters, and the length of the path, I moved 50,820 liters of snow. As a test, I thawed one liter of snow. It yielded about one-fourth of a liter of water. So I moved approximately twelve metric tons. Amazing!

February 21, 1965   Today I completed my hundred thousandth round, reaching exactly 27,000 kilometers.

February 23, 1965   Arnold too has married; Renate will soon be coming to visit. How such events always bring on this feeling of remoteness.

March 18, 1965   A few days ago Hess made a scene with Pelerin because the guard did not come immediately after Hess had signaled. Other guards are understanding about such nervous reactions, but Pelerin reported Hess, although he has long been taking private lessons in German from him and, with Hess's help, recently passed the interpreter's examination.

The punishment was two days' withdrawal of newspapers. But it was ineffective, because Pease simply ignored the order and handed all the newspapers out to Hess.

March 19, 1965   The first crocuses in the garden. I had a modest bonfire burning leaves in celebration of entering my seventh decade. For this sixtieth birthday I received seven records as a present, and in addition a physics lecture by Fritz: "Orthotritium and Paratritium."

March 25, 1965   Yesterday Schirach returned. In spite of all our bickerings I paid him a visit in the infirmary. Schirach was delighted and thanked me stiffly for my good wishes.

He talked uninterruptedly for half an hour, telling me that the hospital staff had been instructed to address him as Herr von Schirach. He had been allowed to choose his meals à la carte daily, since he is reckoned as belonging to the officer class. He had also had radio and television. Now and then in the course of his story he casually wove in such phrases as "my suite with bath" or "I then sat down in my easy chair in the parlor."

The climax of his story was the appearance of an Austrian countess who sent him flowers and a written offer of marriage. She drove by his window every day in her Mercedes sports car, he said. But what had excited him most of all was ordinary everyday life on the street; he was almost bursting with excitement as he described to me the heavy traffic and the well-dressed people.

He is virtually blind in one eye. In the oculist's opinion there is a 25 percent danger that someday the sound eye may also go. Touched by his pitiable condition, I left with a cordial: "Do tell me if there's any way I can help you. I would be glad to." He thanked me in measured words. Altogether, I had the impression that he was rather limp and lacking in energy.

In the evening Pease modified the story somewhat. "You know Schirach. Naturally he had a perfectly ordinary sickroom. The anteroom was meant for the military police, and the lady certainly wasn't driving a Mercedes. It was a Fiat Topolino."

April 10, 1965 Today Schirach was transferred from the infirmary back to the cell. In recent weeks he had in any case been spending more time with us than in the infirmary, had also gone walking in the garden with us; but the return nevertheless showed him that his hopes of release were in vain. With this transfer the acute illness is officially declared to be over.

April 28, 1965 The reports on the Auschwitz trial have completely displaced any public recollection that at this time twenty years ago the Second World War and Hitler's empire were reaching their end. And while images of burning cities, refugees on the roads, tank blockades, and dispersed army units rise before my mind's eye, the figure of Hitler rises with them. A figure grown almost senile, bowed and speaking in a feeble voice; yet nevertheless the center of all that was happening. I have occasionally read that during these last weeks he went insane from fury, impotence, and despair over his wrecked plans; but that is wrong. Rather, at the time it was his entourage that seemed to me insane, or at any rate no longer wholly sane. There was General Busse at Freienwalde Manor, for example, who after Hitler's last visit to the front was deeply moved at how frail the Führer looked, and is said to have exclaimed, "I always imagined Frederick the Great after Kunersdorf like that." Or Robert Ley, who had solemnly assured Hitler, "Mein Führer, all the party functionaries will go on fighting even if the Army surrenders; they will fight like lions, like heroes, like"—he gasped for breath "—just like the Russian partisans. They will ride silently through the woods on bicycles and mercilessly attack the enemy." Or General Keitel and my deputy, Saur, who in the spring of 1945 worked out plans for a fleet of four-engine jet bombers which were to appear over American cities and bomb them until the United States was ready to capitulate. I never heard one of them say in the bunker: "The war is lost. In four weeks it will all be over. Isn't there anyone here who thinks beyond that moment?"

Only one did: Hitler himself. When all had lost their heads, he was the only one who had any idea what was going to come next—if not for Germany, at any rate for him personally. I think that all the apparently contradictory types of behavior, the commands to destroy everything and the commands to hold out, everything he did and said, was directed with amazing consistency toward one single point: how he was going to figure in history. A few days ago I was shown Hitler's "Political Testament," edited by the British historian Hugh R. Trevor-Roper. I actually read it with—there is no other phrase for it—speechless repugnance. For while Hitler was radiating confidence at the military conferences, while he was sending tens of thousands of the Hitler Youth against Russian tanks and declaring that unfortified cities were fortresses, he was coolly, soberly, in the superior tones of a philosopher of history, explaining to posterity why it was inevitable that Germany should lose the war. In other words, he himself had believed none of the things he was always saying. His hypnotic, almost pleading insistence to me that I must believe in victory—it had all been a lie, all cynicism. As I read I sometimes thought that this was not Hitler's diction, but the polished, clever style of Goebbels. Still, that would apply only to the style. The ideas, the grandiose visions, the associative logic—all that was Hitler himself. Scales fell from my eyes. This was the Hitler of whom I had always known only a few facets at a time. He was no madman. Perhaps he no longer had any relationship to reality—but he did have one to history.

May 4, 1965 Recently, in these days full of memories, I have considered how I would probably characterize Hitler today, after the passage of twenty years. I think I am now less sure than I ever was. All reflection magnifies the difficulties, makes him the more incomprehensible. Of course I have no doubts at all about the judgment of history. But I would not know how to describe the man himself. No doubt I could say that he was cruel, unjust, unapproachable, cold, capricious, self-pitying, and vulgar; and in fact he was all of those things. But at the same time he was also the exact opposite of almost all those things. He could be a solicitous paterfamilias, a generous superior, amiable, self-controlled, proud, and capable of enthusiasm for beauty and greatness. I can think of only two concepts that include all his character traits and that are the common denominator of all those many contradictory aspects: opaqueness and dishonesty. Today, in retrospect,

I am completely uncertain when and where he was ever really himself, his image not distorted by playacting, tactical considerations, joy in lying. I could not even say what his feeling toward me actually was—whether he really liked me or merely thought how useful I could be to him.

I don't even know what he felt for Germany. Did he love this country even a little, or was it only an instrument for his plans? And what, I have frequently asked myself ever since our disagreements over my memoranda, did he feel in regard to the downfall of the Reich? Did he suffer on its account? Years ago I came across a sentence of Oscar Wilde's which might apply here. I copied it out: "There is no error more common than that of thinking that those who are the causes or occasions of great tragedies share in the feelings suitable to the tragic mood."

May 6, 1965 Because of a phrase that had remained in my memory, but dimly, I reread Schiller's *Die Braut von Messina* today. At last I found the passage I was looking for:

> Doch nur der Augenblick hat sie geboren.
> Ihres Laufes furchtbare Spur
> Geht verrinnend im Sande verloren;
> Die Zerstörung verkündet sie nur.*

May 8, 1965 According to what I read today in the *Berliner Zeitung* on the anniversary of Germany's surrender, the Presidium of the Soviet Union issued a statement that there can be "no forgiving and forgetting even after twenty years." I pictured these men, survivors of Stalin's purges, whom Ribbentrop felt so close to ("like our old National Socialist Party comrades") who have held millions in their camps, subjugated half of Europe, and annexed large parts of Germany, Poland, Finland, and Rumania—I pictured them speaking of no forgiveness.

May 10, 1965 Yesterday I again went to my imaginary theater. In his play *L'Alouette* Anouilh makes Jeanne d'Arc say to King Charles VII: "I have been afraid always. When you see something insurmountable ahead of you, say to yourself: 'All right! I am afraid. Now that I've been properly afraid, let's go forward.' And you will come

---

* But the moment alone has given them birth,
  And of their lives the terrible traces
  Vanish from the face of the earth
  Telling of ruin and desolate places.

through because you were first afraid. That is the whole secret. The moment you vent your fear and face up to the danger, God comes to your aid. Only you have to take the first step."

After reading that, I once more took out the drawing in which I expressed my fear and loneliness during my second year in Spandau—the man lost on the icy peak of a high mountain.

May 13, 1965 Schirach's case has again become critical; now his left eye shows symptoms of an incipient detachment of the retina. Yesterday came word that the three Western ambassadors and their Soviet colleague have acceded to an operation by Professor Meyer-Schwickerath. Procter, the British director, and a squad of military police accompanied Schirach, who wore the prison garb with his number on his back and his two trouser legs, to the operating room in the German hospital. The retina was fused at eight or ten points with the rear wall of the eyeball. After a brief spell of rest, Schirach has been transferred to the British military hospital.

June 6, 1965 A few days ago Schirach returned from the hospital. He reported on his first meeting with Germans in eighteen years. The doctors were extremely constrained, he said; curious nurses and other staff members had posted themselves in the hallways, and he had been looked at rather like a fabulous beast than with sympathy.

June 25, 1965 A few days ago French General Binoche, in the course of an inspection, pointed to the pictures of my family and said: "*Bientôt vous les verrez!*" Today, regards from George Ball were communicated to me. But I attach no significance to these things. On the contrary, I feel a growing nervousness at the thought of the fifteen months still before me. As though a crisis were looming.

July 7, 1965 George Reiner took a sight-seeing tour through Berlin. As the bus drove across the East-West Axis, the guide pointed out that those streetlamps had been designed by Albert Speer, who was now imprisoned in Spandau. The lanterns are the only remains of my work in Berlin, since the Russians tore down the Chancellery.

July 9, 1965 Today I finished August Koehler's book on lighting technology; he cites me as one of the fathers of light architecture. If my own view is correct, I took the first step in that direction on the occasion of the Paris World's Fair by bathing the German pavilion in dazzling brightness at night by means of skillfully arranged spotlights. The result was to make the architecture of the building emerge sharply outlined against the night, and at the same time to make it unreal. Nevertheless, it was still a combination of architecture and light. Somewhat later I did without constructed architecture altogether. At the Party Rally I experimented with antiaircraft searchlights; I had 150 of them pointed vertically into the night sky, forming a rectangle of light. Inside the rectangle the ritual of the Party Rally took place—a fabulous setting, like one of the imaginary crystal palaces of the Middle Ages. British Ambassador Sir Neville Henderson was carried away by the unearthly effect and described it as a "cathedral of ice."

I feel strangely stirred by the idea that the most successful architectural creation of my life is a chimera, an immaterial phenomenon.

July 25, 1965   Used the Sunday to copy out a batch of notes on the cultural history of the window. Ever since a former associate now employed in the Berlin Central Library has discovered which books might be useful for this work of mine, she has been showering material on me. At the moment I am principally concerned with the comparative costs of glass and other building materials during the period from the Middle Ages to the High Renaissance. Along with this, I want to find out, by comparing wages, what value a square meter of light had at different periods, measured in hours of labor. From home I have recently received word that already more than 600 pages of documentation have piled up.

August 18, 1965   Today Hess was very pleased with the second visit from his lawyer, Dr. Seidl. "When at the end I stated that I was being held here not only for no judicial reasons but for no reason at all, Seidl nodded. And Nadysev, who was present, didn't even raise an objection." Hess takes this incident as a triumph.

September 4, 1965   Hess has been in bed for two days. The doctor could find nothing wrong. Schirach commented to the guards that Hess was laying the grounds for another suicide attempt. By chance I heard Pease tersely reproving Schirach: "After all, it's the last right Hess has; if he makes up his mind to it, it should not be taken from him."

September 5, 1965   Today I passed Los Angeles and tramped on southward in the direction of the Mexican border. Merciless sun on dusty roads. My soles burned on the hot ground, for months without rain. What a strange walking tour, from Europe across Asia to the Bering Strait and to America—with kilometer stones to mark my doleful passage.

September 17, 1965   During the past few days my cardiac rhythm has stopped being accelerated by physical exertion; instead there are three or four very rapid beats followed by fifteen or twenty very slow ones. My pulse returns to normal again only after prolonged rest. At night, these heart symptoms are almost unbearable.

Recently there was an article in the *Frankfurter Allgemeine* on a British government study conducted some time ago to determine how long individuals can be kept in imprisonment without suffering physical or mental harm. Behind this was the thought that while it might be just to punish by imprisonment, the judicial system has no right to inflict permanent damage to health. The conclusion was that nine years are the maximum any individual can bear; thereafter, he is permanently damaged.

As I read that, the cruelty of the Spandau penalty suddenly stood plainly revealed to me. At the Nuremberg trial, high moral and humanitarian principles were voiced. I was sentenced in accordance with them, and I inwardly accepted those principles; I even made myself their advocate to my fellow prisoners and my family when they were unhappy about the verdicts. But I did so without knowing the limits of my own strength. Today I know that I long ago used it up. I am an old man.

In the past twenty years I devoted all my energy to devising a constant succession of new techniques for holding out. But these efforts were rapidly used up. They also used me up. This idiotic organization of emptiness was more enervating than emptiness itself ever could have been. What I am left with in the end is nothing but the foolish satisfaction of having clung to a few resolutions. For more than ten years I have gathered material and piled up abstruse calculations to be used for a history of the window. I have laid out flower beds in this gigantic courtyard, built terraces of bricks, and created a system of paths. And finally I have undertaken a walking tour around the world, Europe, Asia, and now America—but always merely going in a circle. By now it amounts to more than a hundred thousand rounds, utterly meaningless, with imaginary destinations. Isn't that in itself an expression of the madness I was trying to escape by means of all these games? I have always looked down on my fellow prisoners, who have failed to set themselves goals. But what goal did I really have? Isn't the sight of a man marching obstinately in a circle for decades far more absurd and weird than anything they have done or not done? I cannot even congratulate myself on having kept myself in physical shape; for I have circulatory troubles and Hess, who has always done nothing but huddle in his cell, is healthier than he was in the first few years.

I cannot pretend to myself: I have been deformed. Granted, my judges sentenced me to only twenty years' imprisonment to make it plain that I did not deserve a life sentence. But in reality they have physically and mentally destroyed me. Ah, these spokesmen of humanitarianism! Only twenty years! It has really been life. Now irrecoverable. And liberty will restore nothing to me. I'll be an eccentric, fixed on peculiar ideas, pursuing old dreams, never again belonging. A kind of convict on furlough. I tell myself: Don't fool yourself! You're a lifer.

September 22, 1965 There is a lovely lyric, "I wept in my dreams."* This morning I woke with my eyes overflowing with tears. Only now do I understand why strong-nerved Dönitz became more and more subdued and melancholic during his last months, and why he wept quietly during the last hours of his imprisonment.

September 25, 1965 Persistent despair. Shortness of breath and cardiac symptoms. I have not the faintest idea how I am going to manage once I am outside. For the first time I feel real dread. The cell walls are closing in on me. In order to do something, I sat down and made additional excerpts on the history of the window. All day long I took Miltown tablets, and in the evening plenty of Bellergal in addition. I hope for a quiet night.

September 28, 1965 Today for the first time in days I had the feeling that my heart is beginning to beat more regularly. Briefly, I felt like someone who has overcome an illness.

September 30, 1965 This collapse was inevitable. I have shed many burdens. Was that the crisis? Or was it only the beginning of the crisis? I am still rather dazed. I feel no relief at the fact that tomorrow the last year begins.

* Heinrich Heine's "Ich hab' im Traum geweinet," no. 55 of the *Buch der Lieder.*
—*Translators' note.*

The Twentieth Year

October 1, 1965 On this day a year hence I shall no longer be here. Today I kept telling myself that again and again. There was something like an exorcism about it. After the collapse of the past several days I have to remind myself that I will not again experience an October 1 in Spandau.

October 4, 1965 Today George Reiner tried to make me feel better by telling me about psychoses that break out toward the end of long prison terms, sometimes even in the last hours before release. He has heard that prisoners frequently fall prey to a peculiar agitation. Some have severe circulatory disturbances with outbreaks of cold sweat so violent that their clothes become soaked through. Others' legs fail them so that they can walk only with support. Others fight desperately against having to leave their cells. Again I involuntarily thought of Dönitz. Hess listened, pale and keenly attentive. Then he said, "Not exactly a consolation for me that I will be spared such difficulties." He turned on his heel and went to his cell. I felt very sorry for him.

October 7, 1965   Have crossed the Mexican border at Mexicali. It is a dreary region, with here and there preposterous cactuslike plants, which the natives call "boogums," like trees from the backgrounds of Expressionist movies. Now and then I entered one of the churches in small, primitive villages, churches that were built by the Jesuits during the period of Spanish colonization. Welcome stops to cool off in the shade and rest the eyes from the glaring light. One of the churches is built in honor of the Virgin of Guadalupe.

October 18, 1965   For several days three new Russian guards have been here. They sit in the cellblock taking correspondence courses. One of them is learning Near Eastern history and Arabic, another mechanical engineering; I have not yet determined what the third's area of study is. All three arrive every day laden with books, sit down in their places, and study.

John Musker, with the Briton's exaggerated sense of propriety, directed a complaint to the directors a few days ago. He pointed out that one of the Russians was in the habit of staying in our garden after his duty hours; evidently he uses the garden for study. But a guard was not allowed to be inside the prisoners' quarters after hours. Today I asked Colonel Bird not to pursue the complaint, for it would only lead to a poisoning of the atmosphere. Bird agreed.

October 23, 1965   The French doctor has experimentally prescribed Lucidril for me for a week. If the results are satisfactory, he thinks I should take the drug for the last two months before my release. As a matter of fact I feel better balanced and physically stabilized after a few days on it.

October 25, 1965   Today I told Schirach that in preparation for release Dönitz had a suit made, which was brought to the prison for him; his tailor had kept the measurements all these years. "Good idea," Schirach said. "My children will have to find out whether Knize in Vienna still has mine. No doubt he has."

"I'd be inclined to ask about prices first," I said. "I imagine it would come to four to six hundred marks nowadays."

"I would expect eight hundred or a thousand," Schirach replied. "Assuming a thousand, and then five suits and a dinner jacket and three coats and some casual clothes as well, sports jackets, custom-made shirts of course. . . . So, all together, maybe around twelve thousand. What am I saying! Tails, an evening coat, all sorts of other things have to be added in. And then the shoes, the underwear, only the best—let's say, reckoning roughly, twenty."

I was thunderstruck. "But," I said, to do him a kindness, "with the million you'll have for the book you can easily afford that, after all."

Schirach gave me a pitying look. "A million, you say? That's ridiculous. It will be much more. You see, I'm going to write three books."

November 4, 1965   One of my wife's last visits. I wanted to say that to her, and add something about coming home, but my voice failed me. Thereafter I became taciturn and stiff, out of fear of my emotions. At the same time I was afraid that the guard would soon call out "That's all," and we would have to part without having said anything.

November 5, 1965   This evening my first considerations of homecoming. The best thing would be for me to vanish on October 1 for ten days to two weeks. I could go to some hunting lodge, arriving at night. There the whole family ought to be gathered; we'd have peace, would be in the fresh air, could go walking undisturbed, sit in the sun, or watch animals in the twilight. Nearby there should be a small country hotel for the rest of the family, which has expanded so much by now. Then, after two weeks, my release would no longer be news for the tabloids and I could go home in peace.

December 4, 1965   Again more than four weeks without notes. I don't feel like making these entries and do so largely just to wind up an occupation that I have become accustomed to. But I am doing it without interest and mechanically.

Yesterday Professor Meyer-Schwickerath, who operated on Schirach's retina six months ago, was permitted, after a prolonged fuss, to check the results of his operation. Present in the infirmary were not only the four directors, but also two American doctors, interpreters, and the medical aide Mees. Schwickerath determined that the scars had healed well and that Schirach would keep his eyesight. Schirach was deeply touched and beside himself with happiness. Spontaneously, he shook the doctor's hand and thanked him heartily.

December 5, 1965   Today I let Hilde know that I no longer like the idea of being whisked away immediately after release. I'd rather take on a few discomforts and accept some perturbation instead of mysteriously vanishing from sight. In other words, it will be better for me to confront the press right away and get all that behind me. Then the public will be inclined to respect our recuperating quietly alone for a while.

December 6, 1965   Ernst, too, is now going to the university. We had a lively conversation, although all in all, except for the first nineteen months of his life, we have been allowed to see and talk to each other only about fifteen times, for thirty minutes each time—no longer, that is, than an extended afternoon. This was his last visit; next time we will be together in the hunting lodge or somewhere else.

December 7, 1965   There are still a few thousand marks in the Coburg account, so I learned. If I add it all up, friends and acquaintances who felt obligated to me have paid more than 150,000 marks into the "education account" during these years. Spread over approximately one hundred and ninety months, that still amounts to nearly 700 marks a month. I have asked for watch catalogues. As I did so, I imagined just how I would hand over the watch to my wife—initial plans for life on the outside.

December 8, 1965   Hess's heart was found to be quite sound at yesterday's examination. Today I remarked to him, "Many of the guards will fade away in the next few years because of their foolish life, and you will remain."

Ambiguously, he replied, "It's a pity." But in a sense he is already enjoying the fact that an inflated establishment headed by four colonels, visited by generals and commissions of doctors, including a large building and much else, is going to be maintained for him alone. Schirach claims that Hess feels like Napoleon, even if only on St. Helena.

December 10, 1965   Today Colonel Bird informed Schirach that the conference of directors has punished him for shaking hands with Schwickerath; he will not be allowed to write his next letter. The Russian director wanted additional measures, but had not managed to make his wishes prevail.

December 12, 1965   Now at any rate the Spandau clock reads two minutes and thirty-nine seconds after eleven P.M. The last hour has begun!

December 14, 1965 What situation faces me when I return? What will my future be? Will I work as an architect again? Is a new beginning conceivable? I have my doubts.

I do not know my two grandchildren. How will everything turn out? How will I manage with my children? With my wife?

Many questions, more and more attempts to work things out. Sometimes I dream that I am lost outside the prison.

December 18, 1965 Have used up a lot of paper on further excerpts for the history of the window. A rich harvest from many medieval chronicles. On this occasion I have reread Notker for the first time in many years, also Einhard's annals. I was struck by the extent to which these portraits of Charlemagne really present a kind of model of virtue. Classical and Christian standards are curiously mingled to form the ideal image of the great ruler. What fullness and what austerity in the early Middle Ages!

December 19, 1965 This evening Nadysev surprisingly, and contrary to all the rules, brought me a telegram from Albert. He has won first prize of 25,000 marks in a contest for planning a satellite city; forty-seven architects participated. "But I've also brought another surprise," the Russian colonel said, and handed me a printed invitation to a lecture by Albert in Frankfurt's America House, and also some photos of models of the prize-winning design. "Are you happy?" Nadysev asked.

December 20, 1965 Today George Reiner came back from a trip to London and said that he had been on a sight-seeing tour in the Tower and been shown a room where, it was explained, Hess had been held captive for a while.

"What, he was in the Tower?" was Schirach's reaction. "What an honor! Only state prisoners and traitors are admitted there." After a reflective pause he went on, "What I would give to have done only two weeks' time there!"

December 22, 1965 Today I asked the Western directors to shift the beginning of the sleeping period from ten to eleven o'clock. My aim is to break away from the unchanging daily rhythm to which I have been habituated for so many years. As long as no Russians are on duty, the Western directors said, the change would be permitted. But after only a few days I am finding it hard to keep awake until eleven o'clock.

December 27, 1965   Sympathetic guards have made it possible for me to keep the transistor radio with me for four days. In addition, the record player was frequently in operation over Christmas. In four days, therefore, I have heard seventeen hours of music. A curious compulsion to narcotize myself.

December 31, 1965   For days I have been cutting back trees, trimming birches, pruning fruit trees, all to use as material for a high bonfire. It is burning magnificently.

January 1, 1966   At midnight I stood on my stool looking out the high window of my cell at the scanty fireworks display put on by the British garrison. Strangely, while watching I completely forgot that this has been my last New Year's fireworks in Spandau.

This morning, as Schirach and I were tramping our rounds together, Rostlam came across the garden to us and wished us Happy New Year. Then he added, as though casually, "I suppose this may have been your last New Year's Day in prison. Who knows?"

After he had left, Schirach turned anxiously to me. "Did you hear that? Something is going on here." He added that the American doctor had also remarked recently that he was seriously worried about how we would withstand the transition back to normal life.

Schirach became more and more excited. "Do you know what I think? They want to keep us behind bars forever. They'll simply say that it's in our own interest; our health is at stake, they have to observe us for a while. Maybe they'll hold us in a psychiatric hospital."

For a few moments I was infected by his hysteria. Afterwards I asked myself what Rostlam might have meant. Or was it merely the sadistic coldness of a longtime professional?

All these years I have had the feeling of walking on unstable ground. I have never been able to do more than guess what was intended honestly and what hypocritically. In this prison world, dissimulation became second nature on both sides. How much pretense I have had to use solely in order to maintain my contacts with the outside world. Somewhere I once read that prison is the university of crime; it is, at least, the university of moral corruption.

January 2, 1966   Last night, shortly after two o'clock in the morning, one of my "friends" came in and played for me, on a small dictating apparatus, a tape the family had made for me. It was a tremendous experience, one I would not have thought possible. It was not the voices, which after all I know, that stirred me so. It was the acoustic experience of normality: a family chatting and laughing, the shouts of children, the clatter of coffee cups, everyday jokes. At this moment I realized for the first time how unnaturally, how stiffly, we have always behaved toward one another in the visiting room. In eighteen years no one has ever laughed there; we have always shunned the possibility of seeming emotional, banal, or even cheerful. And suddenly all the ambition that I sometimes summon up with regard to life on the outside seemed to be shallow in contrast to this insignificant family scene interrupted by clacking sounds. The felicity of everyday life.

January 5, 1966   At breakfast today Nutall began with Hess and then made a long delay. Three times in recent days he has made me wait in this manner, but today I pressed the signal button. Although he could well imagine what I wanted, he asked with a grumpy official expression, "What d'you want?"

"Just my breakfast," I replied.

When he then growled something about "being able to wait," I brushed right by him and served myself. A sharp discussion ensued, both of us threatening to report the matter to the directors. Nutall became even more excited when I told him it was high time he did his duty and unlocked Schirach's cell also. He literally gasped for breath. "What? You dare to tell me what I'm supposed to do! Who do you think you are? What are you trying to do here?"

I put my hand out to the door. "I want to have my breakfast in peace," I said, and pulled it shut in front of his nose. Oddly, that sobered him down. Without another word, he went over to Schirach.

January 6, 1966   The news has just reached me of the sudden death of Karl Piepenburg, with whom I was planning to open an office. My hopes of a professional future depended very heavily on his friendship and loyalty.

February 7, 1966   This morning Colonel Procter made an inspection tour before the announced visit of Sir Frank Roberts, the British ambassador. In the chapel he saw the big old alarm clock which serves to indicate the end of the concert periods. He commented to his deputy, "We'd better avoid unnecessary things. Take it away."

February 9, 1966 For more than two weeks the *Berliner Zeitung* has been publishing a series of heavy attacks on President Lübke. In East Berlin an international press conference has taken place; the attorney general of the German Democratic Republic intervened, and at the end Heinrich Lübke was represented as one of the chief builders of the concentration camp system.

In reality Lübke was working in a subordinate post in an architectural office that by pure chance was commissioned to build barracks, a few of which were intended for concentration camps. In the Eastern as well as in some of the Western newspapers he appears as my associate. But I barely knew him.

February 11, 1966 Yesterday Musker took a snow shovel and wrote his initials four meters long in the newly fallen snow. I advised him to remove the letters, warning him that this sort of thing would get him into trouble. Out of defiance, he then shoveled his full name in the snow, and by today he had already received a written rebuke. The pilot of an American helicopter who flies along the Berlin border several times a day also checks our terrain. Since the assumption was made that the letters in the snow might be communicating illegal messages, even the secret services were informed.

February 12, 1966 After looking through many catalogues, I have decided on a wristwatch by Jaeger-Lecoultre. I have asked my friend in Coburg to have a dedication engraved on it.

February 13, 1966 A long time since I have thought of Hitler—how long is it, I wonder? But now he has caught up with me in a dream. Last night I dreamed of the days at the beginning of the war. I am in the Chancellery and saying goodbye to him, for he is leaving for his headquarters. Everyone remaining behind says a few words of farewell. I consider what I might best say without seeming subservient. When Hitler turns to me, I limit myself to the sentence: "I wish that you may be able to sleep well." Hitler seems surprised; he looks at me without saying anything, and only then do I notice that he has traces of dry shaving cream foam on his face. As he stands there, the foam spreads out, soon covering his nose and forehead. Embarrassed, I call Hitler's attention to this; and when almost his entire face has vanished in the foam, he coolly shakes hands with me. Then he turns to the waiting generals.

Actually, Hitler was ill-humored and taciturn that time in September 1939, a few days after the declaration of war, when he bade goodbye to us at night in his Berlin apartment. Thinking over this dream I realized that on that day our personal association began breaking down. As a government minister I had much more power, but I was nothing but a member of the government.

February 16, 1966 Godeaux has brought me an article written by Lord Hartley W. Shawcross, the British chief prosecutor at the Nuremberg trial, and published in *Stern*. In it Shawcross states: "Herr Speer, who is still being held prisoner in Spandau, should have been released long ago. Together with John McCloy, the former American High Commissioner in Germany, I have more than once made efforts to obtain his release. But the Soviet government were opposed." A dismal satisfaction that comes too late.

March 17, 1966 Sharkov, who hitherto has always been friendly and helpful, has for the past several weeks been surly and even hostile. I have no idea what the reason is. What strikes me is that his animosity is obviously directed only at me. Today he objected that I had one book too many in my cell; on the other hand, he permitted Schirach two additional books. The other Russians are all the more friendly. Today one of them greeted me from the tower by tossing his cap in the air and with a broad laugh calling out, "General!"

After the afternoon walk, Hess and Schirach returned to the cellblock, but I wanted to go on working. Sharkov pressed Reiner: "All three inside!"

At first the American thought he had misheard. "Two inside."

The Russian said more insistently: "No, all three! Five hasn't worked enough today, only a third of the time. Must go inside also."

I intervened and pointed out that I had worked more than usual.

"No matter," Sharkov insisted. "Must go in too."

Not only the prisoners, the guards too are being deformed. What deforms them most is the right to exhibit any kind of ill-humor.

March 19, 1966 Lovely birthday weather. The yellow crocuses have given me pleasure. Curious thought, that I will never see these again. A kind of farewell feeling filled me today at the flower bed.

And another pleasure: a telegram from Albert informs me that he has won the second prize of 25,000 marks in an architectural design contest for Ludwigshafen.

March 21, 1966   In the course of the past several months Hess has gradually received sixty books sent him by his wife. When Schirach made fun of the heaps of books, Hess replied sadly, ignoring the mockery, "At the moment there are too many, too, but they're a kind of reserve." After a brief pause he added, "For when I'm here alone."

March 26, 1966   Otto Apel has died! On March 19, my birthday. He was, along with Piepenburg, the other of my former associates who had let me know that I could count on him.

How often my career was affected by deaths. For I would never have become Hitler's architect but for the death of Troost, whose designs he so admired. And certainly he would never have appointed me minister of armaments if my predecessor, Todt, had not been killed in an airplane crash. And now this. So it isn't meant to be. At any rate, that is how I understand the meaning of this. All the contacts that I had, all the ideas I was conceiving, all my notions of the future have been shattered by the deaths of these two men.

March 29, 1966   A long walk in the garden today. Almost everything in my life, I thought, has fallen into my lap. Success always came to me. I never had to run after it. I never took part in a contest, like Albert. Now I am too old for that.

Are the twenty years during which I tried to keep up with current work in my profession wasted after all? By myself I cannot build up a new firm. How shall I go on? The old fear of the void.

April 9, 1966   Easter Sunday and another telegram. Albert has won again, first prize in Rothenburg. Nadysev said, laughing, "They'll soon have to apply the antimonopoly laws to your son."

April 10, 1966   After lunch some of the guards gave us small Easter presents. Hess, however, refused to accept them. Later he explained to us, "Recently I've sometimes come to wait for such small acts of friendliness. But I don't want to become dependent on my weaknesses. Therefore I have also resolved to eat only what I receive from the prison. One, two, three!"

April 24, 1966 TV intends to bring me together with Esser for an interview. A horrible thought; I always kept those Bavarian vulgarians in Hitler's retinue, men from the early days of the Party, at arm's length. And they too, those Old-Old Fighters from before 1923, with their incredible conceit, did the same to me. Let Schirach meet with Esser!

April 28, 1966 More and more often I notice that I am thinking about Spandau in the tenses and concepts of the past. Today that even happened to me in a letter home. As though the time were already up.

April 29, 1966 When I think back on the twenty years: would I have been able to survive this time if I had not been permitted to write a single line?

April 30, 1966 I have finally put behind me all thoughts of returning to architecture. Is it really final?
At any rate I sent word to Propyläen Verlag that I was not averse to a publishing contract. I said they would be hearing from me after my release.

May 10, 1966 Today Hess did not emerge from his cell all day; he sent his meals back. A few times I went to his door, but he was sitting bolt upright at his table and seemed to be staring at the nearer wall. I asked Pease whether Hess was sick, but he waved that possibility aside. "It's his mood again." Schirach was offended by the degree of attention that Hess had once again attracted to himself. From his cell I heard Schirach calling, "It's all phony, all phony! He'll probably be back with the stomach cramps soon. The cook is a poisoner, haha!"

May 11, 1966 At night, after everything had quieted down, I remembered that twenty-five years ago yesterday Hess flew off to England. Now he has a quarter of a century in cells behind him. And how much longer before him?

May 14, 1966 Today they imposed a four-day ban on my reading because for the second time at short intervals I was rude to one of the

British guards. I had complained about the monotonous food. I explained my behavior to Procter as a consequence of the nervousness of these last months.

May 22, 1966   Today a power lawnmower arrived. Some of the guards intend to keep the garden in order for Hess later. In addition we received new blue jackets, a kind of teen-ager model with bronze zipper and tabs on the side. I am letting it hang unused in the locker, for I don't want to start anything new here at this point.

May 28, 1966   I hear that the thousandth meeting of the directors was celebrated in the officers' mess with champagne.

June 1, 1966   Today, just as Procter and Letham entered the cell, my notes suddenly began sliding down through my trousers. I was able to prevent the worst only by pressing my calves together convulsively. As soon as the two were gone, I tore all the notes into small pieces and threw them into the toilet.

Of late I have been more nervous than in all the years before. I have repeatedly reacted in a rude and aggressive way toward the friendly guards; once, in fact, I have been punished for this. What worries me most of all is this illegal communication with the outside world—the writing of these notes, handing them over for smuggling out, receiving the illegal mail, hastily reading and getting rid of it—all the thousands of acts of secrecy and hide-and-seek which for years were only an exciting adventure and which now are a strain on my nerves. I can't keep it up.

Today I spontaneously decided to stop writing these notes. I am haunted by the idea that discovery of these contacts stretching back over many years might lead to all sorts of penalties, ultimately even endangering the date of my release. I know, of course, that this is absurd, but my nerves are weaker than my intellect. At this point I no longer want to take any risks.

For the same reason I will no longer accept the transistor radio. I have asked them at home to stop all correspondence and have already informed the liaison people, my friends here.

A strange feeling: the last entry. Sometimes I think that the writing has been only a kind of substitute life, so that on the outside I shall also go on keeping a diary. Then again I think that it will always remain a compensation for a life unlived; and in such moments I swear to myself that on the outside I won't write another line.

In that case this is going to be the last paragraph of my diary. Twenty years! What am I thinking at this moment? I must not fall into an oversolemn mood at this point. How does one conclude a thing like this? And what feelings does one have? Relief, gratitude, anxiety, curiosity, vacancy? . . . I don't know.

July 22, 1966   I am breaking my resolution after all. For last night I had a dream that has been on my mind all day long. For two months I did not miss this diary; on the contrary, I was relieved. Last night I dreamed that I would never return home.

I have just arrived in Heidelberg. Somewhat abstractedly, I take a few steps in the garden, once again fix in my mind the familiar and at the same time strange scene, the house with the low gables, the oaks and beeches on the slope, and the river far below. A low rumbling noise sounds from somewhere, and suddenly, while the sky turns abruptly black, deafening thunder passes over us. Immediately thereafter, red-hot lava pours down the valley from the vicinity of the Hohler Kästenbaum. A second stream is rolling inexorably toward Heidelberg. An inferno has broken loose on both sides of the river. In spite of the distance, I feel the heat burning on my face. Sparks scatter across the sky; the trees begin to burn like torches. Amid all this, a constant series of new thunderclaps. The ground seems to sway, but I stand on my mountain outside the house and have the feeling of safety. Tensely, I watch the spectacle of nature; overwhelmed, I see houses collapse, people fleeing and the lava overtaking them, fiery stone hissing and steaming as it flows into the boiling river. What is going on holds all my senses enthralled, but not my emotions. At this moment I suddenly feel the catastrophe reaching out to my hill. It is already becoming unbearably hot all around me. The leaves on the trees turn brown and wilt. Heat and flying sparks ignite the woods on the slope; the tree trunks crack open with explosive noises; and a windstorm blows the burning branches into the clouds of smoke and flame. Suddenly it is burning on all sides. I do not dare to turn around. But the heat at my back becomes unbearable. I know that my parents' home, in which I spent my youth, to which I was just on the point of returning, is going up in flames.

September 18, 1966   Still thirteen days before my release. Today I completed the last year of my walking tour around the world. Probably it has been the greatest athletic achievement of my life. And at the same time the only tangible result of the Spandau years. At the end of the last segment of my life there is nothing left but statistics, production figures. Here they are:

1954–55	2,367 kilometers
1955–56	3,326
1956–57	3,868
1957–58	2,865
1958–59	2,168
1959–60	1,633
1960–61	1,832
1961–62	1,954
1962–63	2,664
1963–64	2,794
1964–65	3,258
1965–66	3,087
	31,816

The four directors have decided, so I have been informed, that I shall be driven out through the gate before Schirach. So I will have an edge over him of some seconds, as I have hoped for years.

Today, seven days before release, I have written the last official prison letters to my wife. "It is all to the good that we kept on having hopes throughout these years. Had I known that I would have to stick it out until the very last hour—where would I have found the strength? And as so often happens, now that it all has been lived through, the time, the remoteness from you all, shrinks to nothing. . . . At the close of this last letter and this long time, once again I send my thanks to you."

Three days before release, and now many preparations have begun. Once more I weeded the garden, because I would like to leave everything in order. We have received new clothing, but are not permitted to wear it yet. Hilde has brought a suitcase for my possessions. Today was washday for the last time. Hess looks on at all these preparations without visible reaction; his morale is amazing. Not a single bitter remark.

Today, throughout almost the entire day, the next to last, Hess and Schirach went walking in the garden. Hess was obviously framing the messages he wants transmitted to his family. In the course of my work in the flower beds I could easily put together the content of what he was saying from the fragments I overheard. Schirach was trying to persuade Hess that his only chance for release lies in being declared not responsible for his actions; that therefore he must consistently play insane.

As soon as Schirach returned to the cellblock, I went over to Hess and asked him whether he had any commissions for me. But he waved that aside; one person sufficed, he said. When I expressed doubts that Schirach would actually deliver the messages to his family,[1] Hess blew up. Angrily, he berated me: "How can you suspect our comrade Schirach of such a thing! It is outrageous of you to say anything of the kind. No thanks! No thanks to your offer!" And he simply left me there.

In the evening I knocked on his cell door and asked to have a brief talk with him. I told him I thought it wrong to attempt to buy his release by simulating insanity. If he did that, I said, he would be undermining his own image, whereas now, thanks to his consistency, he was regarded with a certain respect even among his enemies. He would only destroy that if he played the madman. It would throw a bad light on his own bearing during the decades that lay behind him, make all that seem merely obsessive behavior. This, I said, was what I had wanted to tell him in all honesty before I no longer could. For a while Hess looked at me wide-eyed, in silence; then he said firmly, "You are absolutely right. I too did not feel good about all that!"

The last day has dawned. Since I drew up those statistics I have tramped an additional 114 kilometers. In a moment I am going into the garden and will cover another ten kilometers, so that I shall be ending my walking tour at kilometer 31,936. And this evening a last violation of the prison rules. At eleven P.M. a telegram is to be sent to my old friend which he should receive around midnight: "Please pick me up thirty-five kilometers south of Guadalajara, Mexico. Holzwege."[2]

[1] I have heard from Wolf Rüdiger Hess that in the following years Schirach neither visited Frau Hess nor contacted Hess's son.

[2] *Holzwege* is the title of a book by Martin Heidegger, which Speer read and then used as his pseudonym in his clandestine correspondence. The word means both "wood roads" and "wrong ways."—*Translators' note.*

And one last item: When I entered the garden a while ago I saw Hess standing in the side court. He had his back to me. I went up to him and stood beside him, just as a gesture of sympathy. Great mounds of coal for the prison were being unloaded in the court. For a while we stood in silence side by side. Then Hess said, "So much coal. And from tomorrow on only for me."

Epilogue

THE LAST PRISON DAY, September 30, 1966, in no way differed from all those that had gone before. The daily routine was followed punctiliously. Only once was there a sign of some excitement, a little whispering, when a guard brought the news that Willy Brandt had sent my daughter a bouquet of carnations.

In the afternoon Hess had himself locked up. The ceremonials of the leave-takings had obviously exhausted his nervous strength. He sent word by the guards that he wished to remain alone. After supper he would take a strong soporific.

After my rounds in the garden—they amounted to six kilometers—I was locked up again; then lunch, newspaper reading, unlocked, more rounds in the garden—four kilometers—then locked up again. The uncertainty of what was to come wiped out all sentiment. Suddenly, too, I was no longer impatient. I addressed a petition to the directors to be allowed to leave my records for Hess. After only a few minutes word came that permission was granted.

Hess did not come out of the cell for supper either. I went to him, but he waved me away. I took his hand; it was as lifeless as his face. "Make it short," he said.

"Goodbye, Herr Hess," I said. "You know——"

He interrupted: "No! No! No! It's . . . Oh, let it go!" Shortly after-wards, Hess asked the chief guard to have the light in his cell turned out.

I lay down on my cot. As my last reading matter I had obtained from the library Heinrich Tessenow's *Handwerk und Kleinstadt*. I wanted once more to read the sentences with which my teacher had concluded his book in 1920, shortly after the First World War. I had never prop-erly understood what he was aiming at: "Perhaps everywhere around us are the truly 'greatest' heroes, uncomprehended, who put up with and smile at even the most gruesome of horrors as unimportant side is-sues. Perhaps, before handicraft and the small town can flourish again, there will have to be something like a rain of fire and brimstone. Per-haps the next great periods of handicraft and the small town will be at-tained by peoples who have passed through hells." I, his favorite pupil, went from his studio straight to the proximity of Hitler, who truly made it rain fire and brimstone.

Resigned, I lay down to rest during the last hours before midnight. Half asleep, I heard someone saying outside the cell: "And he can sleep! I suppose he took a pill." But I had made a point of not taking anything in order to have all my wits about me when I met the press. But also in order to experience with full consciousness the moment I would drive out through the gate.

A tower clock struck many times; then there was some bustle outside the cell. I was brought the old ski jacket in which I had been delivered to Spandau nineteen years before, then an old tie, a shirt, and the cor-duroy trousers.

After dressing I was taken to the directors. It was half past eleven. Never before had I been in these rooms. In a friendly tone the officiat-ing British director asked me to sit down. Schirach came; he looked exhausted. The only formality was completed: I received 2,778 Reichs-marks, no longer valid, which had been taken from me in May 1945. I had no other possessions. In addition, an unsigned, undated receipt was handed to me: "Taken over from F. C. Teich, Jr., Major, director of the Nuremberg Prison, the inmate *Alfred* Speer Ser. No. 32 G 350,037." I also received, because my own identity card had been lost, a temporary paper stating: "Herr Albert Speer can leave Berlin one time by air. Personal data have not been checked. Valid until October 5, 1966. (Stamp) Commissioner of Police, Department II."

A conversation of forced naturalness ensued. All four directors were obviously trying to overcome the difficulty of these last minutes. They, too, felt sympathy for Hess. The cars, one of them said, were already waiting in the yard outside the gate, the small yard through which, handcuffed to an American soldier, I had entered the building of Spandau Prison on *July 18, 1947.* Then it was one minute to twelve. The directors accompanied us to the outer door. I said: "Do everything you can not to make life too hard for Hess." Outside, the person I saw first was my wife. She came quickly up the few steps, followed by my lawyer.

Schirach shook hands with me in parting; we wished each other all the best for the future. A black Mercedes was waiting. Out of habit I went to take my place in the front seat beside the driver, as I had always done in the past. Flächsner pushed me to the rear door; after all, I had to leave the prison at my wife's side.

At the stroke of twelve, both wings of the gate were opened. Suddenly we were bathed in blinding light. Many television spotlights were directed at us. In front, phantoms in the glare, I saw British soldiers running around us. For a moment I thought I recognized Pease in the tumult, and waved to him. We passed through a thunderstorm of flashbulbs; then we turned away. The prison lay behind us. I did not dare look back.

Fourteen quiet days in Schleswig-Holstein. We had rented a house by the Kellersee, and for the first time the whole family was together. Every day I woke at the accustomed time, and I continued to feel the urge to tramp out my kilometers. A harmonious atmosphere prevailed, and everybody tried his best with me, but the family observed my eccentricities with some astonishment. Every so often I had an inkling that there were things I would not be able to adjust to.

I think, as I write this a few days later, that I should not attribute the sense of awkwardness to Spandau. It is even possible that the stiffness with which we sat facing each other in the visiting room is the kind of contact that accords with my nature. Hasn't there always been a sort of wall between me and others? Has not all casualness been only a strategy to make that wall invisible? I was already a stranger in Hitler's entourage, a stranger among my fellow prisoners. How will it be from now on?

My whole life, in fact, appears to me strangely alienated. Architecture I loved, and I hoped to make my name live on in history by building. But my real work consisted in the organization of an enormous system of technology. Since then my life has remained attached to a cause that at bottom I disliked.

But am I not deceiving myself? Since nothing I built has remained, will I at all survive as an architect? And hasn't my achievement as an organizer been outdated and bypassed everywhere? In that case, perhaps the years in prison might be the ladder by which I will after all ascend into the once so longed for heaven of history. My semierotic relationship to Spandau, the fact that perhaps I never really wanted to get away from there, may have something to do with that. When the first people of this outside world start coming to me, what would I rather they talked about—the buildings that glorified a tyranny; the technology that so successfully prolonged the war; or Spandau, which I simply endured?

Nowadays I often have dreams like this: I return to Spandau in order to visit someone. Guards and directors receive me kindly, like someone they have been missing. With alarm I see the neglected garden and the untended paths. Every day I again walk my rounds, read in my cell, or make the signal flap drop. When I want to go home after a few days, it is politely conveyed to me that I must stay. I am told that I had been released only by mistake. My sentence is by no means over. I refer to the twenty years that I waited out to the very last day, but the guards shrug and say: Stay here, we can't do anything about it. A general comes for an inspection, but I do not yet mention that I am being held by mistake. I say that the treatment is satisfactory. The general smiles.

Index

Index